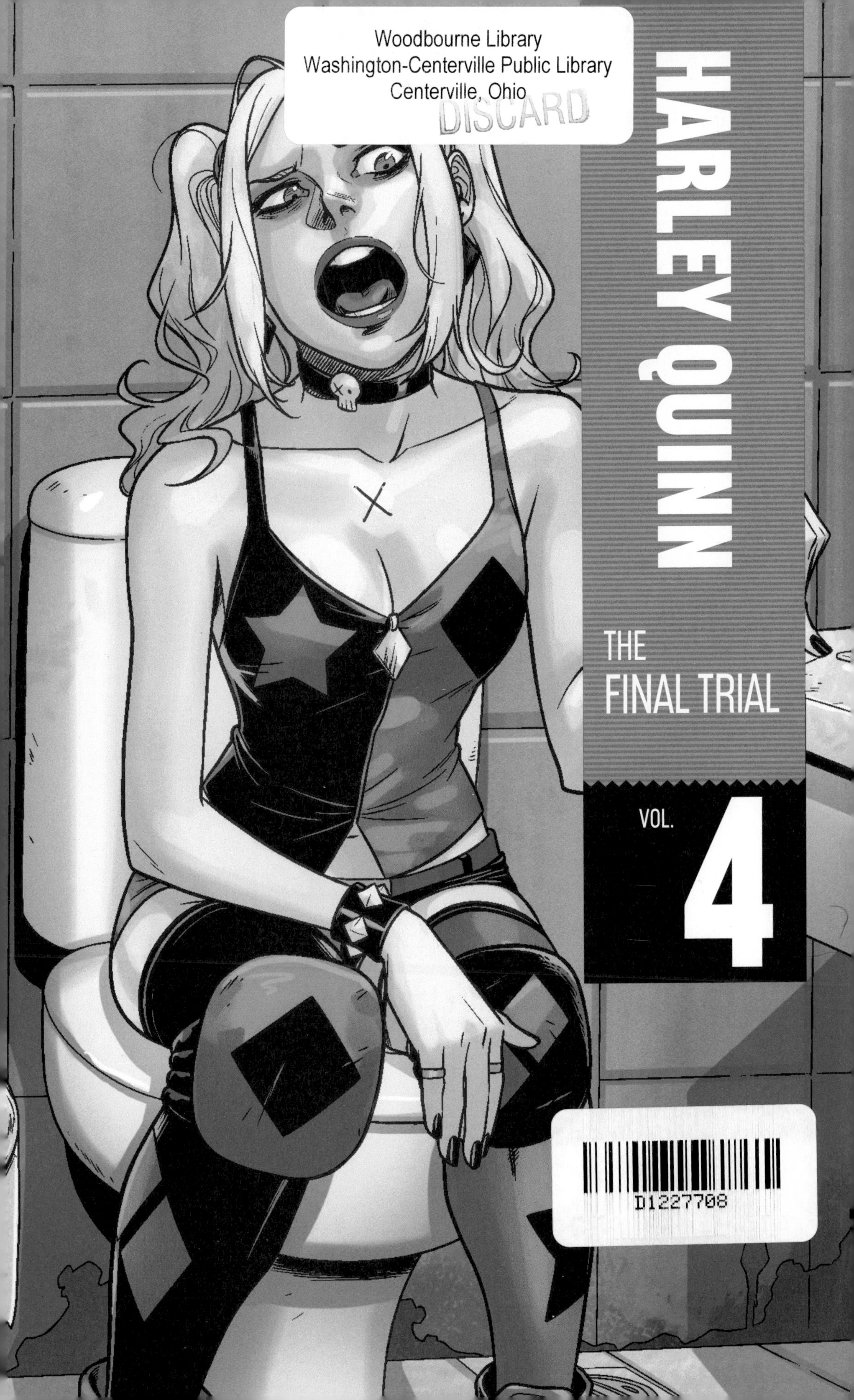

HARLEY QUINN

THE FINAL TRIAL

VOL. 4

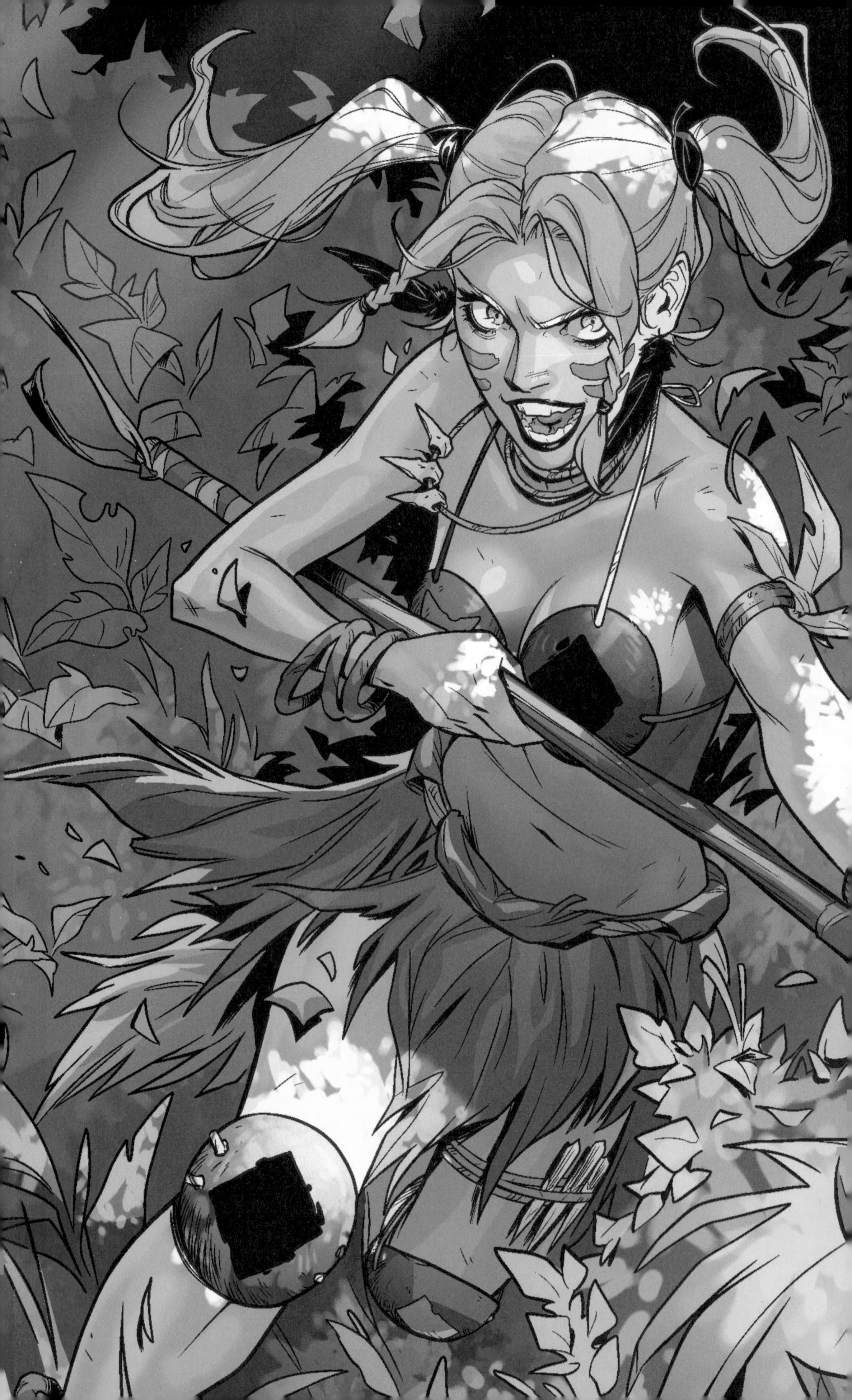

HARLEY QUINN
THE FINAL TRIAL

writers

SAM HUMPHRIES

MARK RUSSELL

artists

SAMI BASRI

MIKE NORTON

DAN JURGENS

NORM RAPMUND

AARON LOPRESTI

MATT RYAN

TOM DERENICK

TREVOR SCOTT

colorists

HI-FI

JESSICA KHOLINNE

IVAN PLASCENCIA

letterers

DAVE SHARPE

STEVE WANDS

collection cover artist

KENNETH ROCAFORT

HARLEY QUINN created by PAUL DINI and BRUCE TIMM

SUPERMAN created by JERRY SIEGEL and JOE SHUSTER
By special arrangement with the Jerry Siegel family

VOL.

4

ALEX ANTONE Editor – Original Series
ANDREA SHEA Associate Editor – Original Series
JEB WOODARD Group Editor – Collected Editions
ROBIN WILDMAN Editor – Collected Edition
STEVE COOK Design Director – Books
JOHN J. HILL Publication Design
SUZANNAH ROWNTREE Publication Production

BOB HARRAS Senior VP – Editor-in-Chief, DC Comics
PAT McCALLUM Executive Editor, DC Comics

DAN DiDIO Publisher
JIM LEE Publisher & Chief Creative Officer
BOBBIE CHASE VP – New Publishing Initiatives & Talent Development
DON FALLETTI VP – Manufacturing Operations & Workflow Management
LAWRENCE GANEM VP – Talent Services
ALISON GILL Senior VP – Manufacturing & Operations
HANK KANALZ Senior VP – Publishing Strategy & Support Services
DAN MIRON VP – Publishing Operations
NICK J. NAPOLITANO VP – Manufacturing Administration & Design
NANCY SPEARS VP – Sales
MICHELE R. WELLS VP & Executive Editor, Young Reader

HARLEY QUINN VOL. 4: THE FINAL TRIAL

DC Comics, 2900 West Alameda Ave., Burbank, CA 91505
Printed by LSC Communications, Owensville, MO, USA. 2/21/20. First Printing.
ISBN: 978-1-4012-9455-7

Library of Congress Cataloging-in-Publication Data is available.

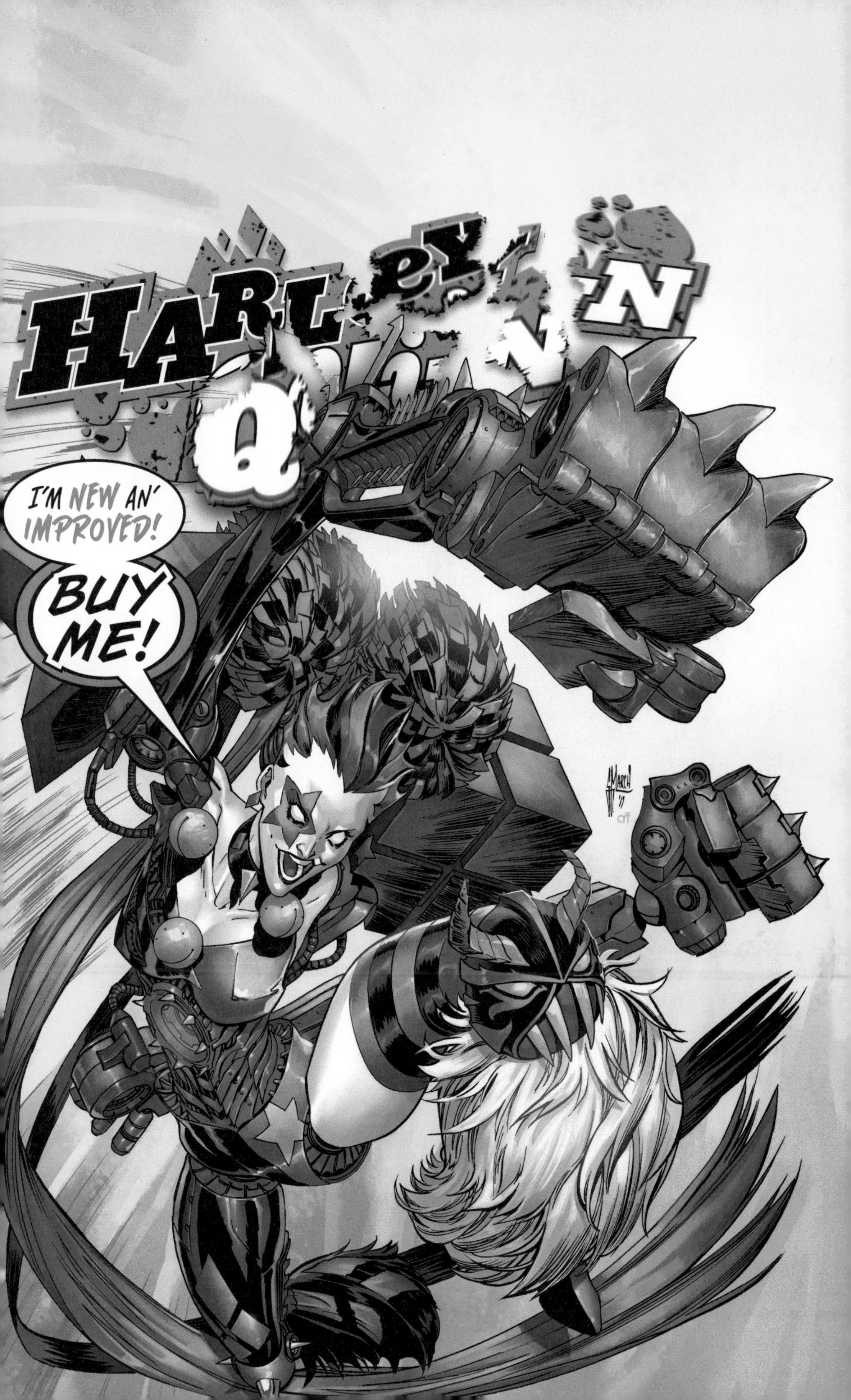
I'M NEW AN' IMPROVED!
BUY ME!

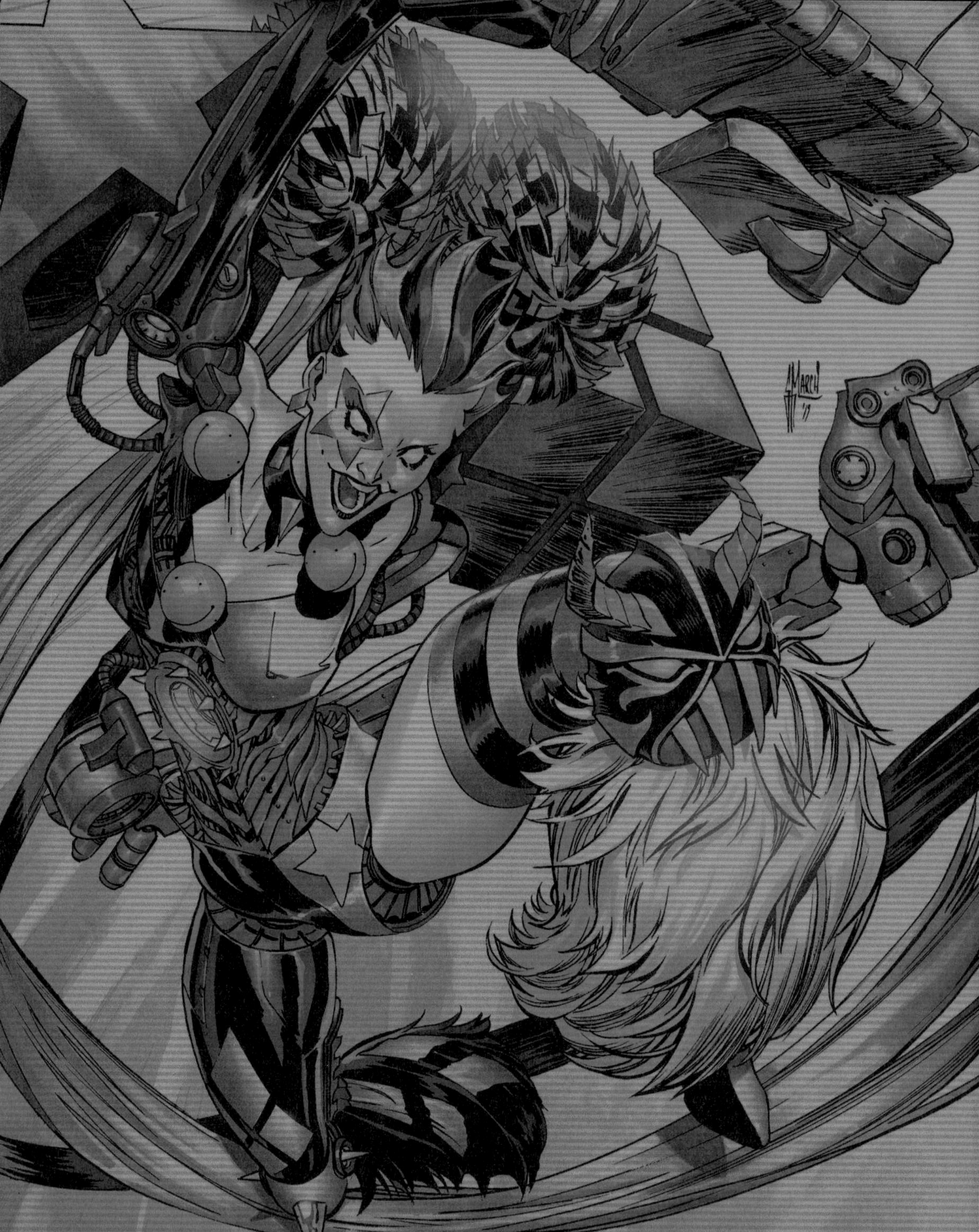

HARLEY QUINN
#64

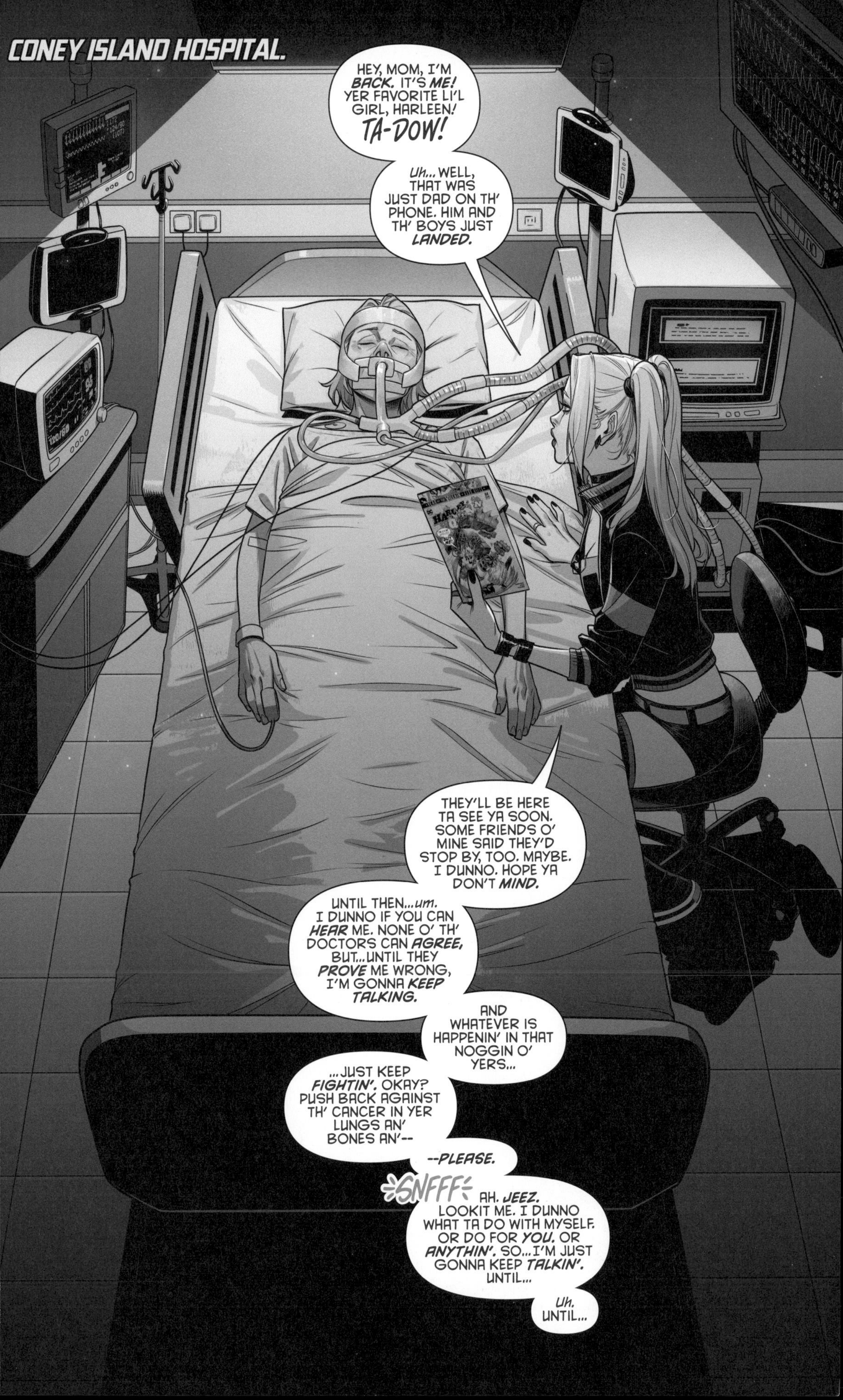
CONEY ISLAND HOSPITAL.
HEY, MOM, I'M BACK. IT'S ME! YER FAVORITE LI'L GIRL, HARLEEN! TA-DOW!
UH... WELL, THAT WAS JUST DAD ON TH' PHONE. HIM AND TH' BOYS JUST LANDED.
THEY'LL BE HERE TA SEE YA SOON. SOME FRIENDS O' MINE SAID THEY'D STOP BY, TOO. MAYBE. I DUNNO. HOPE YA DON'T MIND.
UNTIL THEN...UM. I DUNNO IF YOU CAN HEAR ME. NONE O' TH' DOCTORS CAN AGREE, BUT...UNTIL THEY PROVE ME WRONG, I'M GONNA KEEP TALKING.
AND WHATEVER IS HAPPENIN' IN THAT NOGGIN O' YERS...
...JUST KEEP FIGHTIN'. OKAY? PUSH BACK AGAINST TH' CANCER IN YER LUNGS AN' BONES AN'--
--PLEASE.
SNFFF
AH. JEEZ. LOOKIT ME. I DUNNO WHAT TA DO WITH MYSELF. OR DO FOR YOU. OR ANYTHIN'. SO...I'M JUST GONNA KEEP TALKIN'. UNTIL...
UH. UNTIL...

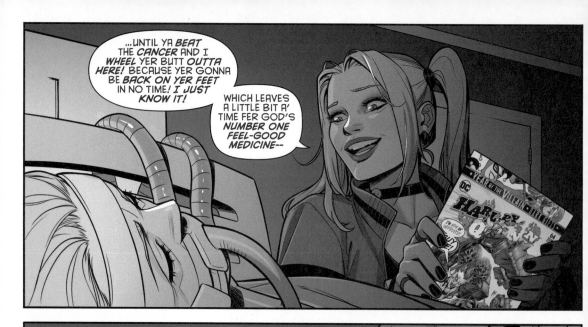

...UNTIL YA BEAT THE CANCER AND I WHEEL YER BUTT OUTTA HERE! BECAUSE YER GONNA BE BACK ON YER FEET IN NO TIME! I JUST KNOW IT!
WHICH LEAVES A LITTLE BIT A' TIME FER GOD'S NUMBER ONE FEEL-GOOD MEDICINE--
YEAR OF THE VILLAIN
DC
HARLEY QUINN
I'M NEW AN' IMPROVED!
64
--COMIC BOOKS! LESSEE, WHERE WERE WE...
OH RIGHT, LEX LUTHOR WAS GONNA MAKE ME AN OFFER!
HELLO, HARLEY QUINN.
IT IS I, LEX LUTHOR!
DUH,
AND MIGHT I SAY, YOU'VE NEVER LOOKED BETTER!
YEAH, YEAH I HEARD ALL ABOUT IT!
I AM TRAVERSING THE UNIVERSE EMPOWERING THE MOST RUTHLESS BEINGS WITH A SINGLE PIECE OF MY TRADEMARK LUTHOR GENEROSITY--
UH, YOU DID?
OF COURSE! IT'S ALL OVER THE INTERNET!
I AM OFFERING, UH, TO HELP YOU REACH THE TOTALITY--
OF MY FULLEST POTENTIAL, YES, I KNOW!
--OF YOUR FULLEST, UM--
CUT THE FANCY SPEECH, LEX! SAVE IT FER SOMEONE WHO CARES! ALL I WANT IS--
--THE OFFER!

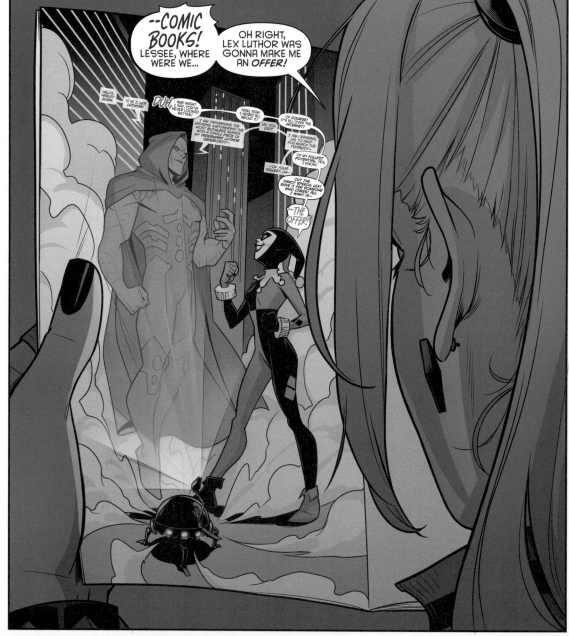

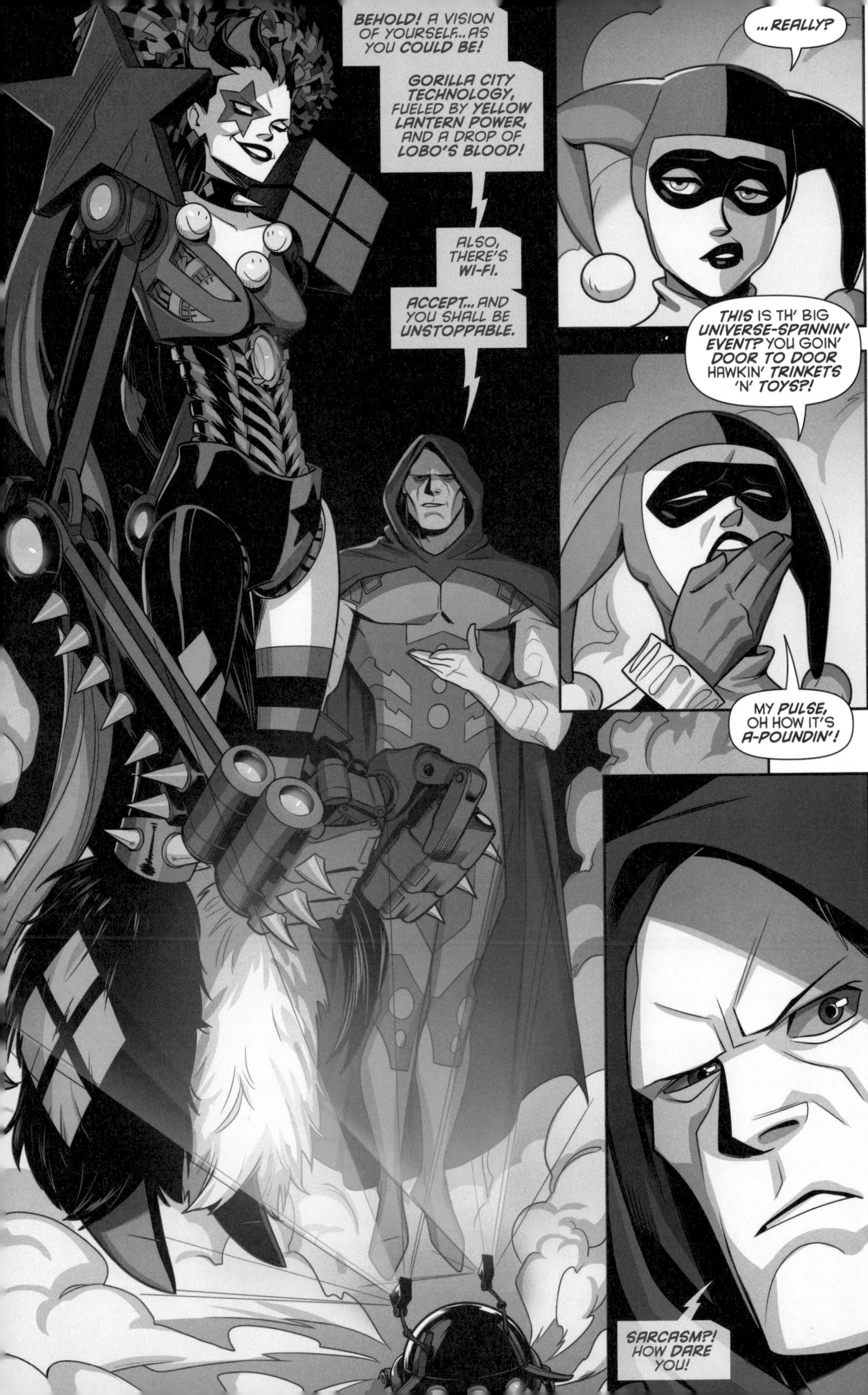
BEHOLD! A VISION OF YOURSELF...AS YOU COULD BE!
GORILLA CITY TECHNOLOGY, FUELED BY YELLOW LANTERN POWER, AND A DROP OF LOBO'S BLOOD!
ALSO, THERE'S WI-FI.
ACCEPT... AND YOU SHALL BE UNSTOPPABLE.
...REALLY?
THIS IS TH' BIG UNIVERSE-SPANNIN' EVENT? YOU GOIN' DOOR TO DOOR HAWKIN' TRINKETS 'N' TOYS?!
MY PULSE, OH HOW IT'S A-POUNDIN'!
SARCASM?! HOW DARE YOU!

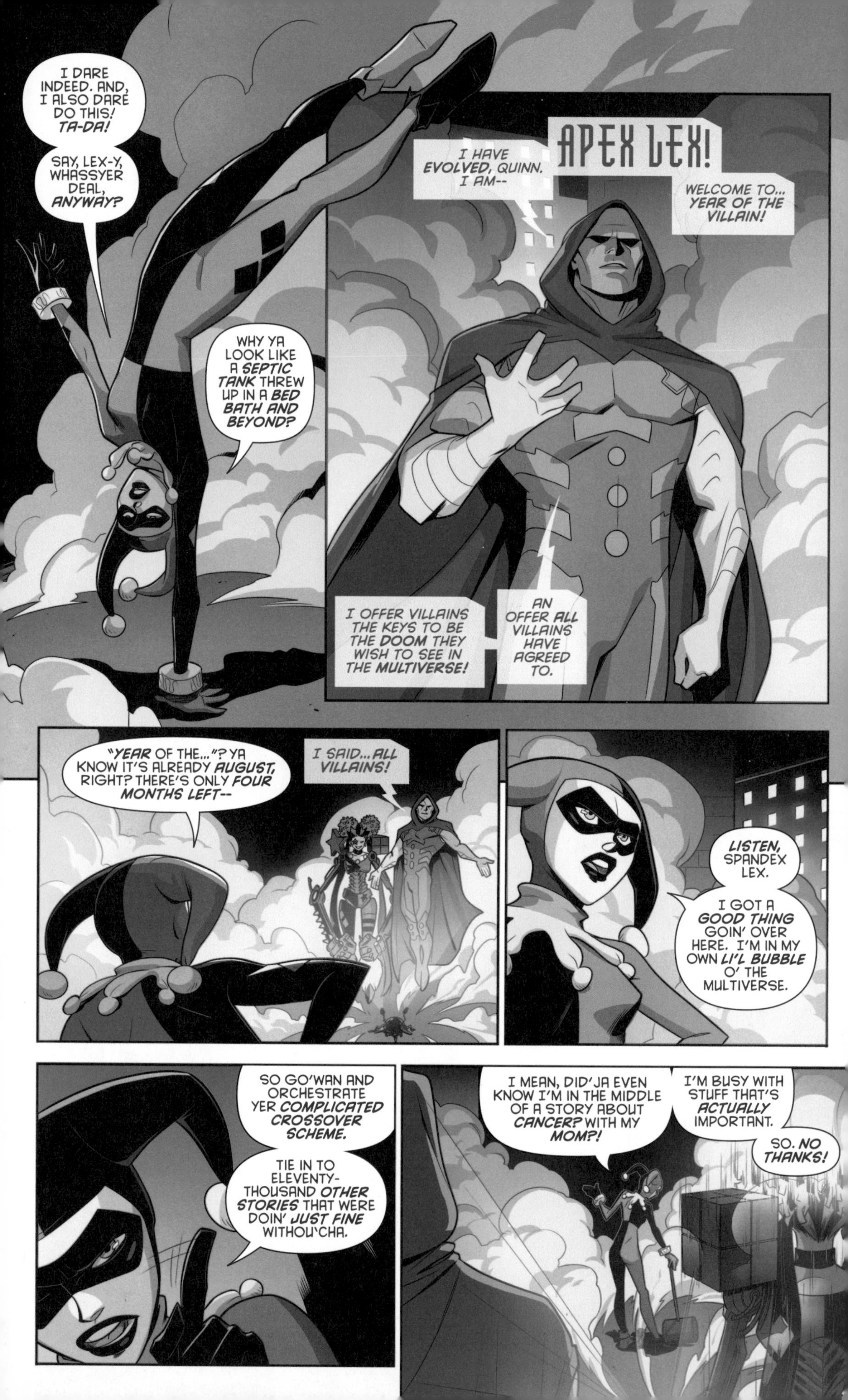
I DARE INDEED. AND, I ALSO DARE DO THIS! TA-DA!
SAY, LEX-Y, WHASSYER DEAL, ANYWAY?
WHY YA LOOK LIKE A SEPTIC TANK THREW UP IN A BED BATH AND BEYOND?
I HAVE EVOLVED, QUINN. I AM--
APEX LEX!
WELCOME TO... YEAR OF THE VILLAIN!
I OFFER VILLAINS THE KEYS TO BE THE DOOM THEY WISH TO SEE IN THE MULTIVERSE!
AN OFFER ALL VILLAINS HAVE AGREED TO.
"YEAR OF THE..."? YA KNOW IT'S ALREADY AUGUST, RIGHT? THERE'S ONLY FOUR MONTHS LEFT--
I SAID...ALL VILLAINS!
LISTEN, SPANDEX LEX.
I GOT A GOOD THING GOIN' OVER HERE. I'M IN MY OWN LI'L BUBBLE O' THE MULTIVERSE.
SO GO'WAN AND ORCHESTRATE YER COMPLICATED CROSSOVER SCHEME.
TIE IN TO ELEVENTY-THOUSAND OTHER STORIES THAT WERE DOIN' JUST FINE WITHOU'CHA.
I MEAN, DID'JA EVEN KNOW I'M IN THE MIDDLE OF A STORY ABOUT CANCER? WITH MY MOM?!
I'M BUSY WITH STUFF THAT'S ACTUALLY IMPORTANT.
SO. NO THANKS!

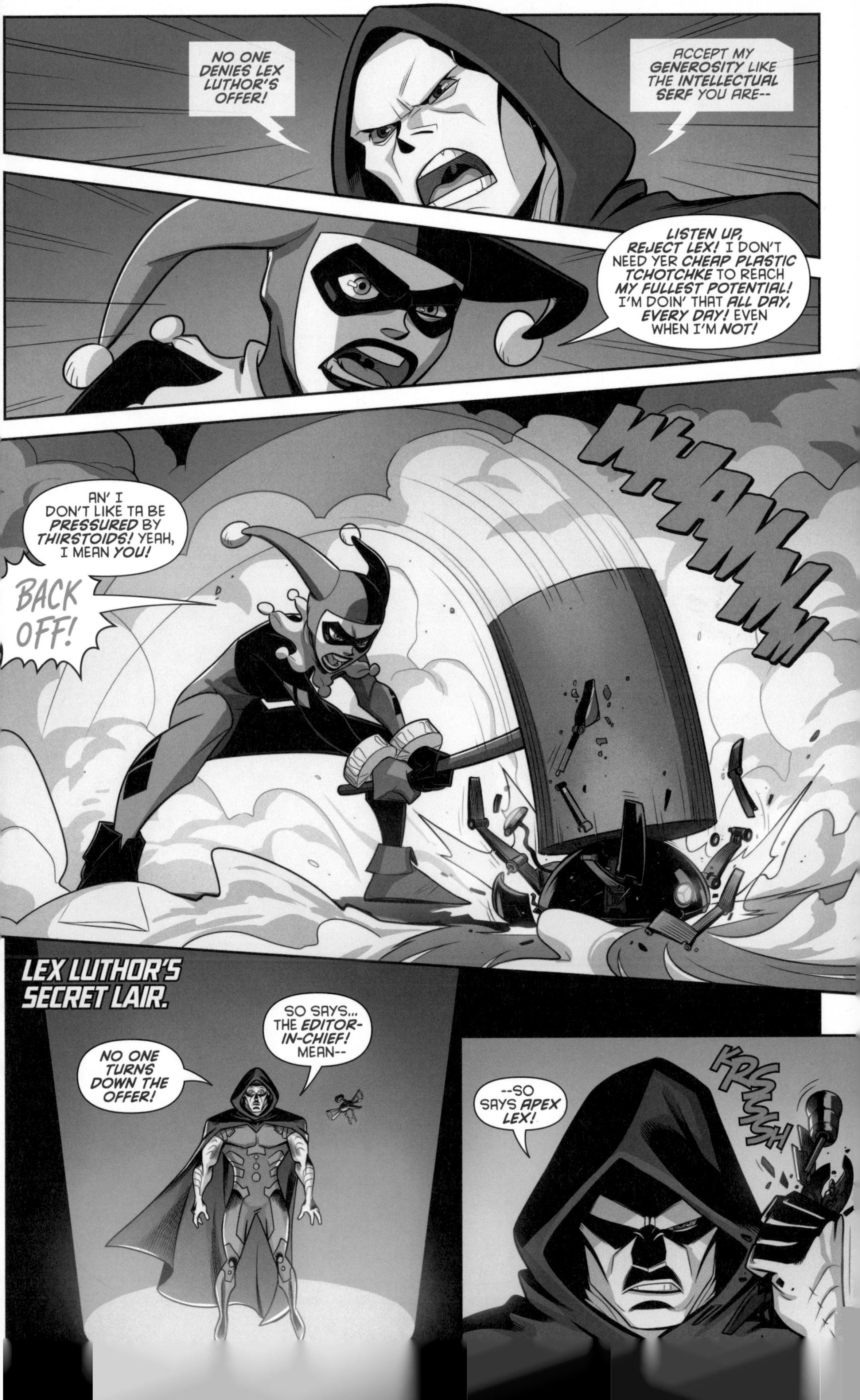
NO ONE DENIES LEX LUTHOR'S OFFER!
ACCEPT MY GENEROSITY LIKE THE INTELLECTUAL SERF YOU ARE--
LISTEN UP, REJECT LEX! I DON'T NEED YER CHEAP PLASTIC TCHOTCHKE TO REACH MY FULLEST POTENTIAL! I'M DOIN' THAT ALL DAY, EVERY DAY! EVEN WHEN I'M NOT!
AN' I DON'T LIKE TA BE PRESSURED BY THIRSTOIDS! YEAH, I MEAN YOU!
BACK OFF!
WHAMM
LEX LUTHOR'S SECRET LAIR.
NO ONE TURNS DOWN THE OFFER!
SO SAYS... THE EDITOR-IN-CHIEF! MEAN--
--SO SAYS APEX LEX!
KRSSSH

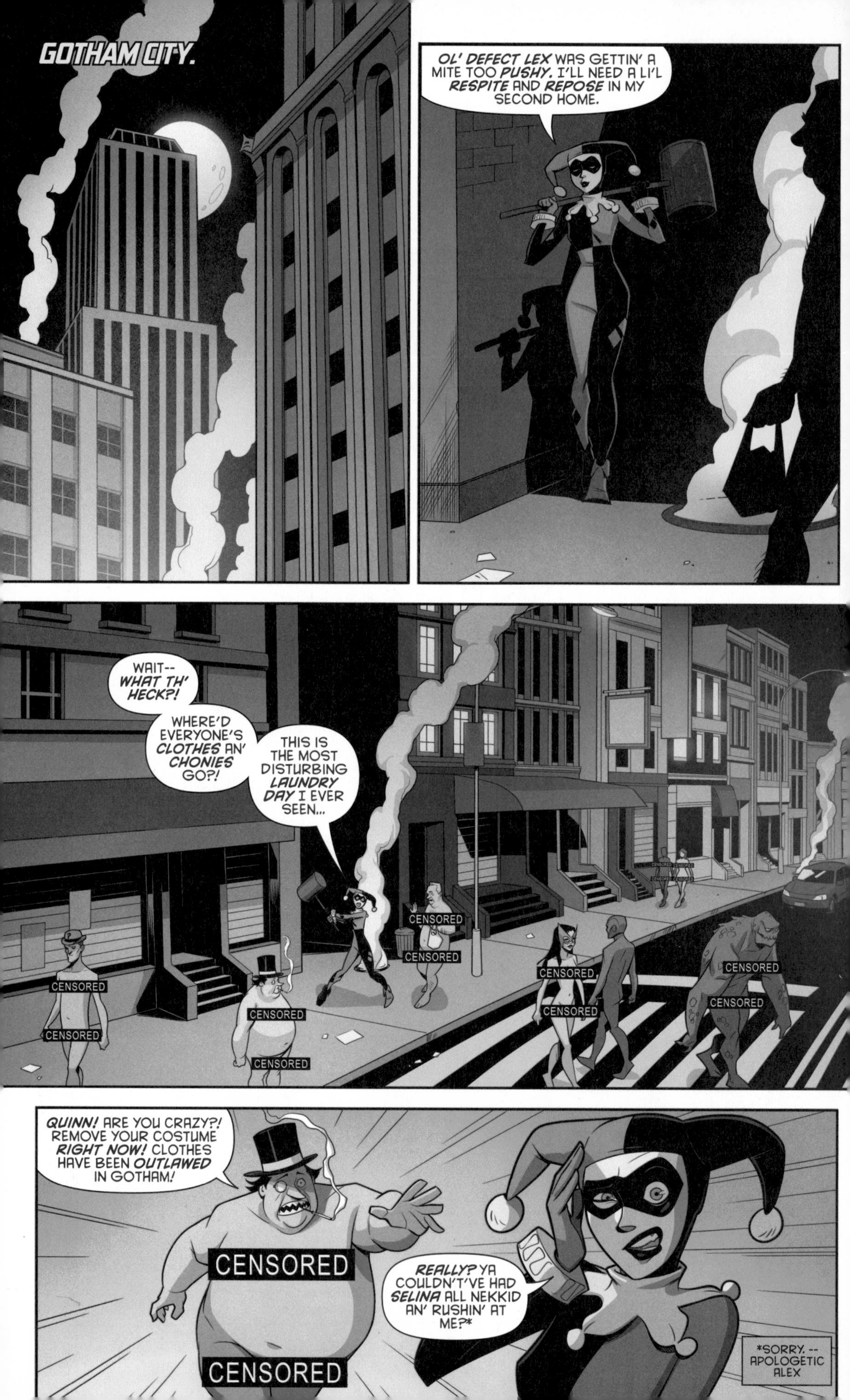
GOTHAM CITY.
OL' DEFECT LEX WAS GETTIN' A MITE TOO PUSHY. I'LL NEED A LI'L RESPITE AND REPOSE IN MY SECOND HOME.
WAIT-- WHAT TH' HECK?!
WHERE'D EVERYONE'S CLOTHES AN' CHONIES GO?!
THIS IS THE MOST DISTURBING LAUNDRY DAY I EVER SEEN...
CENSORED
CENSORED
CENSORED
CENSORED
CENSORED
CENSORED
CENSORED
CENSORED
CENSORED
CENSORED
QUINN! ARE YOU CRAZY?! REMOVE YOUR COSTUME RIGHT NOW! CLOTHES HAVE BEEN OUTLAWED IN GOTHAM!
CENSORED
REALLY? YA COULDN'T'VE HAD SELINA ALL NEKKID AN' RUSHIN' AT ME?*
CENSORED
*SORRY. --APOLOGETIC ALEX

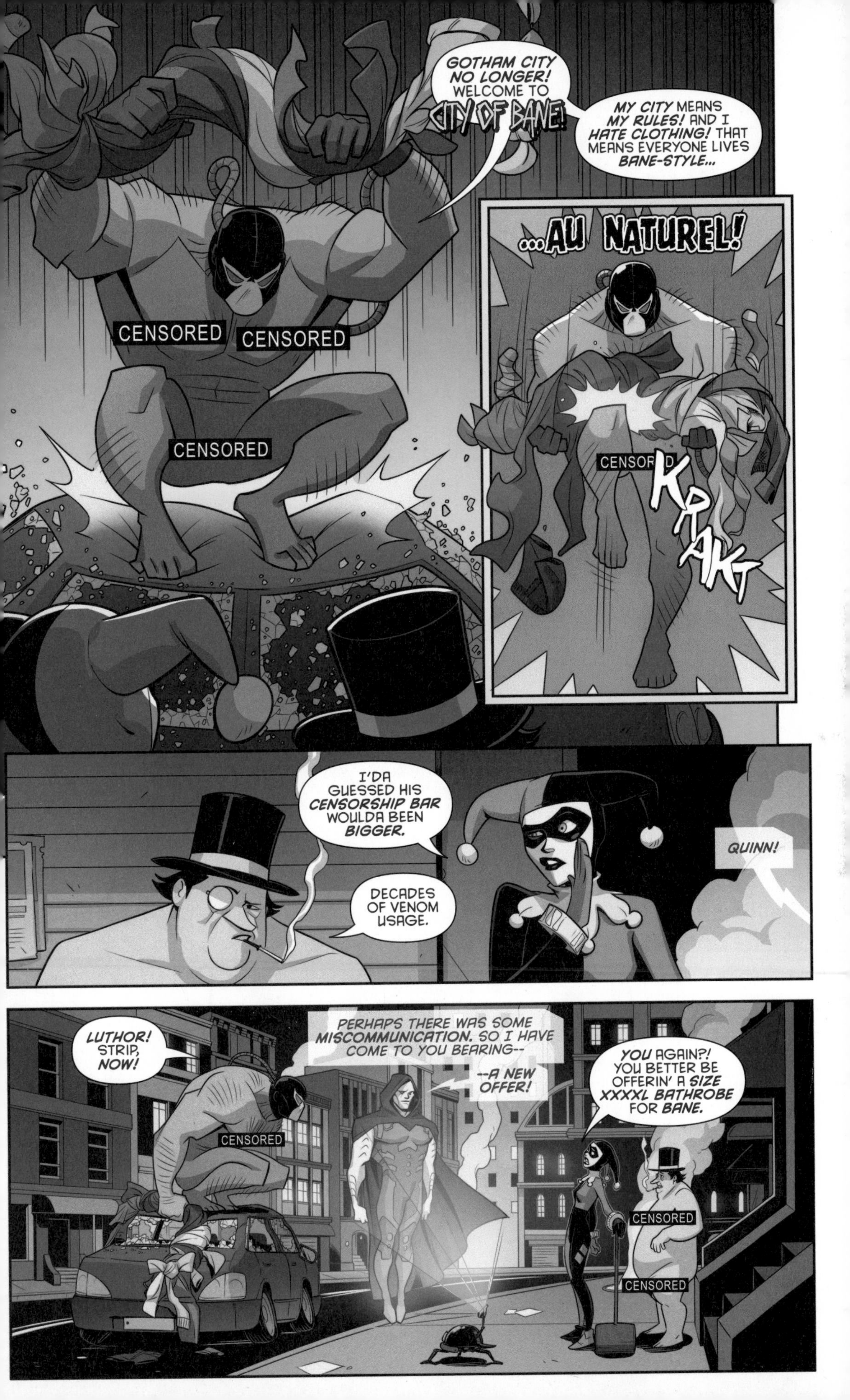
GOTHAM CITY NO LONGER! WELCOME TO CITY OF BANE!
MY CITY MEANS MY RULES! AND I HATE CLOTHING! THAT MEANS EVERYONE LIVES BANE-STYLE...
CENSORED
CENSORED
CENSORED
...AU NATUREL!
CENSORED
KRAKT
I'DA GUESSED HIS CENSORSHIP BAR WOULDA BEEN BIGGER.
DECADES OF VENOM USAGE.
QUINN!
LUTHOR! STRIP, NOW!
PERHAPS THERE WAS SOME MISCOMMUNICATION. SO I HAVE COME TO YOU BEARING--
--A NEW OFFER!
YOU AGAIN?! YOU BETTER BE OFFERIN' A SIZE XXXXL BATHROBE FOR BANE.
CENSORED
CENSORED
CENSORED

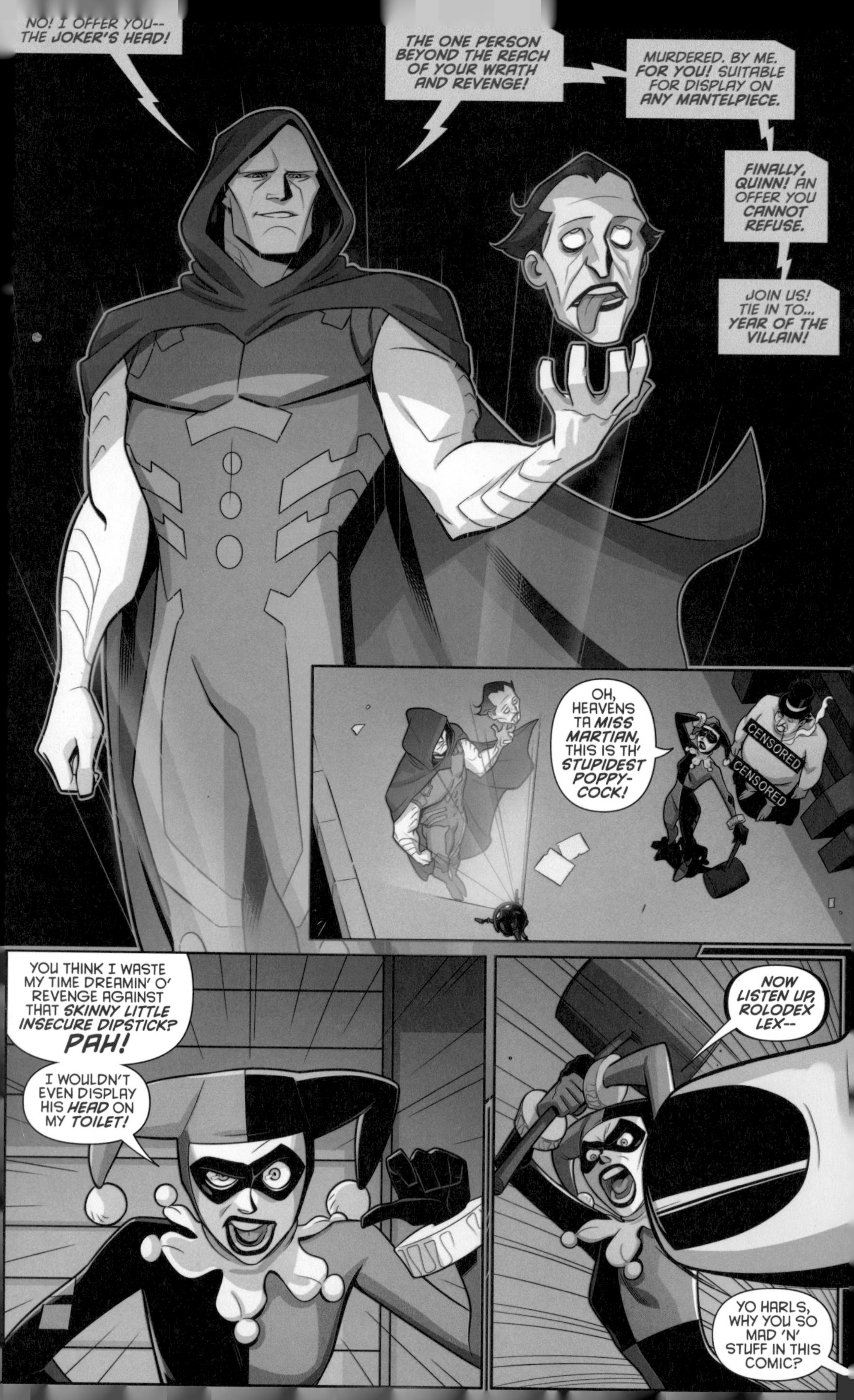

NO! I OFFER YOU-- THE JOKER'S HEAD!
THE ONE PERSON BEYOND THE REACH OF YOUR WRATH AND REVENGE!
MURDERED. BY ME. FOR YOU! SUITABLE FOR DISPLAY ON ANY MANTELPIECE.
FINALLY, QUINN! AN OFFER YOU CANNOT REFUSE.
JOIN US! TIE IN TO... YEAR OF THE VILLAIN!
OH, HEAVENS TA MISS MARTIAN, THIS IS TH' STUPIDEST POPPY-COCK!
CENSORED
CENSORED
CENSORED
YOU THINK I WASTE MY TIME DREAMIN' O' REVENGE AGAINST THAT SKINNY LITTLE INSECURE DIPSTICK? PAH!
I WOULDN'T EVEN DISPLAY HIS HEAD ON MY TOILET!
NOW LISTEN UP, ROLODEX LEX--
YO HARLS, WHY YOU SO MAD 'N' STUFF IN THIS COMIC?

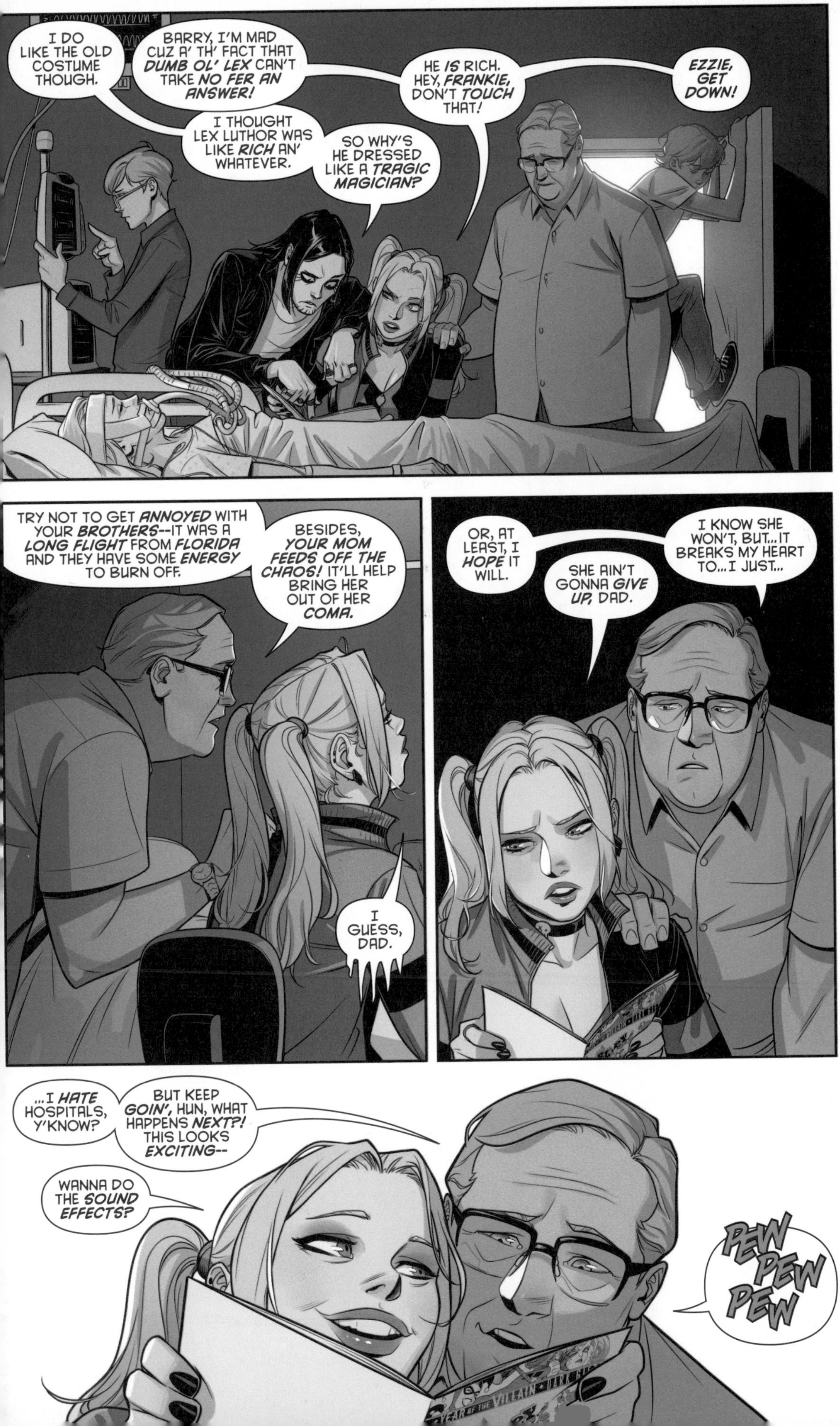

I DO LIKE THE OLD COSTUME THOUGH.
BARRY, I'M MAD CUZ A' TH' FACT THAT DUMB OL' LEX CAN'T TAKE NO FER AN ANSWER!
I THOUGHT LEX LUTHOR WAS LIKE RICH AN' WHATEVER.
SO WHY'S HE DRESSED LIKE A TRAGIC MAGICIAN?
HE IS RICH. HEY, FRANKIE, DON'T TOUCH THAT!
EZZIE, GET DOWN!
TRY NOT TO GET ANNOYED WITH YOUR BROTHERS--IT WAS A LONG FLIGHT FROM FLORIDA AND THEY HAVE SOME ENERGY TO BURN OFF.
BESIDES, YOUR MOM FEEDS OFF THE CHAOS! IT'LL HELP BRING HER OUT OF HER COMA.
I GUESS, DAD.
OR, AT LEAST, I HOPE IT WILL.
SHE AIN'T GONNA GIVE UP, DAD.
I KNOW SHE WON'T, BUT...IT BREAKS MY HEART TO...I JUST...
...I HATE HOSPITALS, Y'KNOW?
BUT KEEP GOIN', HUN, WHAT HAPPENS NEXT?! THIS LOOKS EXCITING--
WANNA DO THE SOUND EFFECTS?
PEW PEW PEW

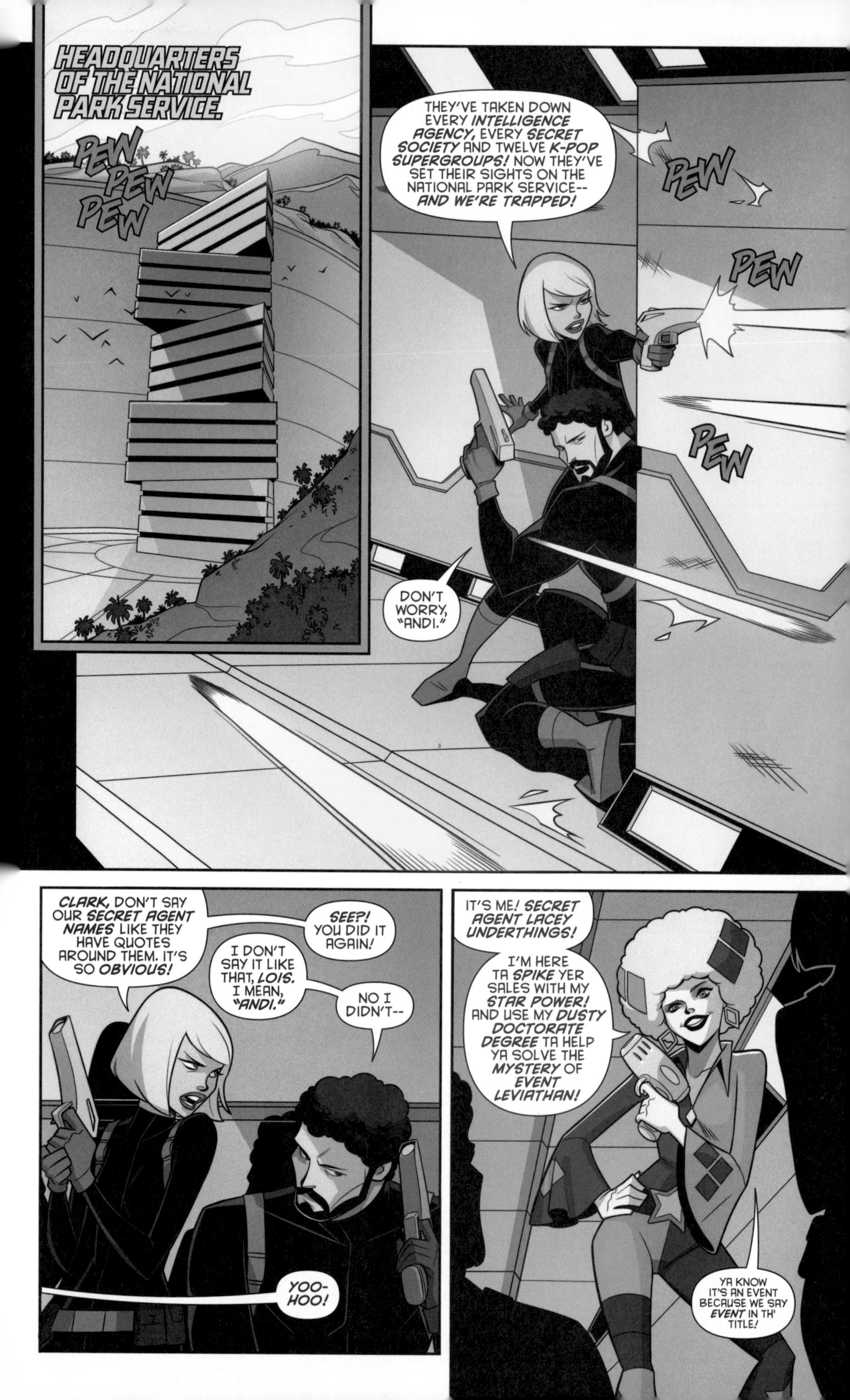
HEADQUARTERS OF THE NATIONAL PARK SERVICE.
PEW PEW PEW
THEY'VE TAKEN DOWN EVERY INTELLIGENCE AGENCY, EVERY SECRET SOCIETY AND TWELVE K-POP SUPERGROUPS! NOW THEY'VE SET THEIR SIGHTS ON THE NATIONAL PARK SERVICE-- AND WE'RE TRAPPED!
PEW
PEW
PEW
DON'T WORRY, "ANDI."
CLARK, DON'T SAY OUR SECRET AGENT NAMES LIKE THEY HAVE QUOTES AROUND THEM. IT'S SO OBVIOUS!
I DON'T SAY IT LIKE THAT, LOIS. I MEAN, "ANDI."
SEE?! YOU DID IT AGAIN!
NO I DIDN'T--
YOO-HOO!
IT'S ME! SECRET AGENT LACEY UNDERTHINGS!
I'M HERE TA SPIKE YER SALES WITH MY STAR POWER! AND USE MY DUSTY DOCTORATE DEGREE TA HELP YA SOLVE THE MYSTERY OF EVENT LEVIATHAN!
YA KNOW IT'S AN EVENT BECAUSE WE SAY EVENT IN TH' TITLE!

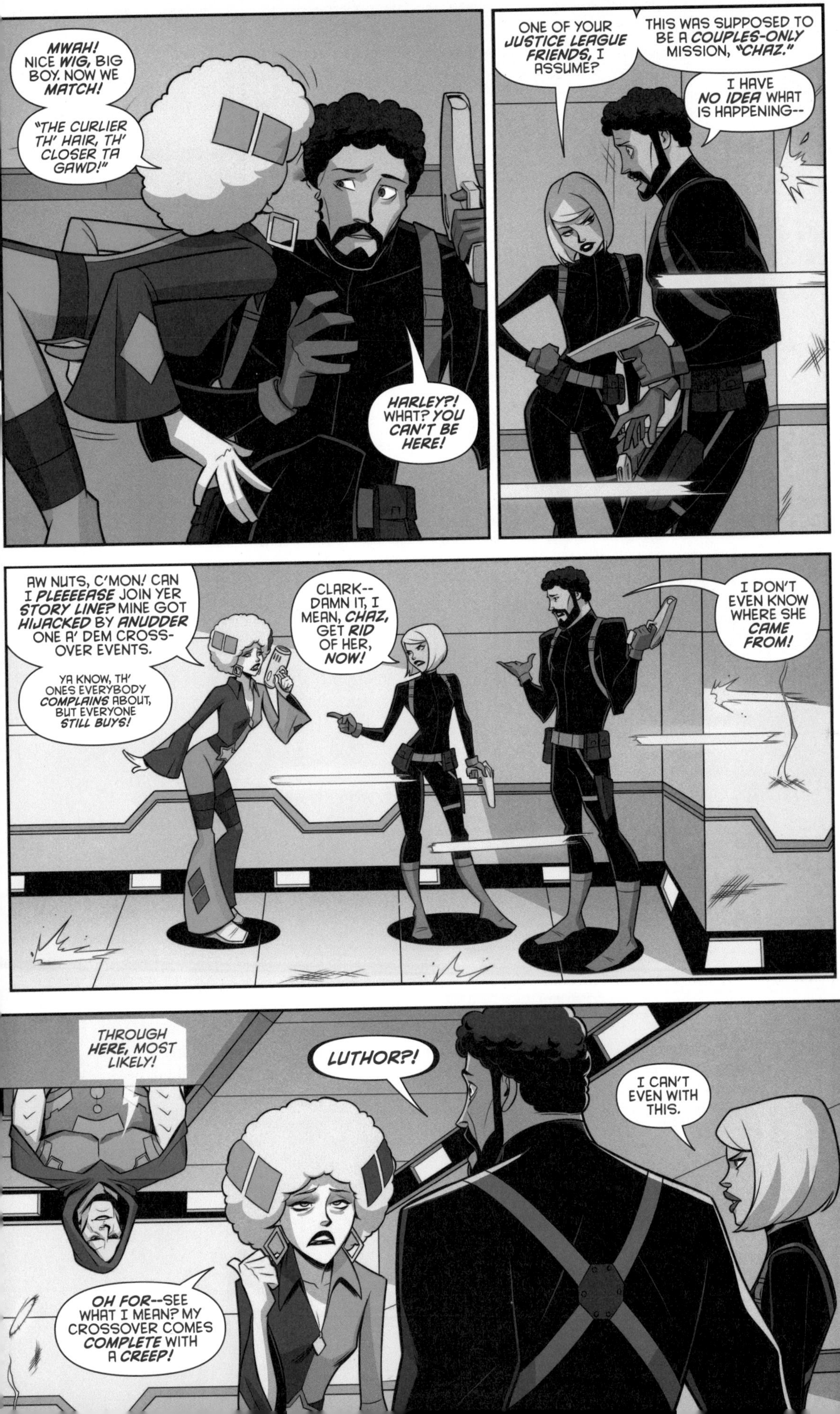
MWAH! NICE WIG, BIG BOY. NOW WE MATCH!
"THE CURLIER TH' HAIR, TH' CLOSER TA GAWD!"
HARLEY?! WHAT? YOU CAN'T BE HERE!
ONE OF YOUR JUSTICE LEAGUE FRIENDS, I ASSUME?
THIS WAS SUPPOSED TO BE A COUPLES-ONLY MISSION, "CHAZ."
I HAVE NO IDEA WHAT IS HAPPENING--
AW NUTS, C'MON! CAN I PLEEEEASE JOIN YER STORY LINE? MINE GOT HIJACKED BY ANUDDER ONE A' DEM CROSS-OVER EVENTS.
YA KNOW, TH' ONES EVERYBODY COMPLAINS ABOUT, BUT EVERYONE STILL BUYS!
CLARK--DAMN IT, I MEAN, CHAZ, GET RID OF HER, NOW!
I DON'T EVEN KNOW WHERE SHE CAME FROM!
THROUGH HERE, MOST LIKELY!
LUTHOR?!
I CAN'T EVEN WITH THIS.
OH FOR--SEE WHAT I MEAN? MY CROSSOVER COMES COMPLETE WITH A CREEP!

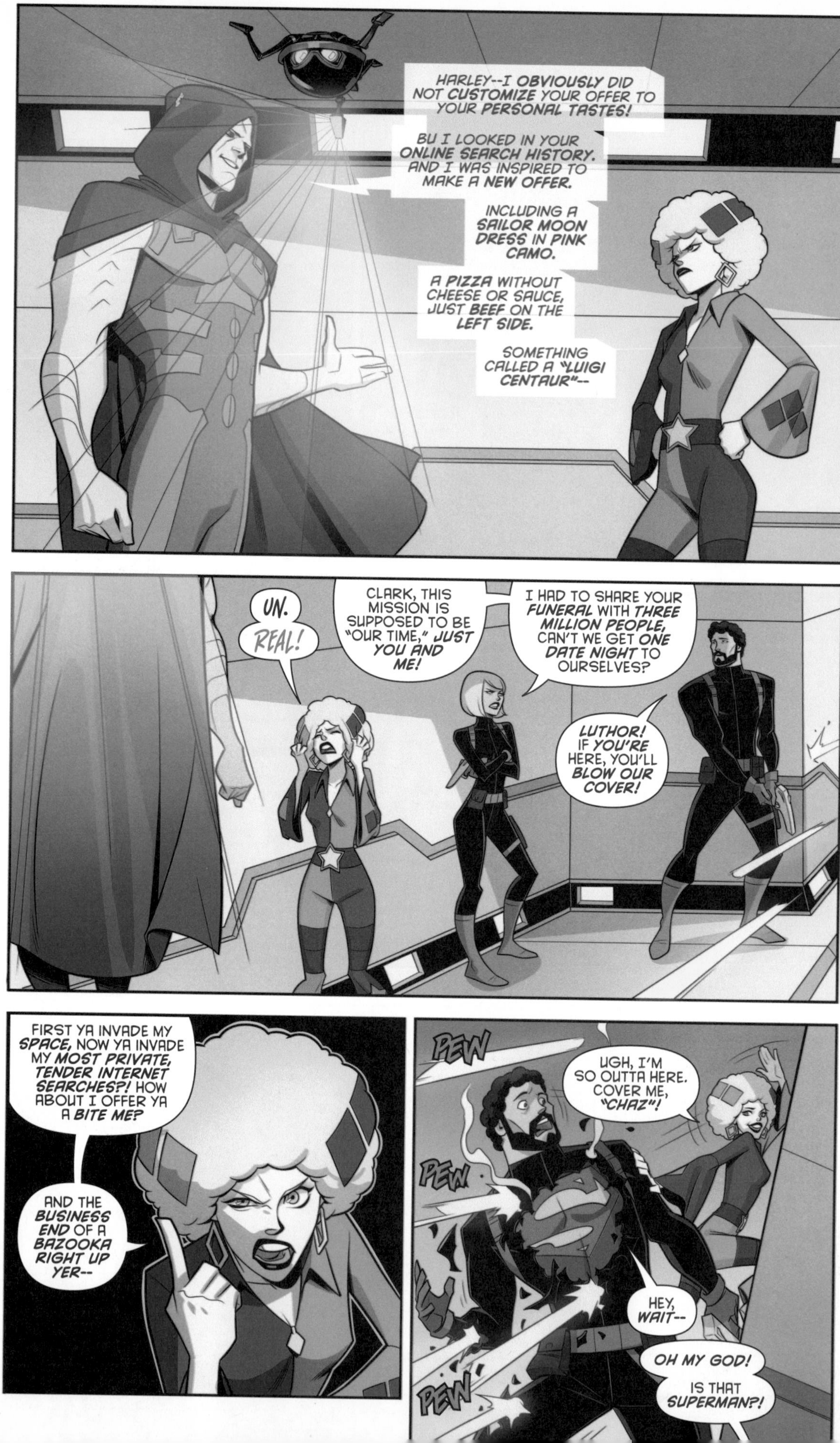
HARLEY--I OBVIOUSLY DID NOT CUSTOMIZE YOUR OFFER TO YOUR PERSONAL TASTES!
BU I LOOKED IN YOUR ONLINE SEARCH HISTORY. AND I WAS INSPIRED TO MAKE A NEW OFFER.
INCLUDING A SAILOR MOON DRESS IN PINK CAMO.
A PIZZA WITHOUT CHEESE OR SAUCE, JUST BEEF ON THE LEFT SIDE.
SOMETHING CALLED A "LUIGI CENTAUR"--
UN. REAL!
CLARK, THIS MISSION IS SUPPOSED TO BE "OUR TIME," JUST YOU AND ME!
I HAD TO SHARE YOUR FUNERAL WITH THREE MILLION PEOPLE, CAN'T WE GET ONE DATE NIGHT TO OURSELVES?
LUTHOR! IF YOU'RE HERE, YOU'LL BLOW OUR COVER!
FIRST YA INVADE MY SPACE, NOW YA INVADE MY MOST PRIVATE, TENDER INTERNET SEARCHES?! HOW ABOUT I OFFER YA A BITE ME?
AND THE BUSINESS END OF A BAZOOKA RIGHT UP YER--
PEW
UGH, I'M SO OUTTA HERE. COVER ME, "CHAZ"!
PEW
HEY, WAIT--
OH MY GOD!
IS THAT SUPERMAN?!
PEW

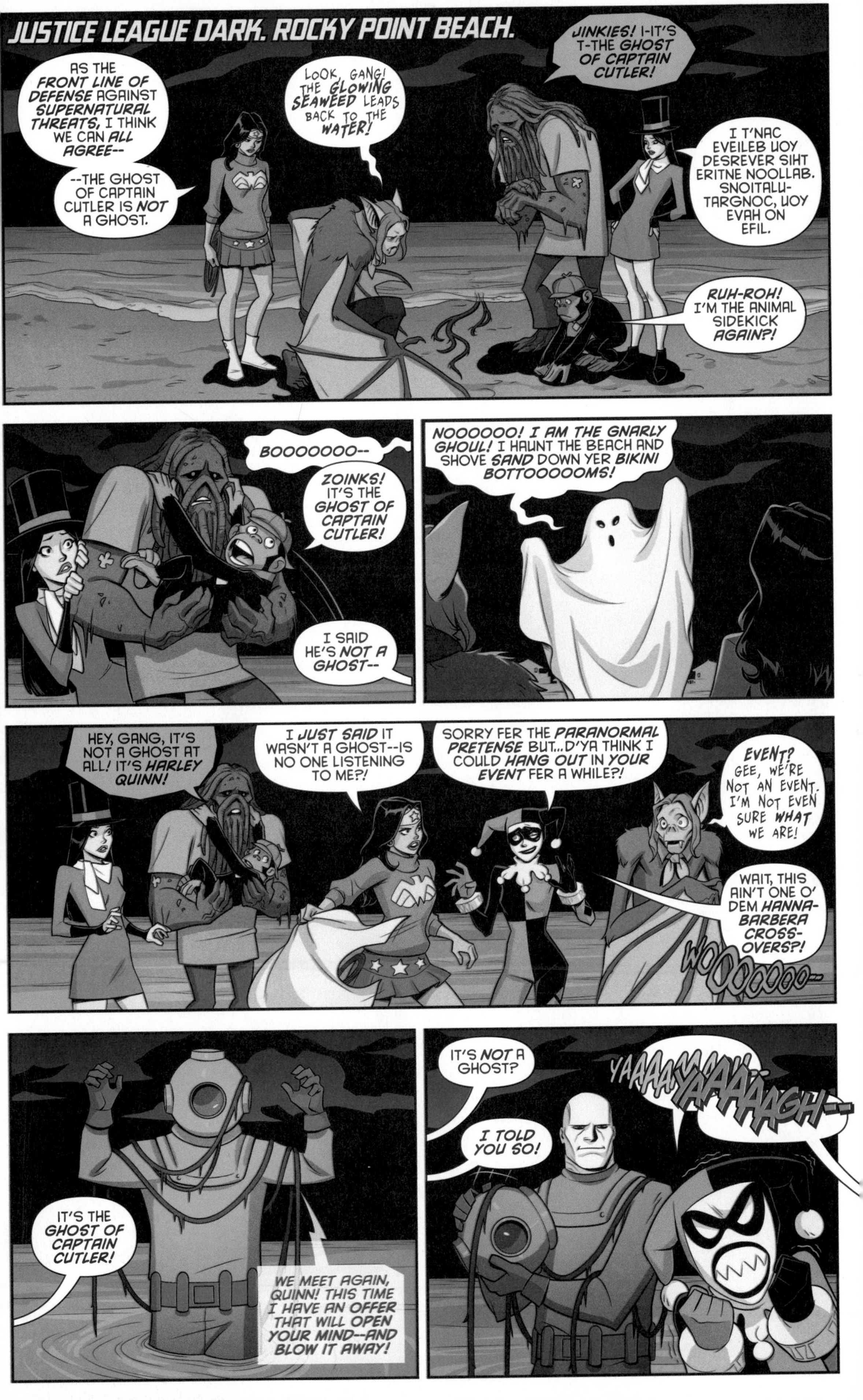
JUSTICE LEAGUE DARK. ROCKY POINT BEACH.
AS THE FRONT LINE OF DEFENSE AGAINST SUPERNATURAL THREATS, I THINK WE CAN ALL AGREE--
--THE GHOST OF CAPTAIN CUTLER IS NOT A GHOST.
LOOK, GANG! THE GLOWING SEAWEED LEADS BACK TO THE WATER!
JINKIES! I-IT'S T-THE GHOST OF CAPTAIN CUTLER!
I T'NAC EVEILEB UOY DESREVER SIHT ERITNE NOOLLAB. SNOITALU-TARGNOC, UOY EVAH ON EFIL.
RUH-ROH! I'M THE ANIMAL SIDEKICK AGAIN?!
BOOOOOOO--
ZOINKS! IT'S THE GHOST OF CAPTAIN CUTLER!
I SAID HE'S NOT A GHOST--
NOOOOOO! I AM THE GNARLY GHOUL! I HAUNT THE BEACH AND SHOVE SAND DOWN YER BIKINI BOTTOOOOOOMS!
HEY, GANG, IT'S NOT A GHOST AT ALL! IT'S HARLEY QUINN!
I JUST SAID IT WASN'T A GHOST--IS NO ONE LISTENING TO ME?!
SORRY FER THE PARANORMAL PRETENSE BUT...D'YA THINK I COULD HANG OUT IN YOUR EVENT FER A WHILE?!
EVENT? GEE, WE'RE NOT AN EVENT. I'M NOT EVEN SURE WHAT WE ARE!
WAIT, THIS AIN'T ONE O' DEM HANNA-BARBERA CROSS-OVERS?!
WOOOOOOO--
IT'S THE GHOST OF CAPTAIN CUTLER!
WE MEET AGAIN, QUINN! THIS TIME I HAVE AN OFFER THAT WILL OPEN YOUR MIND--AND BLOW IT AWAY!
IT'S NOT A GHOST?
I TOLD YOU SO!
YAAAAAAAAH--
YAAAAAAGH--

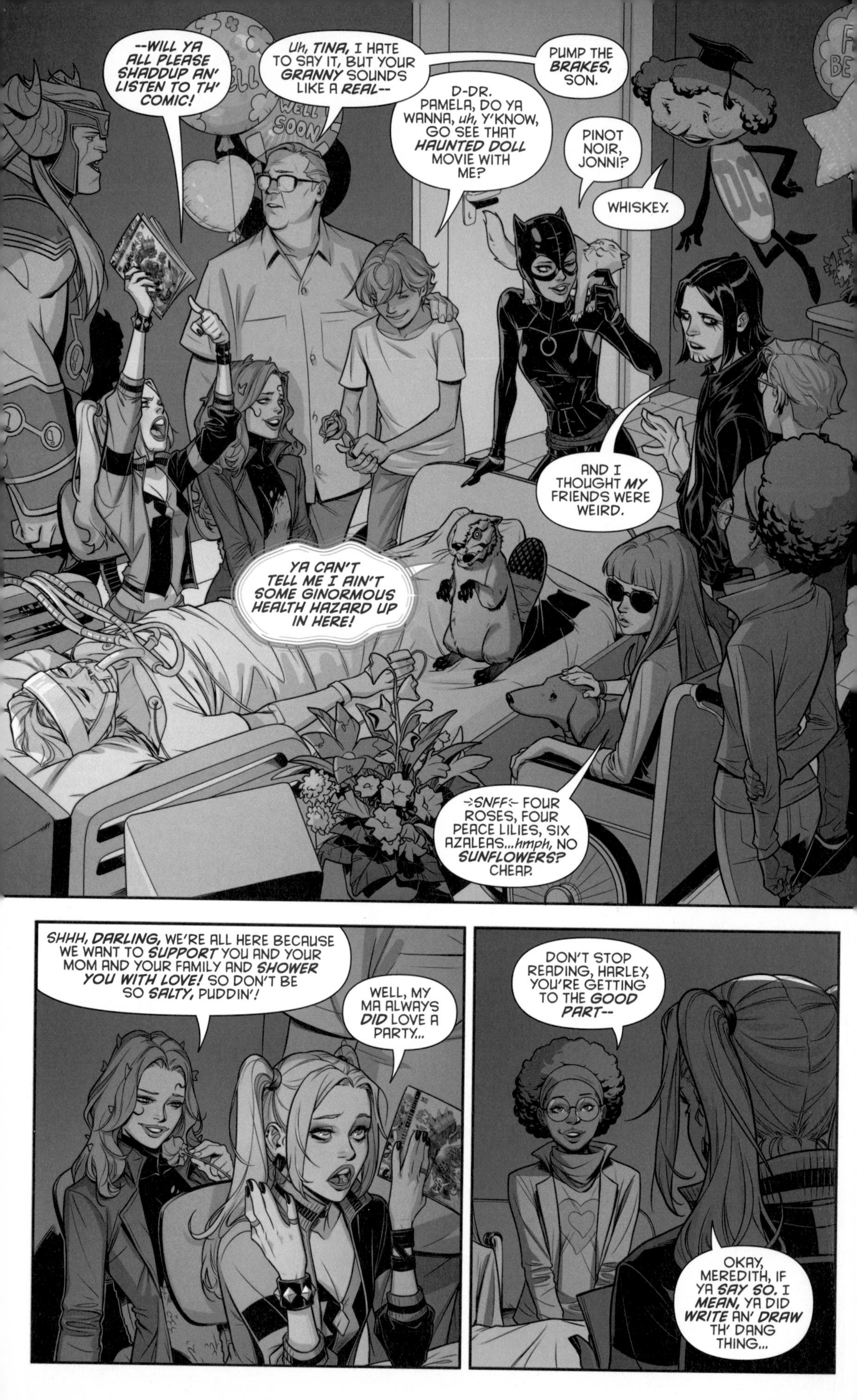
--WILL YA ALL PLEASE SHADDUP AN' LISTEN TO TH' COMIC!
UH, TINA, I HATE TO SAY IT, BUT YOUR GRANNY SOUNDS LIKE A REAL--
PUMP THE BRAKES, SON.
D-DR. PAMELA, DO YA WANNA, UH, Y'KNOW, GO SEE THAT HAUNTED DOLL MOVIE WITH ME?
PINOT NOIR, JONNI?
WHISKEY.
AND I THOUGHT MY FRIENDS WERE WEIRD.
YA CAN'T TELL ME I AIN'T SOME GINORMOUS HEALTH HAZARD UP IN HERE!
SNFF FOUR ROSES, FOUR PEACE LILIES, SIX AZALEAS...HMPH, NO SUNFLOWERS? CHEAP.
SHHH, DARLING, WE'RE ALL HERE BECAUSE WE WANT TO SUPPORT YOU AND YOUR MOM AND YOUR FAMILY AND SHOWER YOU WITH LOVE! SO DON'T BE SO SALTY, PUDDIN'!
WELL, MY MA ALWAYS DID LOVE A PARTY...
DON'T STOP READING, HARLEY, YOU'RE GETTING TO THE GOOD PART--
OKAY, MEREDITH, IF YA SAY SO. I MEAN, YA DID WRITE AN' DRAW TH' DANG THING...

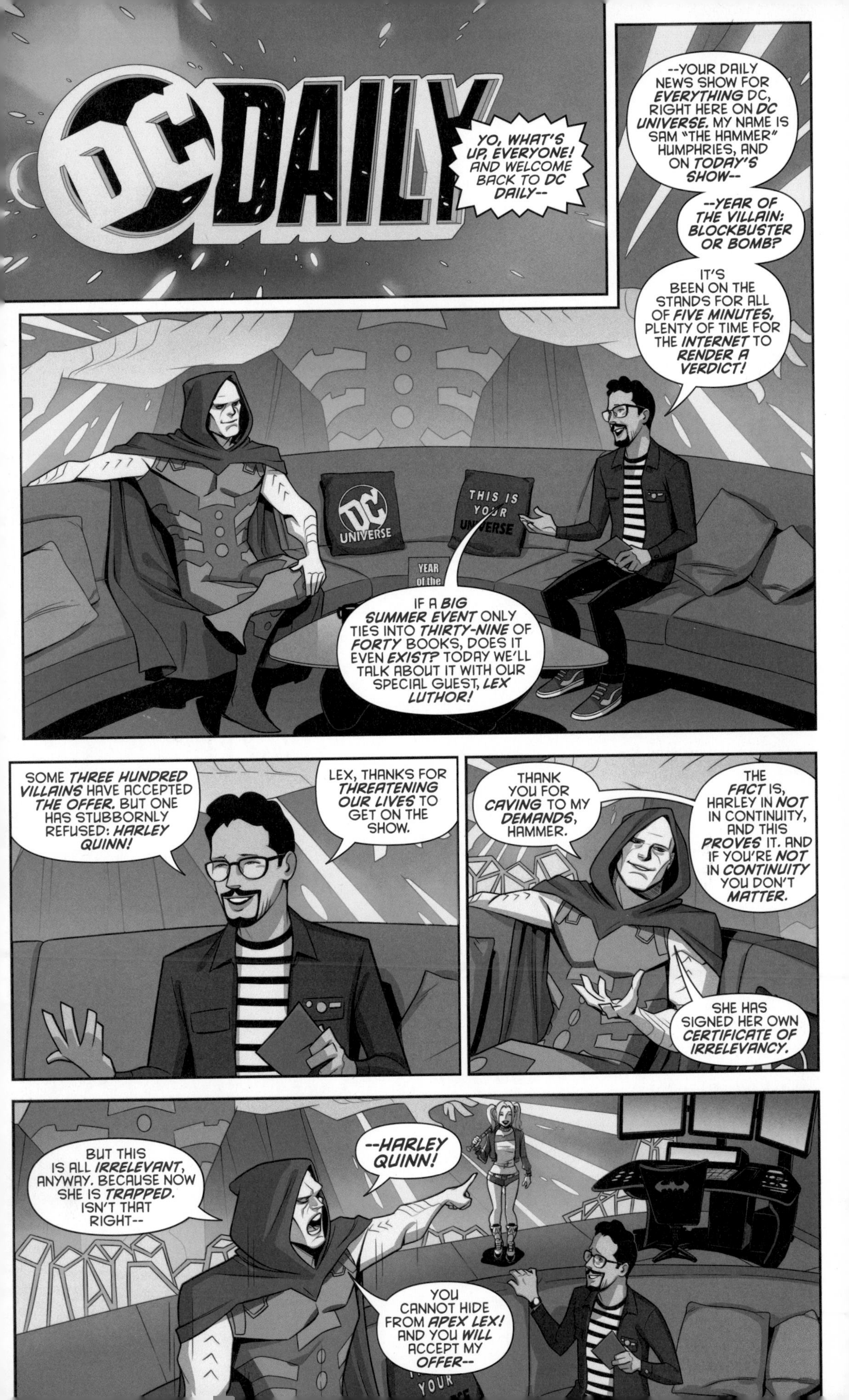
DC DAILY
YO, WHAT'S UP, EVERYONE! AND WELCOME BACK TO DC DAILY--
--YOUR DAILY NEWS SHOW FOR EVERYTHING DC, RIGHT HERE ON DC UNIVERSE. MY NAME IS SAM "THE HAMMER" HUMPHRIES, AND ON TODAY'S SHOW--
--YEAR OF THE VILLAIN: BLOCKBUSTER OR BOMB?
IT'S BEEN ON THE STANDS FOR ALL OF FIVE MINUTES, PLENTY OF TIME FOR THE INTERNET TO RENDER A VERDICT!
DC UNIVERSE
THIS IS YOUR UNIVERSE
YEAR of the
IF A BIG SUMMER EVENT ONLY TIES INTO THIRTY-NINE OF FORTY BOOKS, DOES IT EVEN EXIST? TODAY WE'LL TALK ABOUT IT WITH OUR SPECIAL GUEST, LEX LUTHOR!
SOME THREE HUNDRED VILLAINS HAVE ACCEPTED THE OFFER. BUT ONE HAS STUBBORNLY REFUSED: HARLEY QUINN!
LEX, THANKS FOR THREATENING OUR LIVES TO GET ON THE SHOW.
THANK YOU FOR CAVING TO MY DEMANDS, HAMMER.
THE FACT IS, HARLEY IN NOT IN CONTINUITY, AND THIS PROVES IT. AND IF YOU'RE NOT IN CONTINUITY YOU DON'T MATTER.
SHE HAS SIGNED HER OWN CERTIFICATE OF IRRELEVANCY.
BUT THIS IS ALL IRRELEVANT, ANYWAY. BECAUSE NOW SHE IS TRAPPED. ISN'T THAT RIGHT--
--HARLEY QUINN!
YOU CANNOT HIDE FROM APEX LEX! AND YOU WILL ACCEPT MY OFFER--

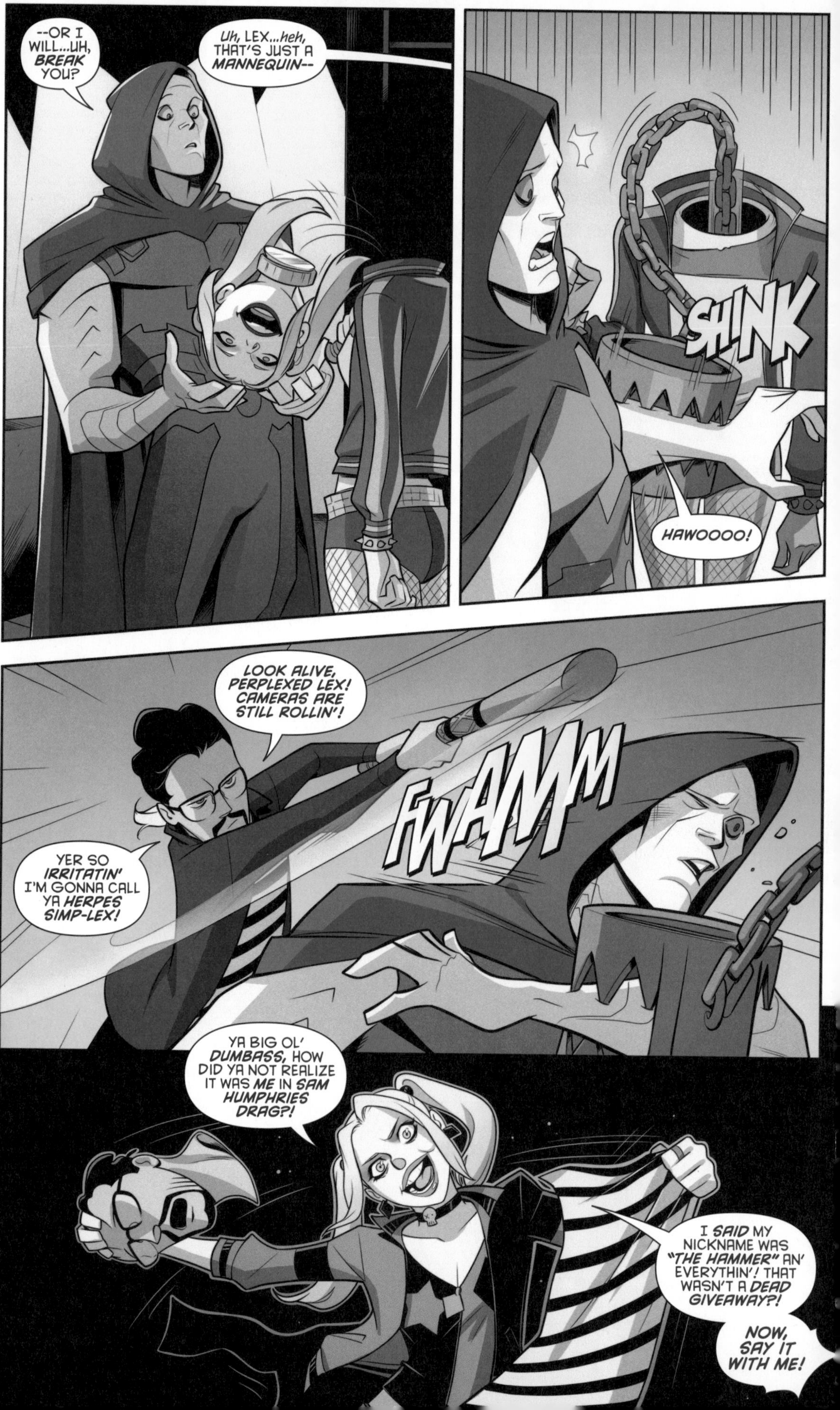
--OR I WILL...UH, BREAK YOU?
UH, LEX...heh, THAT'S JUST A MANNEQUIN--
SHINK
HAWOOOO!
LOOK ALIVE, PERPLEXED LEX! CAMERAS ARE STILL ROLLIN'!
FWAMM
YER SO IRRITATIN' I'M GONNA CALL YA HERPES SIMP-LEX!
YA BIG OL' DUMBASS, HOW DID YA NOT REALIZE IT WAS ME IN SAM HUMPHRIES DRAG?!
I SAID MY NICKNAME WAS "THE HAMMER" AN' EVERYTHIN'! THAT WASN'T A DEAD GIVEAWAY?!
NOW, SAY IT WITH ME!

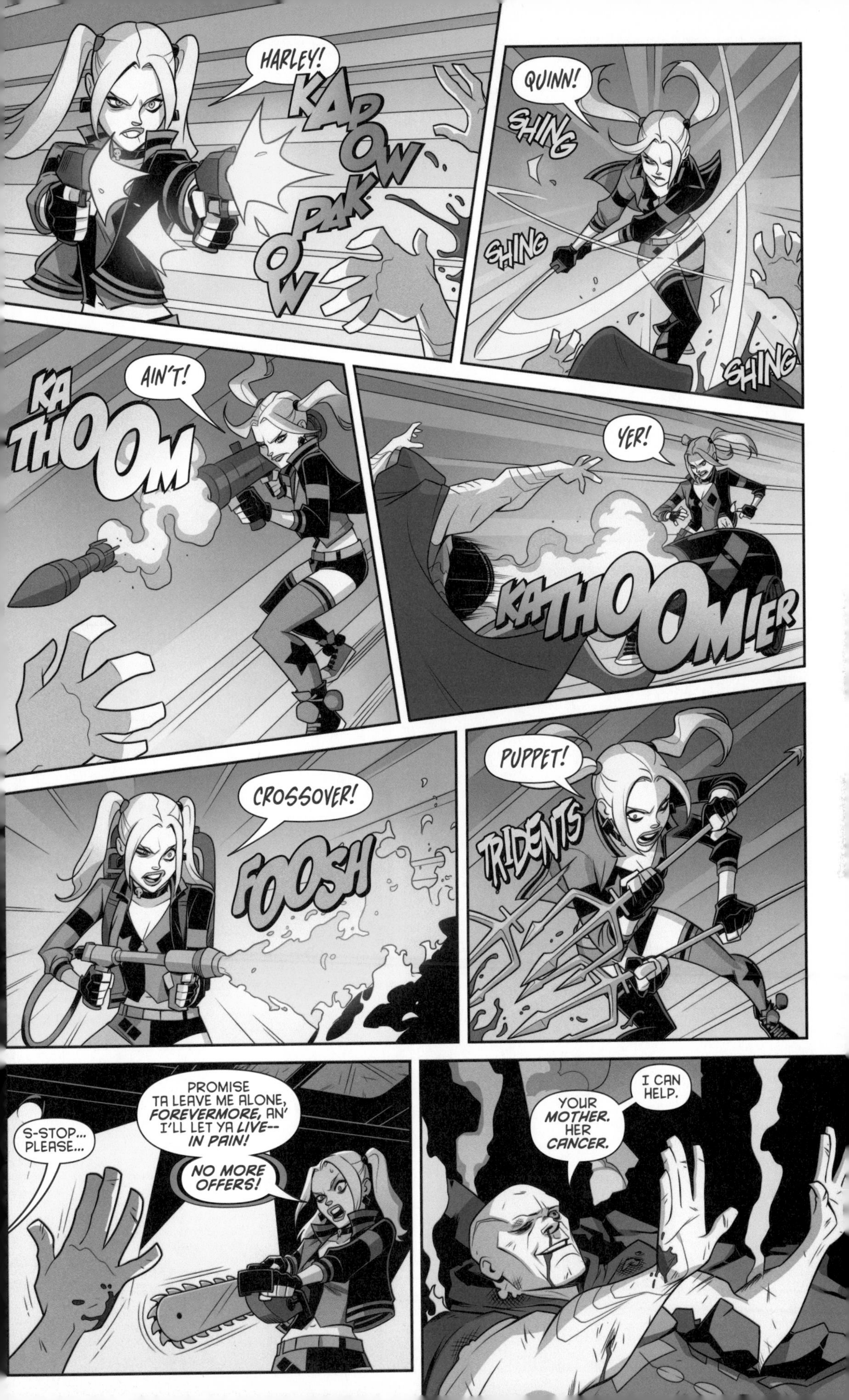

HARLEY!
KAPOW
PAK
POW
QUINN!
SHING
SHING
SHING
KA THOOM
AIN'T!
YER!
KATHOOMIER
CROSSOVER!
FOOSH
PUPPET!
TRIDENTS
S-STOP... PLEASE...
PROMISE TA LEAVE ME ALONE, FOREVERMORE, AN' I'LL LET YA LIVE-- IN PAIN!
NO MORE OFFERS!
I CAN HELP.
YOUR MOTHER. HER CANCER.

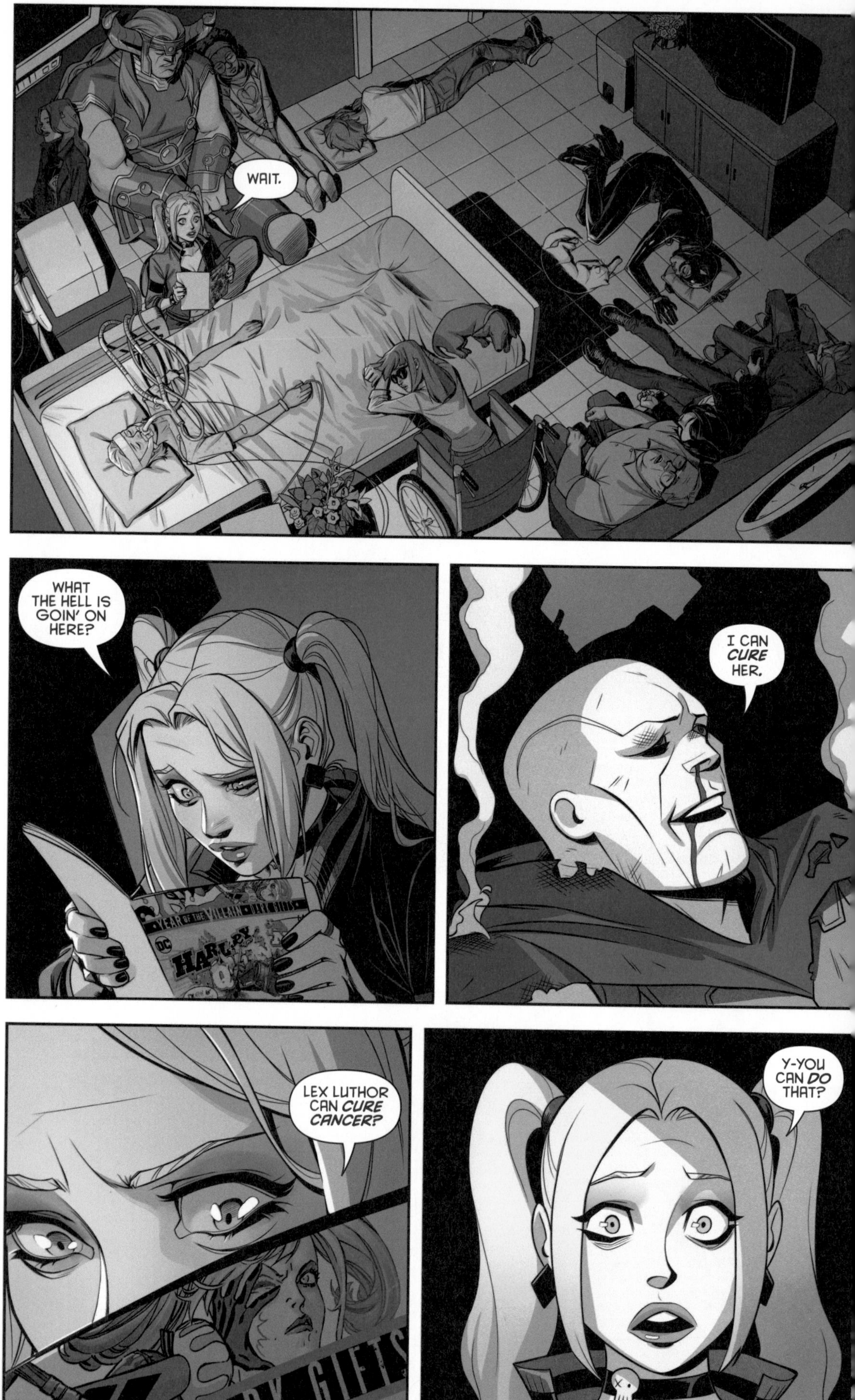
WAIT.
WHAT THE HELL IS GOIN' ON HERE?
I CAN *CURE* HER.
LEX LUTHOR CAN *CURE CANCER?*
Y-YOU CAN *DO* THAT?

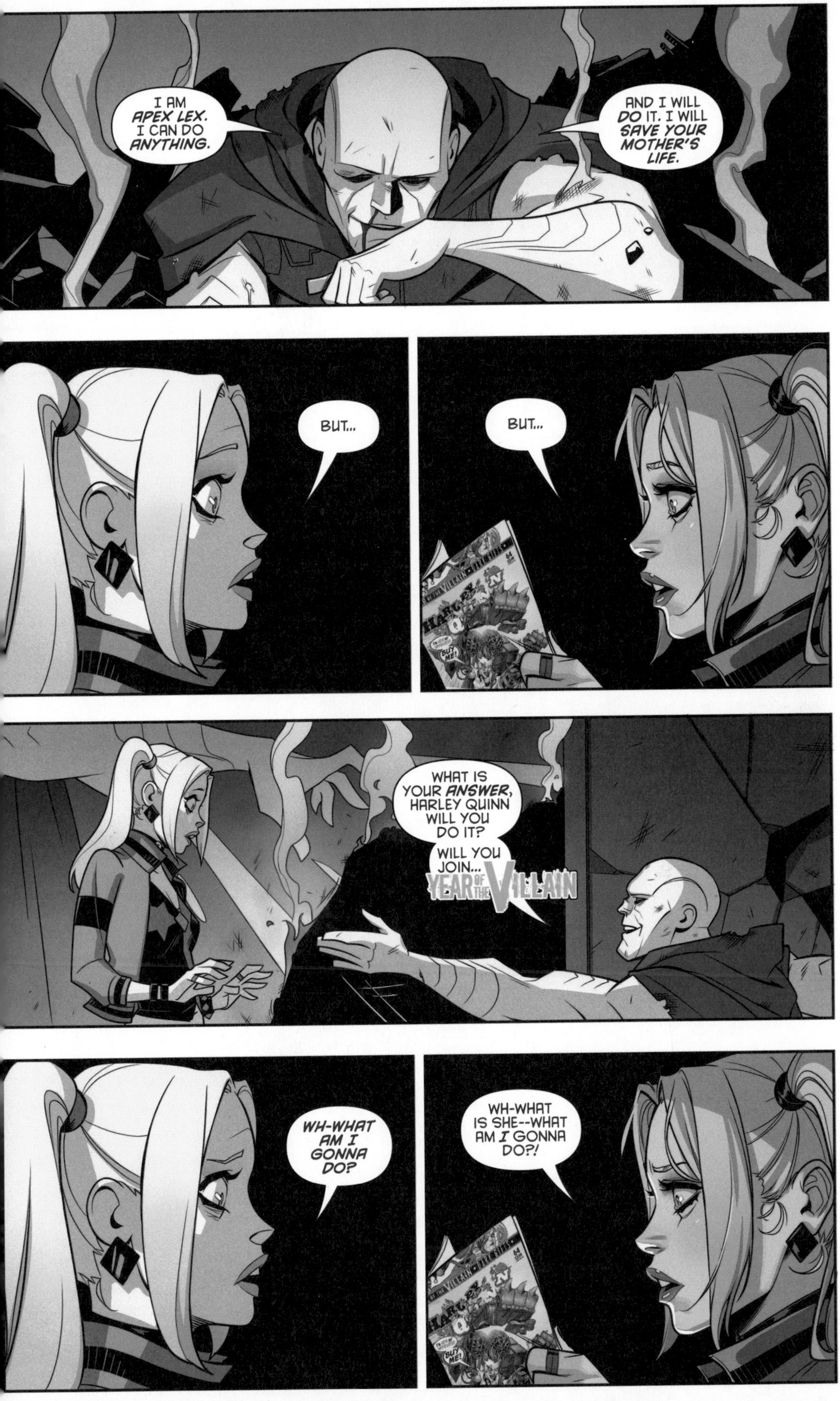
I AM APEX LEX. I CAN DO ANYTHING.
AND I WILL DO IT. I WILL SAVE YOUR MOTHER'S LIFE.
BUT...
BUT...
WHAT IS YOUR ANSWER, HARLEY QUINN WILL YOU DO IT?
WILL YOU JOIN... YEAR OF THE VILLAIN
WH-WHAT AM I GONNA DO?
WH-WHAT IS SHE--WHAT AM I GONNA DO?!

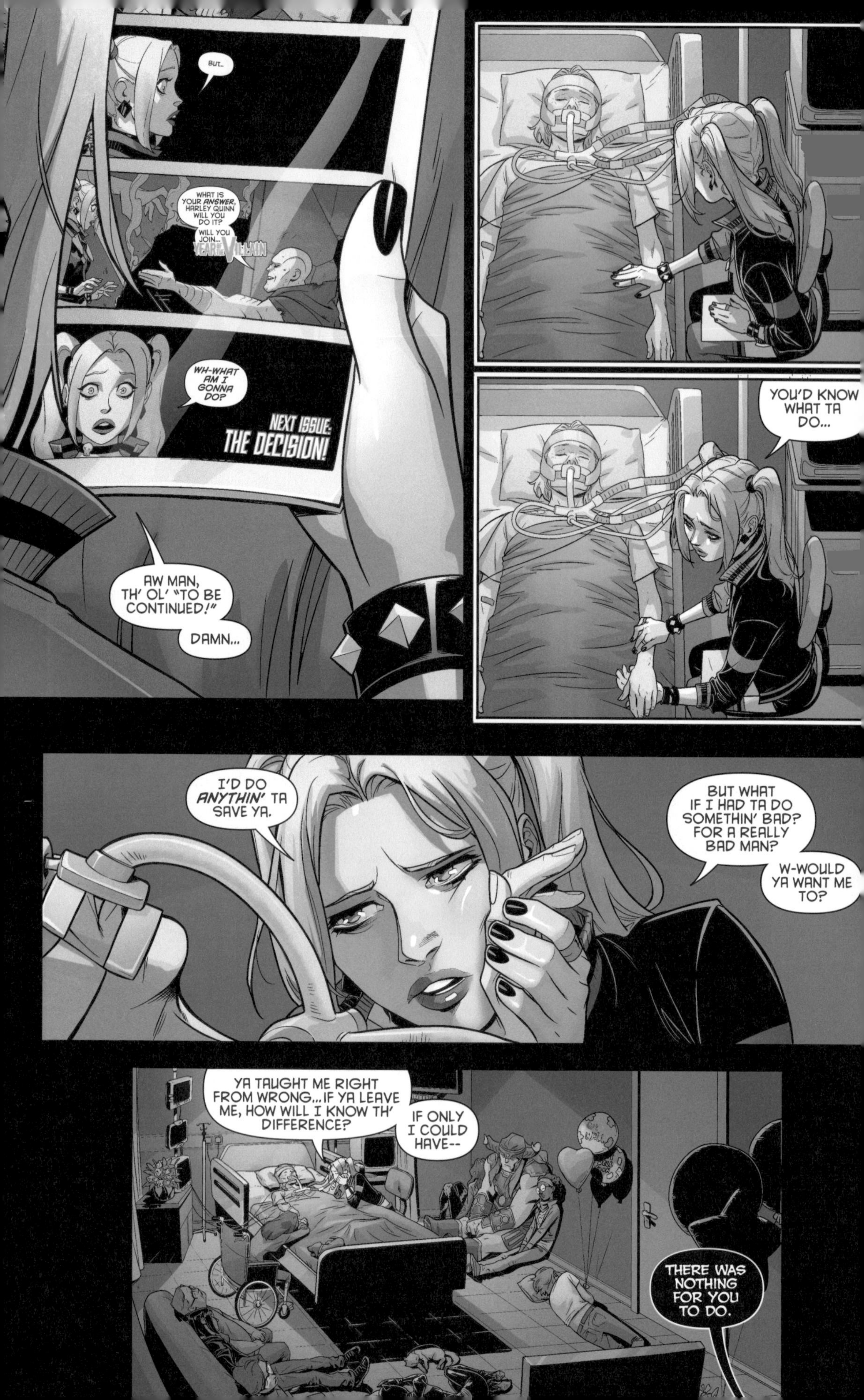
BUT...
WHAT IS YOUR ANSWER, HARLEY QUINN WILL YOU DO IT? WILL YOU JOIN... YEAR OF THE VILLAIN
WH-WHAT AM I GONNA DO?
NEXT ISSUE: THE DECISION!
AW MAN, TH' OL' "TO BE CONTINUED!"
DAMN...
YOU'D KNOW WHAT TA DO...
I'D DO ANYTHIN' TA SAVE YA.
BUT WHAT IF I HAD TA DO SOMETHIN' BAD? FOR A REALLY BAD MAN?
W-WOULD YA WANT ME TO?
YA TAUGHT ME RIGHT FROM WRONG...IF YA LEAVE ME, HOW WILL I KNOW TH' DIFFERENCE?
IF ONLY I COULD HAVE--
THERE WAS NOTHING FOR YOU TO DO.

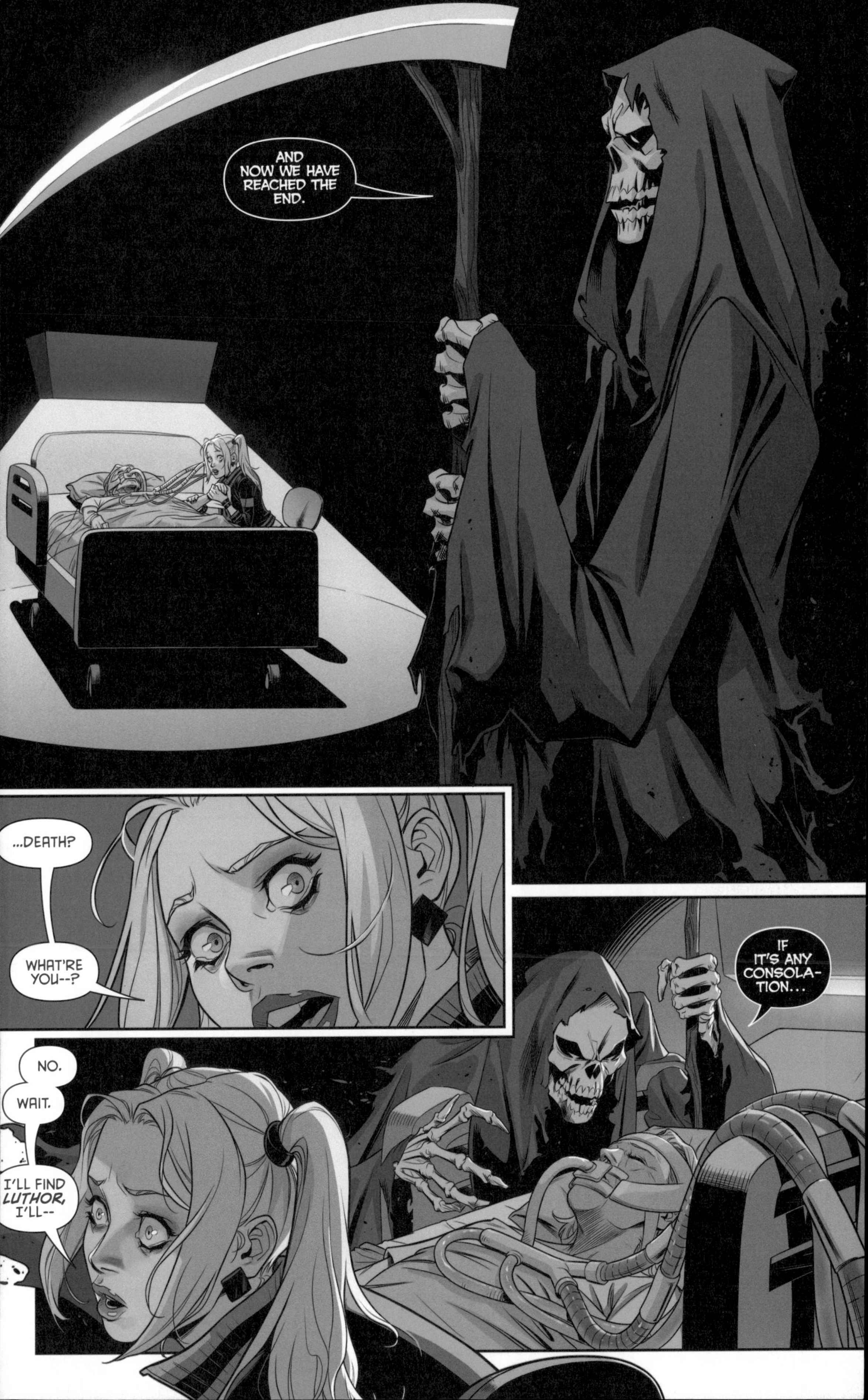
AND NOW WE HAVE REACHED THE END.
...DEATH?
WHAT'RE YOU--?
IF IT'S ANY CONSOLA-TION...
NO.
WAIT.
I'LL FIND *LUTHOR,* I'LL--

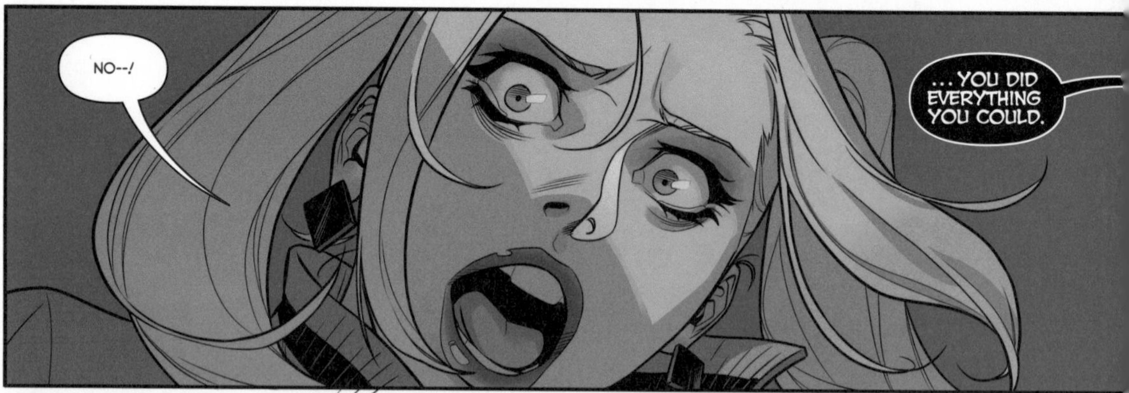
NO--!
...YOU DID EVERYTHING YOU COULD.

THE OFFER

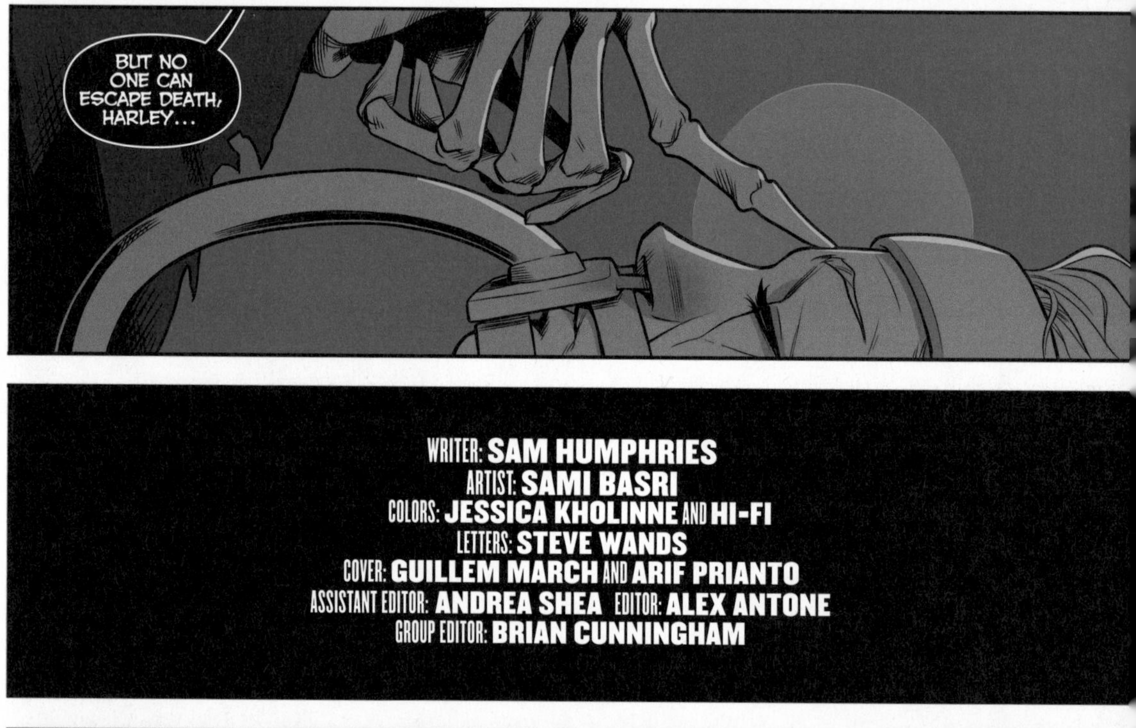
BUT NO ONE CAN ESCAPE DEATH, HARLEY...

WRITER: **SAM HUMPHRIES**
ARTIST: **SAMI BASRI**
COLORS: **JESSICA KHOLINNE** AND **HI-FI**
LETTERS: **STEVE WANDS**
COVER: **GUILLEM MARCH** AND **ARIF PRIANTO**
ASSISTANT EDITOR: **ANDREA SHEA** EDITOR: **ALEX ANTONE**
GROUP EDITOR: **BRIAN CUNNINGHAM**

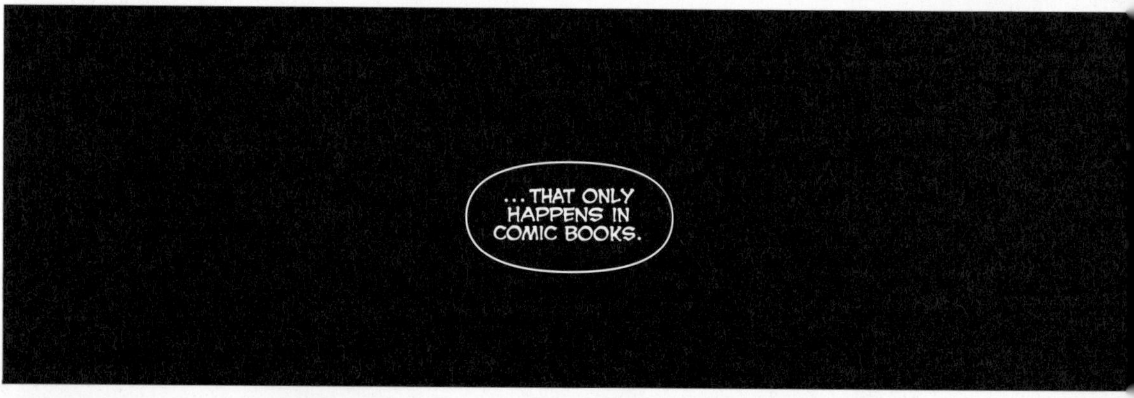
...THAT ONLY HAPPENS IN COMIC BOOKS.

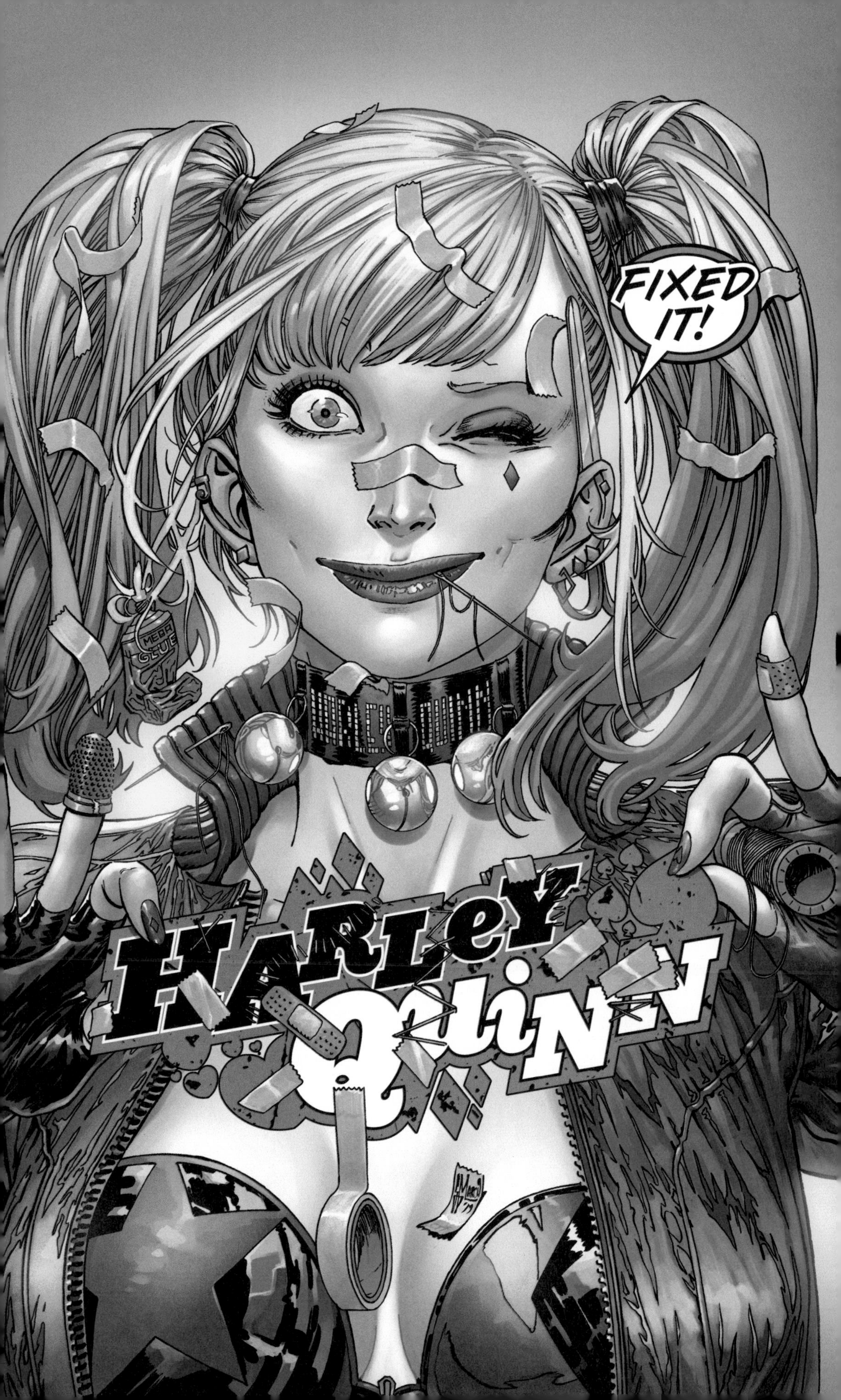

FIXED IT!
HARLEY QUINN

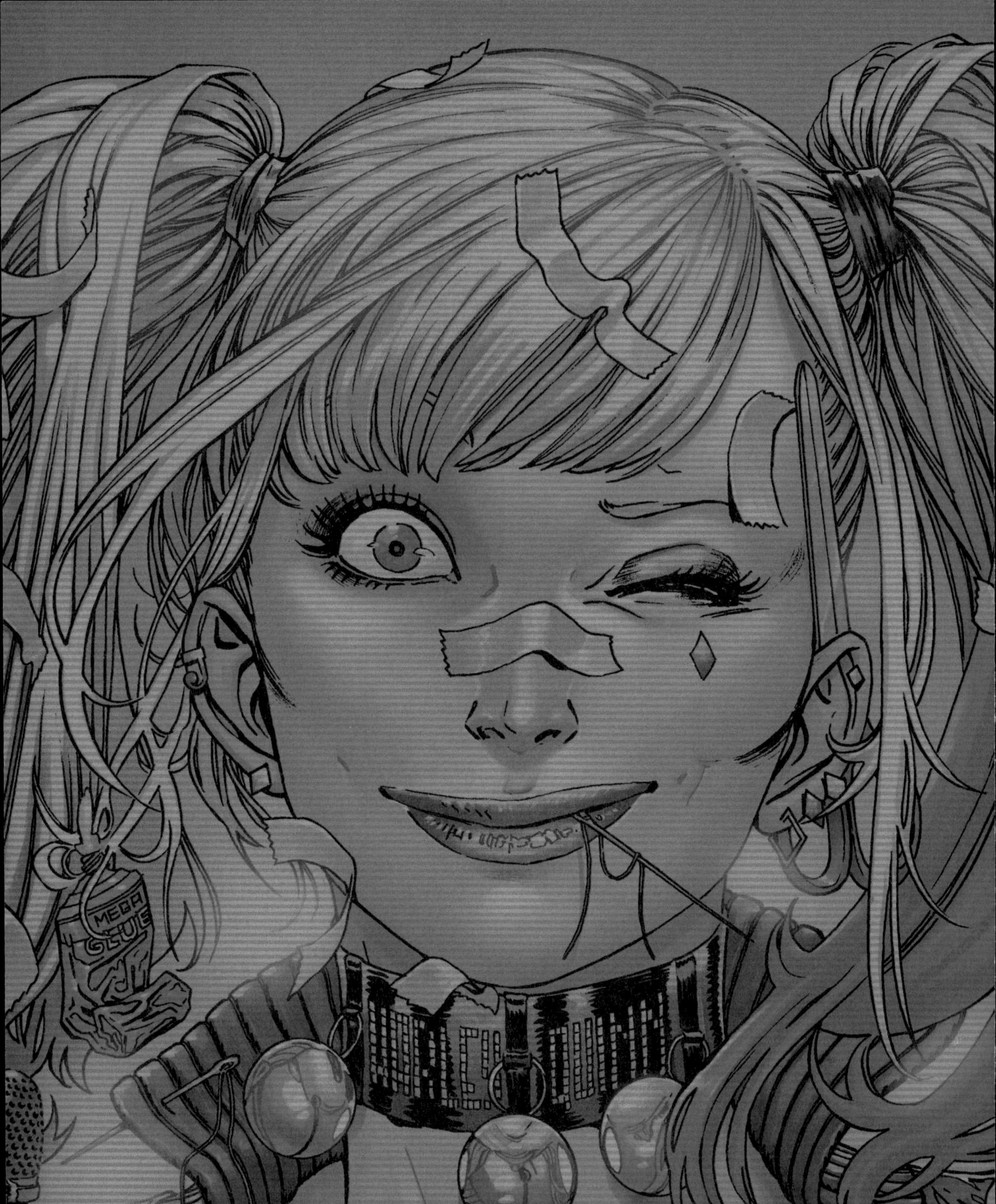
MEGA GLUE

HARLEY QUINN
#65

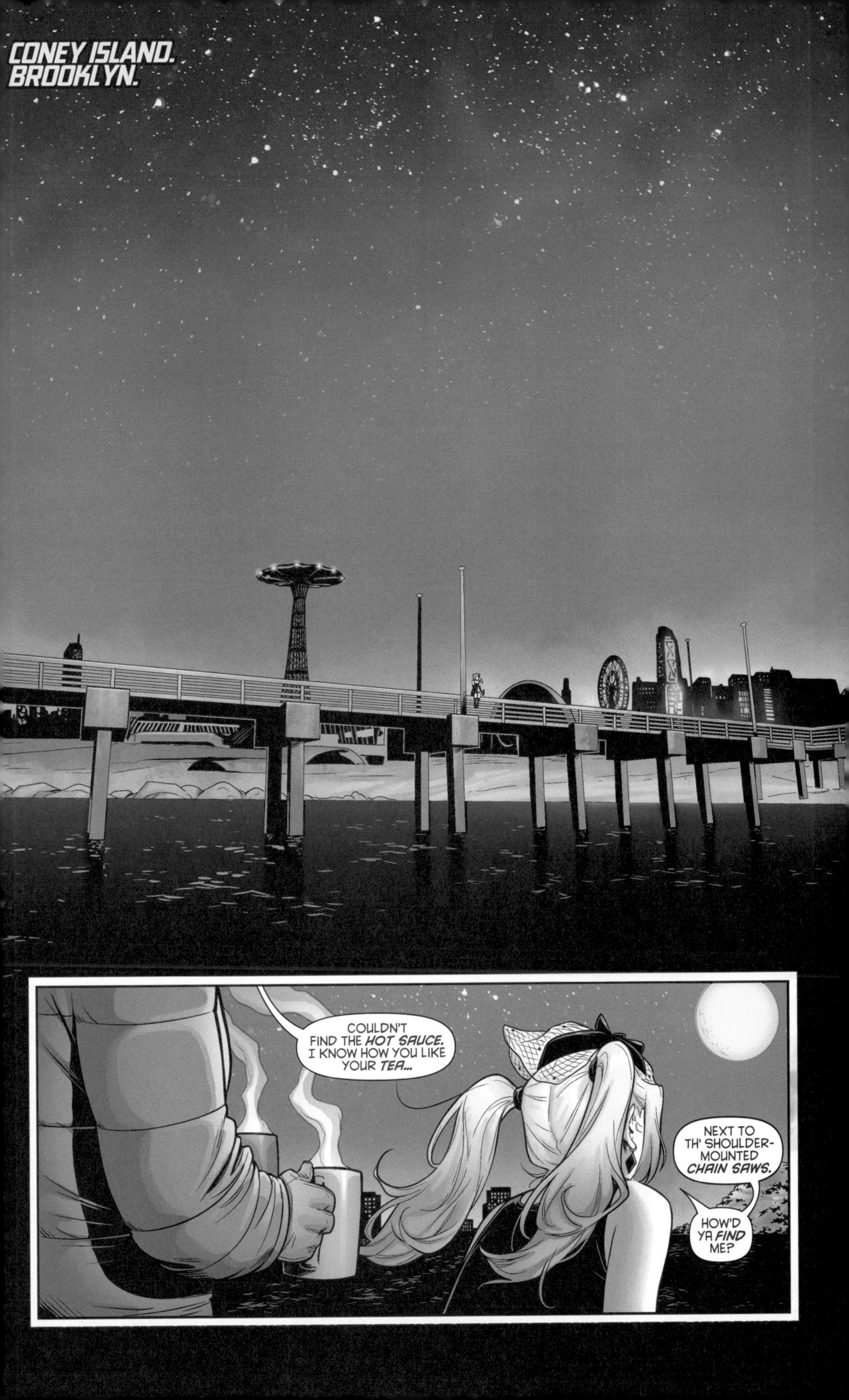
CONEY ISLAND. BROOKLYN.
COULDN'T FIND THE HOT SAUCE. I KNOW HOW YOU LIKE YOUR TEA...
NEXT TO TH' SHOULDER-MOUNTED CHAIN SAWS.
HOW'D YA FIND ME?

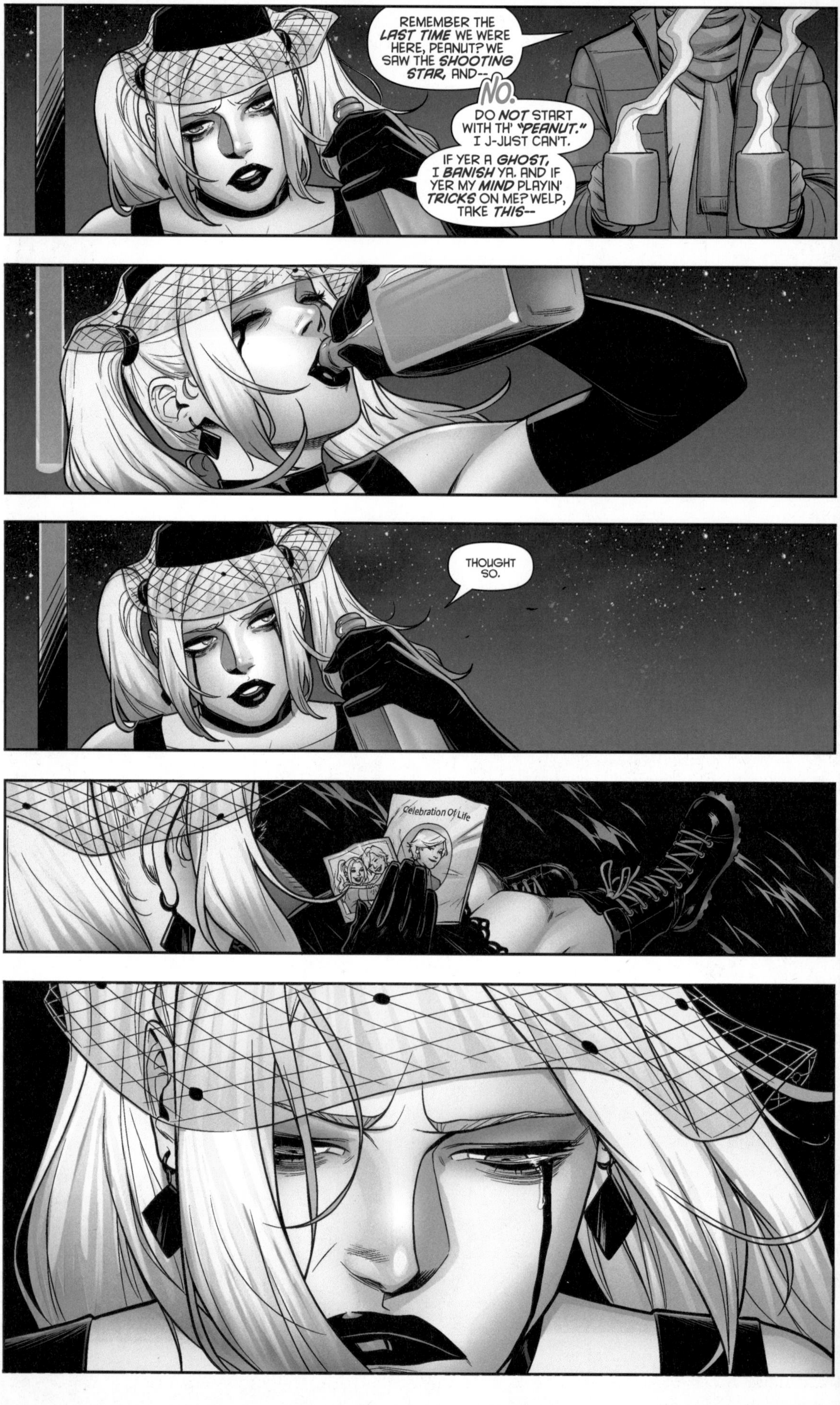
REMEMBER THE LAST TIME WE WERE HERE, PEANUT? WE SAW THE SHOOTING STAR, AND--
NO.
DO NOT START WITH TH' "PEANUT." I J-JUST CAN'T.
IF YER A GHOST, I BANISH YA. AND IF YER MY MIND PLAYIN' TRICKS ON ME? WELP, TAKE THIS--
THOUGHT SO.
Celebration Of Life

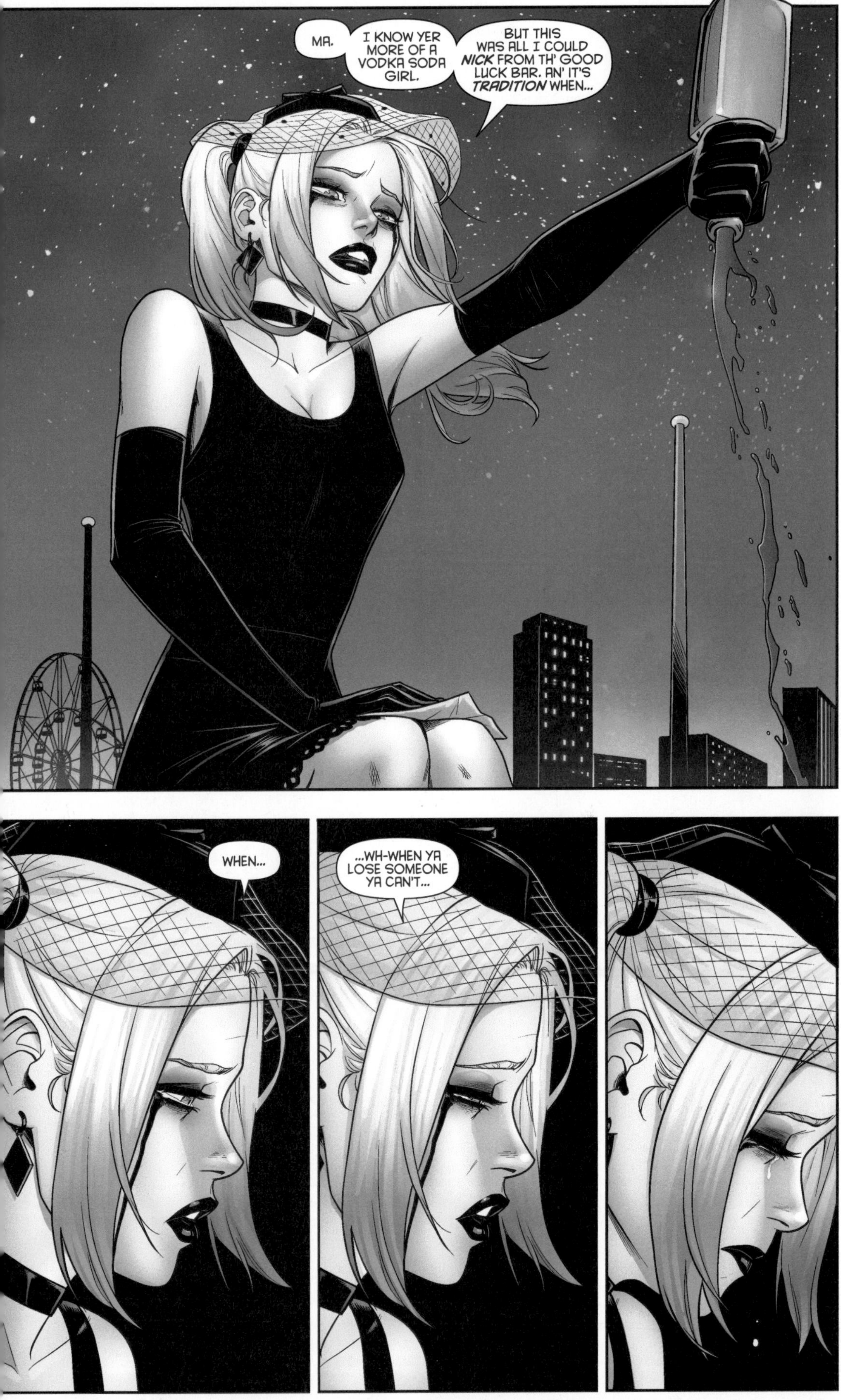
MA.
I KNOW YER MORE OF A VODKA SODA GIRL.
BUT THIS WAS ALL I COULD NICK FROM TH' GOOD LUCK BAR. AN' IT'S TRADITION WHEN...
WHEN...
...WH-WHEN YA LOSE SOMEONE YA CAN'T...

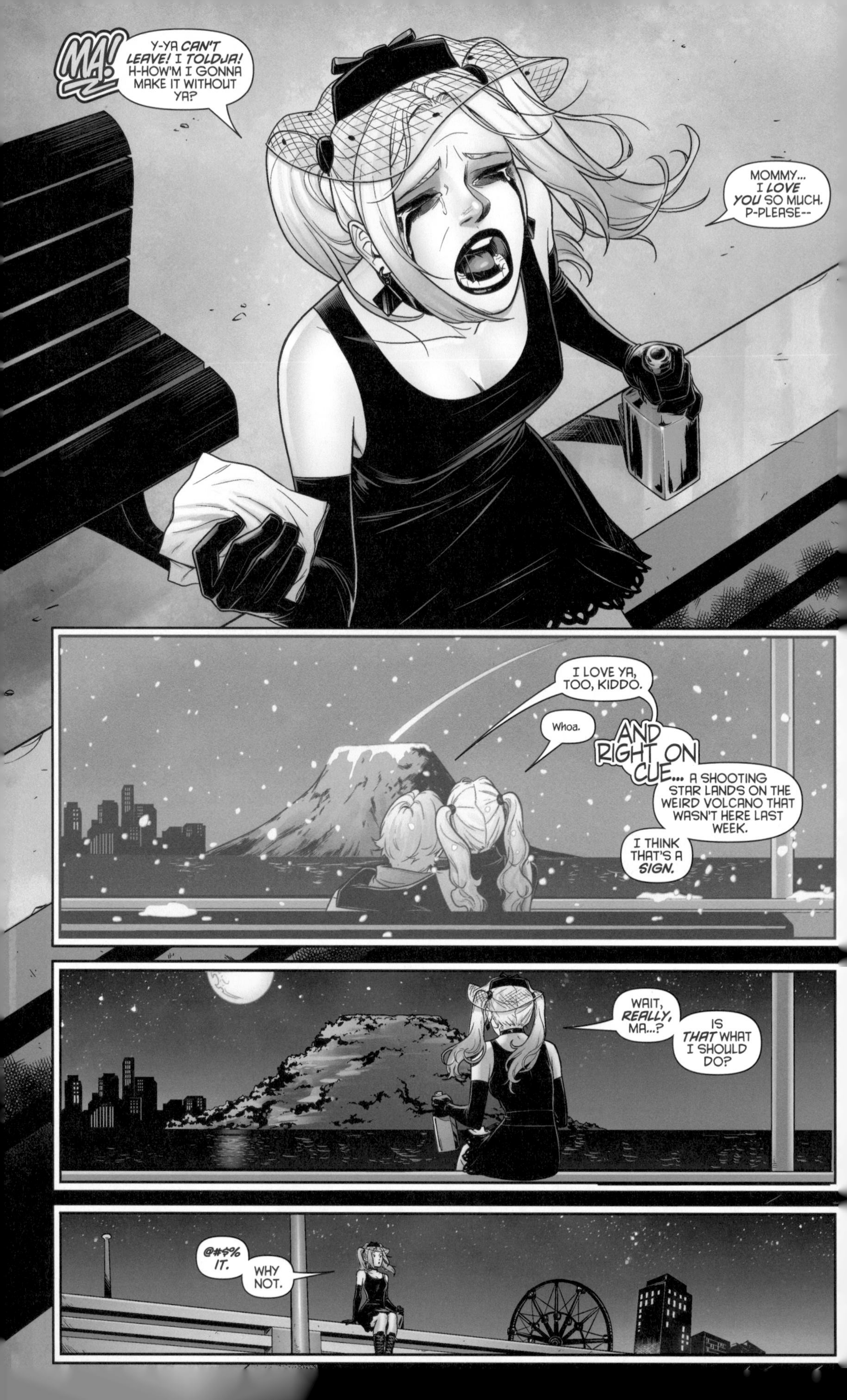
MA!
Y-YA CAN'T LEAVE! I TOLDJA! H-HOW'M I GONNA MAKE IT WITHOUT YA?
MOMMY... I LOVE YOU SO MUCH. P-PLEASE--
I LOVE YA, TOO, KIDDO.
Whoa.
AND RIGHT ON CUE... A SHOOTING STAR LANDS ON THE WEIRD VOLCANO THAT WASN'T HERE LAST WEEK.
I THINK THAT'S A SIGN.
WAIT, REALLY, MA...?
IS THAT WHAT I SHOULD DO?
@#$% IT.
WHY NOT.

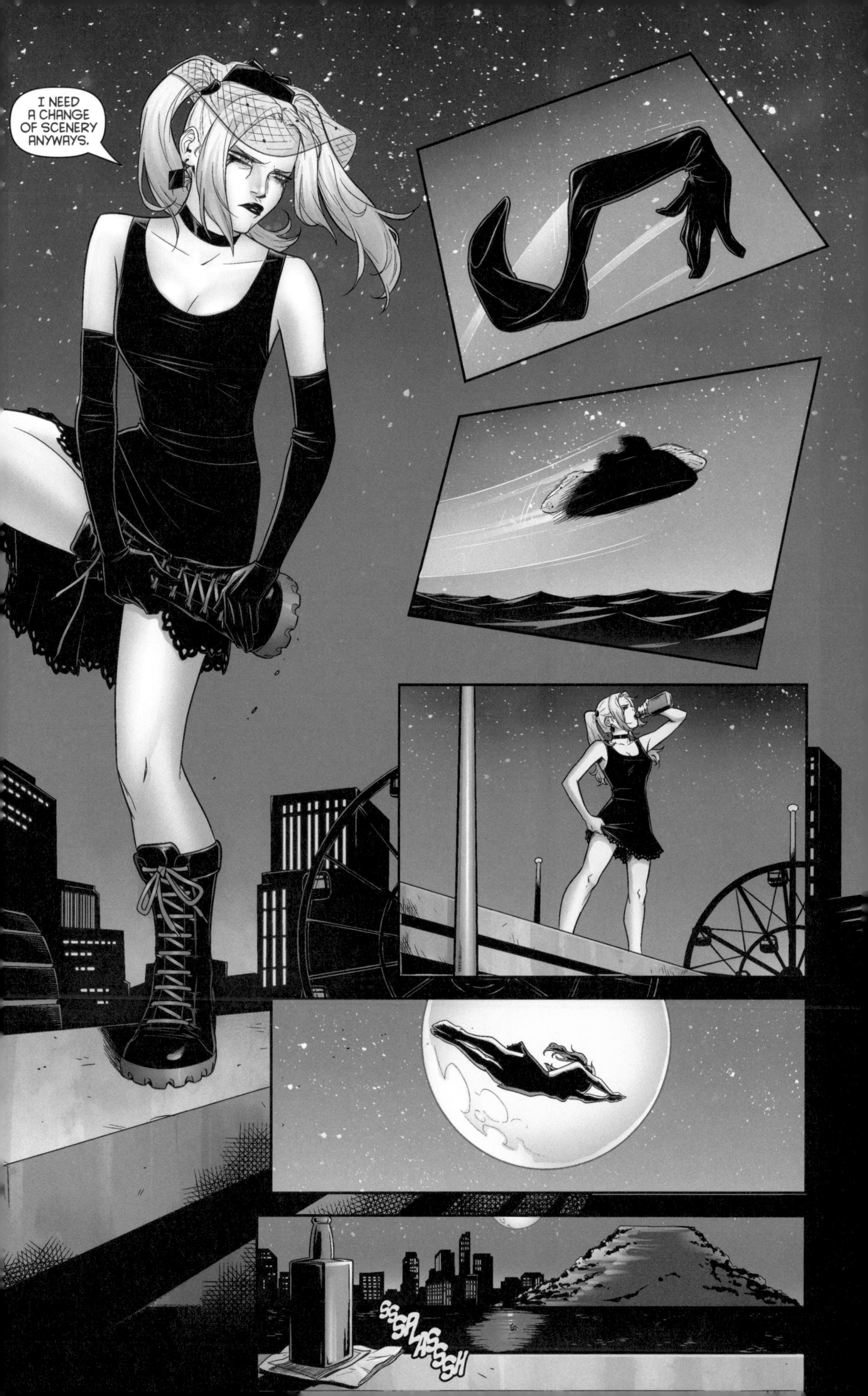
I NEED A CHANGE OF SCENERY ANYWAYS.
SSSPLASSSH

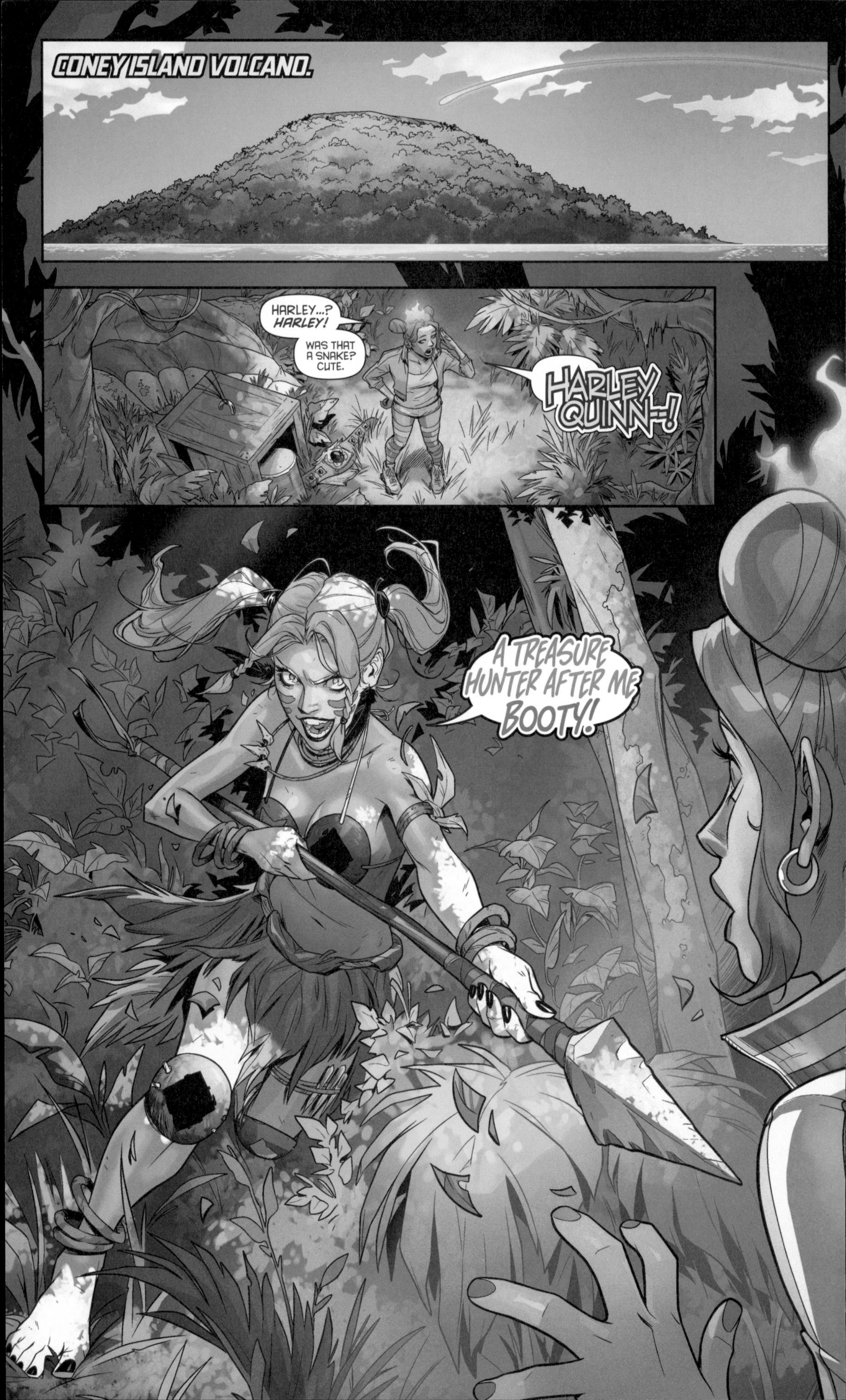
CONEY ISLAND VOLCANO.
HARLEY...? HARLEY!
WAS THAT A SNAKE? CUTE.
HARLEY QUINN--!
A TREASURE HUNTER AFTER ME BOOTY!

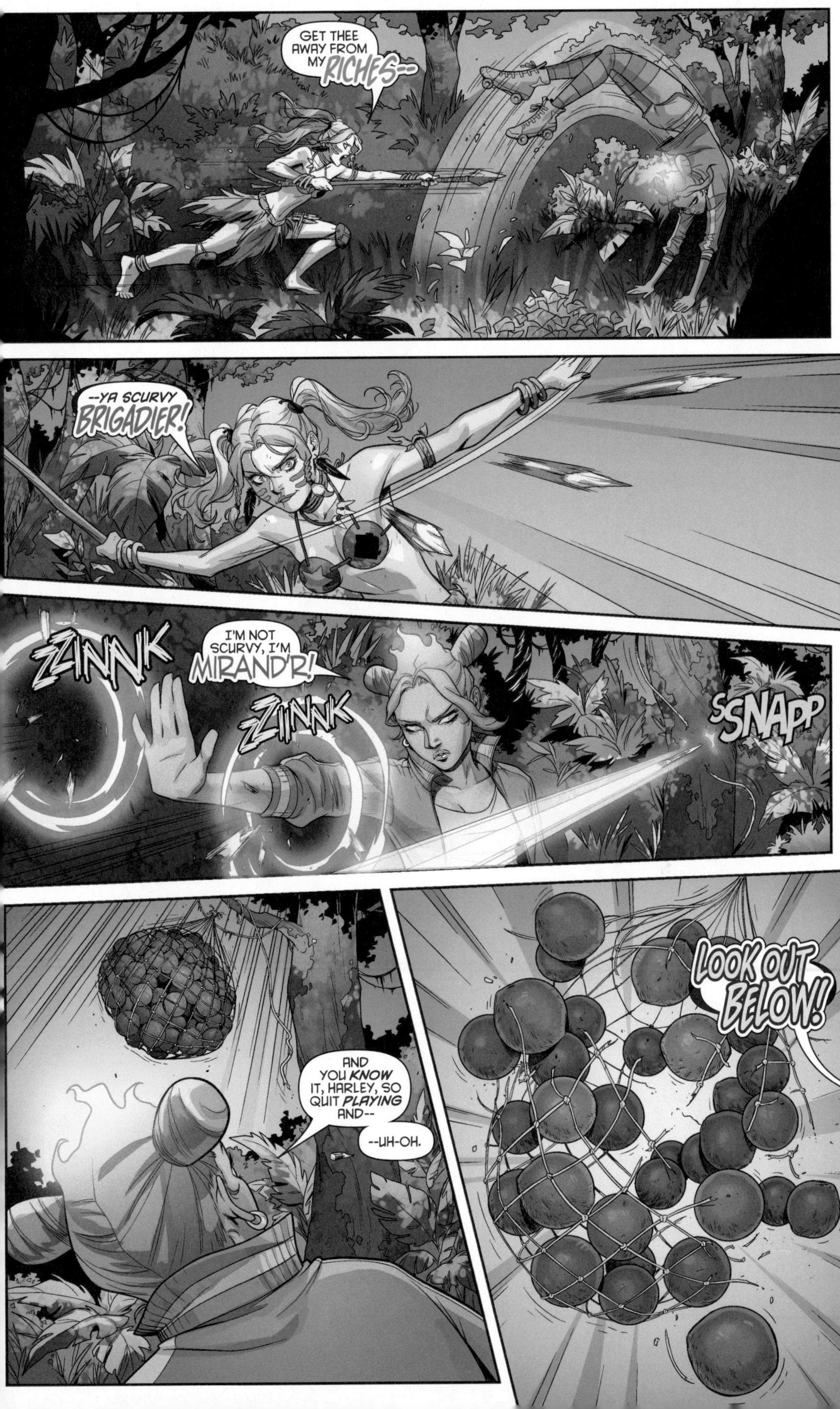
GET THEE AWAY FROM MY RICHES--
--YA SCURVY BRIGADIER!
ZZINNK
I'M NOT SCURVY, I'M MIRAND'R!
ZZINNK
SSNAPP
AND YOU KNOW IT, HARLEY, SO QUIT PLAYING AND--
--UH-OH.
LOOK OUT BELOW!

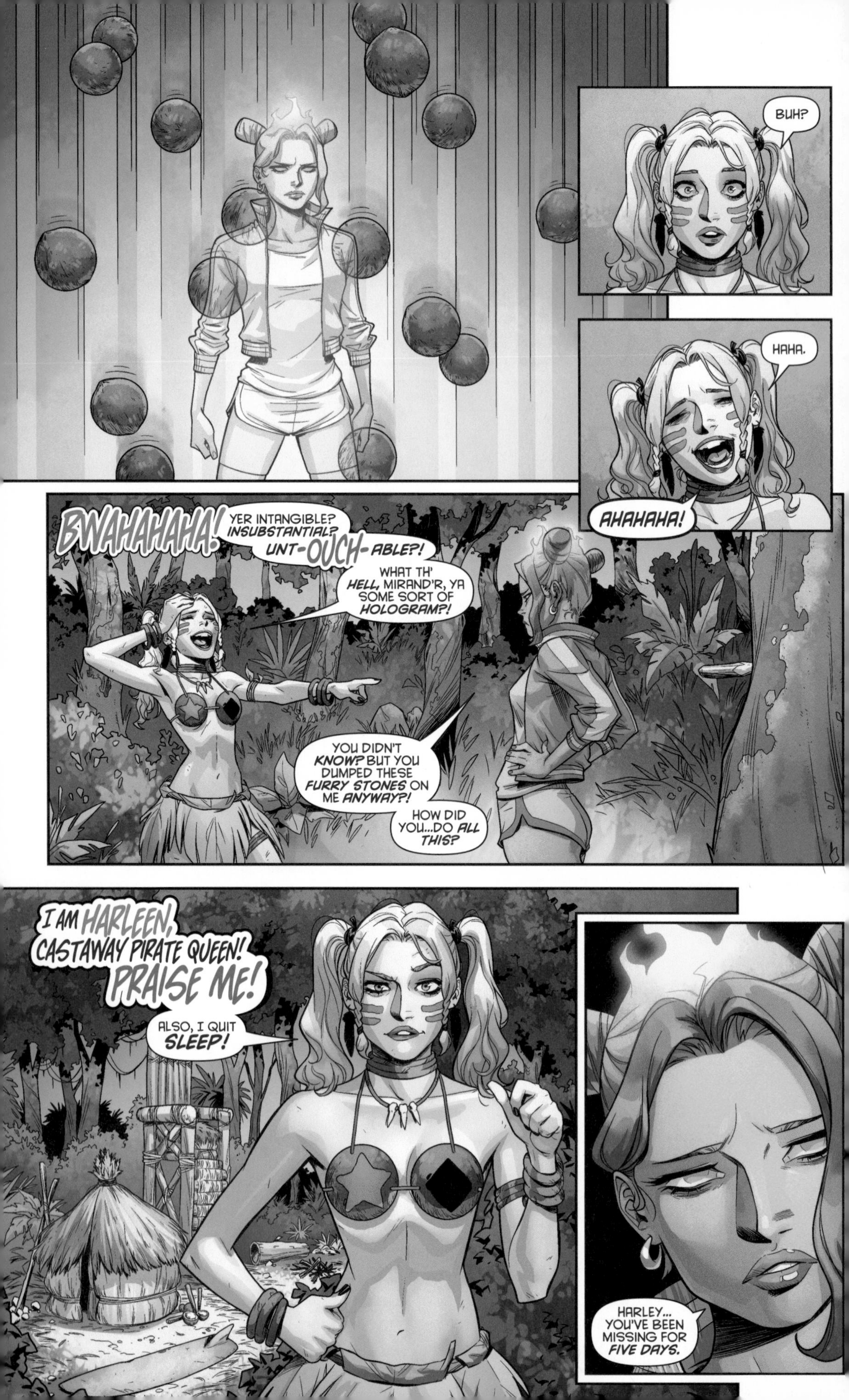
BUH?
HAHA.
AHAHAHA!
BWAHAHAHA!
YER INTANGIBLE? INSUBSTANTIAL? UNT-OUCH-ABLE?!
WHAT TH' HELL, MIRAND'R, YA SOME SORT OF HOLOGRAM?!
YOU DIDN'T KNOW? BUT YOU DUMPED THESE FURRY STONES ON ME ANYWAY?!
HOW DID YOU...DO ALL THIS?
I AM HARLEEN, CASTAWAY PIRATE QUEEN! PRAISE ME!
ALSO, I QUIT SLEEP!
HARLEY... YOU'VE BEEN MISSING FOR FIVE DAYS.

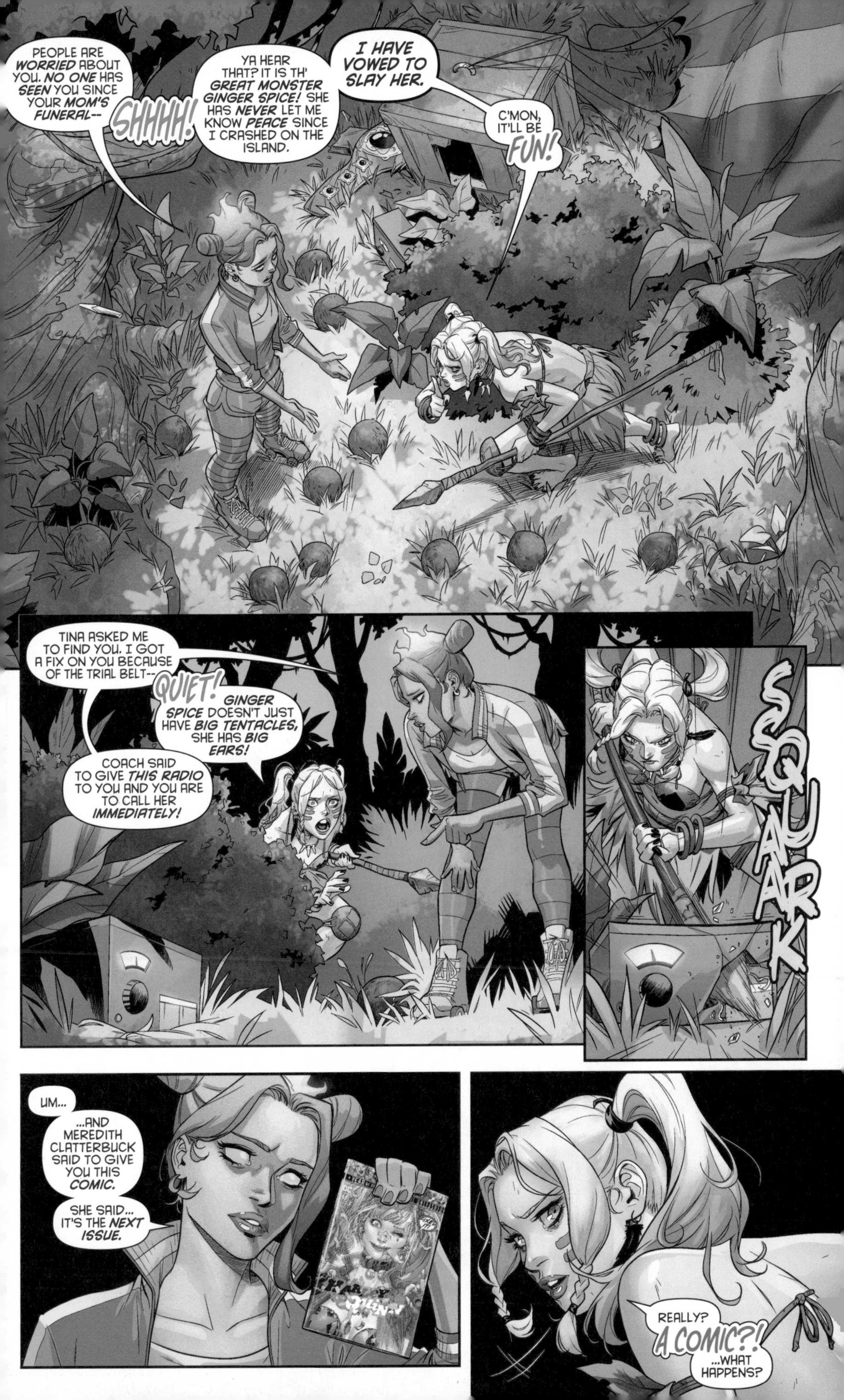

PEOPLE ARE WORRIED ABOUT YOU. NO ONE HAS SEEN YOU SINCE YOUR MOM'S FUNERAL--
SHHHH!
YA HEAR THAT? IT IS TH' GREAT MONSTER GINGER SPICE! SHE HAS NEVER LET ME KNOW PEACE SINCE I CRASHED ON THE ISLAND.
I HAVE VOWED TO SLAY HER.
C'MON, IT'LL BE FUN!
TINA ASKED ME TO FIND YOU. I GOT A FIX ON YOU BECAUSE OF THE TRIAL BELT--
QUIET!
GINGER SPICE DOESN'T JUST HAVE BIG TENTACLES, SHE HAS BIG EARS!
COACH SAID TO GIVE THIS RADIO TO YOU AND YOU ARE TO CALL HER IMMEDIATELY!
SQUAARK
UM...
...AND MEREDITH CLATTERBUCK SAID TO GIVE YOU THIS COMIC.
SHE SAID... IT'S THE NEXT ISSUE.
REALLY? A COMIC?!
...WHAT HAPPENS?

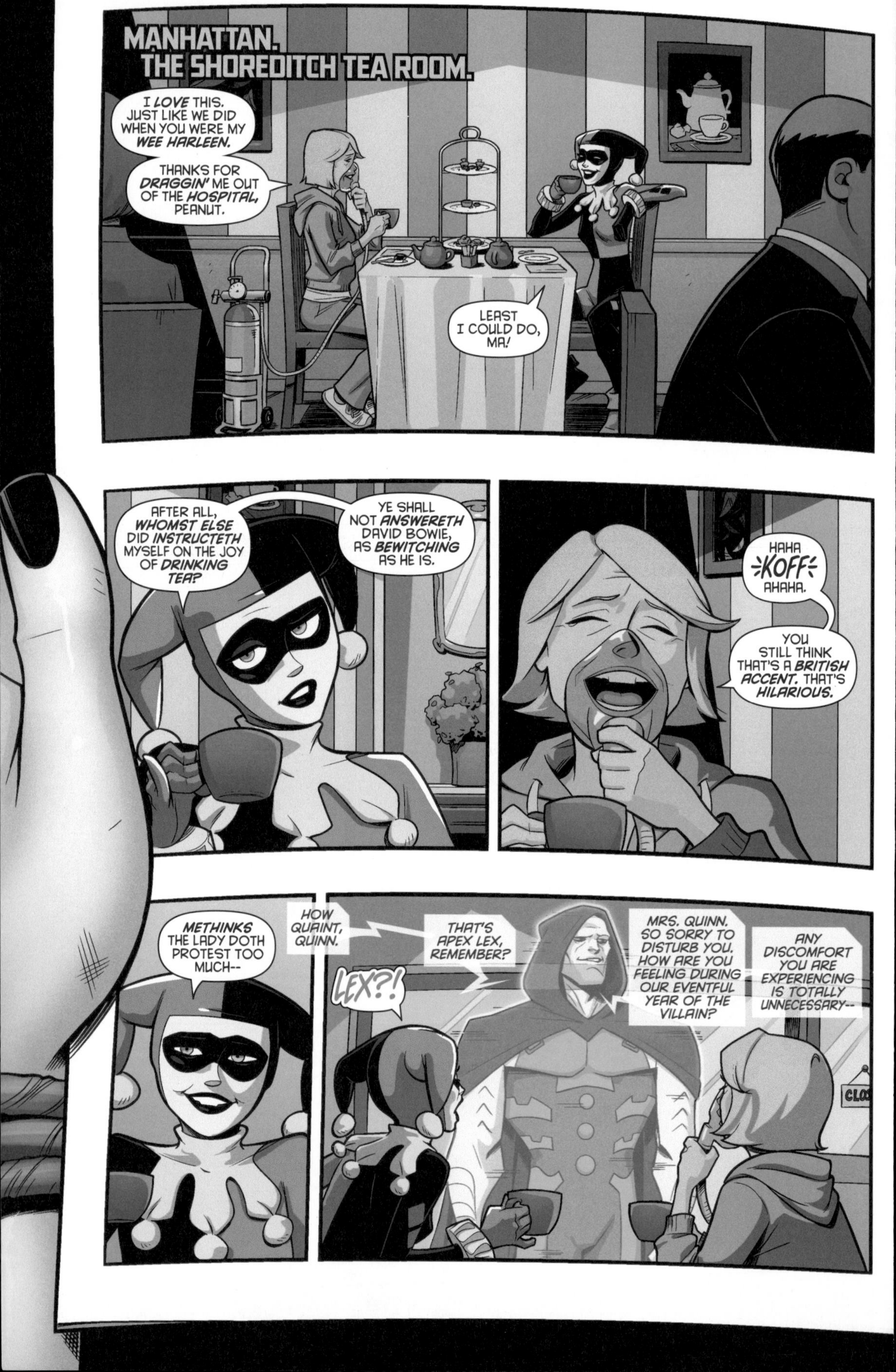
MANHATTAN. THE SHOREDITCH TEA ROOM.
I LOVE THIS. JUST LIKE WE DID WHEN YOU WERE MY WEE HARLEEN.
THANKS FOR DRAGGIN' ME OUT OF THE HOSPITAL, PEANUT.
LEAST I COULD DO, MA!
AFTER ALL, WHOMST ELSE DID INSTRUCTETH MYSELF ON THE JOY OF DRINKING TEA?
YE SHALL NOT ANSWERETH DAVID BOWIE, AS BEWITCHING AS HE IS.
HAHA *KOFF* AHAHA.
YOU STILL THINK THAT'S A BRITISH ACCENT. THAT'S HILARIOUS.
METHINKS THE LADY DOTH PROTEST TOO MUCH--
HOW QUAINT, QUINN.
LEX?!
THAT'S APEX LEX, REMEMBER?
MRS. QUINN. SO SORRY TO DISTURB YOU. HOW ARE YOU FEELING DURING OUR EVENTFUL YEAR OF THE VILLAIN?
ANY DISCOMFORT YOU ARE EXPERIENCING IS TOTALLY UNNECESSARY--

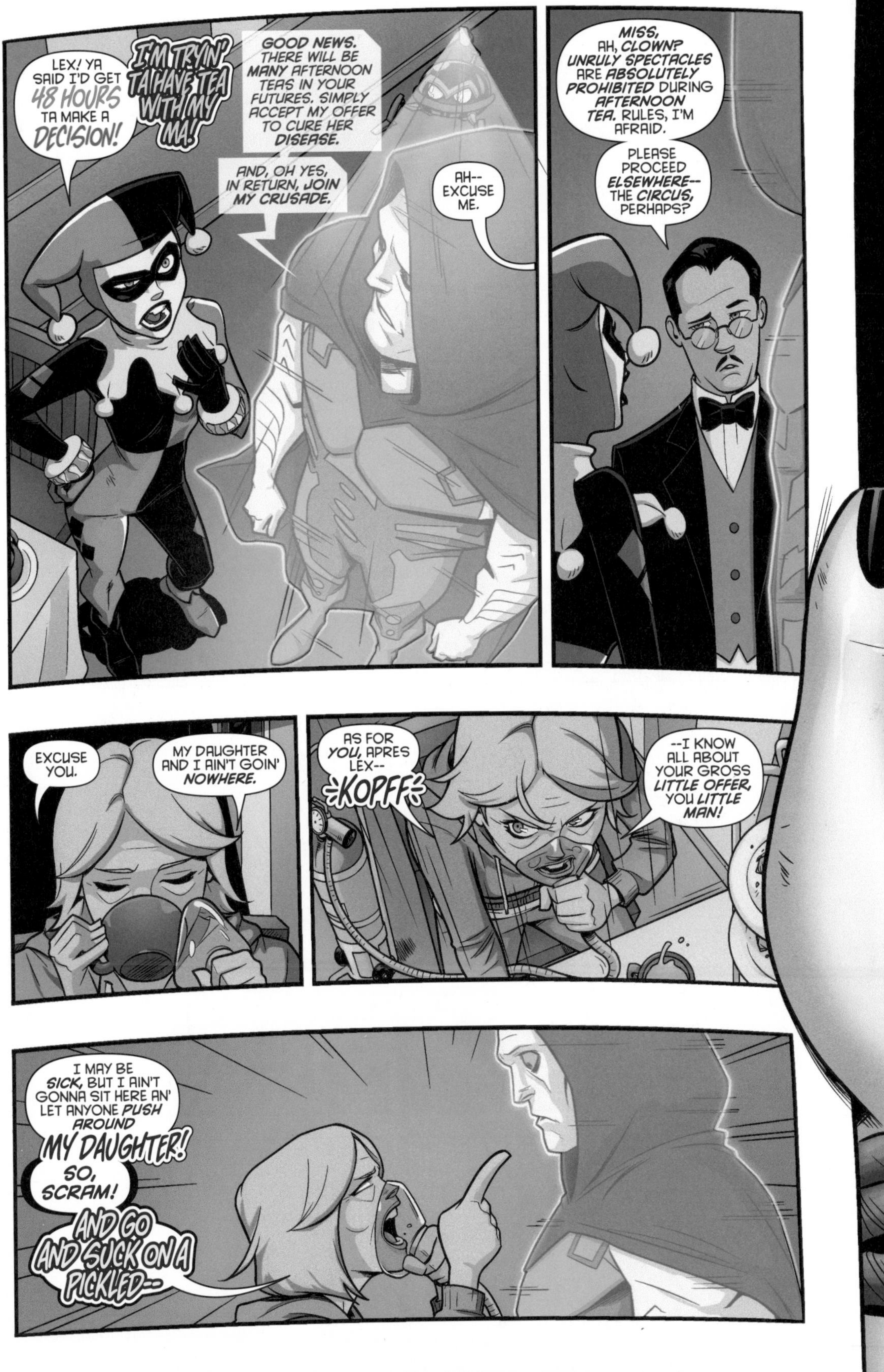
LEX! YA SAID I'D GET 48 HOURS TA MAKE A DECISION!
I'M TRYIN' TA HAVE TEA WITH MY MA!
GOOD NEWS. THERE WILL BE MANY AFTERNOON TEAS IN YOUR FUTURES. SIMPLY ACCEPT MY OFFER TO CURE HER DISEASE.
AND, OH YES, IN RETURN, JOIN MY CRUSADE.
AH-- EXCUSE ME.
MISS, AH, CLOWN? UNRULY SPECTACLES ARE ABSOLUTELY PROHIBITED DURING AFTERNOON TEA. RULES, I'M AFRAID.
PLEASE PROCEED ELSEWHERE-- THE CIRCUS, PERHAPS?
EXCUSE YOU.
MY DAUGHTER AND I AIN'T GOIN' NOWHERE.
AS FOR YOU, APRES LEX--
KOPFF
--I KNOW ALL ABOUT YOUR GROSS LITTLE OFFER, YOU LITTLE MAN!
I MAY BE SICK, BUT I AIN'T GONNA SIT HERE AN' LET ANYONE PUSH AROUND MY DAUGHTER!
SO, SCRAM!
AND GO AND SUCK ON A PICKLED--

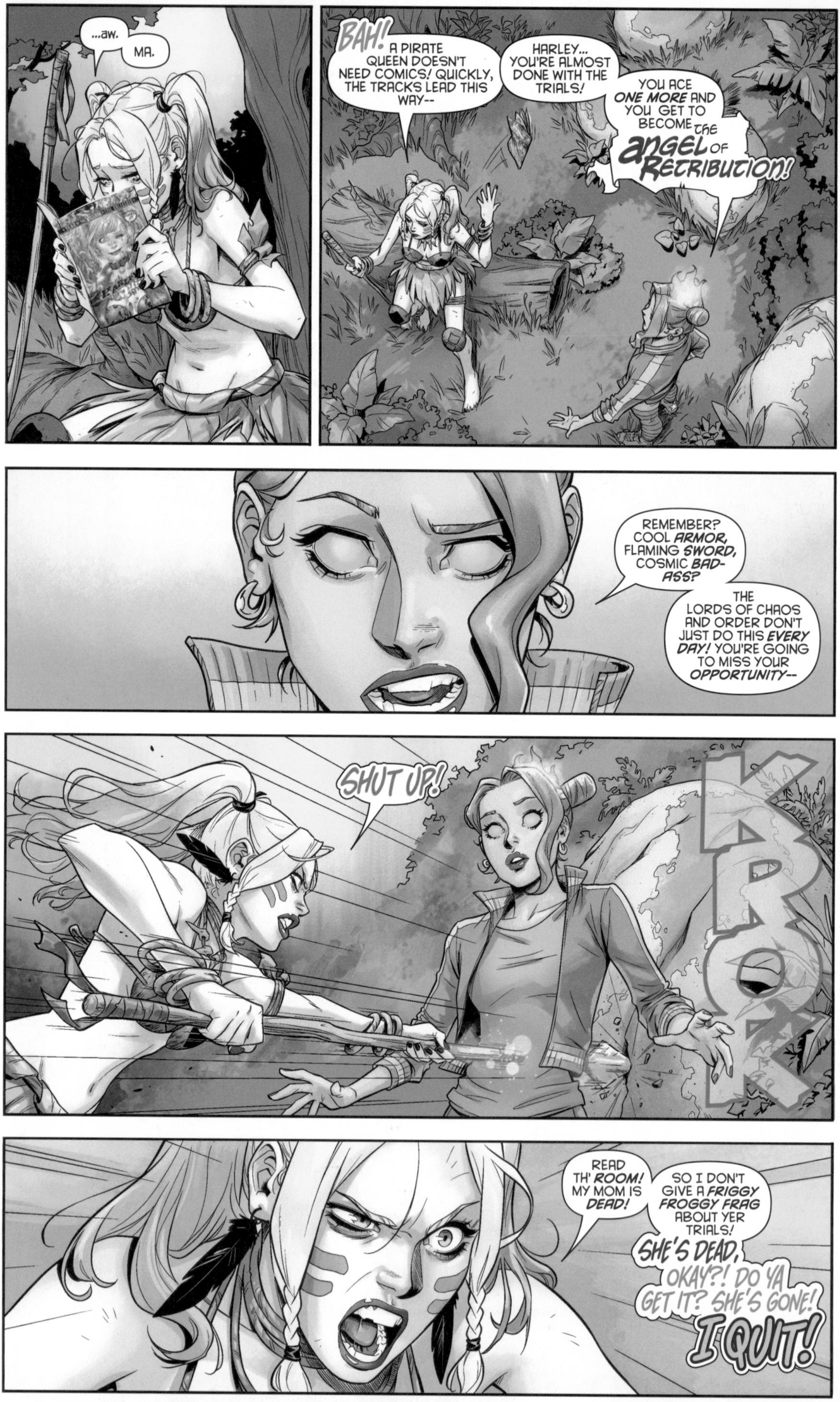
...aw.
MA.
BAH!
A PIRATE QUEEN DOESN'T NEED COMICS! QUICKLY, THE TRACKS LEAD THIS WAY--
HARLEY... YOU'RE ALMOST DONE WITH THE TRIALS!
YOU ACE ONE MORE AND YOU GET TO BECOME THE ANGEL OF RETRIBUTION!
REMEMBER? COOL ARMOR, FLAMING SWORD, COSMIC BAD-ASS?
THE LORDS OF CHAOS AND ORDER DON'T JUST DO THIS EVERY DAY! YOU'RE GOING TO MISS YOUR OPPORTUNITY--
SHUT UP!
KROK
READ TH' ROOM! MY MOM IS DEAD!
SO I DON'T GIVE A FRIGGY FROGGY FRAG ABOUT YER TRIALS!
SHE'S DEAD, OKAY?! DO YA GET IT? SHE'S GONE!
I QUIT!

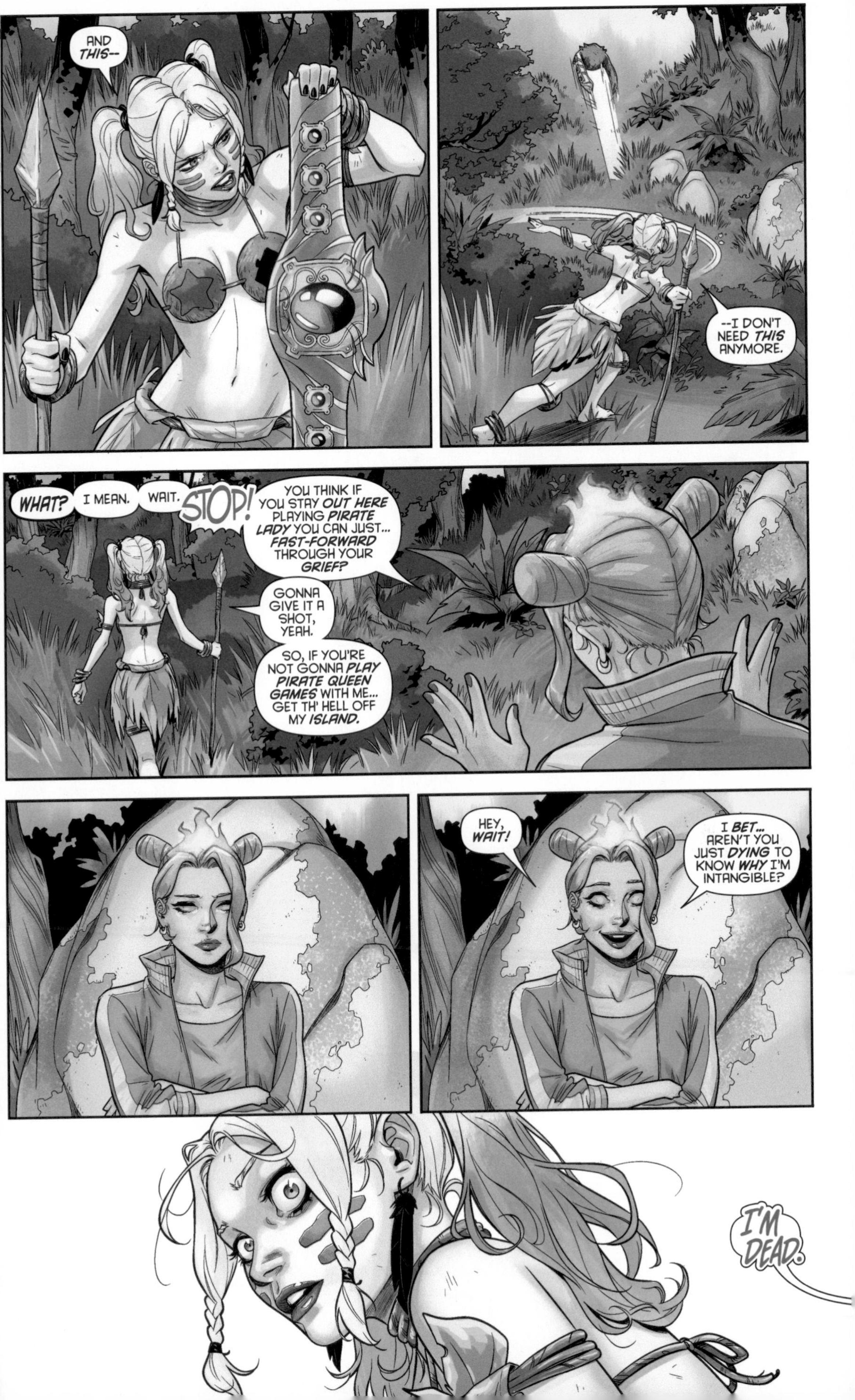

AND *THIS*--
--I DON'T NEED *THIS* ANYMORE.
WHAT?
I MEAN.
WAIT.
STOP!
YOU THINK IF YOU STAY *OUT HERE* PLAYING *PIRATE LADY* YOU CAN JUST... *FAST-FORWARD* THROUGH YOUR *GRIEF?*
GONNA GIVE IT A SHOT, YEAH.
SO, IF YOU'RE NOT GONNA *PLAY PIRATE QUEEN GAMES* WITH ME... GET TH' HELL OFF MY *ISLAND.*
HEY, *WAIT!*
I *BET*... AREN'T YOU JUST *DYING* TO KNOW *WHY* I'M INTANGIBLE?
I'M DEAD.

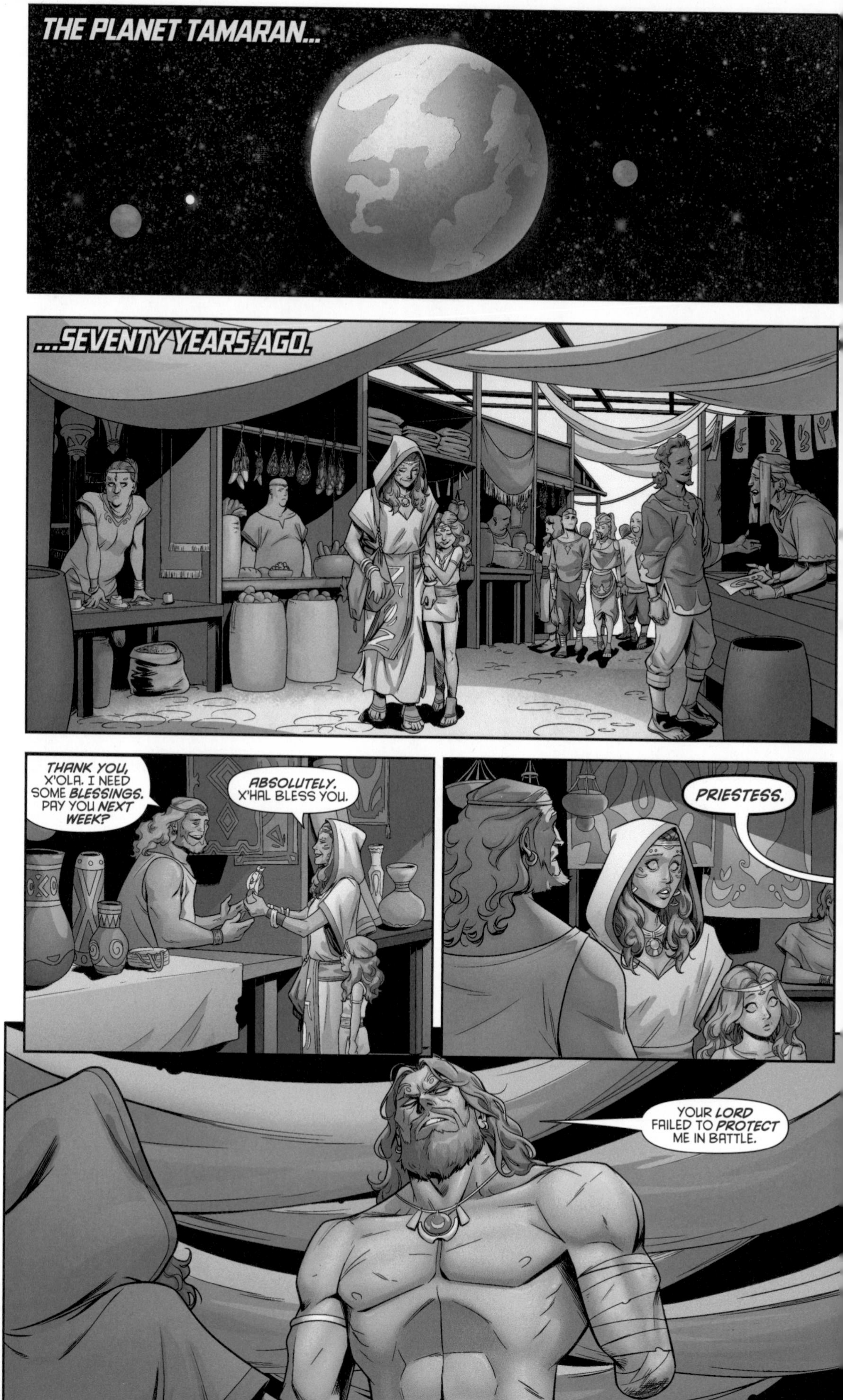

THE PLANET TAMARAN...
...SEVENTY YEARS AGO.
THANK YOU, X'OLA. I NEED SOME BLESSINGS. PAY YOU NEXT WEEK?
ABSOLUTELY. X'HAL BLESS YOU.
PRIESTESS.
YOUR LORD FAILED TO PROTECT ME IN BATTLE.

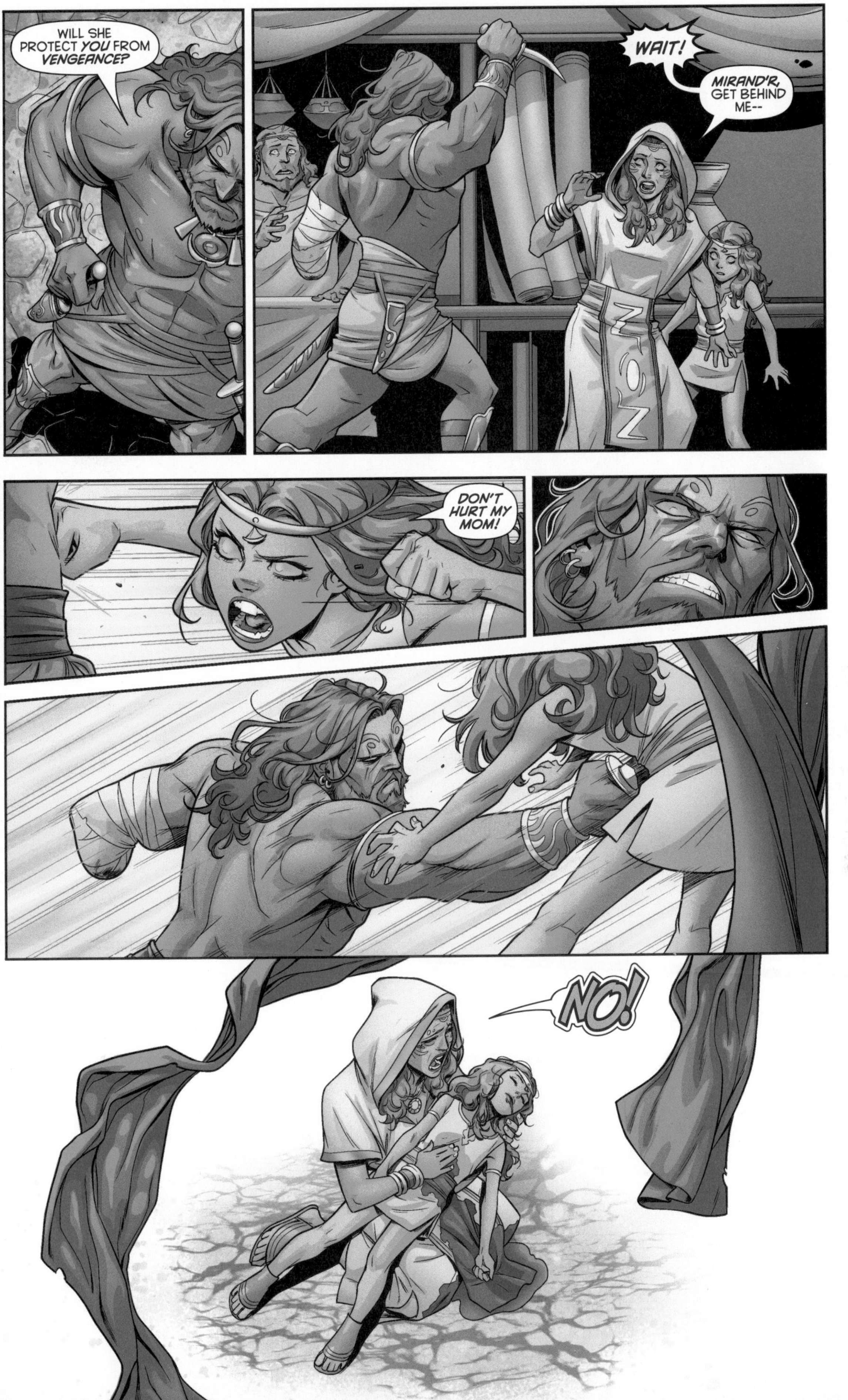
WILL SHE PROTECT YOU FROM VENGEANCE?
WAIT!
MIRAND'R, GET BEHIND ME--
DON'T HURT MY MOM!
NO!

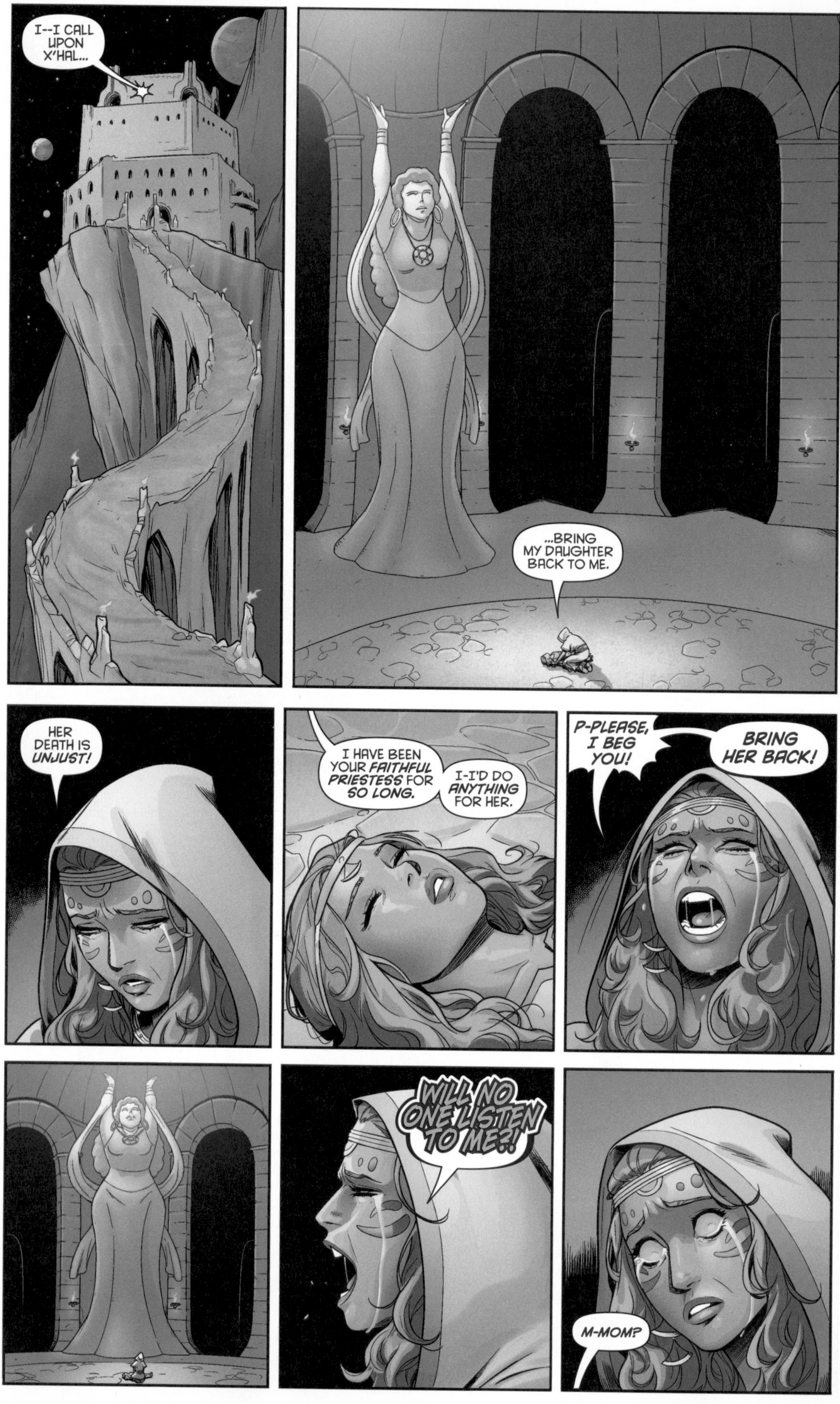
I--I CALL UPON X'HAL...
...BRING MY DAUGHTER BACK TO ME.
HER DEATH IS UNJUST!
I HAVE BEEN YOUR FAITHFUL PRIESTESS FOR SO LONG.
I-I'D DO ANYTHING FOR HER.
P-PLEASE, I BEG YOU!
BRING HER BACK!
WILL NO ONE LISTEN TO ME?!
M-MOM?

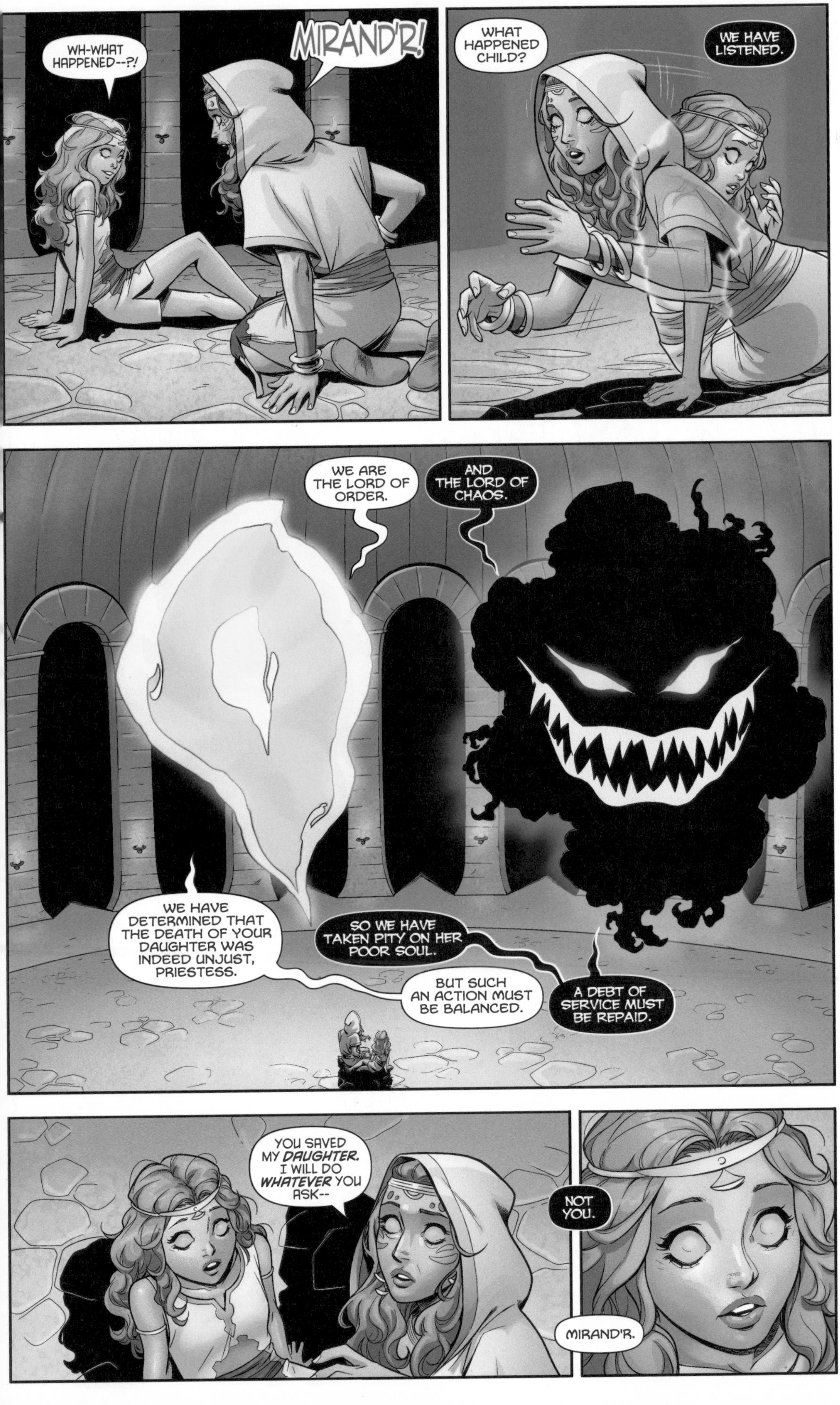
WH-WHAT HAPPENED--?!
MIRAND'R!
WHAT HAPPENED CHILD?
WE HAVE LISTENED.
WE ARE THE LORD OF ORDER.
AND THE LORD OF CHAOS.
WE HAVE DETERMINED THAT THE DEATH OF YOUR DAUGHTER WAS INDEED UNJUST, PRIESTESS.
SO WE HAVE TAKEN PITY ON HER POOR SOUL.
BUT SUCH AN ACTION MUST BE BALANCED.
A DEBT OF SERVICE MUST BE REPAID.
YOU SAVED MY DAUGHTER. I WILL DO WHATEVER YOU ASK--
NOT YOU.
MIRAND'R.

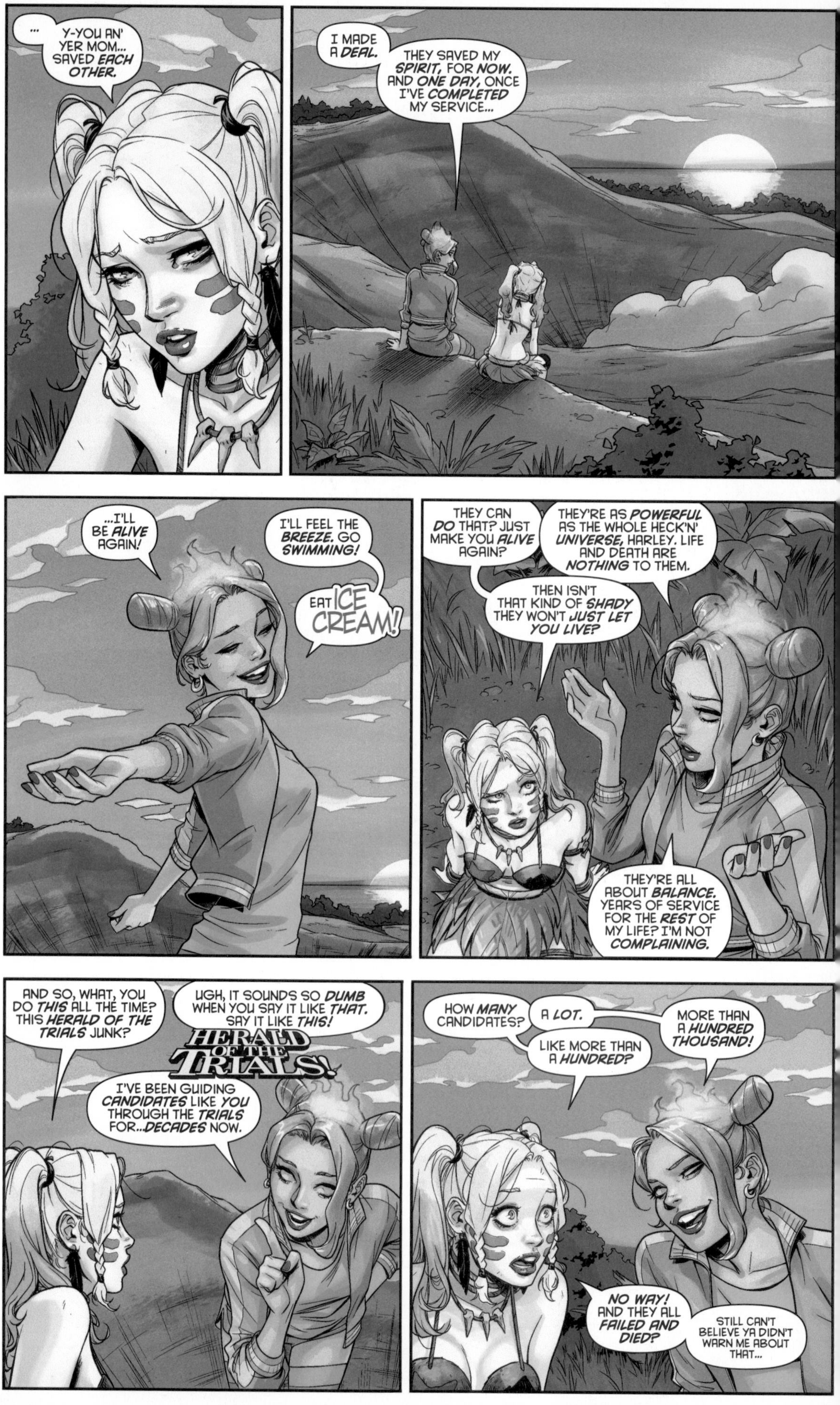
...
Y-YOU AN' YER MOM... SAVED EACH OTHER.
I MADE A DEAL.
THEY SAVED MY SPIRIT, FOR NOW. AND ONE DAY, ONCE I'VE COMPLETED MY SERVICE...
...I'LL BE ALIVE AGAIN!
I'LL FEEL THE BREEZE. GO SWIMMING!
EAT ICE CREAM!
THEY CAN DO THAT? JUST MAKE YOU ALIVE AGAIN?
THEY'RE AS POWERFUL AS THE WHOLE HECK'N' UNIVERSE, HARLEY. LIFE AND DEATH ARE NOTHING TO THEM.
THEN ISN'T THAT KIND OF SHADY THEY WON'T JUST LET YOU LIVE?
THEY'RE ALL ABOUT BALANCE. YEARS OF SERVICE FOR THE REST OF MY LIFE? I'M NOT COMPLAINING.
AND SO, WHAT, YOU DO THIS ALL THE TIME? THIS HERALD OF THE TRIALS JUNK?
UGH, IT SOUNDS SO DUMB WHEN YOU SAY IT LIKE THAT. SAY IT LIKE THIS!
HERALD OF THE TRIALS!
I'VE BEEN GUIDING CANDIDATES LIKE YOU THROUGH THE TRIALS FOR...DECADES NOW.
HOW MANY CANDIDATES?
A LOT.
LIKE MORE THAN A HUNDRED?
MORE THAN A HUNDRED THOUSAND!
NO WAY! AND THEY ALL FAILED AND DIED?
STILL CAN'T BELIEVE YA DIDN'T WARN ME ABOUT THAT...

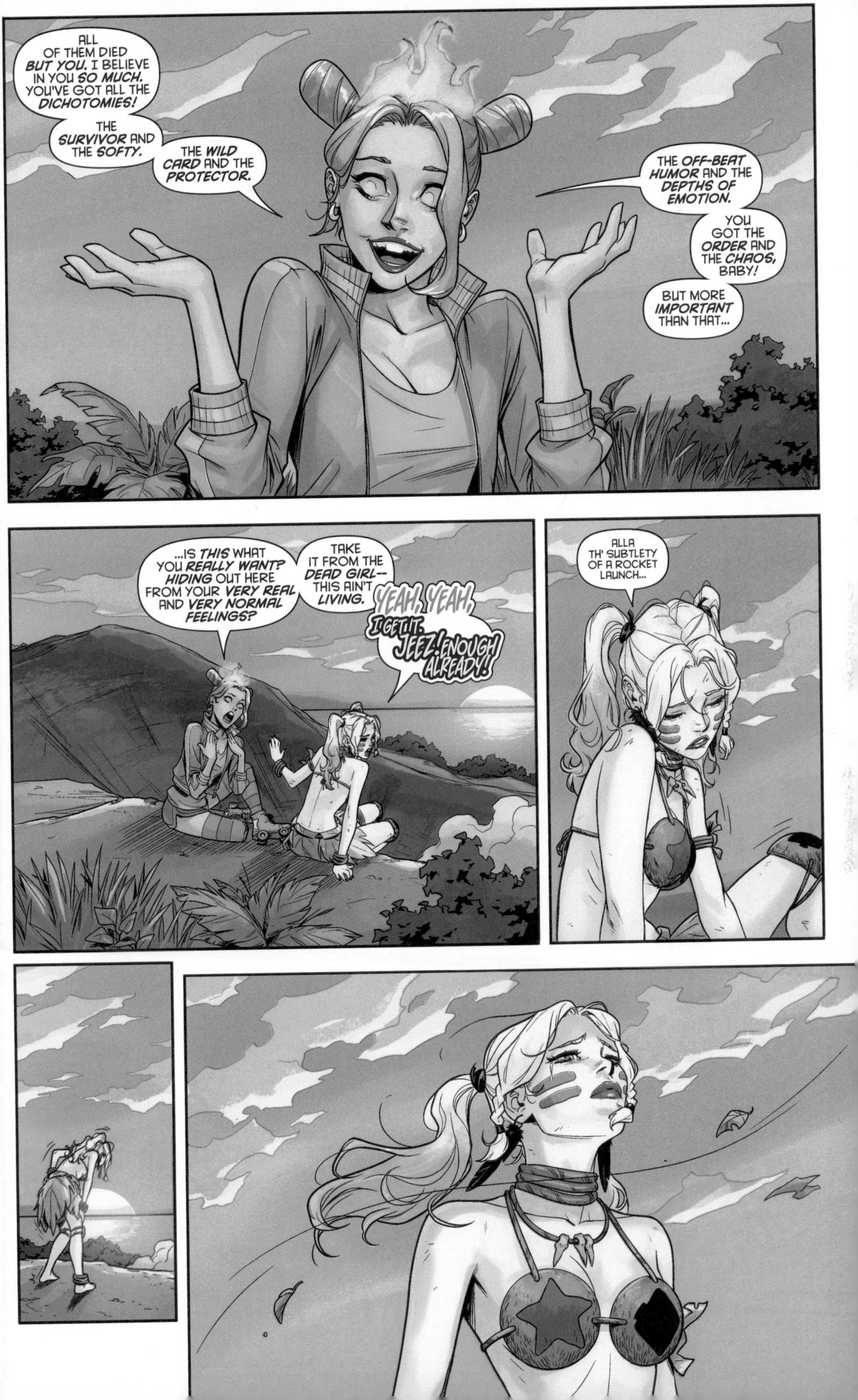

ALL OF THEM DIED BUT YOU. I BELIEVE IN YOU SO MUCH. YOU'VE GOT ALL THE DICHOTOMIES!
THE SURVIVOR AND THE SOFTY.
THE WILD CARD AND THE PROTECTOR.
THE OFF-BEAT HUMOR AND THE DEPTHS OF EMOTION.
YOU GOT THE ORDER AND THE CHAOS, BABY!
BUT MORE IMPORTANT THAN THAT...
...IS THIS WHAT YOU REALLY WANT? HIDING OUT HERE FROM YOUR VERY REAL AND VERY NORMAL FEELINGS?
TAKE IT FROM THE DEAD GIRL-- THIS AIN'T LIVING.
YEAH, YEAH, I GET IT. JEEZ! ENOUGH ALREADY!
ALLA TH' SUBTLETY OF A ROCKET LAUNCH...

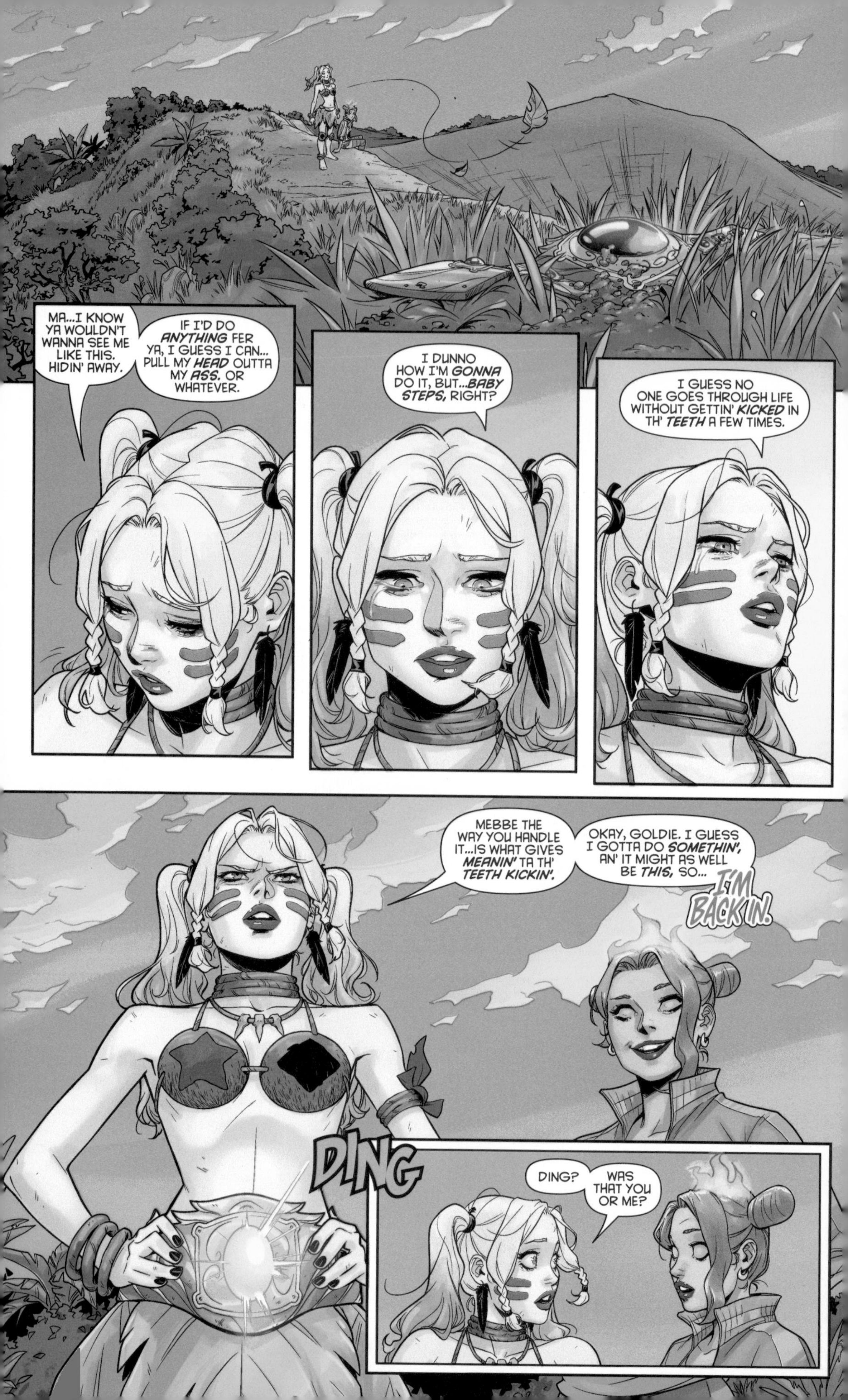
MA...I KNOW YA WOULDN'T WANNA SEE ME LIKE THIS. HIDIN' AWAY.
IF I'D DO *ANYTHING* FER YA, I GUESS I CAN... PULL MY *HEAD* OUTTA MY *ASS.* OR WHATEVER.
I DUNNO HOW I'M *GONNA* DO IT, BUT...*BABY STEPS,* RIGHT?
I GUESS NO ONE GOES THROUGH LIFE WITHOUT GETTIN' *KICKED* IN TH' *TEETH* A FEW TIMES.
MEBBE THE WAY YOU HANDLE IT...IS WHAT GIVES *MEANIN'* TA TH' *TEETH KICKIN'.*
OKAY, GOLDIE. I GUESS I GOTTA DO *SOMETHIN',* AN' IT MIGHT AS WELL BE *THIS,* SO...
I'M BACK IN.
DING
DING?
WAS THAT YOU OR ME?

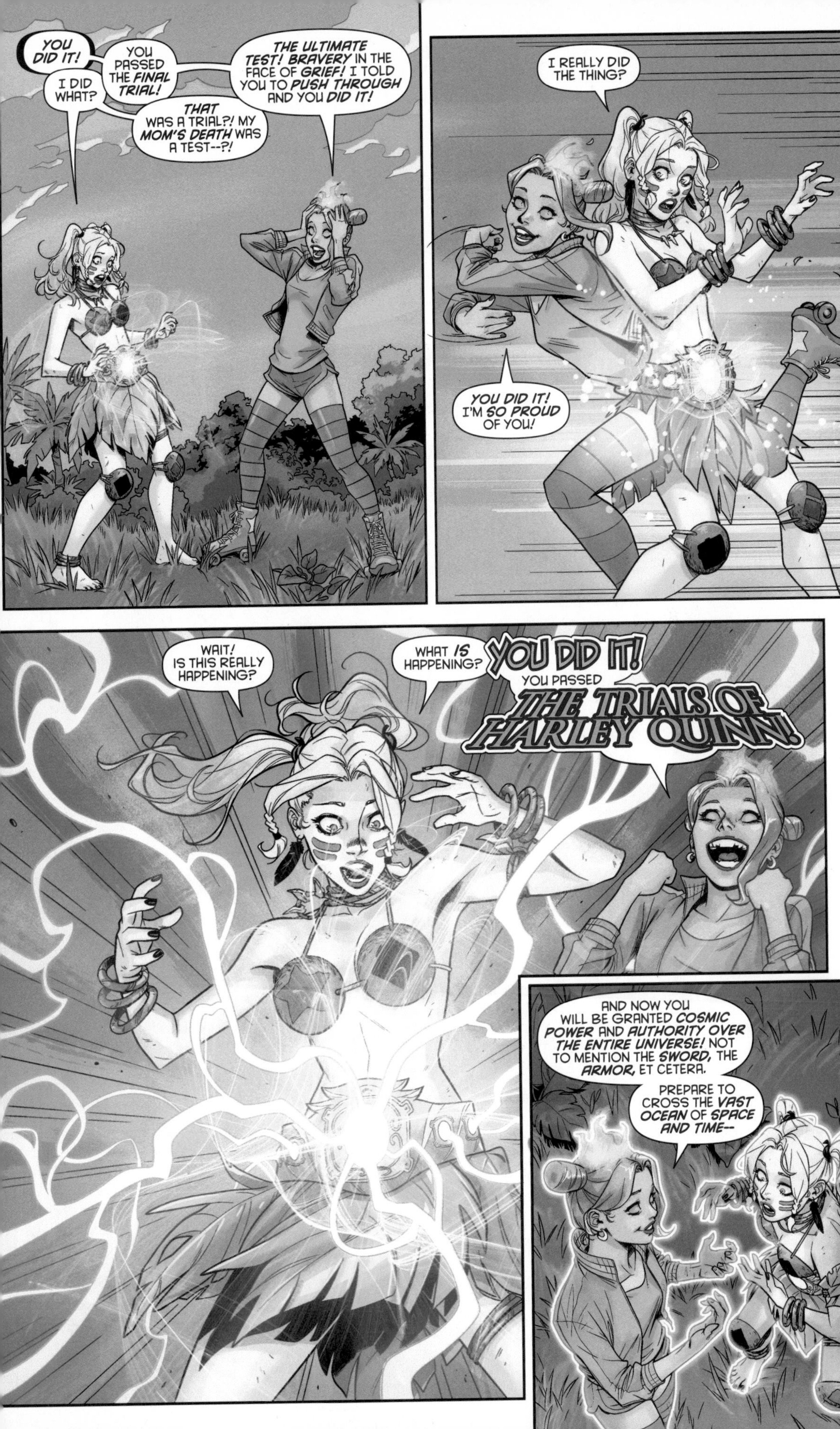
YOU DID IT!
YOU PASSED THE FINAL TRIAL!
I DID WHAT?
THE ULTIMATE TEST! BRAVERY IN THE FACE OF GRIEF! I TOLD YOU TO PUSH THROUGH AND YOU DID IT!
THAT WAS A TRIAL?! MY MOM'S DEATH WAS A TEST--?!
I REALLY DID THE THING?
YOU DID IT! I'M SO PROUD OF YOU!
WAIT! IS THIS REALLY HAPPENING?
WHAT IS HAPPENING?
YOU DID IT! YOU PASSED THE TRIALS OF HARLEY QUINN!
AND NOW YOU WILL BE GRANTED COSMIC POWER AND AUTHORITY OVER THE ENTIRE UNIVERSE! NOT TO MENTION THE SWORD, THE ARMOR, ET CETERA.
PREPARE TO CROSS THE VAST OCEAN OF SPACE AND TIME--

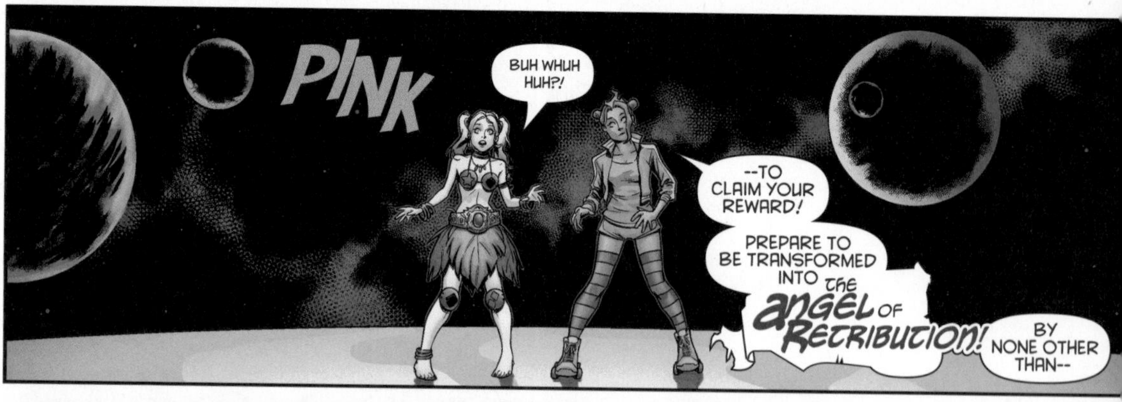
PINK
BUH WHUH HUH?!
--TO CLAIM YOUR REWARD!
PREPARE TO BE TRANSFORMED INTO THE ANGEL OF RETRIBUTION!
BY NONE OTHER THAN--

Castaway Quinn

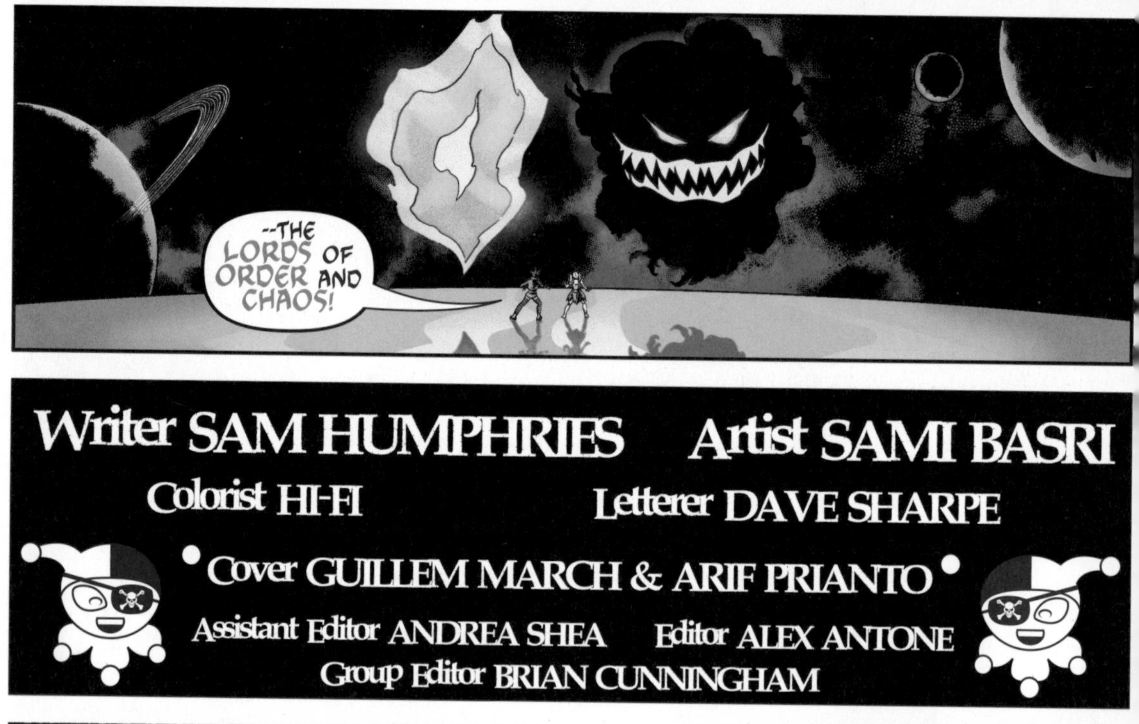
--THE LORDS OF ORDER AND CHAOS!

Writer SAM HUMPHRIES Artist SAMI BASRI
Colorist HI-FI Letterer DAVE SHARPE
Cover GUILLEM MARCH & ARIF PRIANTO
Assistant Editor ANDREA SHEA Editor ALEX ANTONE
Group Editor BRIAN CUNNINGHAM

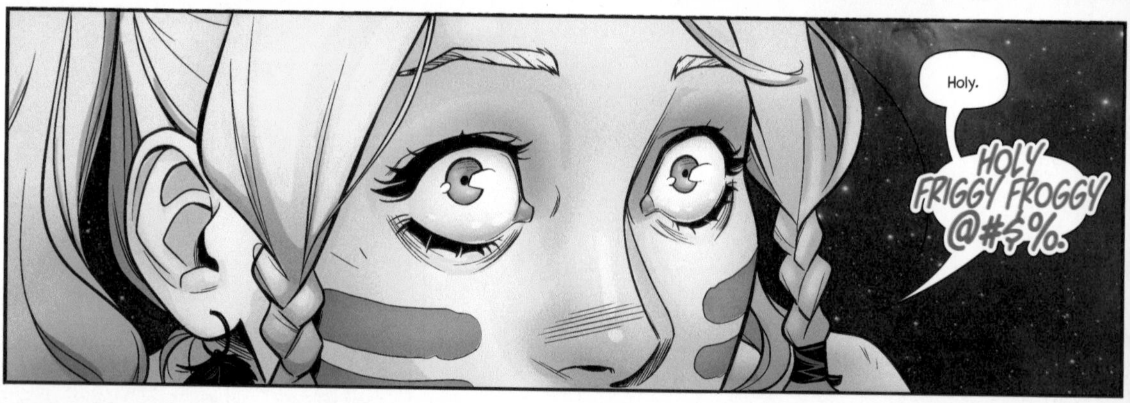
Holy.
HOLY FRIGGY FROGGY @#$%.

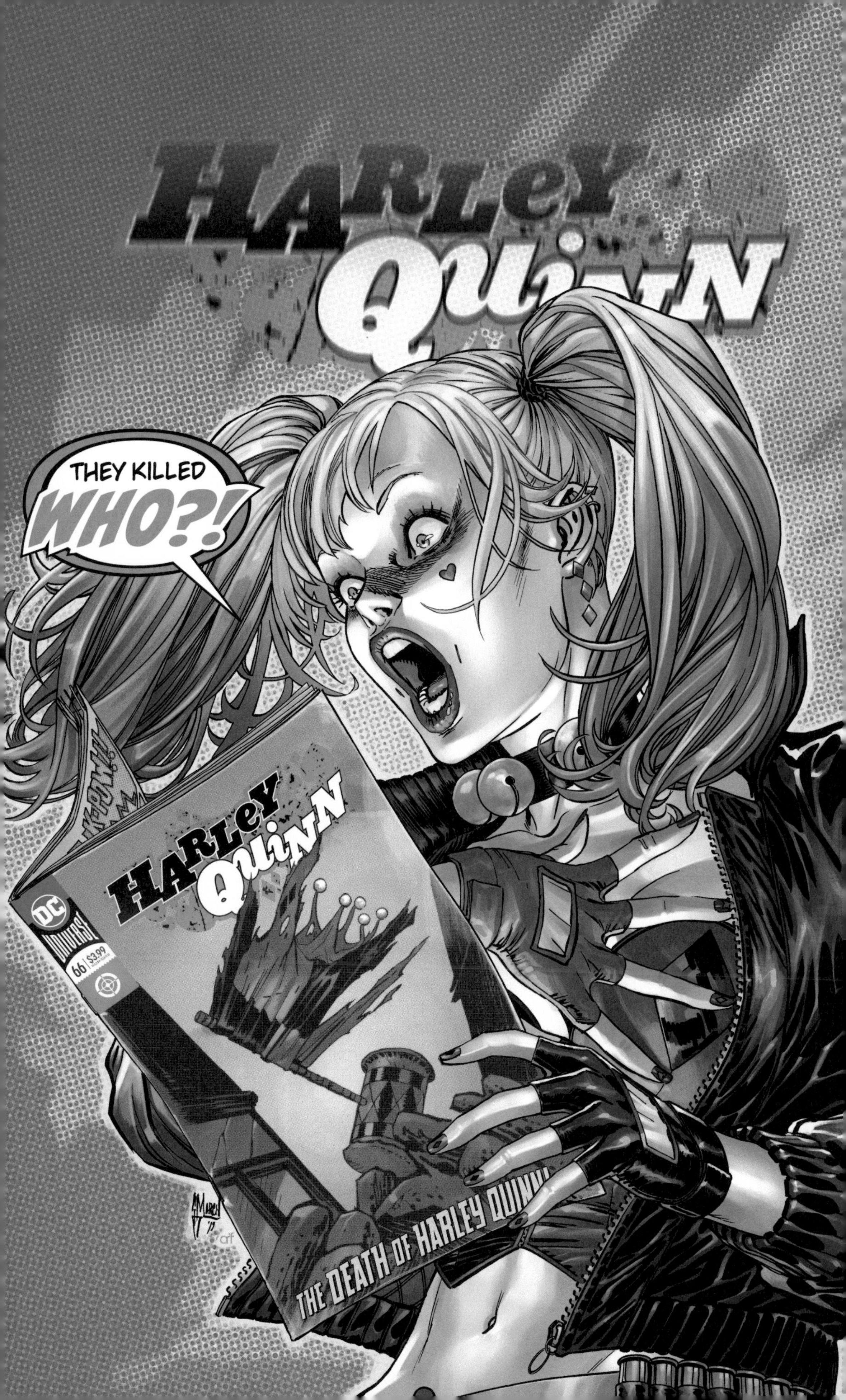

HARLEY QUINN
THEY KILLED WHO?!
HARLEY QUINN
DC UNIVERSE
66 $3.99
THE DEATH OF HARLEY QUINN

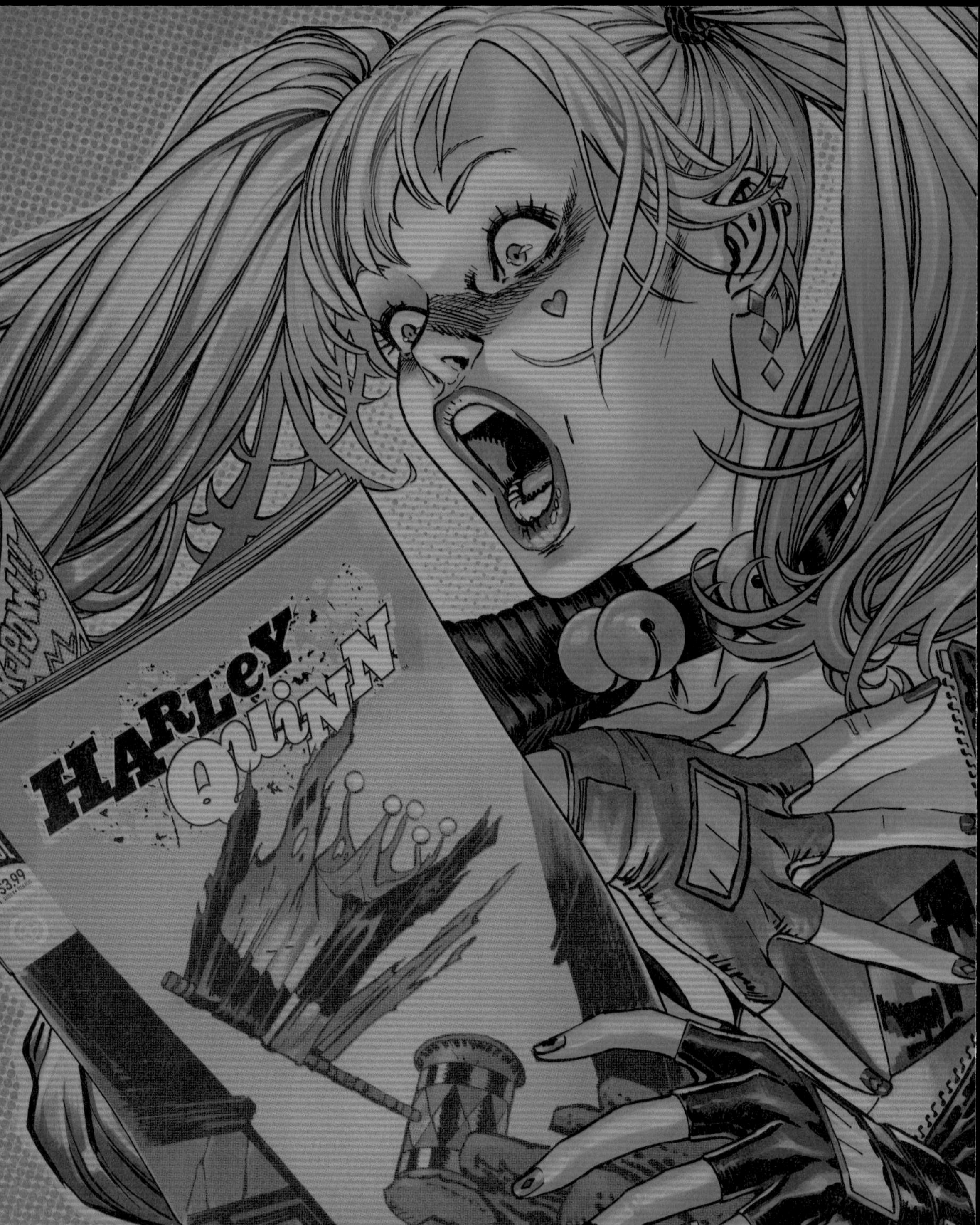
HARLEY QUINN
$3.99

HARLEY QUINN
#66

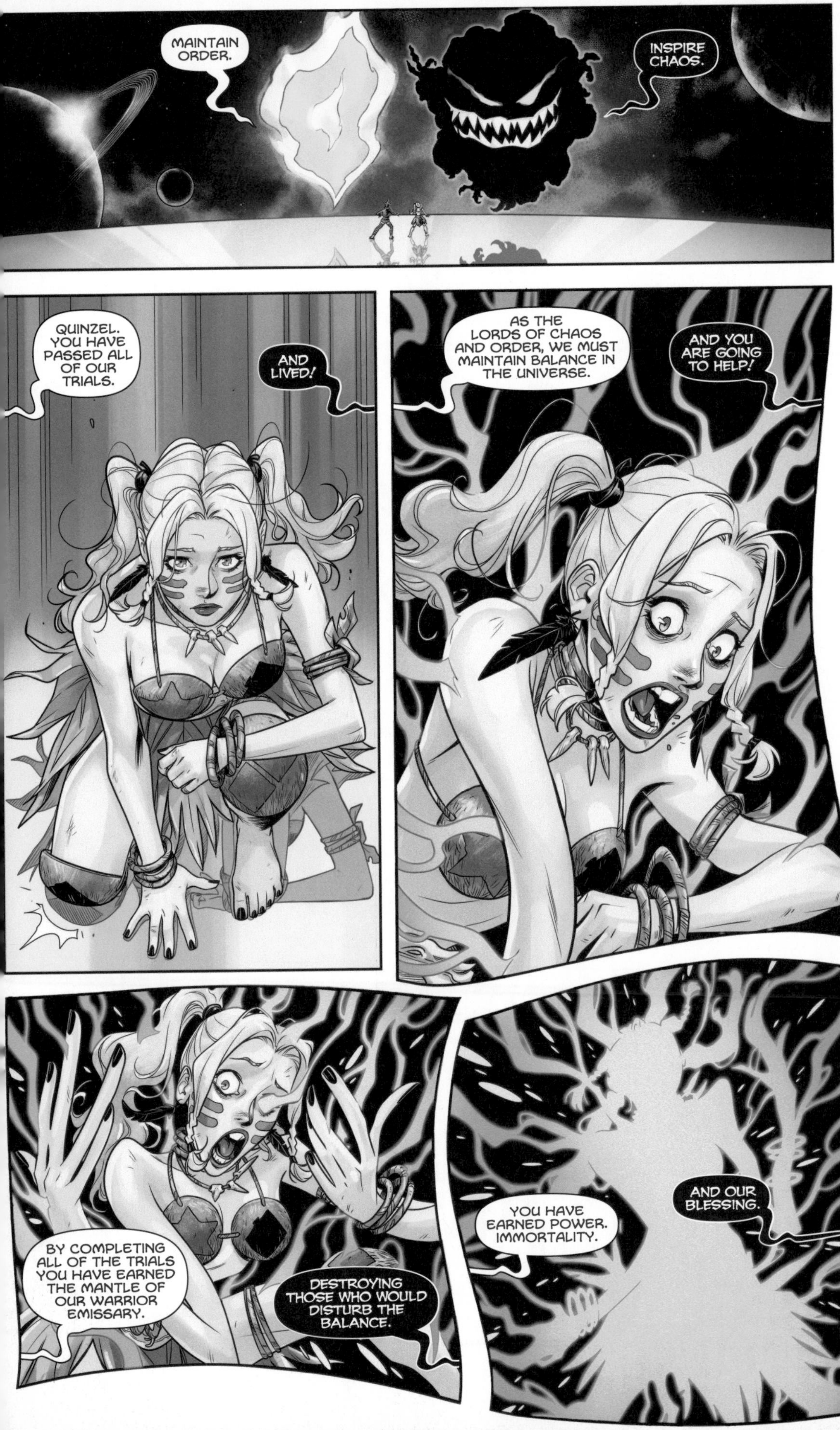
MAINTAIN ORDER.
INSPIRE CHAOS.
QUINZEL. YOU HAVE PASSED ALL OF OUR TRIALS.
AND LIVED!
AS THE LORDS OF CHAOS AND ORDER, WE MUST MAINTAIN BALANCE IN THE UNIVERSE.
AND YOU ARE GOING TO HELP!
BY COMPLETING ALL OF THE TRIALS YOU HAVE EARNED THE MANTLE OF OUR WARRIOR EMISSARY.
DESTROYING THOSE WHO WOULD DISTURB THE BALANCE.
YOU HAVE EARNED POWER. IMMORTALITY.
AND OUR BLESSING.

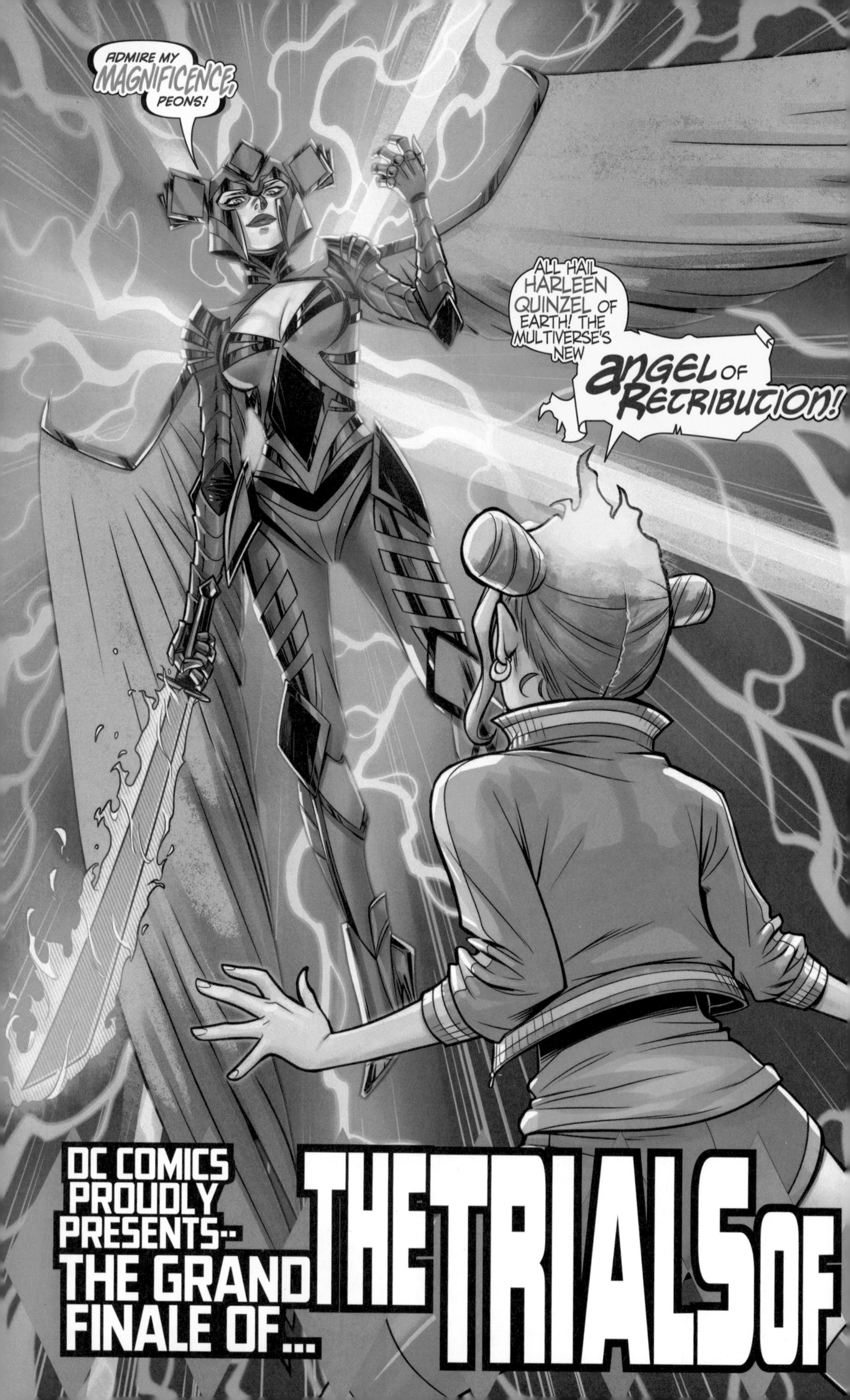
ADMIRE MY MAGNIFICENCE, PEONS!
ALL HAIL HARLEEN QUINZEL OF EARTH! THE MULTIVERSE'S NEW ANGEL OF RETRIBUTION!
DC COMICS PROUDLY PRESENTS-- THE GRAND FINALE OF...
THE TRIALS OF

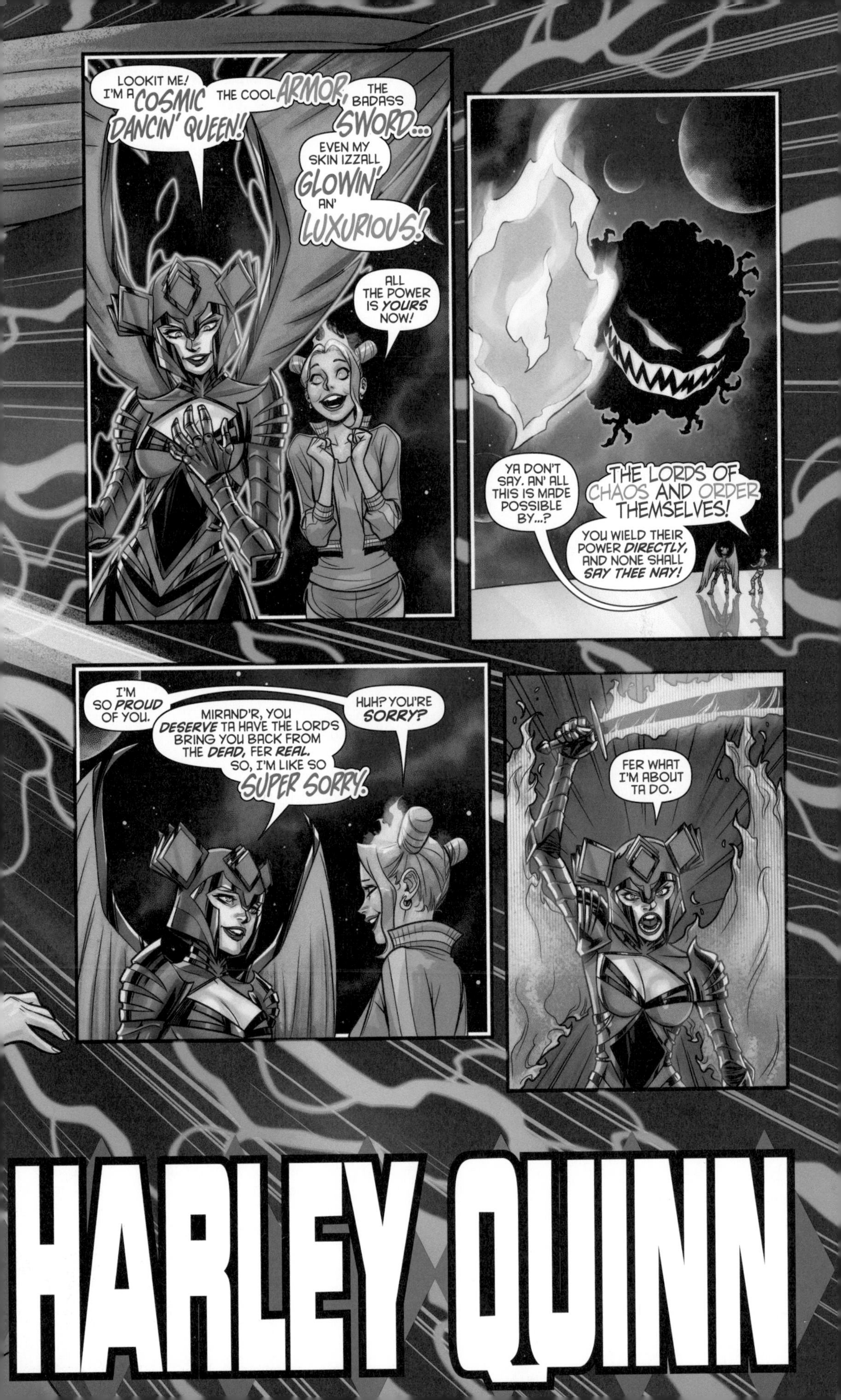
LOOKIT ME! I'M A COSMIC DANCIN' QUEEN!
THE COOL ARMOR,
THE BADASS SWORD...
EVEN MY SKIN IZZALL GLOWIN' AN' LUXURIOUS!
ALL THE POWER IS YOURS NOW!
YA DON'T SAY. AN' ALL THIS IS MADE POSSIBLE BY...?
THE LORDS OF CHAOS AND ORDER THEMSELVES!
YOU WIELD THEIR POWER DIRECTLY, AND NONE SHALL SAY THEE NAY!
I'M SO PROUD OF YOU.
MIRAND'R, YOU DESERVE TA HAVE THE LORDS BRING YOU BACK FROM THE DEAD, FER REAL. SO, I'M LIKE SO SUPER SORRY.
HUH? YOU'RE SORRY?
FER WHAT I'M ABOUT TA DO.
HARLEY QUINN

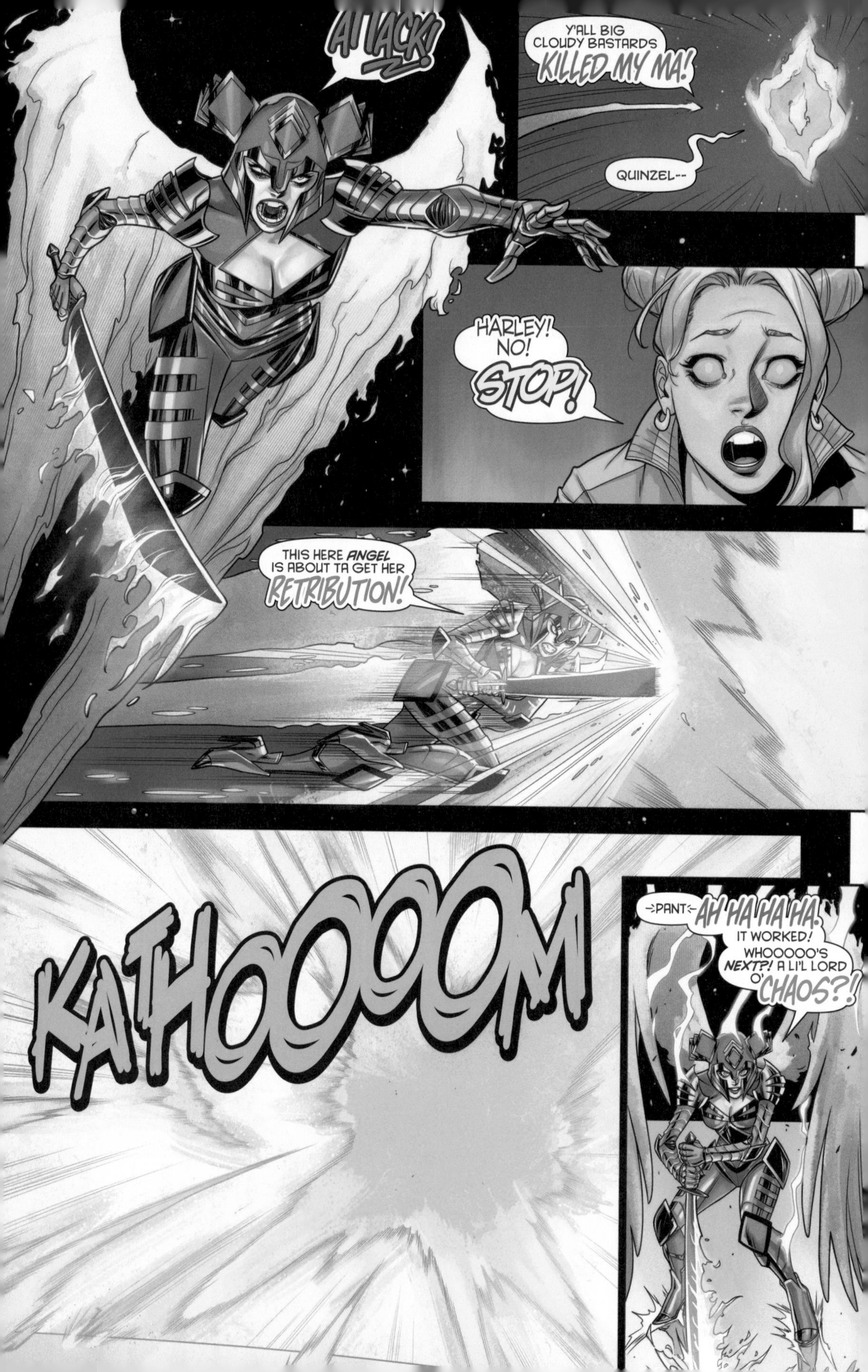
ATTACK!
Y'ALL BIG CLOUDY BASTARDS KILLED MY MA!
QUINZEL--
HARLEY! NO! STOP!
THIS HERE ANGEL IS ABOUT TA GET HER RETRIBUTION!
KATHOOOOM
-PANT- AH HA HA HA.
IT WORKED! WHOOOOO'S NEXT?! A LI'L LORD O' CHAOS?!

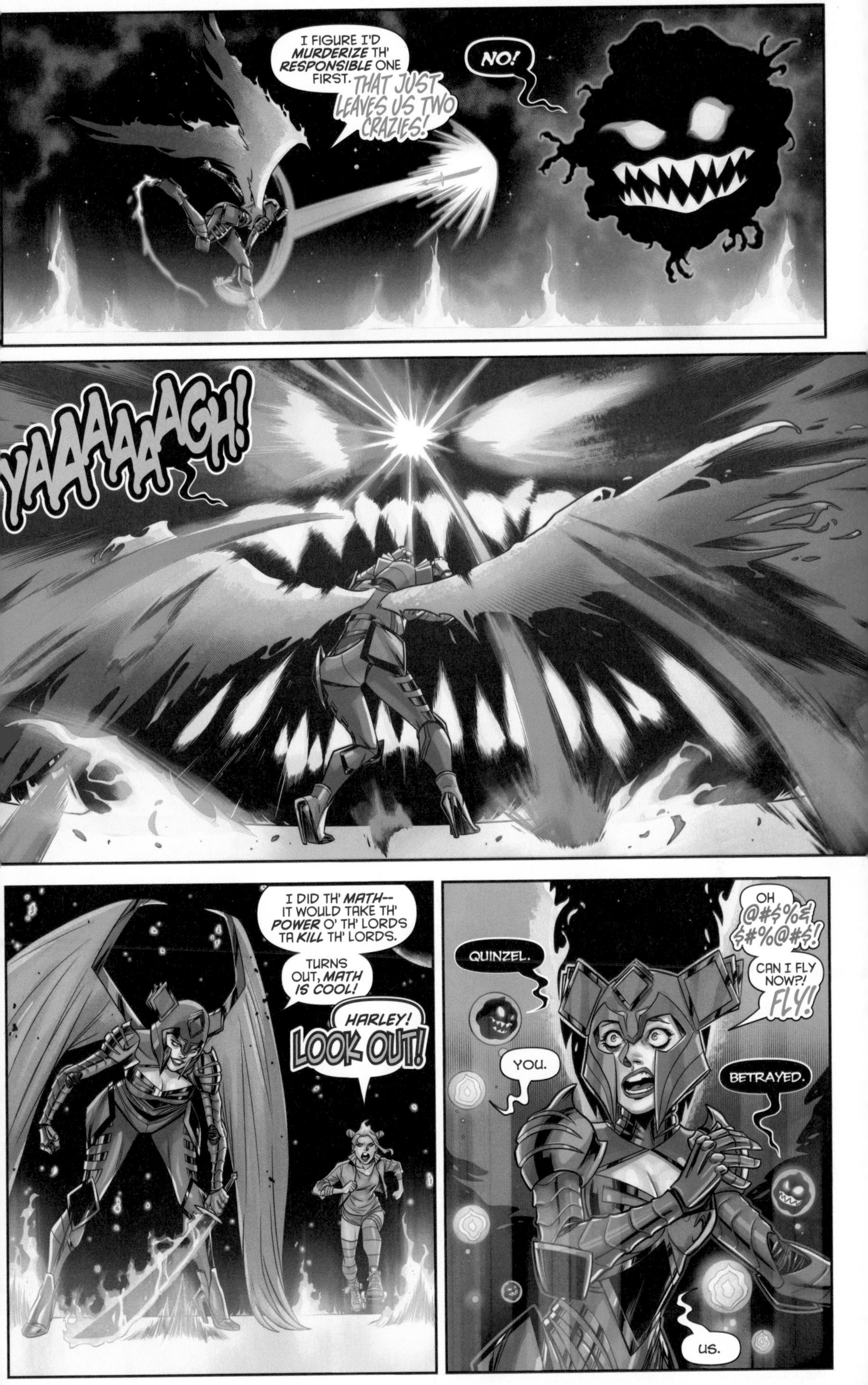
I FIGURE I'D MURDERIZE TH' RESPONSIBLE ONE FIRST.
THAT JUST LEAVES US TWO CRAZIES!
NO!
YAAAAAAGH!
I DID TH' MATH-- IT WOULD TAKE TH' POWER O' TH' LORDS TA KILL TH' LORDS.
TURNS OUT, MATH IS COOL!
HARLEY! LOOK OUT!
OH @#$%& $#%@#$!
CAN I FLY NOW?! FLY!
QUINZEL.
YOU.
BETRAYED.
US.

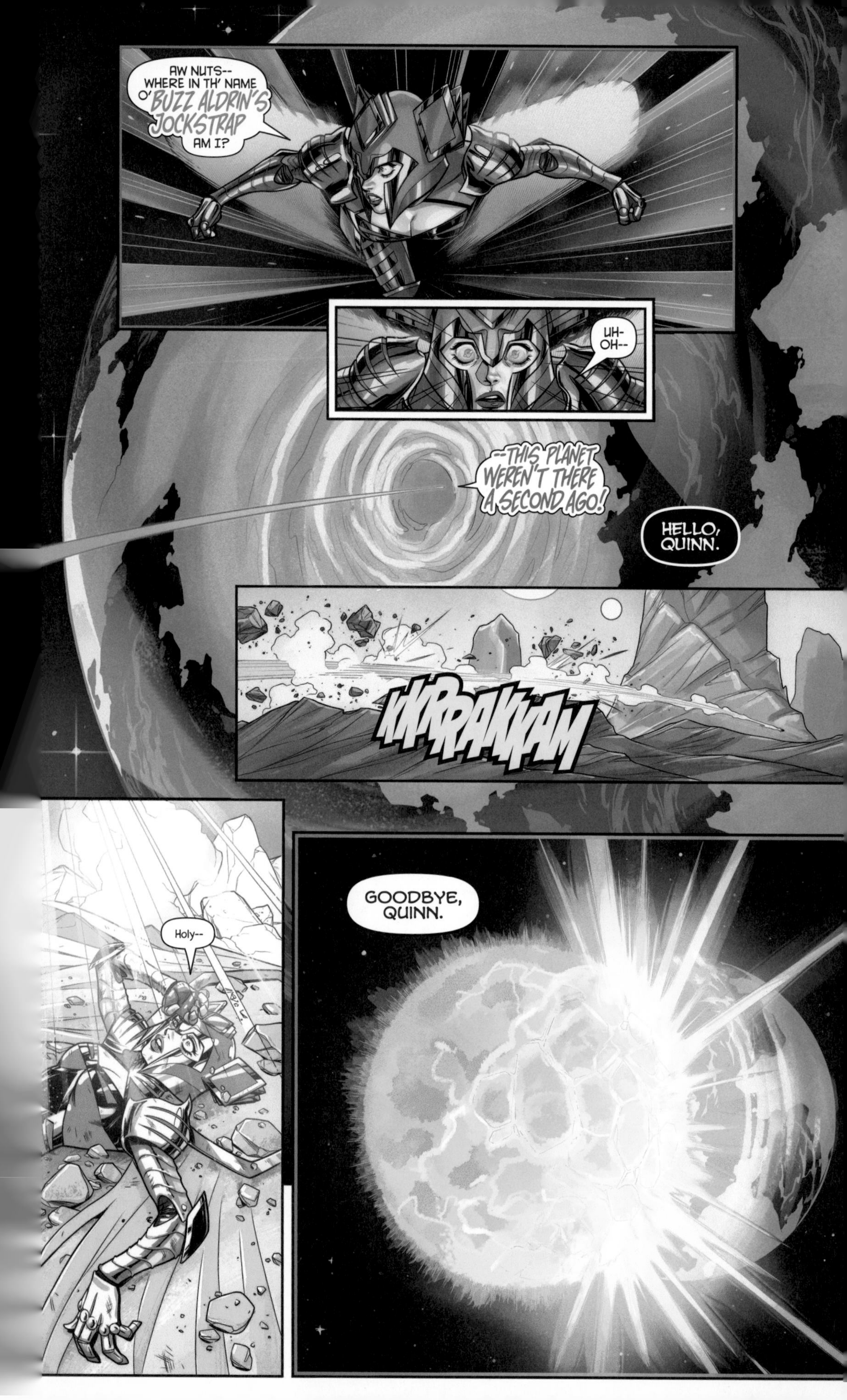
AW NUTS-- WHERE IN TH' NAME O' BUZZ ALDRIN'S JOCKSTRAP AM I?
UH-OH--
--THIS PLANET WEREN'T THERE A SECOND AGO!
HELLO, QUINN.
KKRRAKKAM
Holy--
GOODBYE, QUINN.

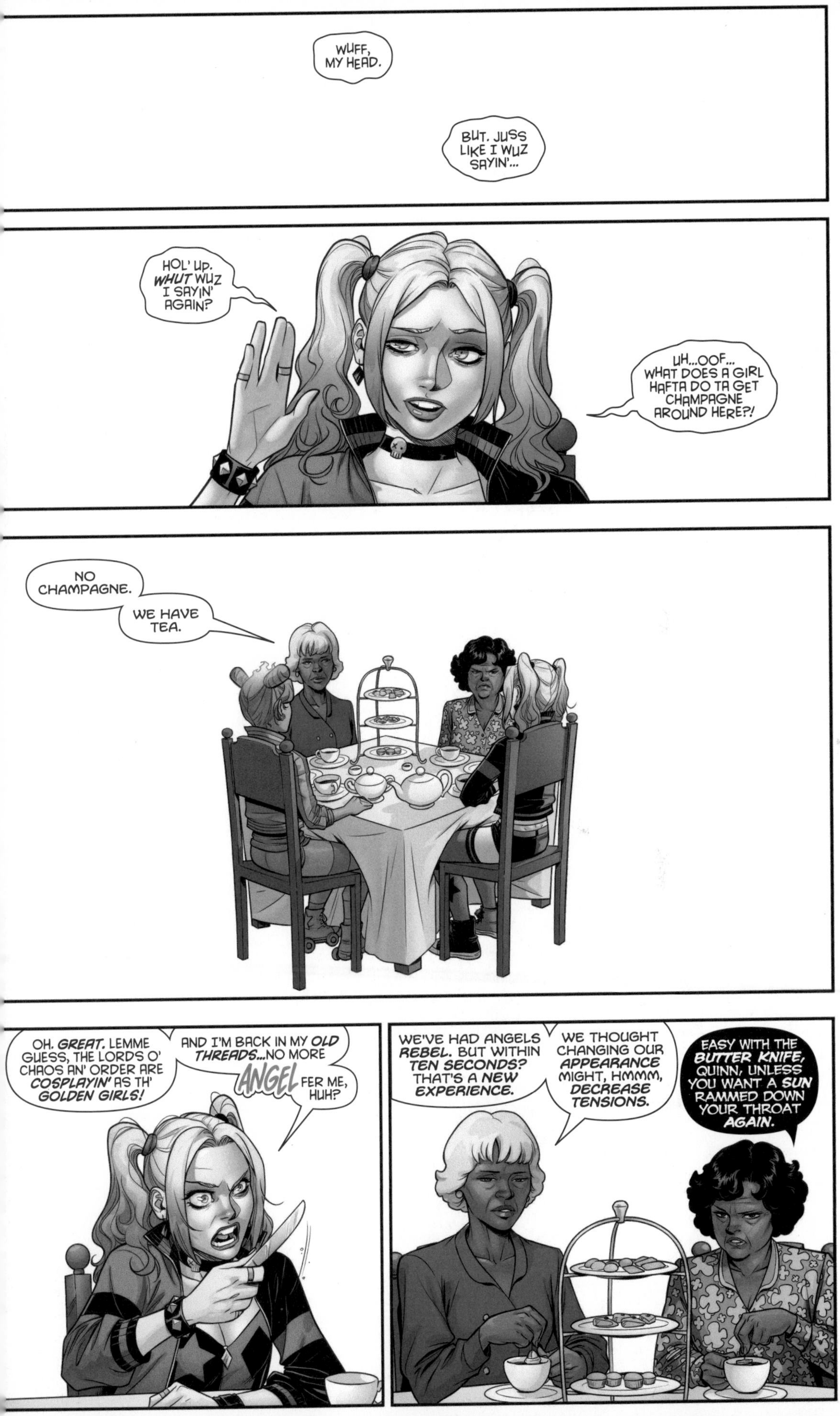
WUFF, MY HEAD.
BUT. JUSS LIKE I WUZ SAYIN'...
HOL' UP. WHUT WUZ I SAYIN' AGAIN?
UH...OOF... WHAT DOES A GIRL HAFTA DO TA GET CHAMPAGNE AROUND HERE?!
NO CHAMPAGNE.
WE HAVE TEA.
OH. GREAT. LEMME GUESS, THE LORDS O' CHAOS AN' ORDER ARE COSPLAYIN' AS TH' GOLDEN GIRLS!
AND I'M BACK IN MY OLD THREADS...NO MORE ANGEL FER ME, HUH?
WE'VE HAD ANGELS REBEL. BUT WITHIN TEN SECONDS? THAT'S A NEW EXPERIENCE.
WE THOUGHT CHANGING OUR APPEARANCE MIGHT, HMMM, DECREASE TENSIONS.
EASY WITH THE BUTTER KNIFE, QUINN, UNLESS YOU WANT A SUN RAMMED DOWN YOUR THROAT AGAIN.

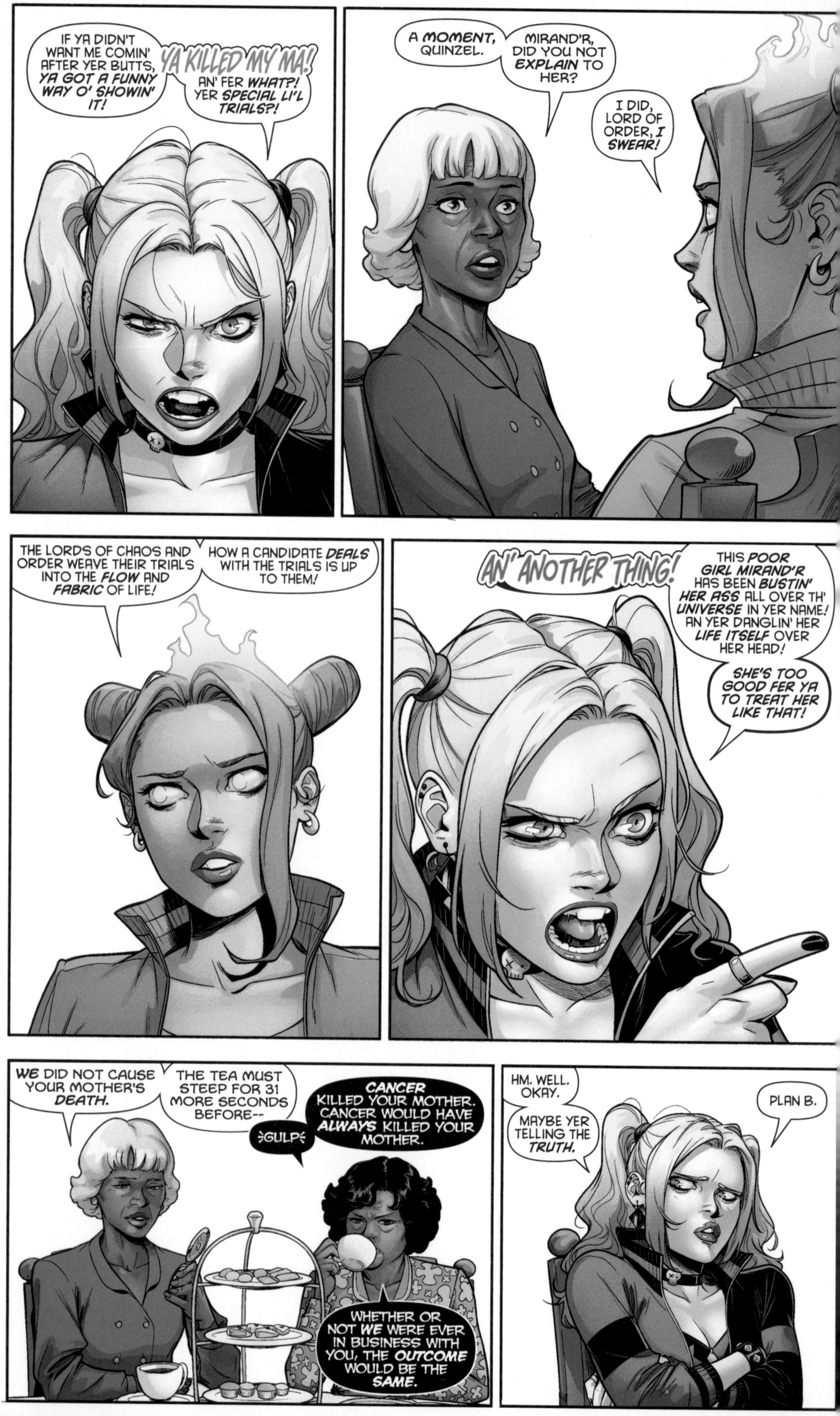

IF YA DIDN'T WANT ME COMIN' AFTER YER BUTTS, YA GOT A FUNNY WAY O' SHOWIN' IT!
YA KILLED MY MA!
AN' FER WHAT?! YER SPECIAL LI'L TRIALS?!
A MOMENT, QUINZEL.
MIRAND'R, DID YOU NOT EXPLAIN TO HER?
I DID, LORD OF ORDER, I SWEAR!
THE LORDS OF CHAOS AND ORDER WEAVE THEIR TRIALS INTO THE FLOW AND FABRIC OF LIFE!
HOW A CANDIDATE DEALS WITH THE TRIALS IS UP TO THEM!
AN' ANOTHER THING!
THIS POOR GIRL MIRAND'R HAS BEEN BUSTIN' HER ASS ALL OVER TH' UNIVERSE IN YER NAME! AN YER DANGLIN' HER LIFE ITSELF OVER HER HEAD!
SHE'S TOO GOOD FER YA TO TREAT HER LIKE THAT!
WE DID NOT CAUSE YOUR MOTHER'S DEATH.
THE TEA MUST STEEP FOR 31 MORE SECONDS BEFORE--
GULP
CANCER KILLED YOUR MOTHER. CANCER WOULD HAVE ALWAYS KILLED YOUR MOTHER.
WHETHER OR NOT WE WERE EVER IN BUSINESS WITH YOU, THE OUTCOME WOULD BE THE SAME.
HM. WELL. OKAY.
MAYBE YER TELLING THE TRUTH.
PLAN B.

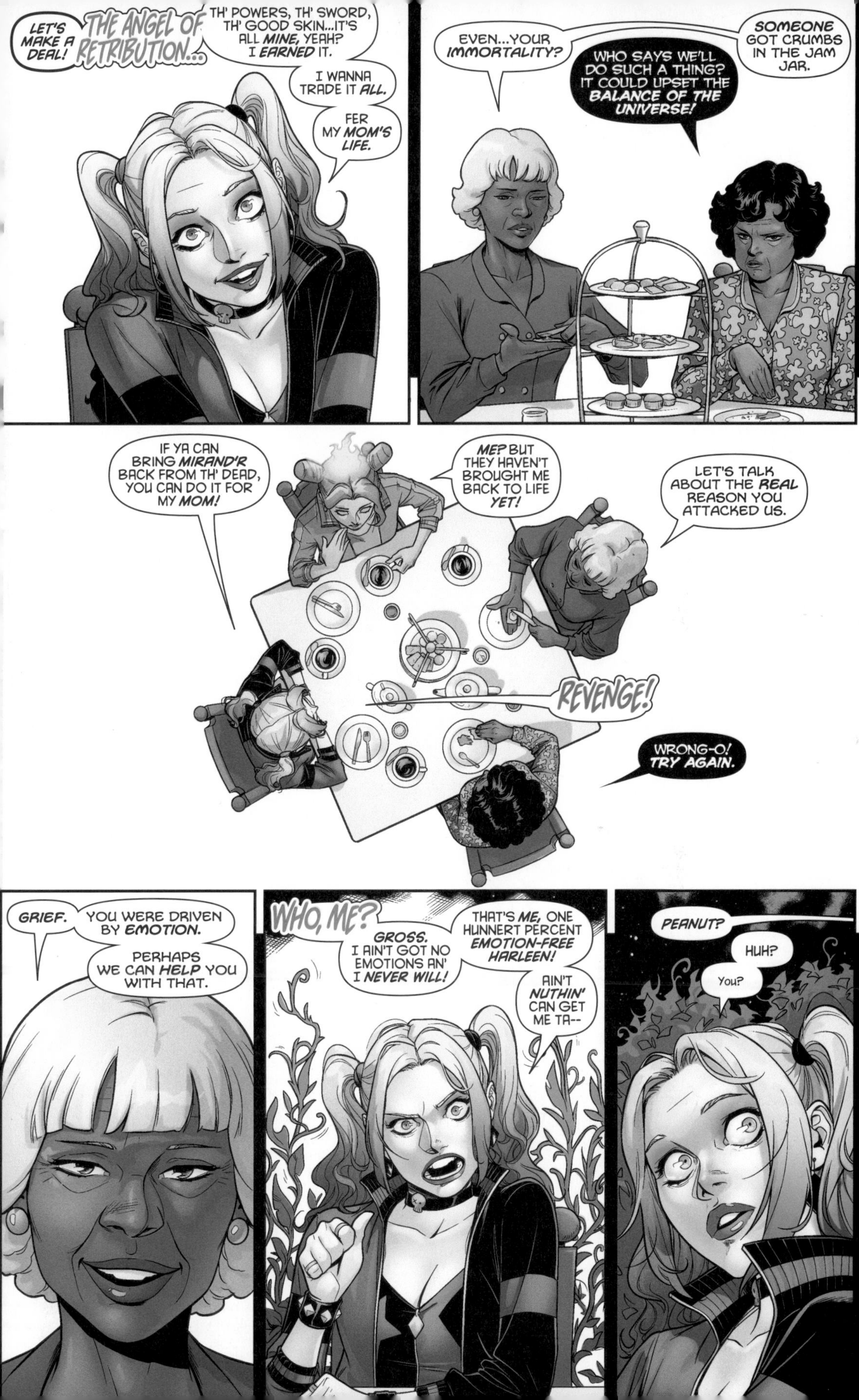

LET'S MAKE A DEAL!
THE ANGEL OF RETRIBUTION...
TH' POWERS, TH' SWORD, TH' GOOD SKIN...IT'S ALL MINE, YEAH? I EARNED IT.
I WANNA TRADE IT ALL.
FER MY MOM'S LIFE.
EVEN...YOUR IMMORTALITY?
SOMEONE GOT CRUMBS IN THE JAM JAR.
WHO SAYS WE'LL DO SUCH A THING? IT COULD UPSET THE BALANCE OF THE UNIVERSE!
IF YA CAN BRING MIRAND'R BACK FROM TH' DEAD, YOU CAN DO IT FOR MY MOM!
ME? BUT THEY HAVEN'T BROUGHT ME BACK TO LIFE YET!
LET'S TALK ABOUT THE REAL REASON YOU ATTACKED US.
REVENGE!
WRONG-O! TRY AGAIN.
GRIEF.
YOU WERE DRIVEN BY EMOTION.
PERHAPS WE CAN HELP YOU WITH THAT.
WHO, ME?
GROSS. I AIN'T GOT NO EMOTIONS AN' I NEVER WILL!
THAT'S ME, ONE HUNNERT PERCENT EMOTION-FREE HARLEEN!
AIN'T NUTHIN' CAN GET ME TA--
PEANUT?
HUH?
You?

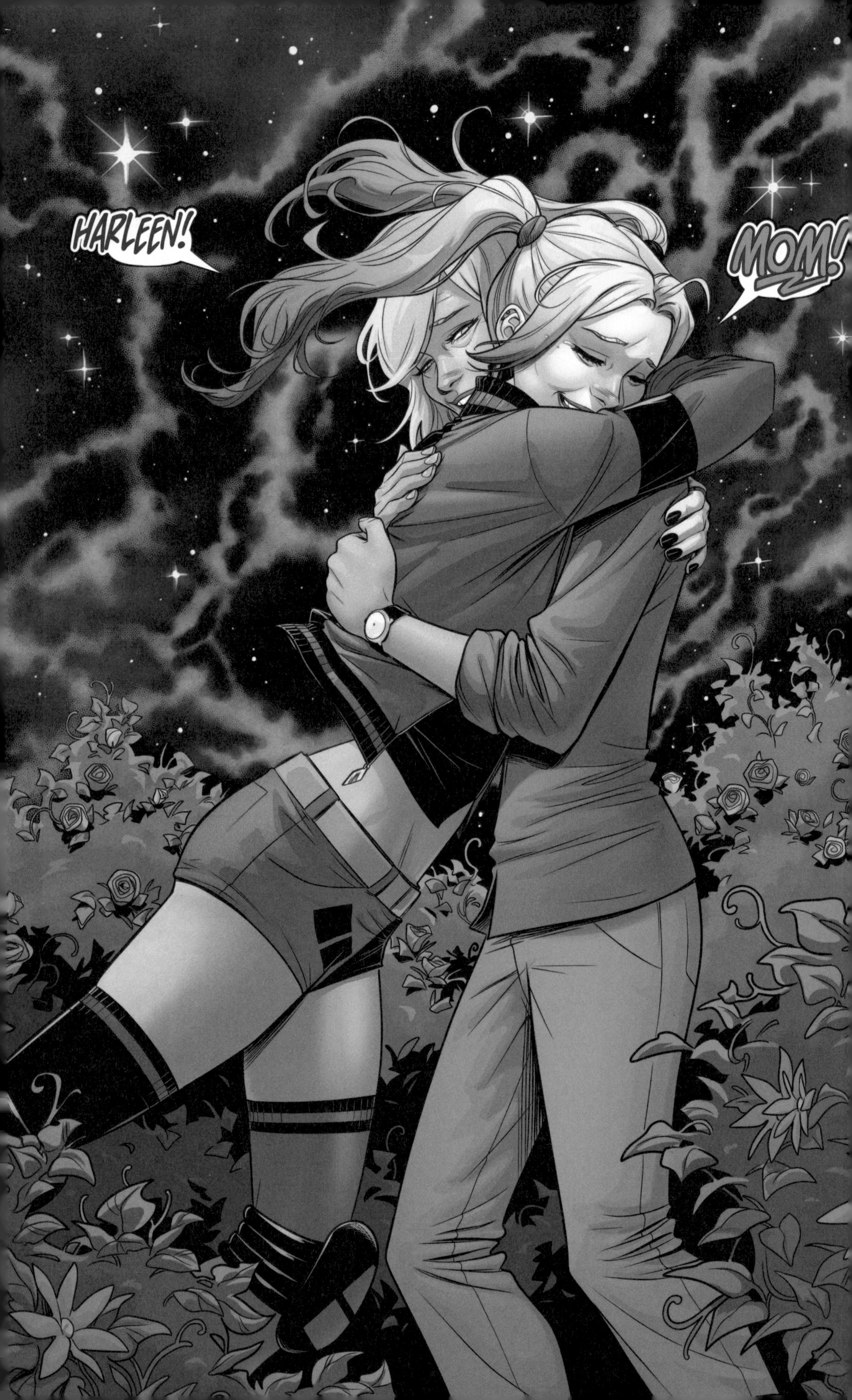
HARLEEN!
MOM!

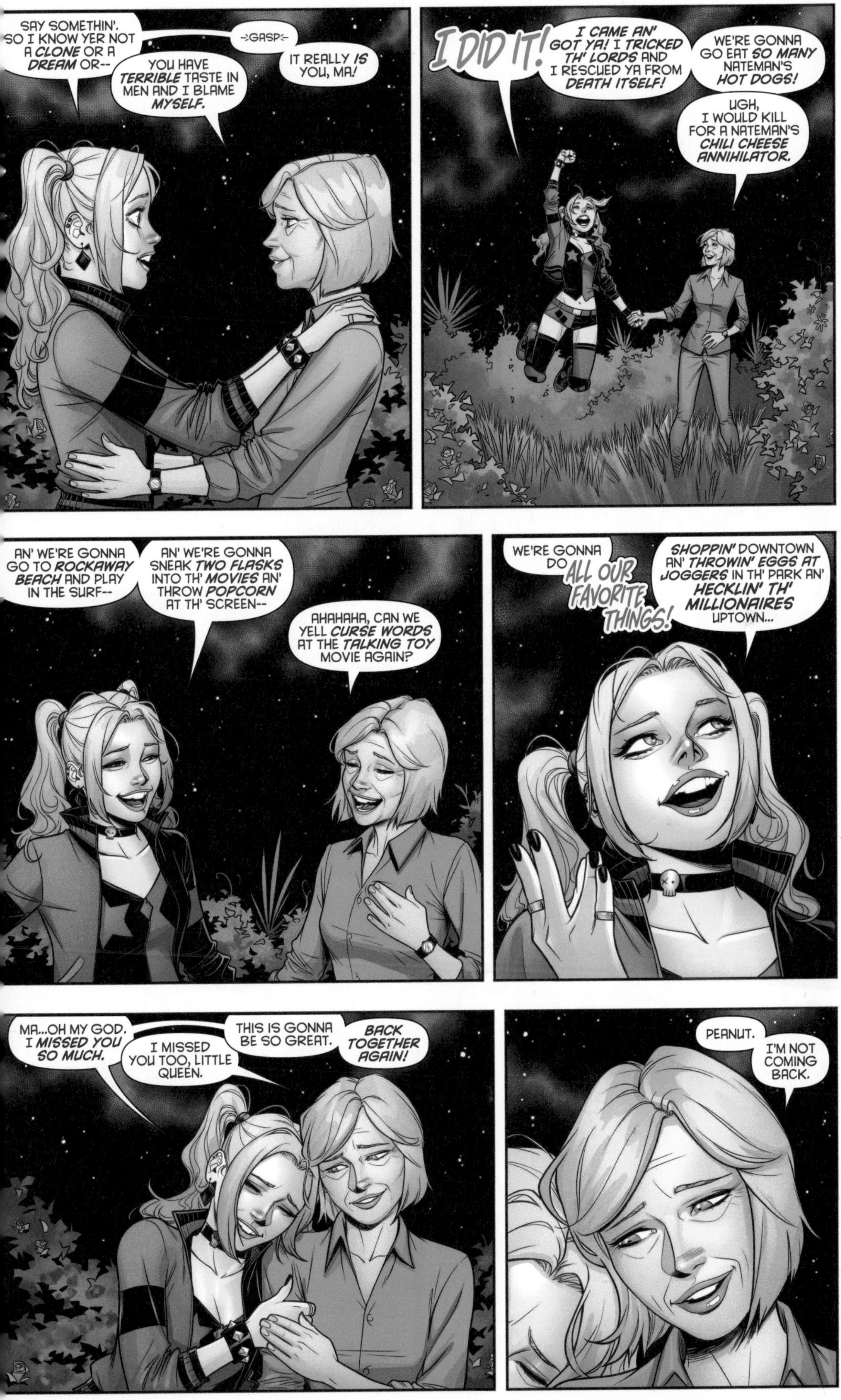
SAY SOMETHIN'. SO I KNOW YER NOT A CLONE OR A DREAM OR--
-GASP-
YOU HAVE TERRIBLE TASTE IN MEN AND I BLAME MYSELF.
IT REALLY IS YOU, MA!
I DID IT!
I CAME AN' GOT YA! I TRICKED TH' LORDS AND I RESCUED YA FROM DEATH ITSELF!
WE'RE GONNA GO EAT SO MANY NATEMAN'S HOT DOGS!
UGH, I WOULD KILL FOR A NATEMAN'S CHILI CHEESE ANNIHILATOR.
AN' WE'RE GONNA GO TO ROCKAWAY BEACH AND PLAY IN THE SURF--
AN' WE'RE GONNA SNEAK TWO FLASKS INTO TH' MOVIES AN' THROW POPCORN AT TH' SCREEN--
AHAHAHA, CAN WE YELL CURSE WORDS AT THE TALKING TOY MOVIE AGAIN?
WE'RE GONNA DO ALL OUR FAVORITE THINGS!
SHOPPIN' DOWNTOWN AN' THROWIN' EGGS AT JOGGERS IN TH' PARK AN' HECKLIN' TH' MILLIONAIRES UPTOWN...
MA...OH MY GOD. I MISSED YOU SO MUCH.
I MISSED YOU TOO, LITTLE QUEEN.
THIS IS GONNA BE SO GREAT.
BACK TOGETHER AGAIN!
PEANUT.
I'M NOT COMING BACK.

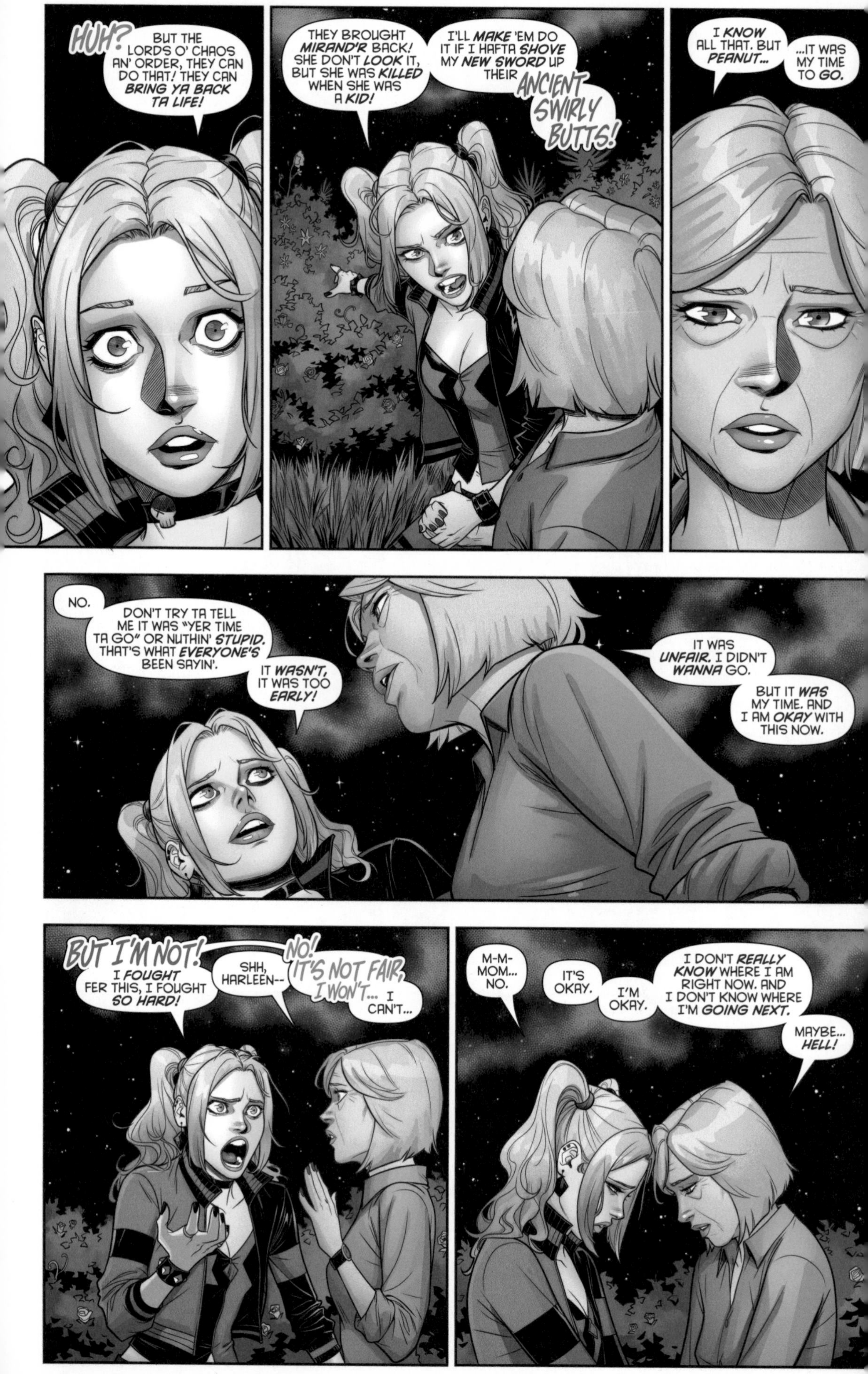
HUH?
BUT THE LORDS O' CHAOS AN' ORDER, THEY CAN DO THAT! THEY CAN BRING YA BACK TA LIFE!
THEY BROUGHT MIRAND'R BACK! SHE DON'T LOOK IT, BUT SHE WAS KILLED WHEN SHE WAS A KID!
I'LL MAKE 'EM DO IT IF I HAFTA SHOVE MY NEW SWORD UP THEIR ANCIENT SWIRLY BUTTS!
I KNOW ALL THAT. BUT PEANUT...
...IT WAS MY TIME TO GO.
NO.
DON'T TRY TA TELL ME IT WAS "YER TIME TA GO" OR NUTHIN' STUPID. THAT'S WHAT EVERYONE'S BEEN SAYIN'.
IT WASN'T, IT WAS TOO EARLY!
IT WAS UNFAIR. I DIDN'T WANNA GO.
BUT IT WAS MY TIME. AND I AM OKAY WITH THIS NOW.
BUT I'M NOT!
I FOUGHT FER THIS, I FOUGHT SO HARD!
SHH, HARLEEN--
NO! IT'S NOT FAIR, I WON'T... I CAN'T...
M-M-MOM... NO.
IT'S OKAY.
I'M OKAY.
I DON'T REALLY KNOW WHERE I AM RIGHT NOW. AND I DON'T KNOW WHERE I'M GOING NEXT.
MAYBE... HELL!

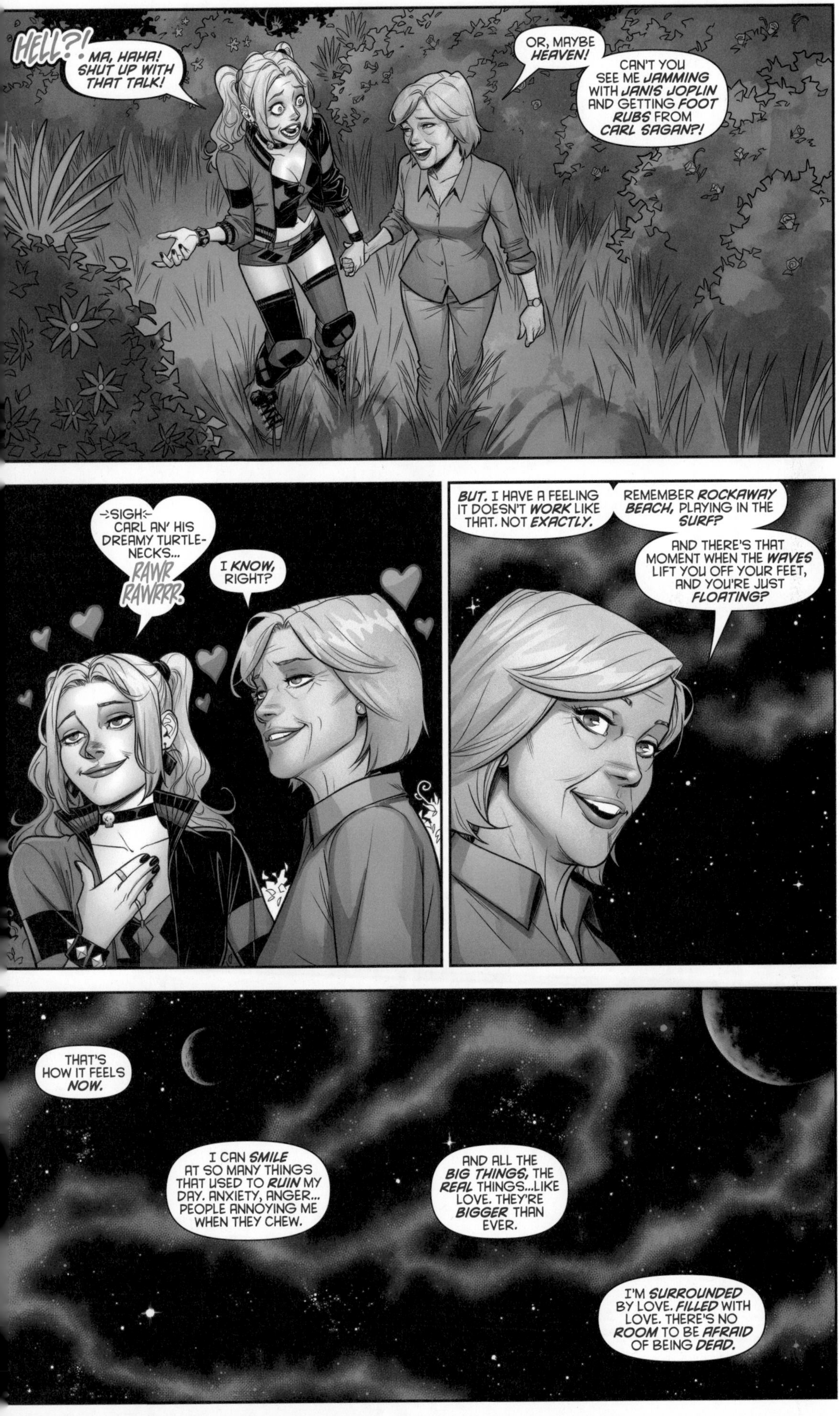
HELL?!
MA, HAHA! SHUT UP WITH THAT TALK!
OR, MAYBE HEAVEN!
CAN'T YOU SEE ME JAMMING WITH JANIS JOPLIN AND GETTING FOOT RUBS FROM CARL SAGAN?!
-SIGH- CARL AN' HIS DREAMY TURTLE-NECKS... RAWR RAWRRR.
I KNOW, RIGHT?
BUT. I HAVE A FEELING IT DOESN'T WORK LIKE THAT. NOT EXACTLY.
REMEMBER ROCKAWAY BEACH, PLAYING IN THE SURF?
AND THERE'S THAT MOMENT WHEN THE WAVES LIFT YOU OFF YOUR FEET, AND YOU'RE JUST FLOATING?
THAT'S HOW IT FEELS NOW.
I CAN SMILE AT SO MANY THINGS THAT USED TO RUIN MY DAY. ANXIETY, ANGER... PEOPLE ANNOYING ME WHEN THEY CHEW.
AND ALL THE BIG THINGS, THE REAL THINGS...LIKE LOVE. THEY'RE BIGGER THAN EVER.
I'M SURROUNDED BY LOVE. FILLED WITH LOVE. THERE'S NO ROOM TO BE AFRAID OF BEING DEAD.

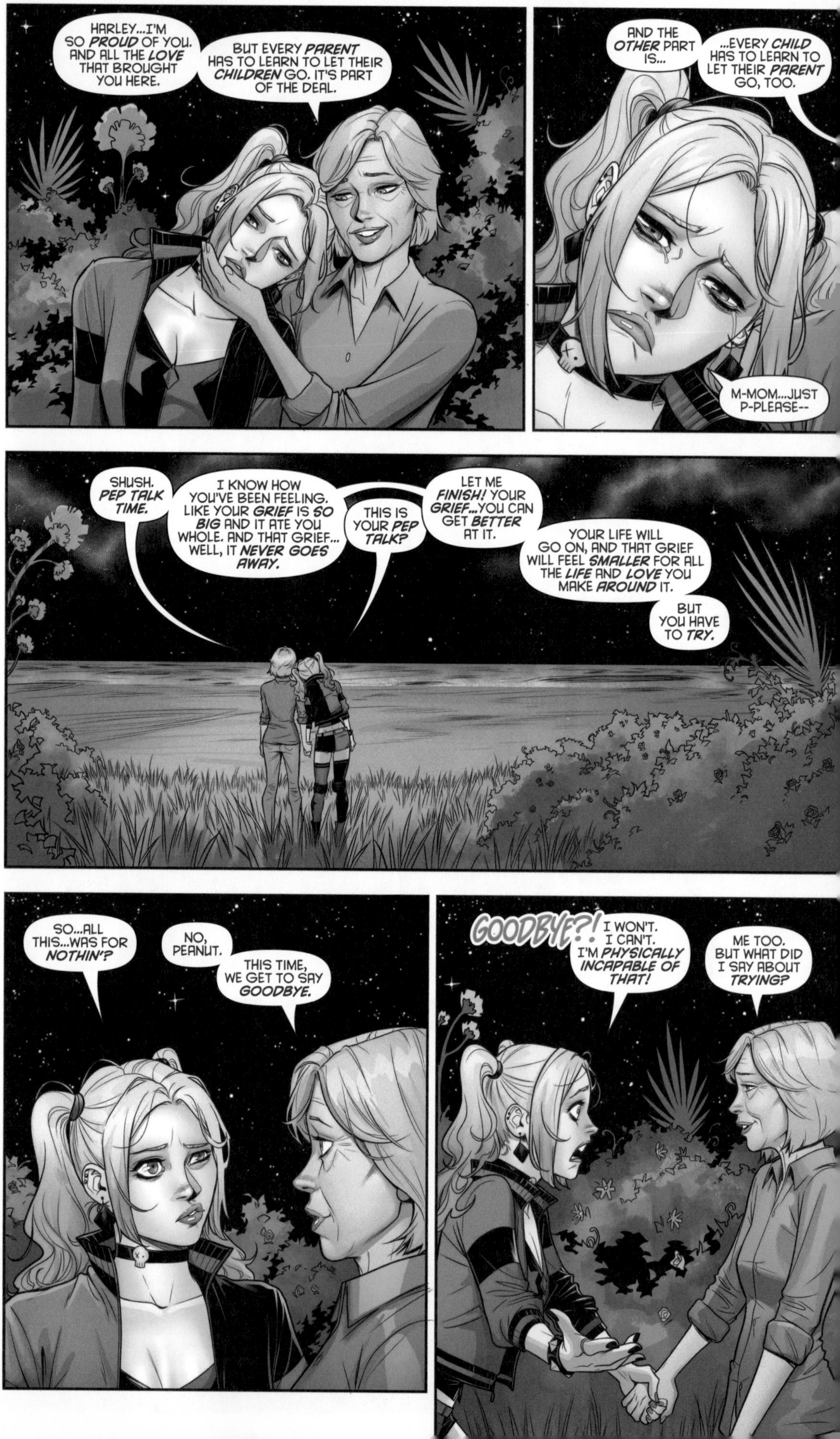
HARLEY...I'M SO PROUD OF YOU. AND ALL THE LOVE THAT BROUGHT YOU HERE.
BUT EVERY PARENT HAS TO LEARN TO LET THEIR CHILDREN GO. IT'S PART OF THE DEAL.
AND THE OTHER PART IS...
...EVERY CHILD HAS TO LEARN TO LET THEIR PARENT GO, TOO.
M-MOM...JUST P-PLEASE--
SHUSH. PEP TALK TIME.
I KNOW HOW YOU'VE BEEN FEELING. LIKE YOUR GRIEF IS SO BIG AND IT ATE YOU WHOLE. AND THAT GRIEF... WELL, IT NEVER GOES AWAY.
THIS IS YOUR PEP TALK?
LET ME FINISH! YOUR GRIEF...YOU CAN GET BETTER AT IT.
YOUR LIFE WILL GO ON, AND THAT GRIEF WILL FEEL SMALLER FOR ALL THE LIFE AND LOVE YOU MAKE AROUND IT.
BUT YOU HAVE TO TRY.
SO...ALL THIS...WAS FOR NOTHIN'?
NO, PEANUT.
THIS TIME, WE GET TO SAY GOODBYE.
GOODBYE?!
I WON'T. I CAN'T. I'M PHYSICALLY INCAPABLE OF THAT!
ME TOO. BUT WHAT DID I SAY ABOUT TRYING?

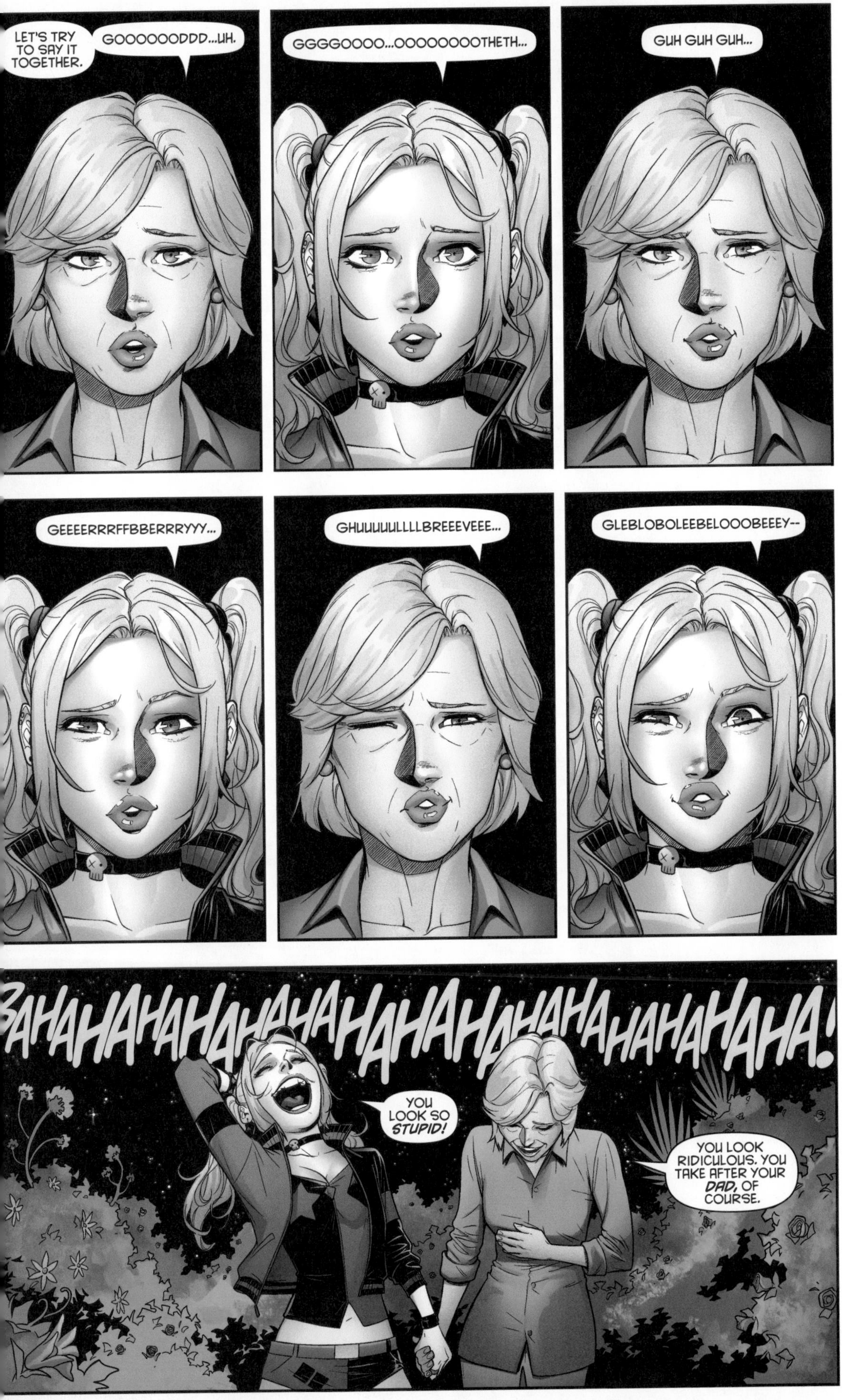
LET'S TRY TO SAY IT TOGETHER.
GOOOOOOODDD...UH.
GGGGOOOO...OOOOOOOOTHETH...
GUH GUH GUH...
GEEEERRRFFBBERRRYYY...
GHUUUUULLLLBREEEVEEE...
GLEBLOBOLEEBELOOOBEEEY--
HAHAHAHAHAHAHAHAHAHAHAHAHAHAHAHAHAHAHA!
YOU LOOK SO STUPID!
YOU LOOK RIDICULOUS. YOU TAKE AFTER YOUR DAD, OF COURSE.

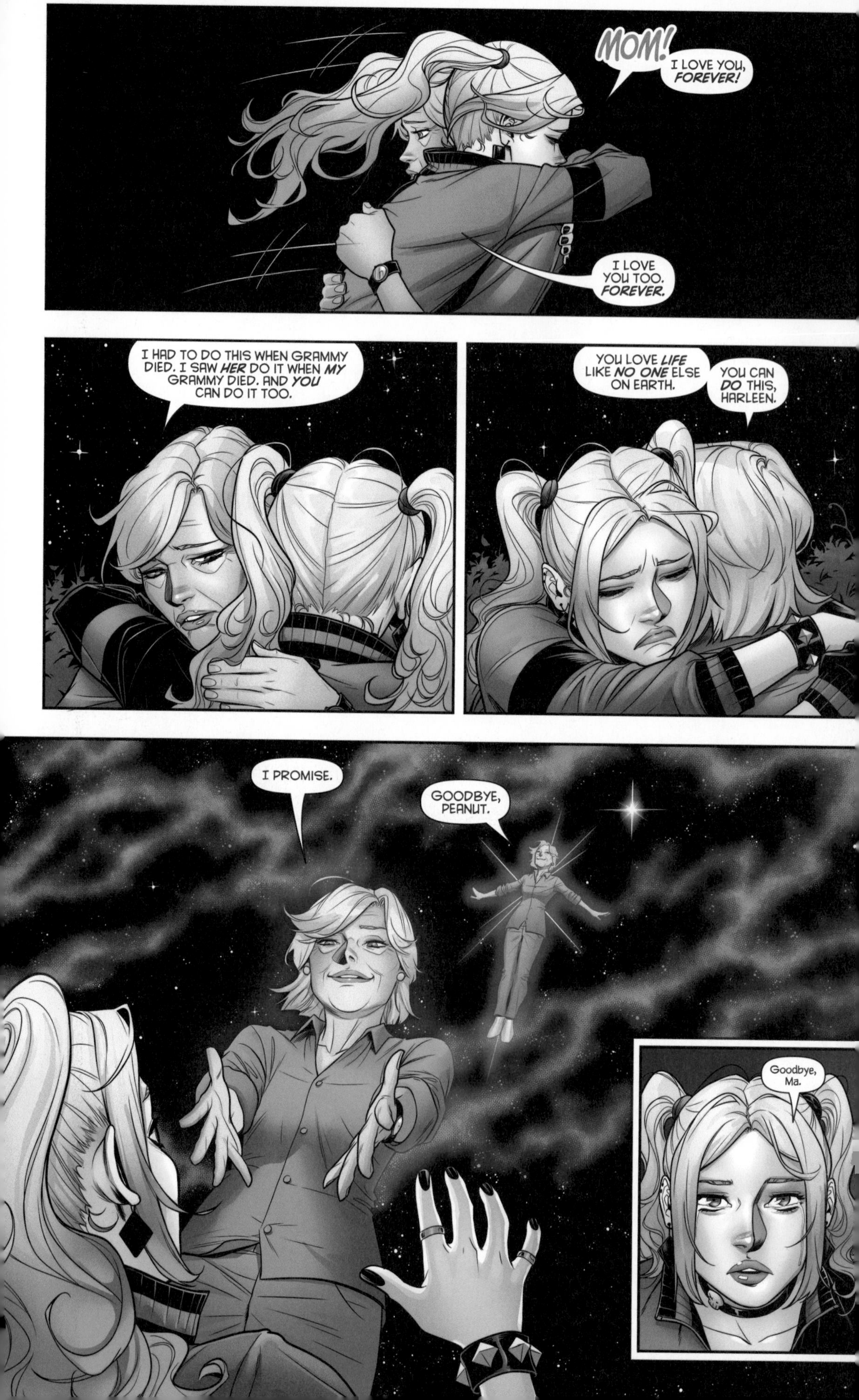
MOM! I LOVE YOU, FOREVER!
I LOVE YOU TOO. FOREVER.
I HAD TO DO THIS WHEN GRAMMY DIED. I SAW HER DO IT WHEN MY GRAMMY DIED. AND YOU CAN DO IT TOO.
YOU LOVE LIFE LIKE NO ONE ELSE ON EARTH.
YOU CAN DO THIS, HARLEEN.
I PROMISE.
GOODBYE, PEANUT.
Goodbye, Ma.

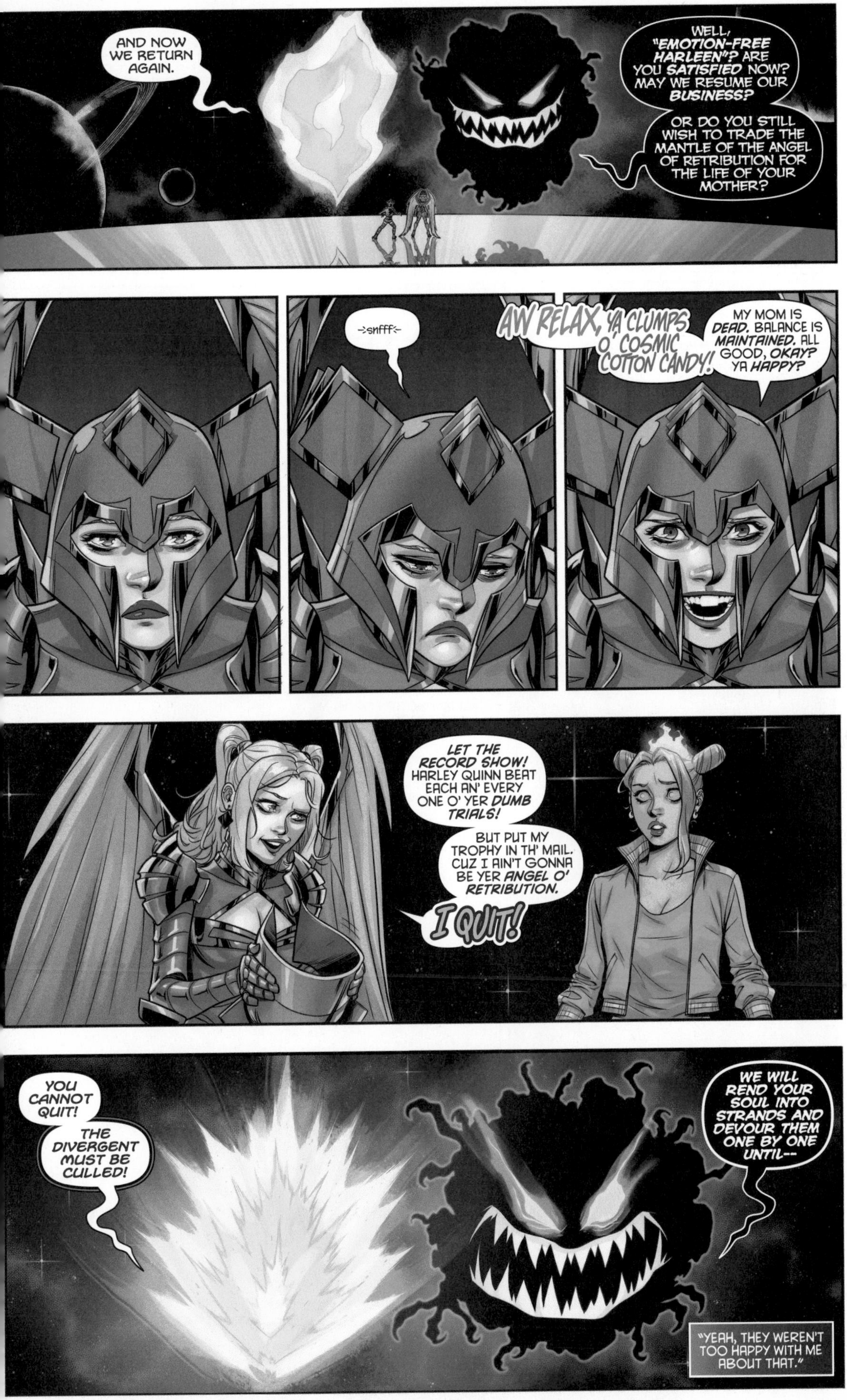
AND NOW WE RETURN AGAIN.
WELL, "EMOTION-FREE HARLEEN"? ARE YOU SATISFIED NOW? MAY WE RESUME OUR BUSINESS?
OR DO YOU STILL WISH TO TRADE THE MANTLE OF THE ANGEL OF RETRIBUTION FOR THE LIFE OF YOUR MOTHER?
-snfff-
AW RELAX, YA CLUMPS O' COSMIC COTTON CANDY!
MY MOM IS DEAD. BALANCE IS MAINTAINED. ALL GOOD, OKAY? YA HAPPY?
LET THE RECORD SHOW! HARLEY QUINN BEAT EACH AN' EVERY ONE O' YER DUMB TRIALS!
BUT PUT MY TROPHY IN TH' MAIL. CUZ I AIN'T GONNA BE YER ANGEL O' RETRIBUTION.
I QUIT!
YOU CANNOT QUIT!
THE DIVERGENT MUST BE CULLED!
WE WILL REND YOUR SOUL INTO STRANDS AND DEVOUR THEM ONE BY ONE UNTIL--
"YEAH, THEY WEREN'T TOO HAPPY WITH ME ABOUT THAT."

BUT, HEY, LET 'EM CRY INTO THEIR *COSMIC KLEENEX* ABOUT IT FER ALL I CARE.

I'M DONE MESSIN' AROUND WITH ALLA THAT *META-PHYSI-CASTICAL STUFF.*

IT GIVES ME *ARTHRITIS* OF TH' *PRIVATE PARTS* AN' *NOTHIN' GOOD* COMES OF IT!

HARLEY...I'M SORRY THAT YOUR *MOM...* SHE DIDN'T WANT TO...

OLD HISTORY, TINA SWEETIE TREATIE. *SO!* WHAT'S *NEWS* AROUND HERE?

HOLD ON. THE LORDS *NEED* AN ANGEL OF RETRIBUTION, RIGHT? BALANCE OF THE *UNIVERSE!*

SO WHAT ARE THEY GONNA DO NOW THAT YOU *QUIT?*

START THE TRIALS *OVER AGAIN* FOR SOME OTHER *POOR SUCKER?*

NOPE. I HAD AN IDEA, COACH. *A GOOD ONE,* THIS TIME!

I TOLD 'EM ONLY *ONE PERSON* KNEW TH' JOB *INSIDE AND OUT.* TH' BALANCE BETWEEN *GOOD* AN' *EVIL...*

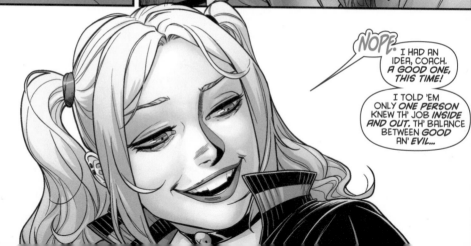

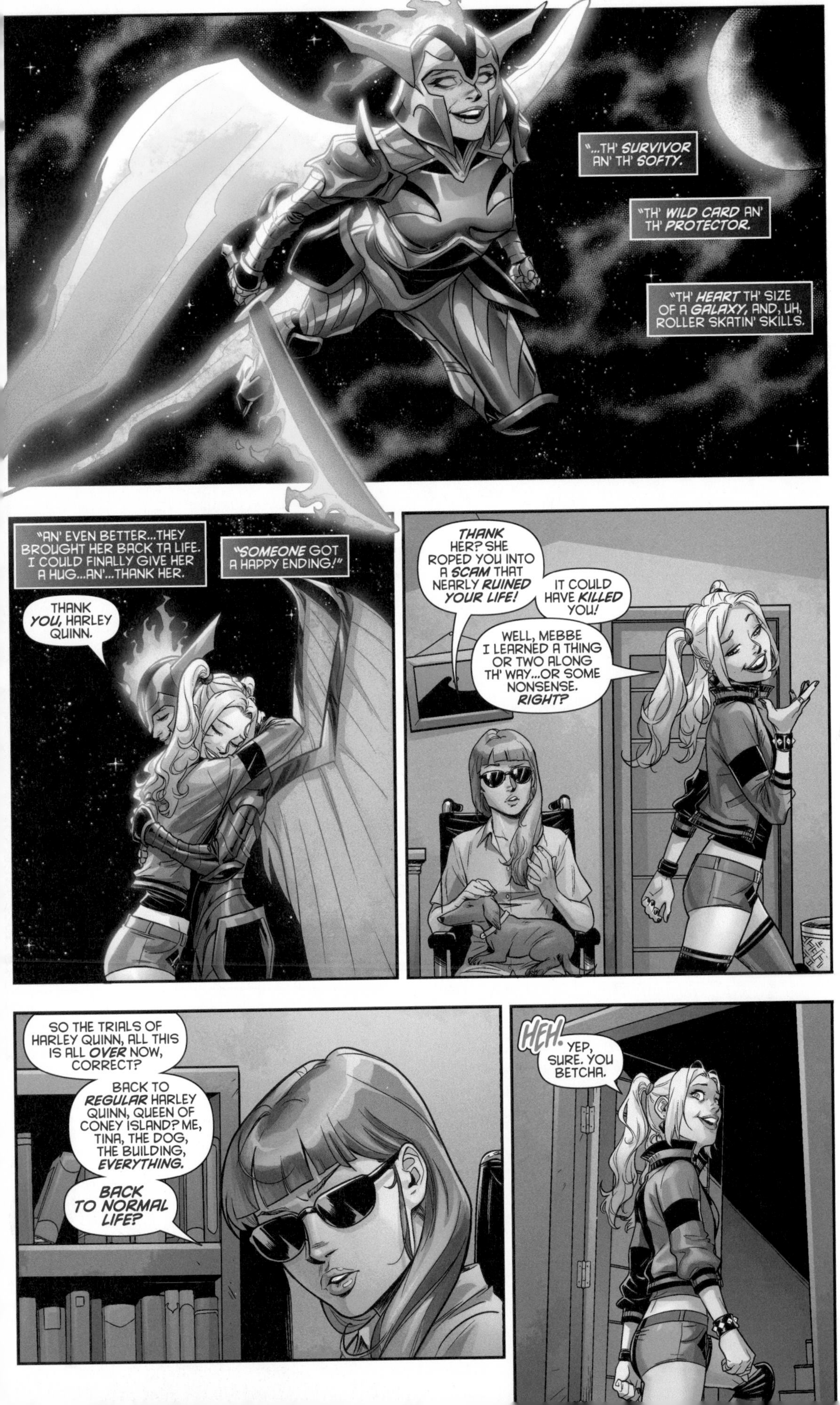

"...TH' SURVIVOR AN' TH' SOFTY.
"TH' WILD CARD AN' TH' PROTECTOR.
"TH' HEART TH' SIZE OF A GALAXY, AND, UH, ROLLER SKATIN' SKILLS.
"AN' EVEN BETTER...THEY BROUGHT HER BACK TA LIFE. I COULD FINALLY GIVE HER A HUG...AN'...THANK HER.
"SOMEONE GOT A HAPPY ENDING!"
THANK YOU, HARLEY QUINN.
THANK HER? SHE ROPED YOU INTO A SCAM THAT NEARLY RUINED YOUR LIFE!
IT COULD HAVE KILLED YOU!
WELL, MEBBE I LEARNED A THING OR TWO ALONG TH' WAY...OR SOME NONSENSE. RIGHT?
SO THE TRIALS OF HARLEY QUINN, ALL THIS IS ALL OVER NOW, CORRECT?
BACK TO REGULAR HARLEY QUINN, QUEEN OF CONEY ISLAND? ME, TINA, THE DOG, THE BUILDING, EVERYTHING.
BACK TO NORMAL LIFE?
HEH.
YEP, SURE. YOU BETCHA.

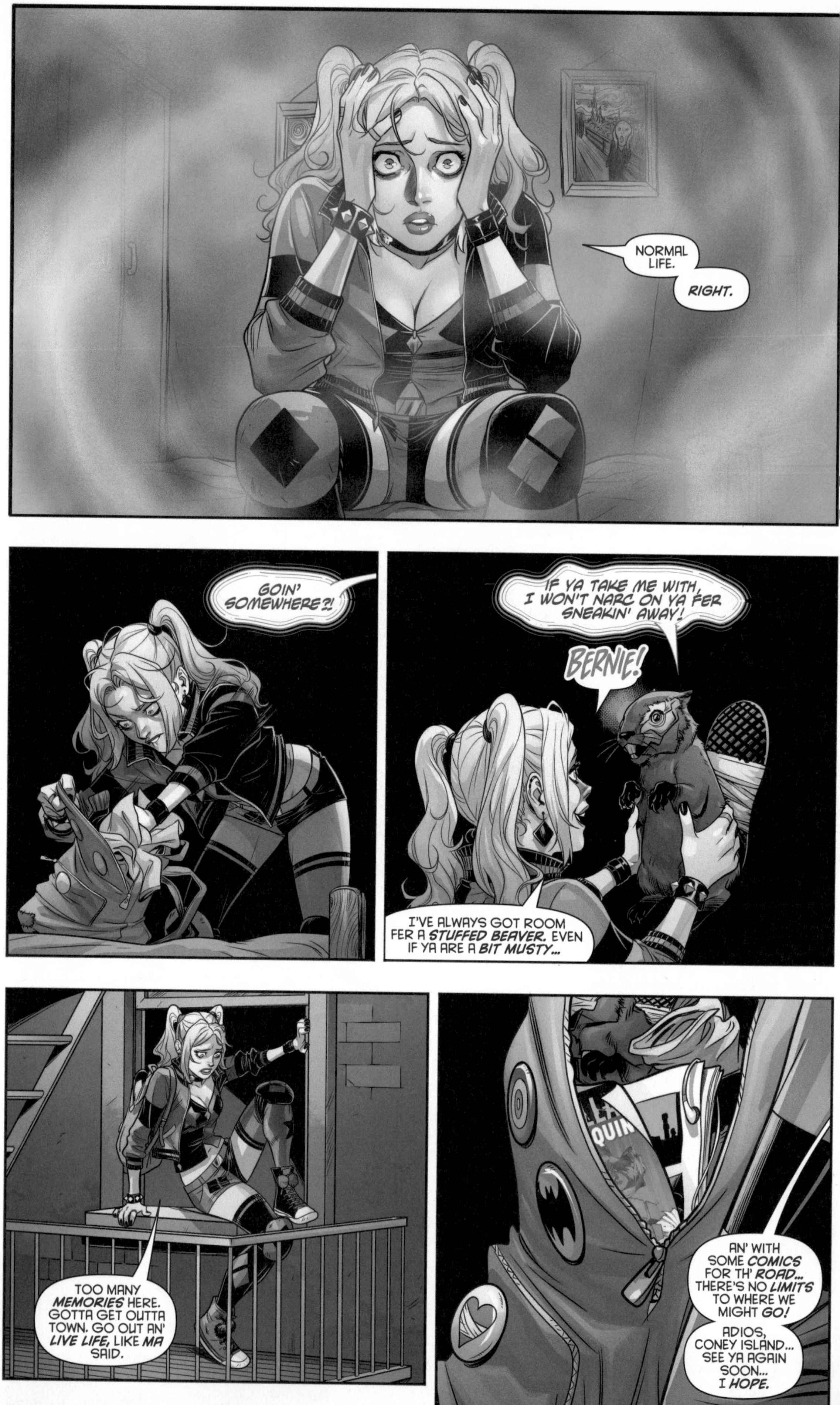
NORMAL LIFE.
RIGHT.
GOIN' SOMEWHERE?!
IF YA TAKE ME WITH, I WON'T NARC ON YA FER SNEAKIN' AWAY!
BERNIE!
I'VE ALWAYS GOT ROOM FER A STUFFED BEAVER. EVEN IF YA ARE A BIT MUSTY...
TOO MANY MEMORIES HERE. GOTTA GET OUTTA TOWN. GO OUT AN' LIVE LIFE, LIKE MA SAID.
AN' WITH SOME COMICS FOR TH' ROAD... THERE'S NO LIMITS TO WHERE WE MIGHT GO!
ADIOS, CONEY ISLAND... SEE YA AGAIN SOON... I HOPE.

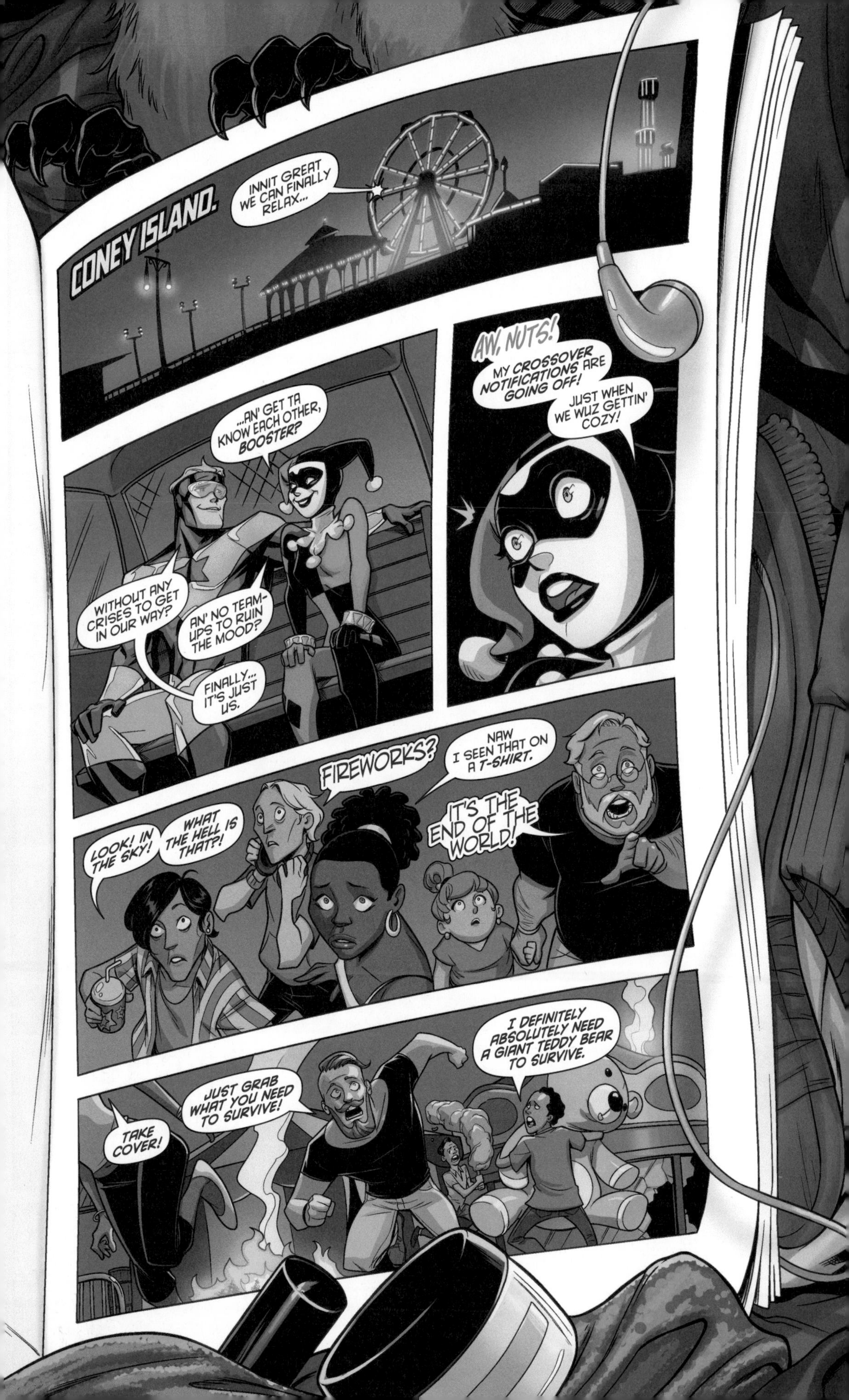
CONEY ISLAND.
INNIT GREAT WE CAN FINALLY RELAX...
...AN' GET TA KNOW EACH OTHER, BOOSTER?
WITHOUT ANY CRISES TO GET IN OUR WAY?
AN' NO TEAM-UPS TO RUIN THE MOOD?
FINALLY... IT'S JUST US.
AW, NUTS!
MY CROSSOVER NOTIFICATIONS ARE GOING OFF!
JUST WHEN WE WUZ GETTIN' COZY!
LOOK! IN THE SKY!
WHAT THE HELL IS THAT?!
FIREWORKS?
NAW I SEEN THAT ON A T-SHIRT.
IT'S THE END OF THE WORLD!
TAKE COVER!
JUST GRAB WHAT YOU NEED TO SURVIVE!
I DEFINITELY ABSOLUTELY NEED A GIANT TEDDY BEAR TO SURVIVE.

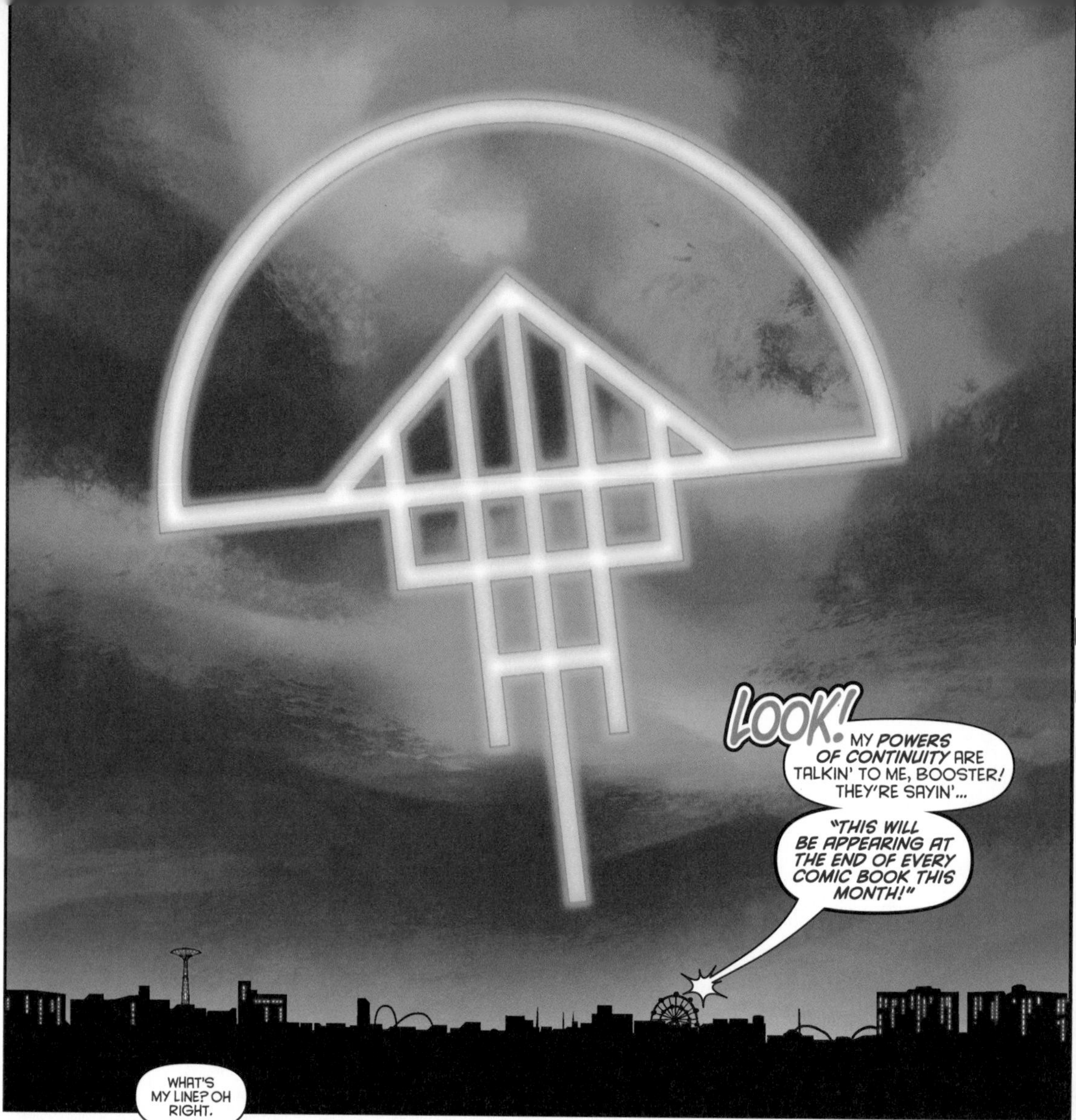
LOOK! MY POWERS OF CONTINUITY ARE TALKIN' TO ME, BOOSTER! THEY'RE SAYIN'...
"THIS WILL BE APPEARING AT THE END OF EVERY COMIC BOOK THIS MONTH!"
WHAT'S MY LINE? OH RIGHT.

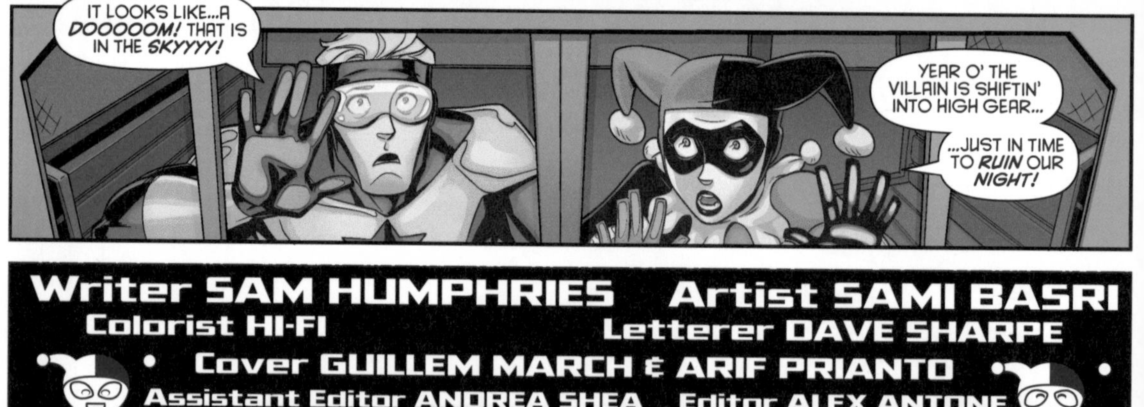
IT LOOKS LIKE...A DOOOOOM! THAT IS IN THE SKYYYY!
YEAR O' THE VILLAIN IS SHIFTIN' INTO HIGH GEAR...
...JUST IN TIME TO RUIN OUR NIGHT!

Writer SAM HUMPHRIES **Artist** SAMI BASRI
Colorist HI-FI **Letterer** DAVE SHARPE
Cover GUILLEM MARCH & ARIF PRIANTO
Assistant Editor ANDREA SHEA **Editor** ALEX ANTONE
Group Editor BRIAN CUNNINGHAM

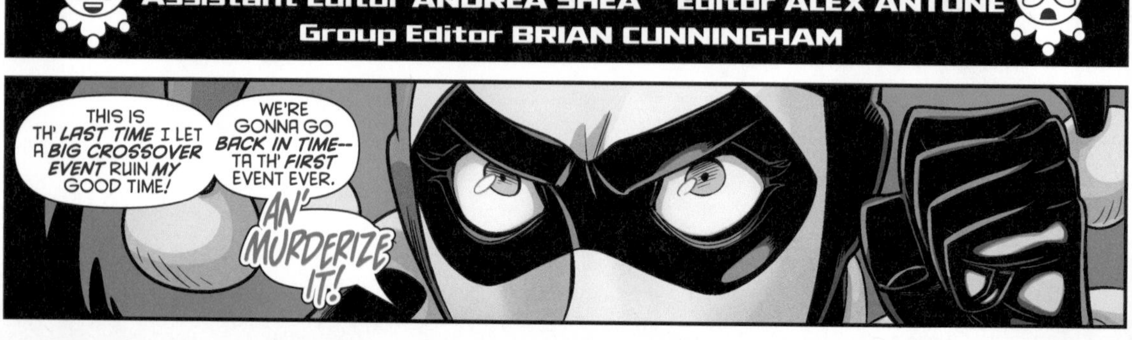
THIS IS TH' LAST TIME I LET A BIG CROSSOVER EVENT RUIN MY GOOD TIME!
WE'RE GONNA GO BACK IN TIME-- TA TH' FIRST EVENT EVER.
AN' MURDERIZE IT!

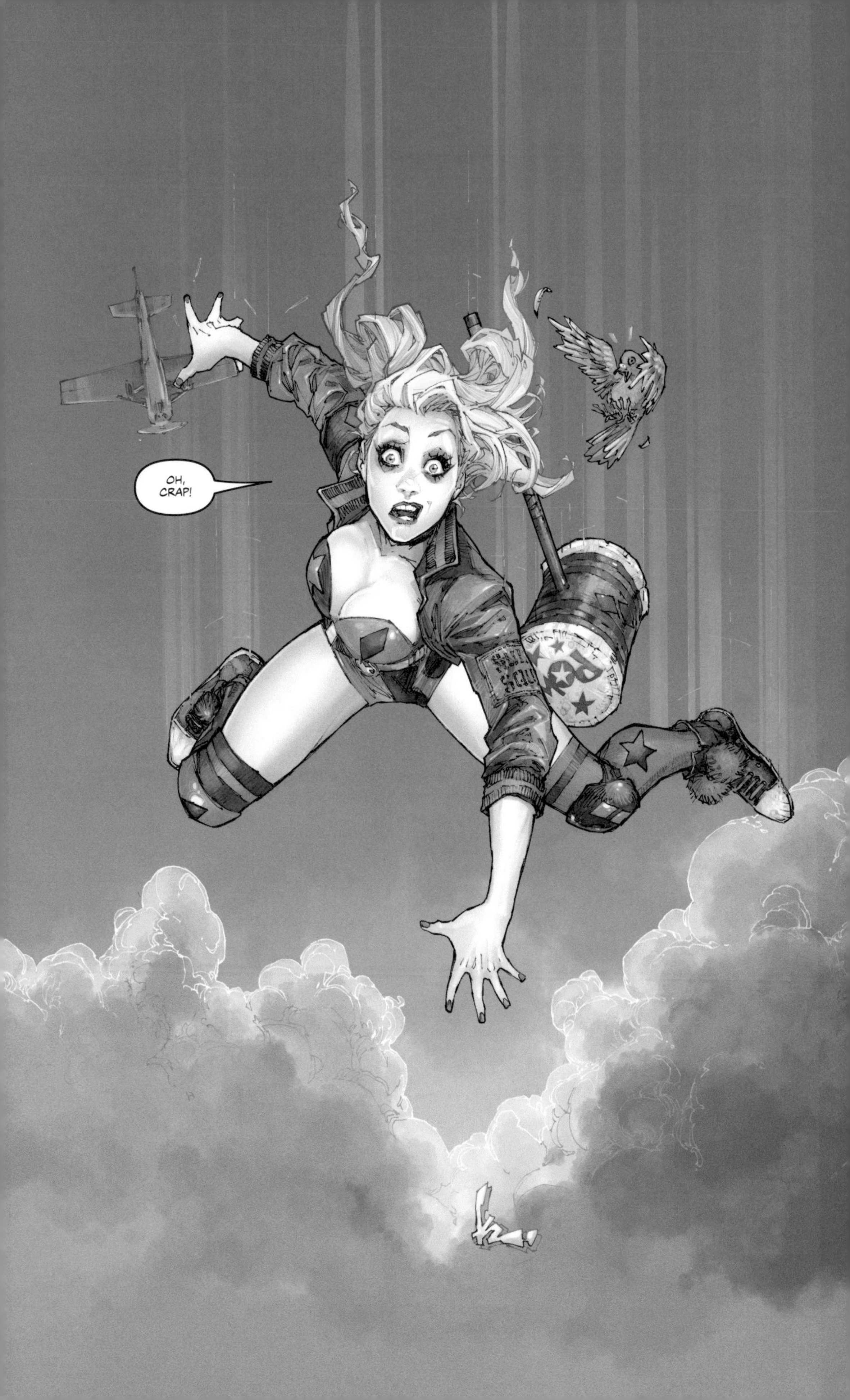
OH, CRAP!

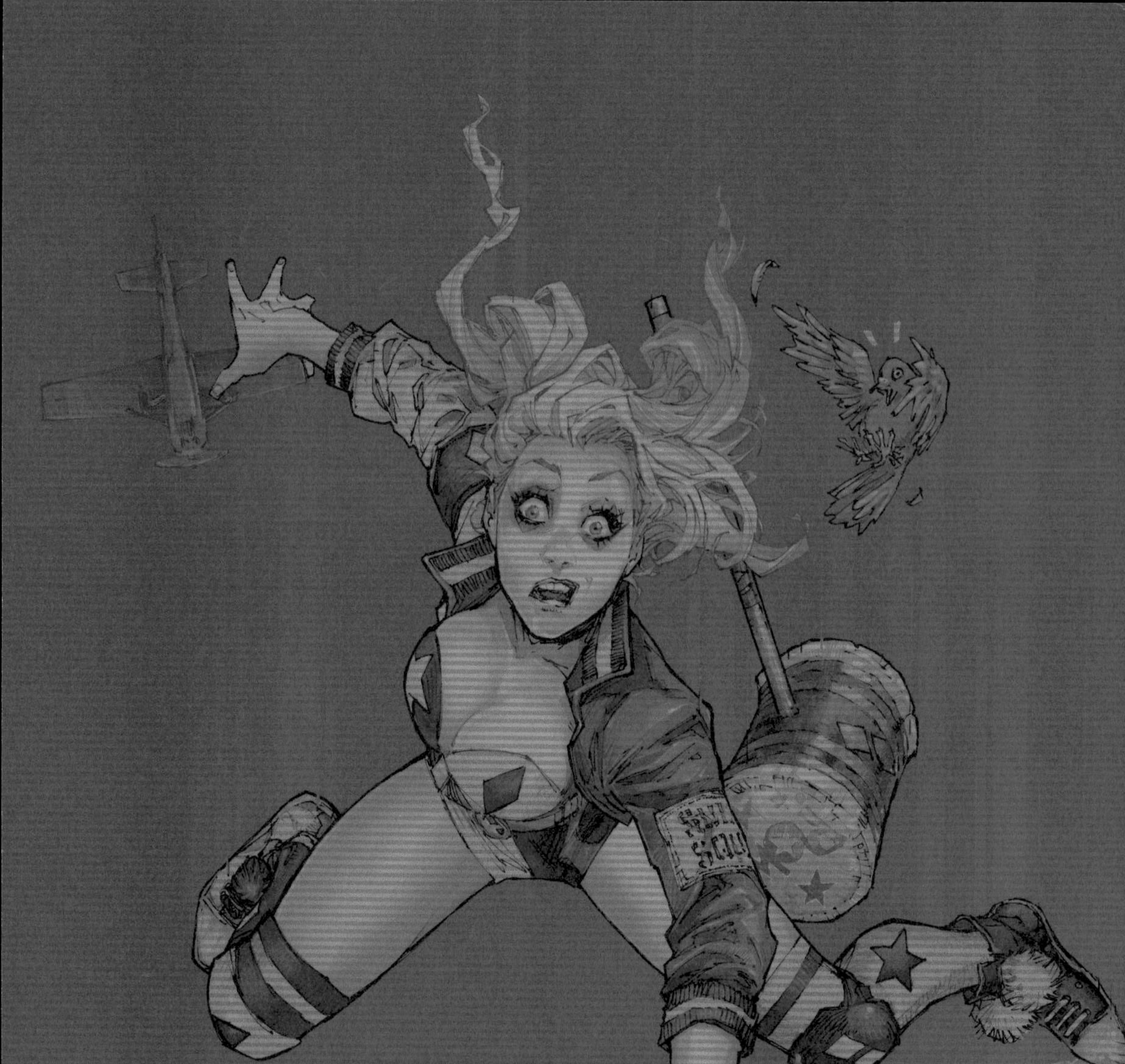

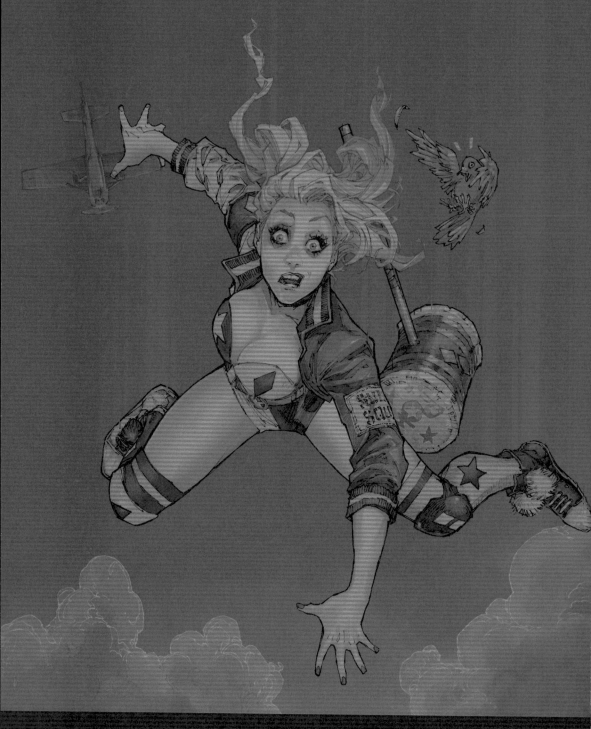

HARLEY QUINN
#67

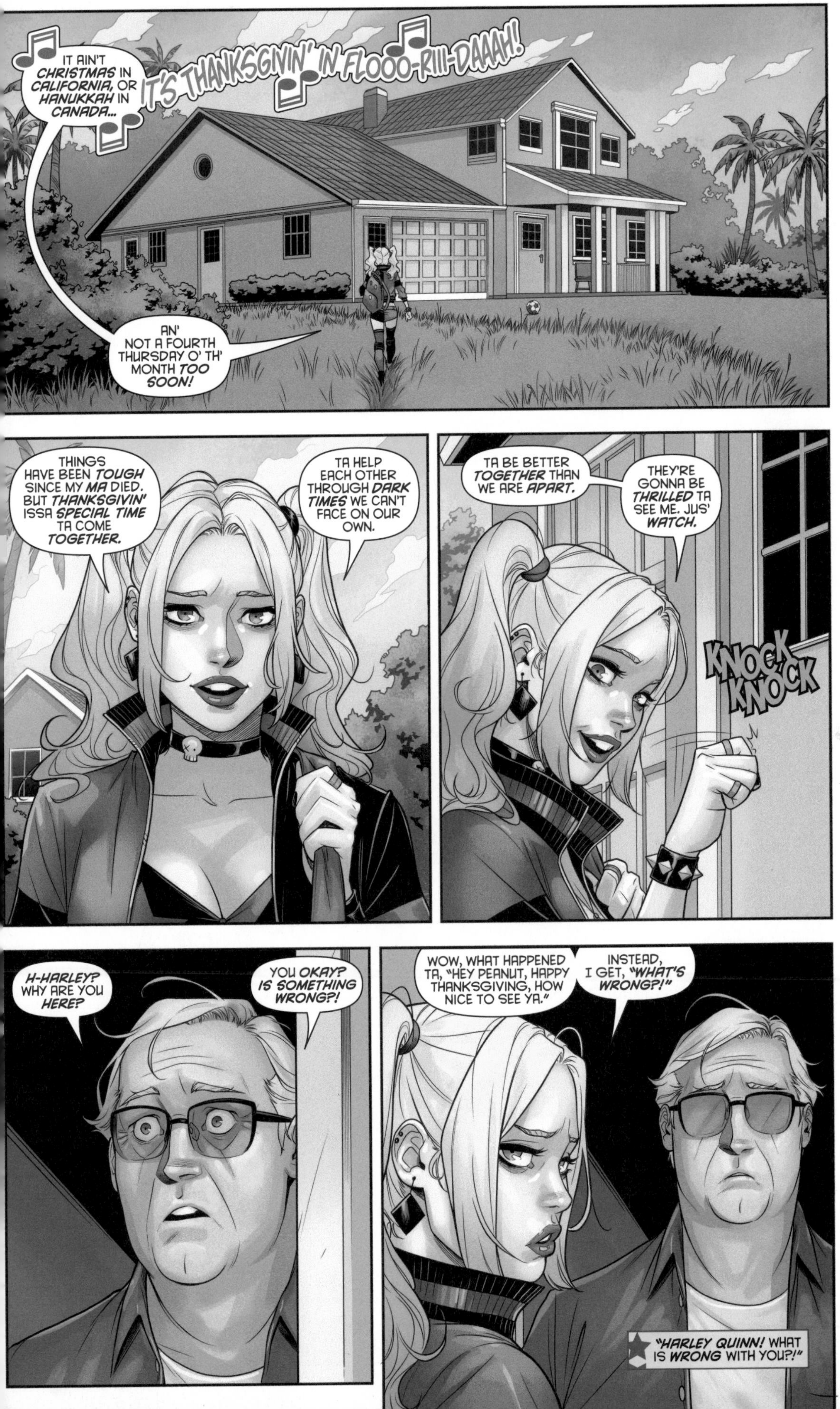

IT AIN'T CHRISTMAS IN CALIFORNIA, OR HANUKKAH IN CANADA...
IT'S THANKSGIVIN' IN FLOOO-RIII-DAAAH!
AN' NOT A FOURTH THURSDAY O' TH' MONTH TOO SOON!
THINGS HAVE BEEN TOUGH SINCE MY MA DIED. BUT THANKSGIVIN' ISSA SPECIAL TIME TA COME TOGETHER.
TA HELP EACH OTHER THROUGH DARK TIMES WE CAN'T FACE ON OUR OWN.
TA BE BETTER TOGETHER THAN WE ARE APART.
THEY'RE GONNA BE THRILLED TA SEE ME. JUS' WATCH.
KNOCK KNOCK
H-HARLEY? WHY ARE YOU HERE?
YOU OKAY? IS SOMETHING WRONG?!
WOW, WHAT HAPPENED TA, "HEY PEANUT, HAPPY THANKSGIVING, HOW NICE TO SEE YA."
INSTEAD, I GET, "WHAT'S WRONG?!"
"HARLEY QUINN! WHAT IS WRONG WITH YOU?!"

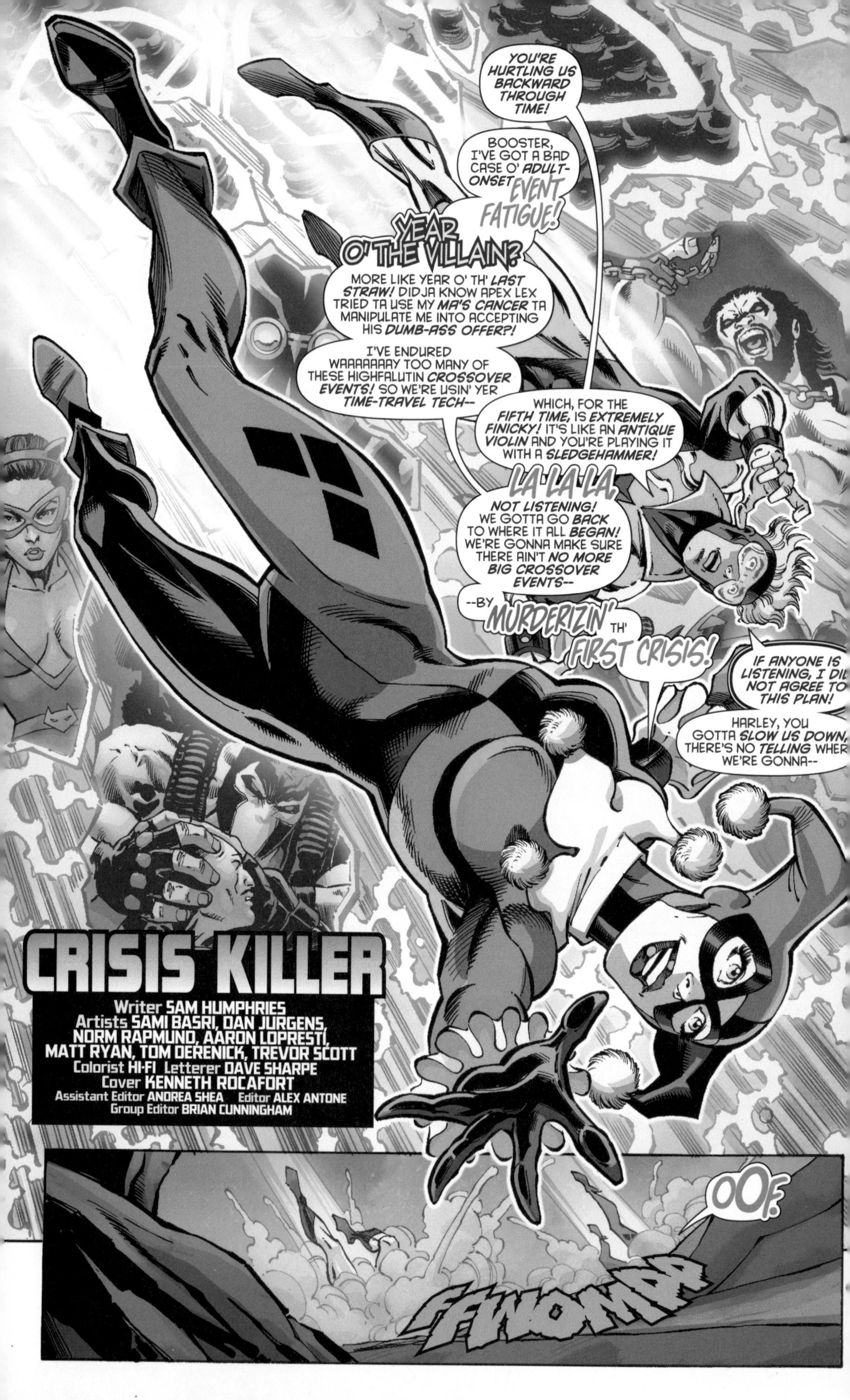

YOU'RE HURTLING US BACKWARD THROUGH TIME!
BOOSTER, I'VE GOT A BAD CASE O' ADULT-ONSET EVENT FATIGUE!
YEAR O' THE VILLAIN?
MORE LIKE YEAR O' TH' LAST STRAW! DIDJA KNOW APEX LEX TRIED TA USE MY MA'S CANCER TA MANIPULATE ME INTO ACCEPTING HIS DUMB-ASS OFFER?!
I'VE ENDURED WAAAAAAAY TOO MANY OF THESE HIGHFALUTIN CROSSOVER EVENTS! SO WE'RE USIN' YER TIME-TRAVEL TECH--
WHICH, FOR THE FIFTH TIME, IS EXTREMELY FINICKY! IT'S LIKE AN ANTIQUE VIOLIN AND YOU'RE PLAYING IT WITH A SLEDGEHAMMER!
LA LA LA NOT LISTENING! WE GOTTA GO BACK TO WHERE IT ALL BEGAN! WE'RE GONNA MAKE SURE THERE AIN'T NO MORE BIG CROSSOVER EVENTS--
--BY MURDERIZIN' TH' FIRST CRISIS!
IF ANYONE IS LISTENING, I DI NOT AGREE TO THIS PLAN!
HARLEY, YOU GOTTA SLOW US DOWN, THERE'S NO TELLING WHER WE'RE GONNA--
CRISIS KILLER
Writer SAM HUMPHRIES
Artists SAMI BASRI, DAN JURGENS, NORM RAPMUND, AARON LOPRESTI, MATT RYAN, TOM DERENICK, TREVOR SCOTT
Colorist HI-FI Letterer DAVE SHARPE
Cover KENNETH ROCAFORT
Assistant Editor ANDREA SHEA Editor ALEX ANTONE
Group Editor BRIAN CUNNINGHAM
OOF.
FFWOMP

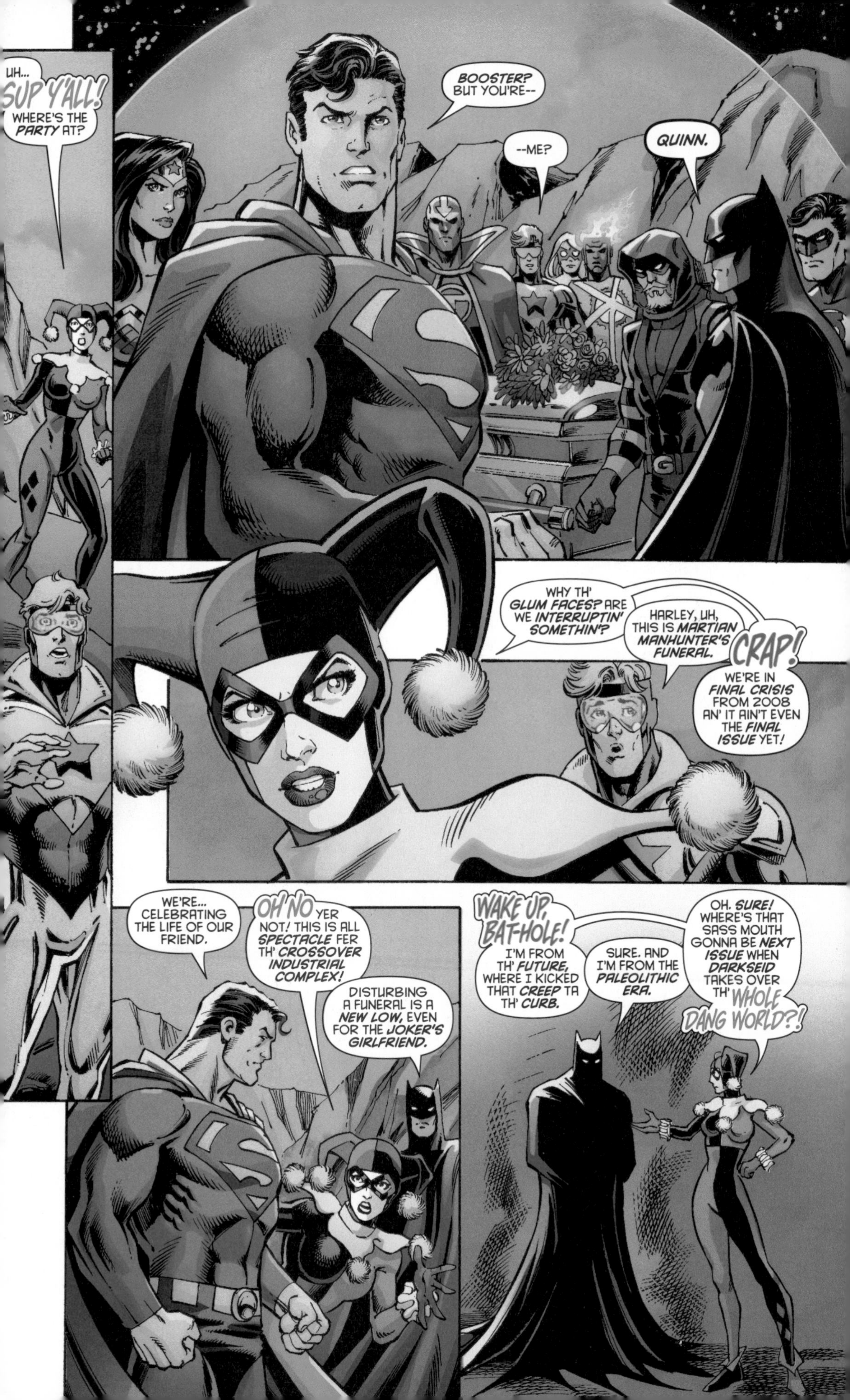
UH... SUP Y'ALL! WHERE'S THE PARTY AT?
BOOSTER? BUT YOU'RE--
--ME?
QUINN.
WHY TH' GLUM FACES? ARE WE INTERRUPTIN' SOMETHIN'?
HARLEY, UH, THIS IS MARTIAN MANHUNTER'S FUNERAL.
CRAP!
WE'RE IN FINAL CRISIS FROM 2008 AN' IT AIN'T EVEN THE FINAL ISSUE YET!
WE'RE... CELEBRATING THE LIFE OF OUR FRIEND.
OH NO YER NOT! THIS IS ALL SPECTACLE FER TH' CROSSOVER INDUSTRIAL COMPLEX!
DISTURBING A FUNERAL IS A NEW LOW, EVEN FOR THE JOKER'S GIRLFRIEND.
WAKE UP, BAT-HOLE!
I'M FROM TH' FUTURE, WHERE I KICKED THAT CREEP TA TH' CURB.
SURE. AND I'M FROM THE PALEOLITHIC ERA.
OH. SURE! WHERE'S THAT SASS MOUTH GONNA BE NEXT ISSUE WHEN DARKSEID TAKES OVER TH' WHOLE DANG WORLD?!

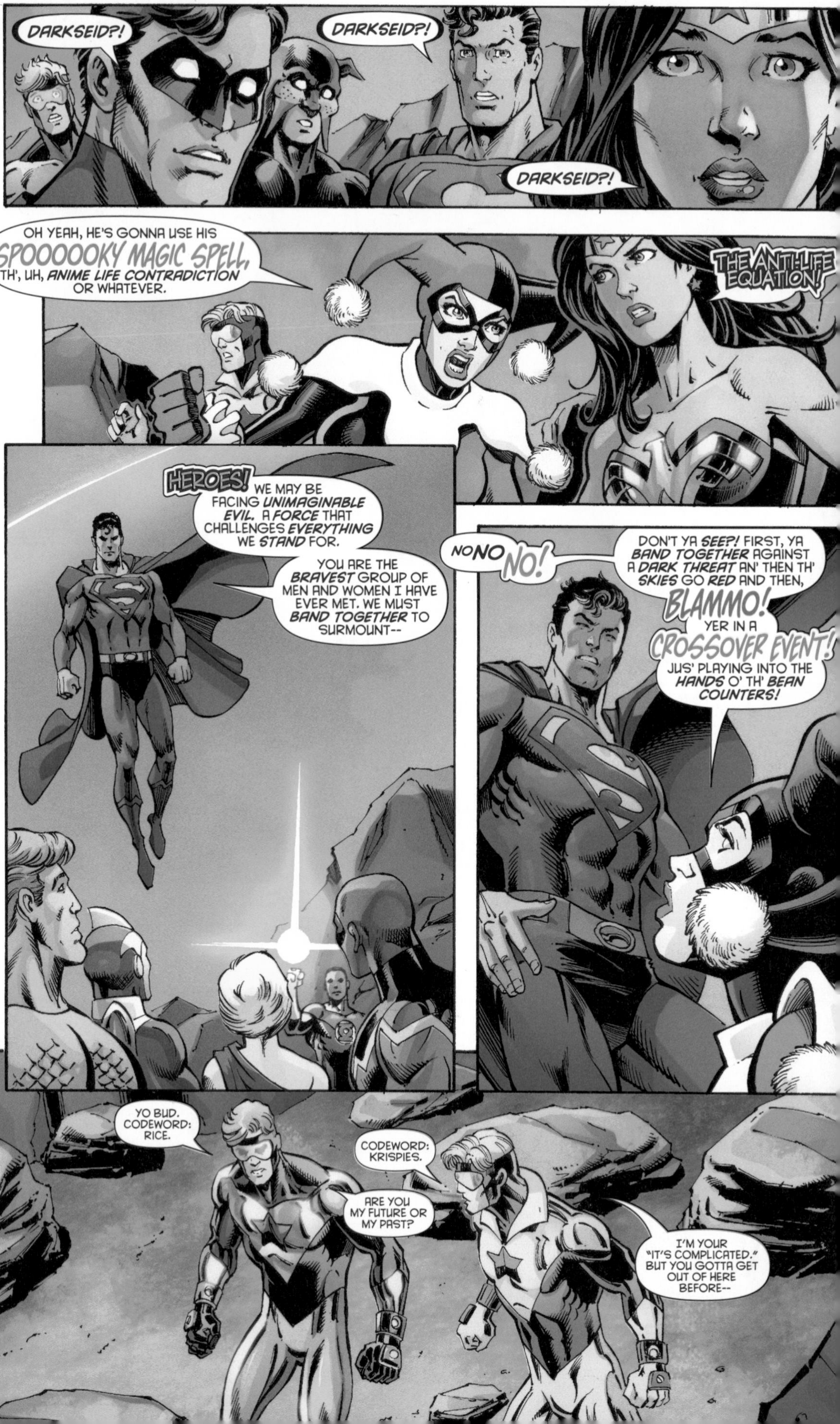

DARKSEID?!
DARKSEID?!
DARKSEID?!
OH YEAH, HE'S GONNA USE HIS SPOOOOOKY MAGIC SPELL, TH', UH, ANIME LIFE CONTRADICTION OR WHATEVER.
THE ANTI-LIFE EQUATION!
HEROES! WE MAY BE FACING UNIMAGINABLE EVIL. A FORCE THAT CHALLENGES EVERYTHING WE STAND FOR.
YOU ARE THE BRAVEST GROUP OF MEN AND WOMEN I HAVE EVER MET. WE MUST BAND TOGETHER TO SURMOUNT--
NO NO NO!
DON'T YA SEE?! FIRST, YA BAND TOGETHER AGAINST A DARK THREAT AN' THEN TH' SKIES GO RED AND THEN, BLAMMO! YER IN A CROSSOVER EVENT! JUS' PLAYING INTO THE HANDS O' TH' BEAN COUNTERS!
YO BUD. CODEWORD: RICE.
CODEWORD: KRISPIES.
ARE YOU MY FUTURE OR MY PAST?
I'M YOUR "IT'S COMPLICATED." BUT YOU GOTTA GET OUT OF HERE BEFORE--

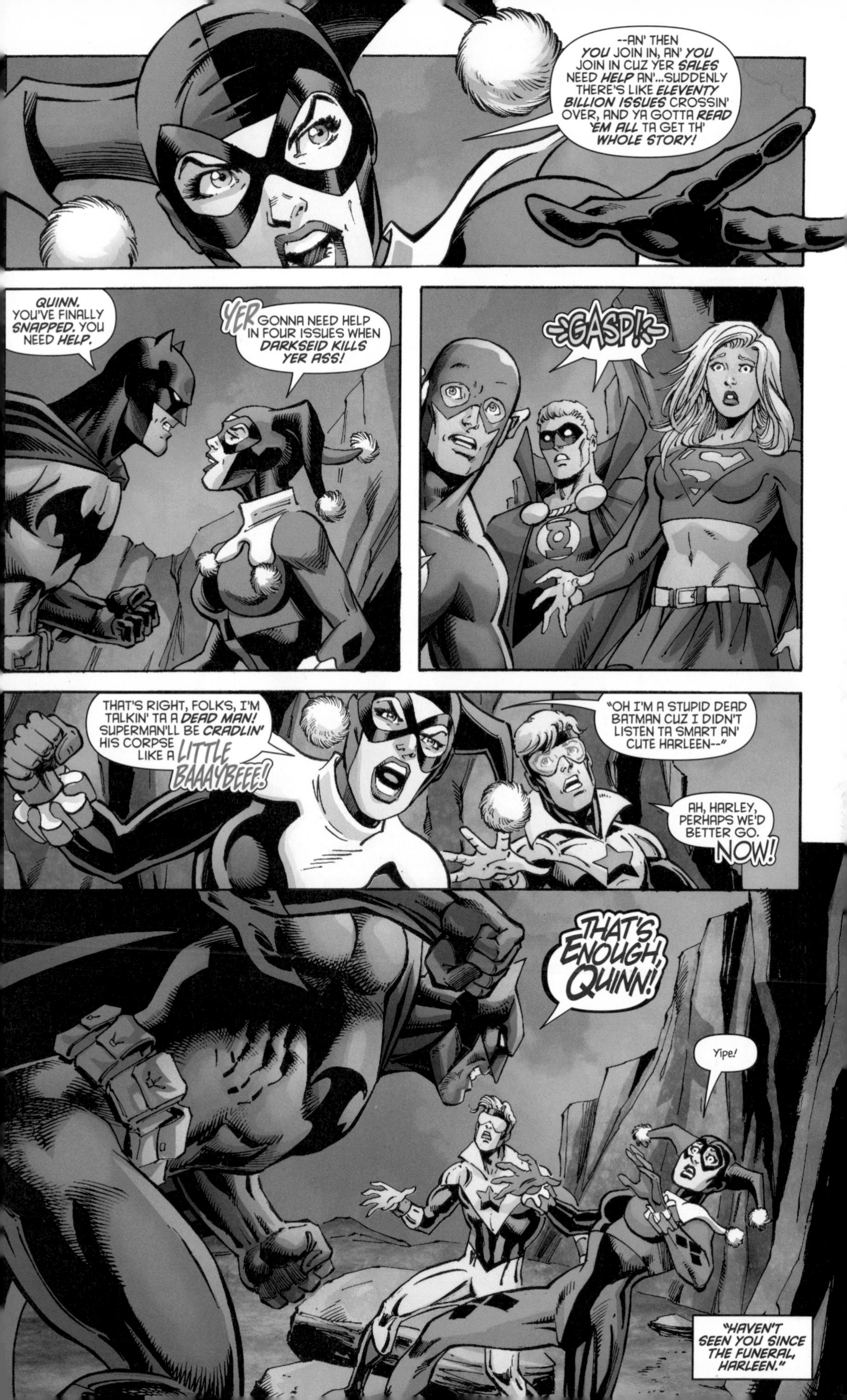
--AN' THEN YOU JOIN IN, AN' YOU JOIN IN CUZ YER SALES NEED HELP AN'...SUDDENLY THERE'S LIKE ELEVENTY BILLION ISSUES CROSSIN' OVER, AND YA GOTTA READ 'EM ALL TA GET TH' WHOLE STORY!
QUINN. YOU'VE FINALLY SNAPPED. YOU NEED HELP.
YER GONNA NEED HELP IN FOUR ISSUES WHEN DARKSEID KILLS YER ASS!
GASP!
THAT'S RIGHT, FOLKS, I'M TALKIN' TA A DEAD MAN! SUPERMAN'LL BE CRADLIN' HIS CORPSE LIKE A LITTLE BAAAYBEEE!
"OH I'M A STUPID DEAD BATMAN CUZ I DIDN'T LISTEN TA SMART AN' CUTE HARLEEN--"
AH, HARLEY, PERHAPS WE'D BETTER GO. NOW!
THAT'S ENOUGH, QUINN!
Yipe!
"HAVEN'T SEEN YOU SINCE THE FUNERAL, HARLEEN."

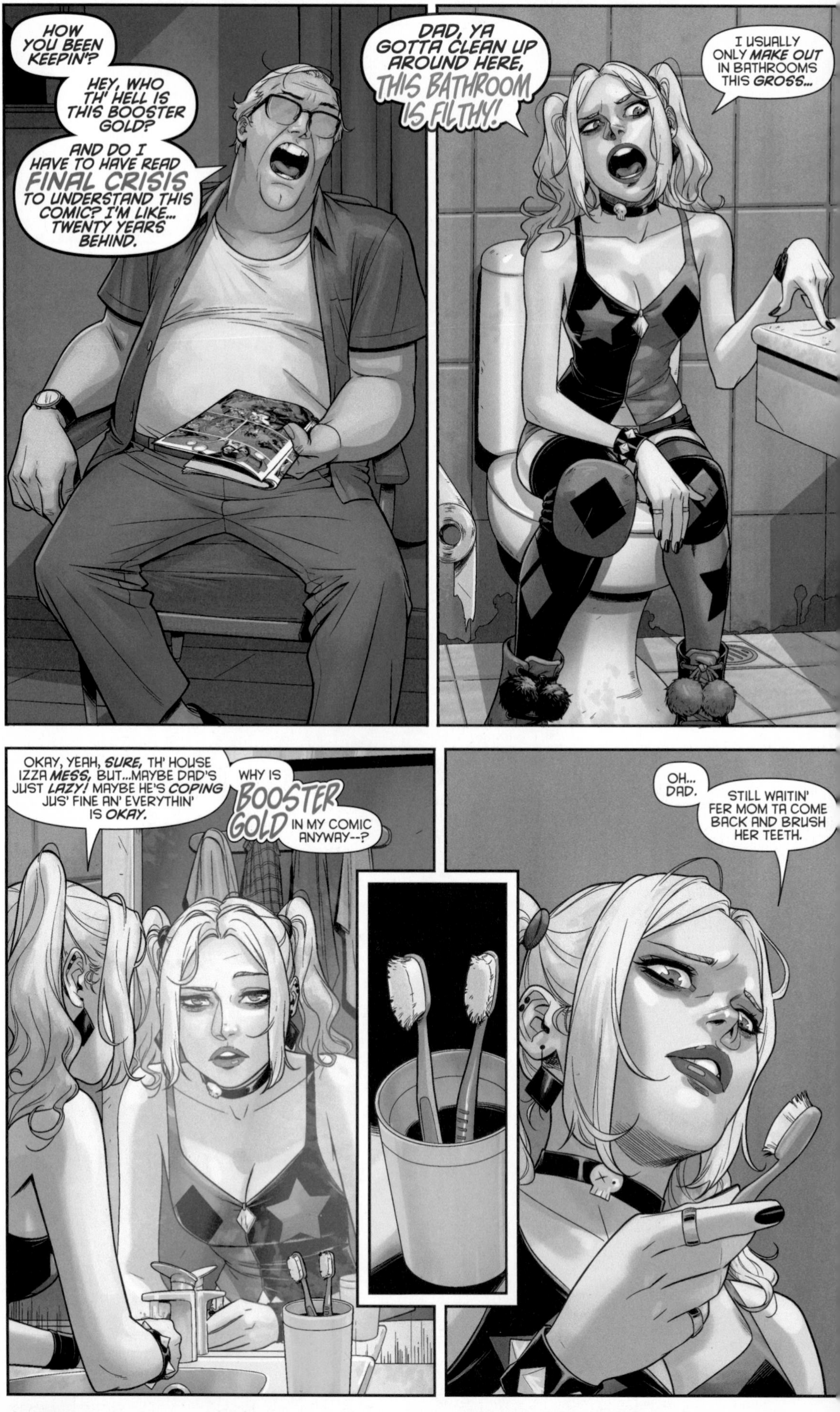
HOW YOU BEEN KEEPIN'?
HEY, WHO TH' HELL IS THIS BOOSTER GOLD?
AND DO I HAVE TO HAVE READ FINAL CRISIS TO UNDERSTAND THIS COMIC? I'M LIKE... TWENTY YEARS BEHIND.
DAD, YA GOTTA CLEAN UP AROUND HERE, THIS BATHROOM IS FILTHY!
I USUALLY ONLY MAKE OUT IN BATHROOMS THIS GROSS...
OKAY, YEAH, SURE, TH' HOUSE IZZA MESS, BUT...MAYBE DAD'S JUST LAZY! MAYBE HE'S COPING JUS' FINE AN' EVERYTHIN' IS OKAY.
WHY IS BOOSTER GOLD IN MY COMIC ANYWAY--?
OH... DAD.
STILL WAITIN' FER MOM TA COME BACK AND BRUSH HER TEETH.

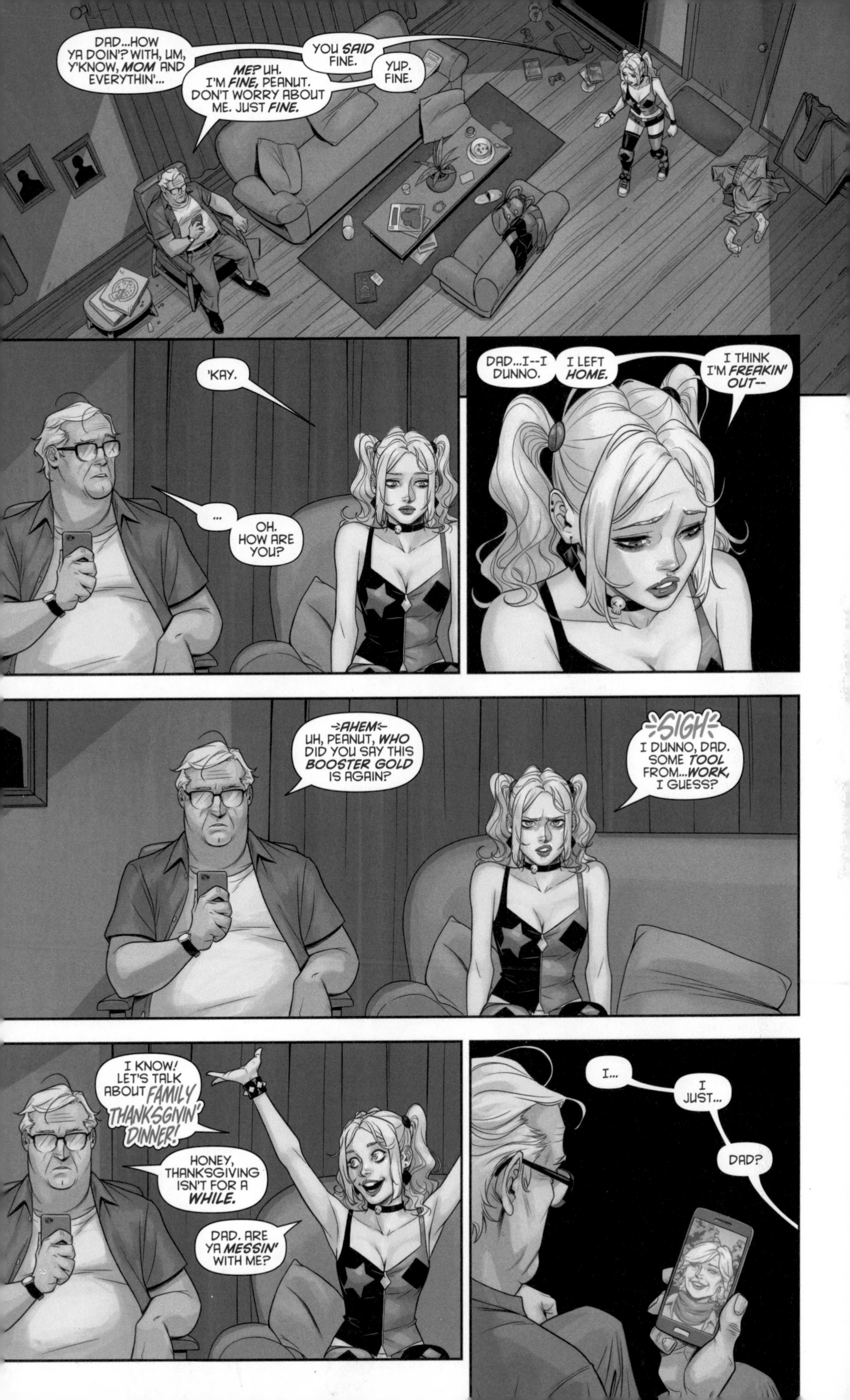
DAD...HOW YA DOIN'? WITH, UM, Y'KNOW, MOM AND EVERYTHIN'...
ME? UH. I'M FINE, PEANUT. DON'T WORRY ABOUT ME. JUST FINE.
YOU SAID FINE.
YUP. FINE.
'KAY.
...
OH. HOW ARE YOU?
DAD...I--I DUNNO.
I LEFT HOME.
I THINK I'M FREAKIN' OUT--
AHEM
UH, PEANUT, WHO DID YOU SAY THIS BOOSTER GOLD IS AGAIN?
SIGH
I DUNNO, DAD. SOME TOOL FROM...WORK, I GUESS?
I KNOW! LET'S TALK ABOUT FAMILY THANKSGIVIN' DINNER!
HONEY, THANKSGIVING ISN'T FOR A WHILE.
DAD. ARE YA MESSIN' WITH ME?
I...
I JUST...
DAD?

DAD! THANKSGIVIN' IS *TOMORROW!*

CRAP. *REALLY?*

SO THERE'S NO PLAN FER FAMILY *THANKSGIVIN'* DINNER?!

NOT UNLESS ONE OF YOUR *BROTHERS* MADE A PLAN.

BWAHAHAHAHAHAHAHAHA HAHAHAHAHAHAHAHAHA HAHAHAHAHAHAHAHA HAHAHAHAHA

LET *ME* DO IT! I'LL MAKE IT HAPPEN! *PLEASE?* I *KNOW* TH' HOUSE IS A *MESS* AN'--

WAIT!

LET'S DO IT AT *MANDY'S DINER!* C'MON! JUS' LIKE *OLD TIMES!*

I DUNNO, PEANUT, I DON'T GO OUT MUCH ANYMORE. MAYBE WE JUST... *SKIP* IT?

DAD, WE *GOTTA* HAVE *FAMILY THANKSGIVIN' DINNER!* NOW MORE THAN *EVER!*

WE *NEED* TA KEEP THIS FAMILY HAND IN HAND. ONLY *TOGETHER* CAN I *DEAL* WITH THIS.

I MEAN, *WE.* ONLY TOGETHER CAN *WE* DEAL WITH THIS.

PLEASE, DAD. *PLEASE?*

O-OKAY. IF YOU CONVINCE THE *BOYS.*

EASY AS *PUMPKIN PIE.* WHERE ARE THEY?

WELL, YOU'LL PROBABLY FIND *BARRY* AT--

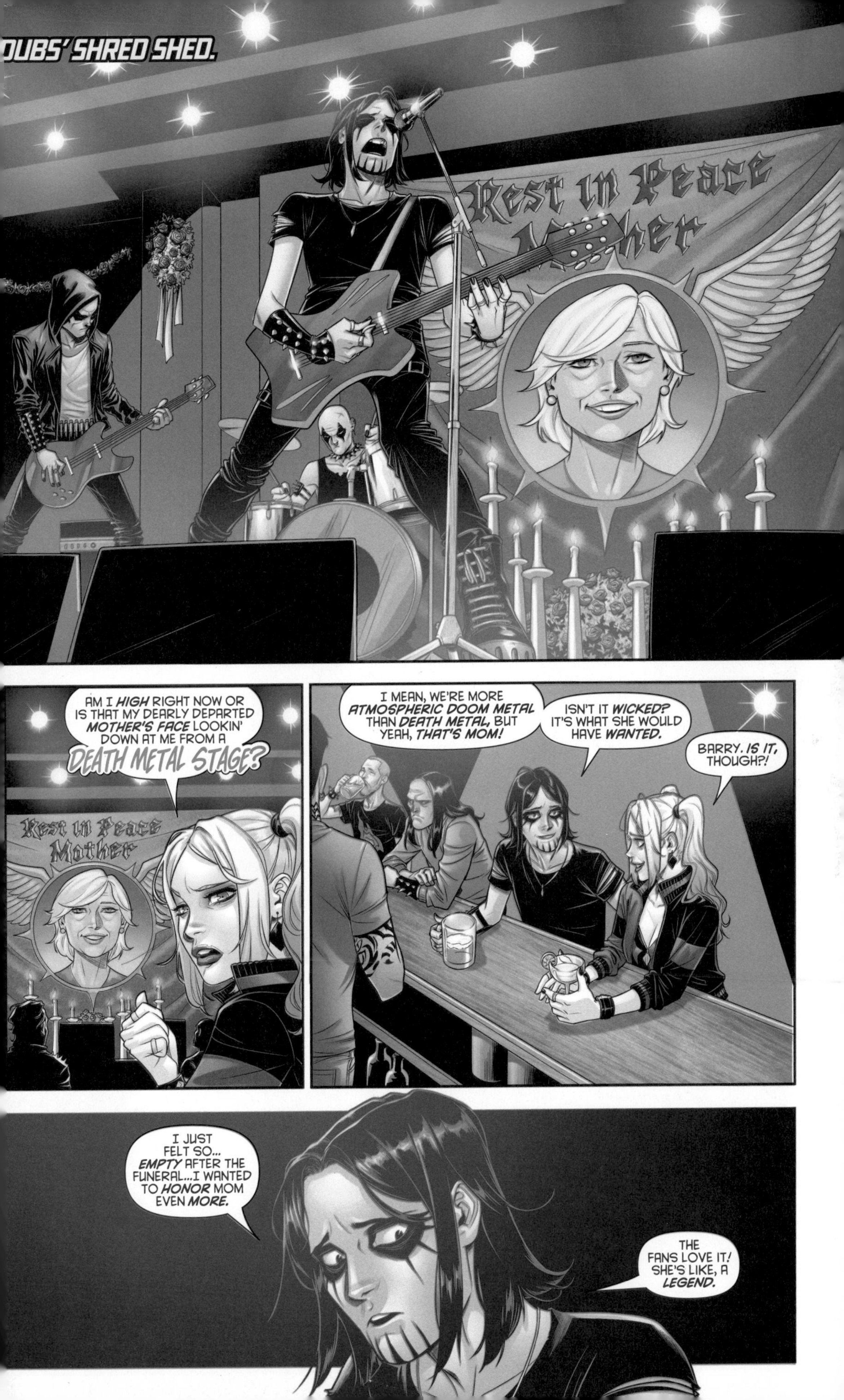
DUBS' SHRED SHED.
Rest in Peace Mother
AM I HIGH RIGHT NOW OR IS THAT MY DEARLY DEPARTED MOTHER'S FACE LOOKIN' DOWN AT ME FROM A DEATH METAL STAGE?
Rest in Peace Mother
I MEAN, WE'RE MORE ATMOSPHERIC DOOM METAL THAN DEATH METAL, BUT YEAH, THAT'S MOM!
ISN'T IT WICKED? IT'S WHAT SHE WOULD HAVE WANTED.
BARRY. IS IT, THOUGH?!
I JUST FELT SO... EMPTY AFTER THE FUNERAL...I WANTED TO HONOR MOM EVEN MORE.
THE FANS LOVE IT! SHE'S LIKE, A LEGEND.

OH WAIT, I HAVEN'T SEEN YOU SINCE I GOT *THIS!* DOESN'T IT *SHRED?*

YUP. SUPER SHREDS. MEGA *SHREDS.*

Yikes.

BARRY, LET'S TALK *TURKEY.* AN' BY THAT I MEAN, *FAMILY THANKSGIVIN' DINNER!*

WE HAVEN'T ALL BEEN TOGETHER SINCE TH' *FUNERAL.* DAD IS HAVIN' A *HARD TIME...* WHAT BETTER WAY TA HONOR *MOM* THAN--

OH, YOU'RE HERE FOR *THANKSGIVING!* I THOUGHT YOU WERE ABOUT TO TELL ME SOMETHING'S *WRONG.*

YOU MEAN *BESIDES* A *ROADIE* WEARIN' A *BANDANNA* WITH *MA'S FACE* ON IT?

EVERYTHIN' IS *FINE,* WHY CAN'T I COME SEE MY FAMILY ON *THANKSGIVIN'?*

WELL-ELL-ELL--

LOOK, HARLS...WE'RE NOT *KIDS* ANYMORE. DIDJA SEE *DAD?* HE'S NOT UP TO THIS. WITHOUT MOM? IT'S GONNA BE SO *DEPRESSING...*

TOMORROW'S NOT GOOD FOR ME ANYWAY. REHEARSAL FOR *FANGSGIVING* FESTIVAL.

REHEARSAL? ON A HOLIDAY? THAT'S NOT VERY *METAL* O' YA!

C'MON, BARRY, *PLEASE PLEASE PLEASE....* I REALLY NEED THIS. CAN'TCHA MAKE TIME FER BOTH? FER ME?!

UH, *MAYBE--*

HEY! IS THAT ANOTHER COMIC BY YOUR FRIEND MEREDITH? *LEMME READ IT--*

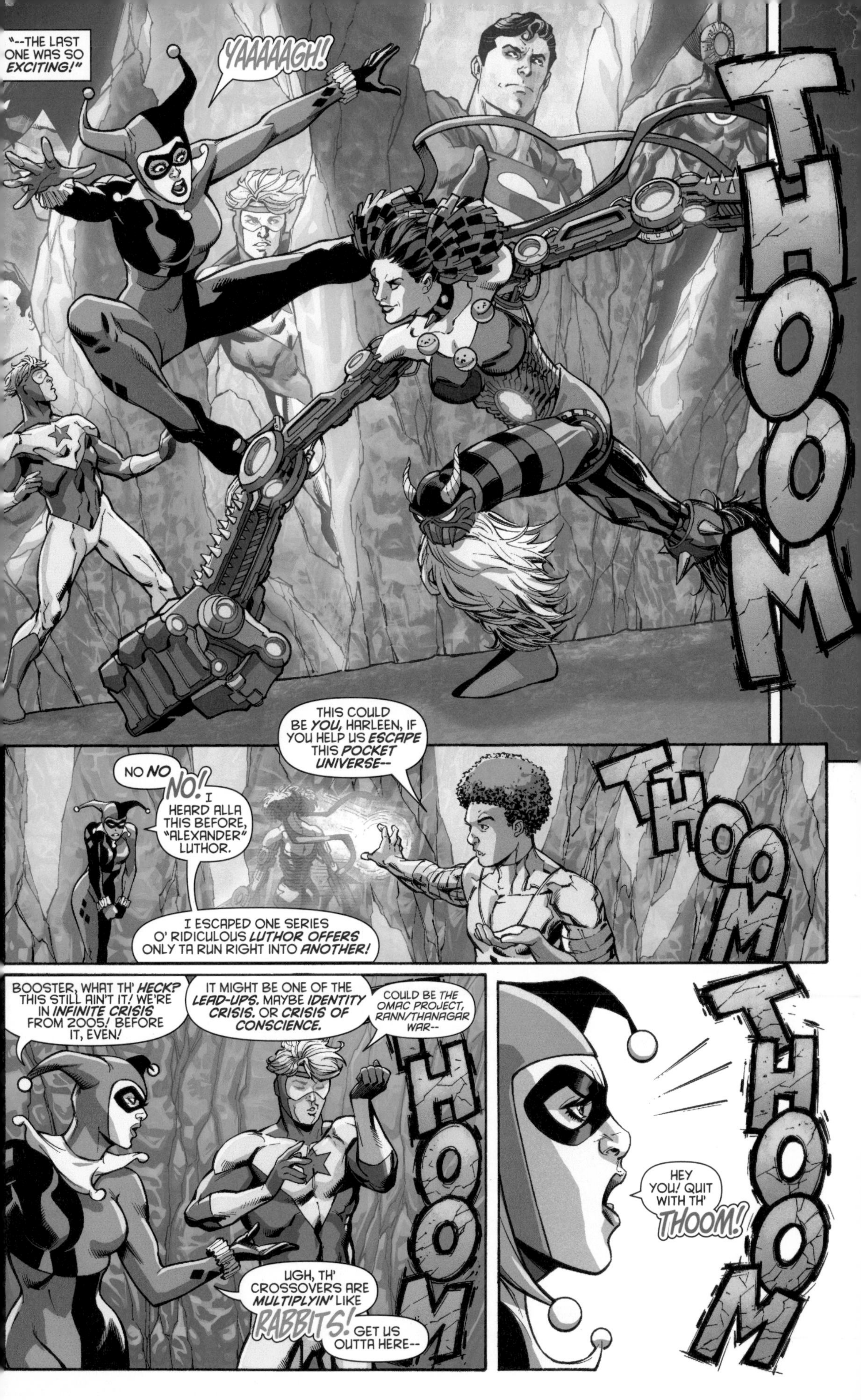
"--THE LAST ONE WAS SO EXCITING!"
YAAAAAGH!
THOOM
NO NO NO! I HEARD ALLA THIS BEFORE, "ALEXANDER" LUTHOR.
THIS COULD BE YOU, HARLEEN, IF YOU HELP US ESCAPE THIS POCKET UNIVERSE--
I ESCAPED ONE SERIES O' RIDICULOUS LUTHOR OFFERS ONLY TA RUN RIGHT INTO ANOTHER!
THOOM
BOOSTER, WHAT TH' HECK? THIS STILL AIN'T IT! WE'RE IN INFINITE CRISIS FROM 2005! BEFORE IT, EVEN!
IT MIGHT BE ONE OF THE LEAD-UPS. MAYBE IDENTITY CRISIS. OR CRISIS OF CONSCIENCE.
COULD BE THE OMAC PROJECT, RANN/THANAGAR WAR--
THOOM
UGH, TH' CROSSOVERS ARE MULTIPLYIN' LIKE RABBITS! GET US OUTTA HERE--
HEY YOU! QUIT WITH TH' THOOM!
THOOM

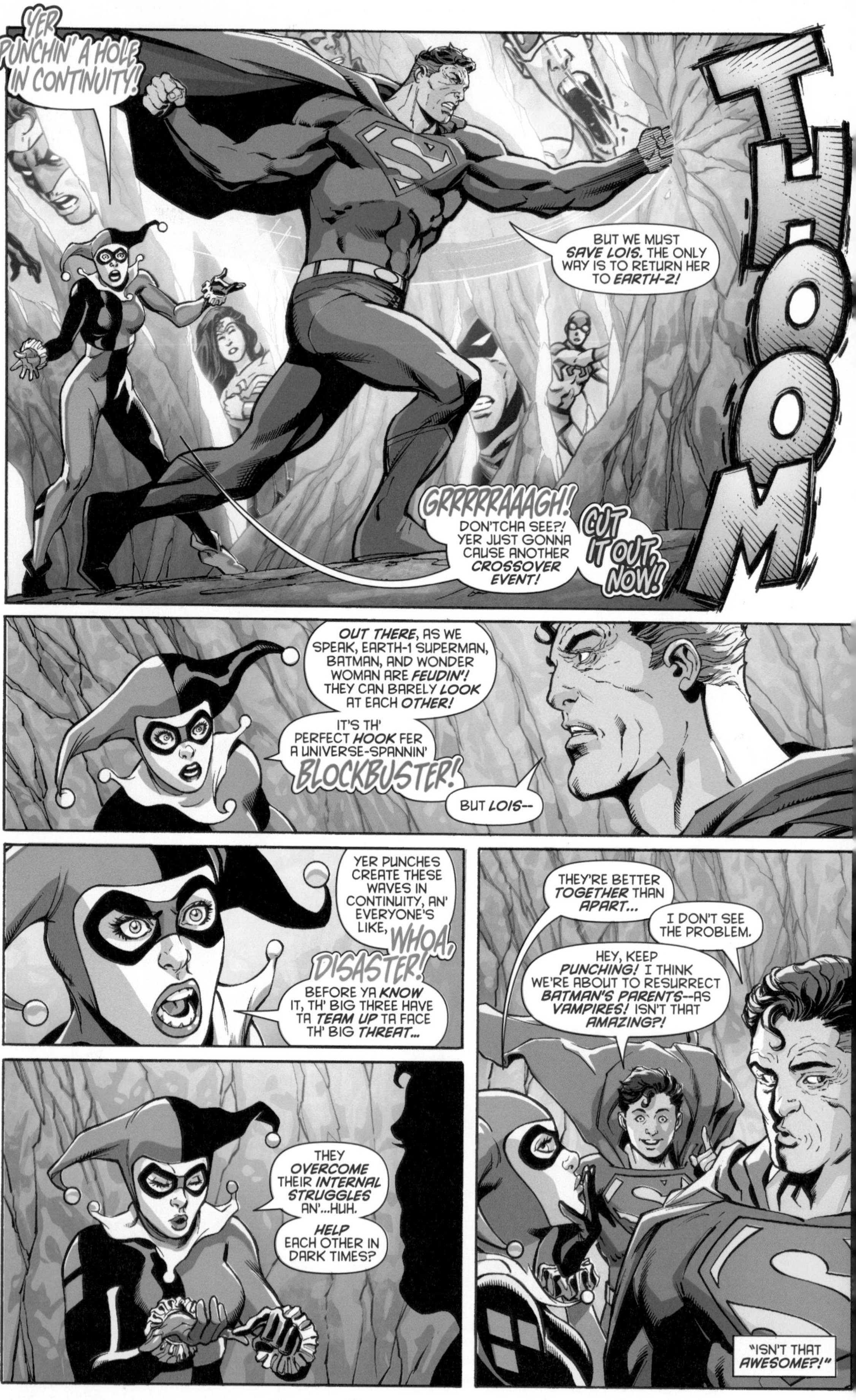
YER PUNCHIN' A HOLE IN CONTINUITY!
BUT WE MUST SAVE LOIS. THE ONLY WAY IS TO RETURN HER TO EARTH-2!
THOOM
GRRRRRAAAGH!
DON'TCHA SEE?! YER JUST GONNA CAUSE ANOTHER CROSSOVER EVENT!
CUT IT OUT, NOW!
OUT THERE, AS WE SPEAK, EARTH-1 SUPERMAN, BATMAN, AND WONDER WOMAN ARE FEUDIN'! THEY CAN BARELY LOOK AT EACH OTHER!
IT'S TH' PERFECT HOOK FER A UNIVERSE-SPANNIN' BLOCKBUSTER!
BUT LOIS--
YER PUNCHES CREATE THESE WAVES IN CONTINUITY, AN' EVERYONE'S LIKE, WHOA, DISASTER!
BEFORE YA KNOW IT, TH' BIG THREE HAVE TA TEAM UP TA FACE TH' BIG THREAT...
THEY OVERCOME THEIR INTERNAL STRUGGLES AN'...HUH.
HELP EACH OTHER IN DARK TIMES?
THEY'RE BETTER TOGETHER THAN APART...
I DON'T SEE THE PROBLEM.
HEY, KEEP PUNCHING! I THINK WE'RE ABOUT TO RESURRECT BATMAN'S PARENTS--AS VAMPIRES! ISN'T THAT AMAZING?!
"ISN'T THAT AWESOME?!"

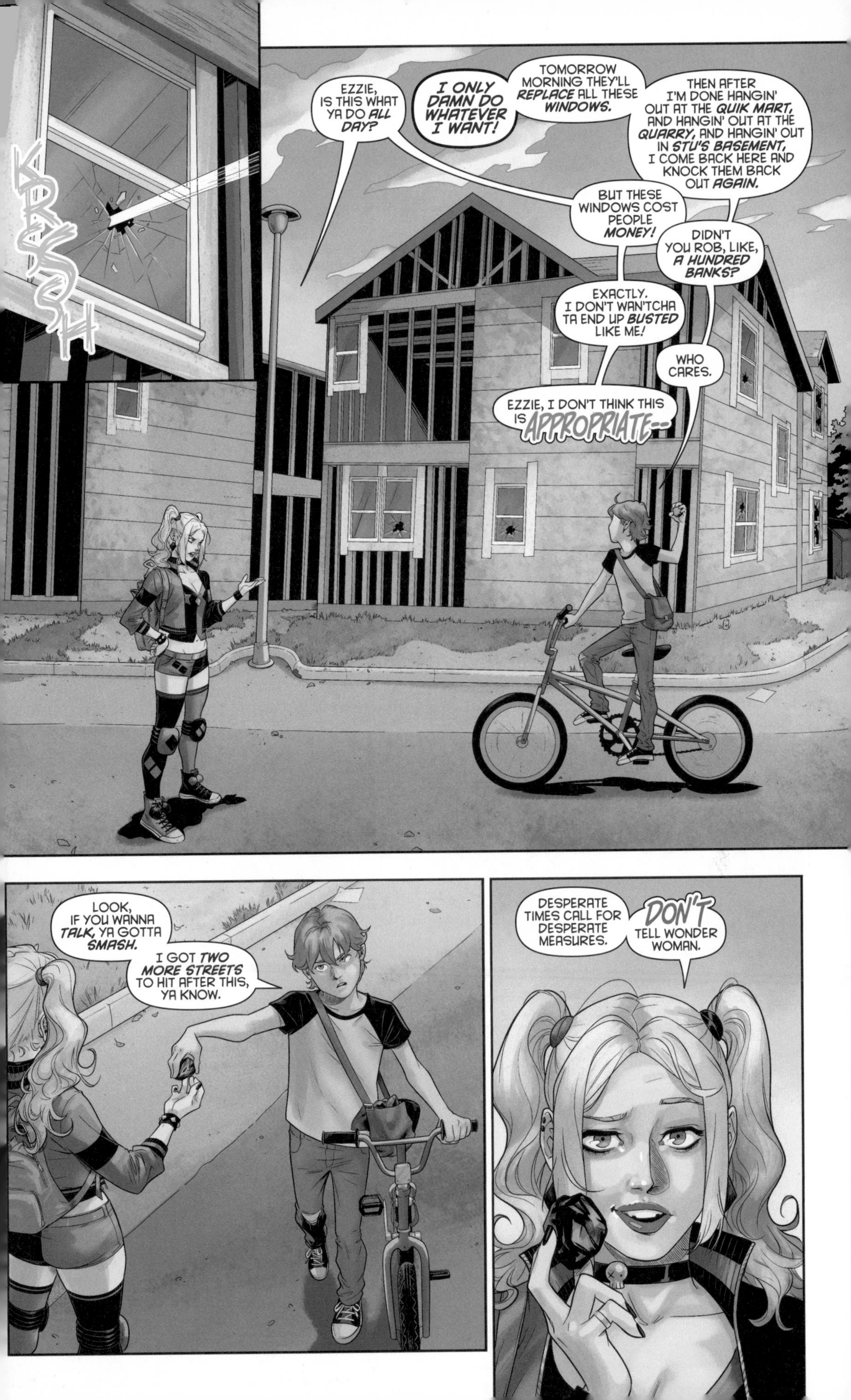
KRSSH
EZZIE, IS THIS WHAT YA DO ALL DAY?
I ONLY DAMN DO WHATEVER I WANT!
TOMORROW MORNING THEY'LL REPLACE ALL THESE WINDOWS.
THEN AFTER I'M DONE HANGIN' OUT AT THE QUIK MART, AND HANGIN' OUT AT THE QUARRY, AND HANGIN' OUT IN STU'S BASEMENT, I COME BACK HERE AND KNOCK THEM BACK OUT AGAIN.
BUT THESE WINDOWS COST PEOPLE MONEY!
DIDN'T YOU ROB, LIKE, A HUNDRED BANKS?
EXACTLY. I DON'T WAN'TCHA TA END UP BUSTED LIKE ME!
WHO CARES.
EZZIE, I DON'T THINK THIS IS APPROPRIATE--
LOOK, IF YOU WANNA TALK, YA GOTTA SMASH.
I GOT TWO MORE STREETS TO HIT AFTER THIS, YA KNOW.
DESPERATE TIMES CALL FOR DESPERATE MEASURES.
DON'T TELL WONDER WOMAN.

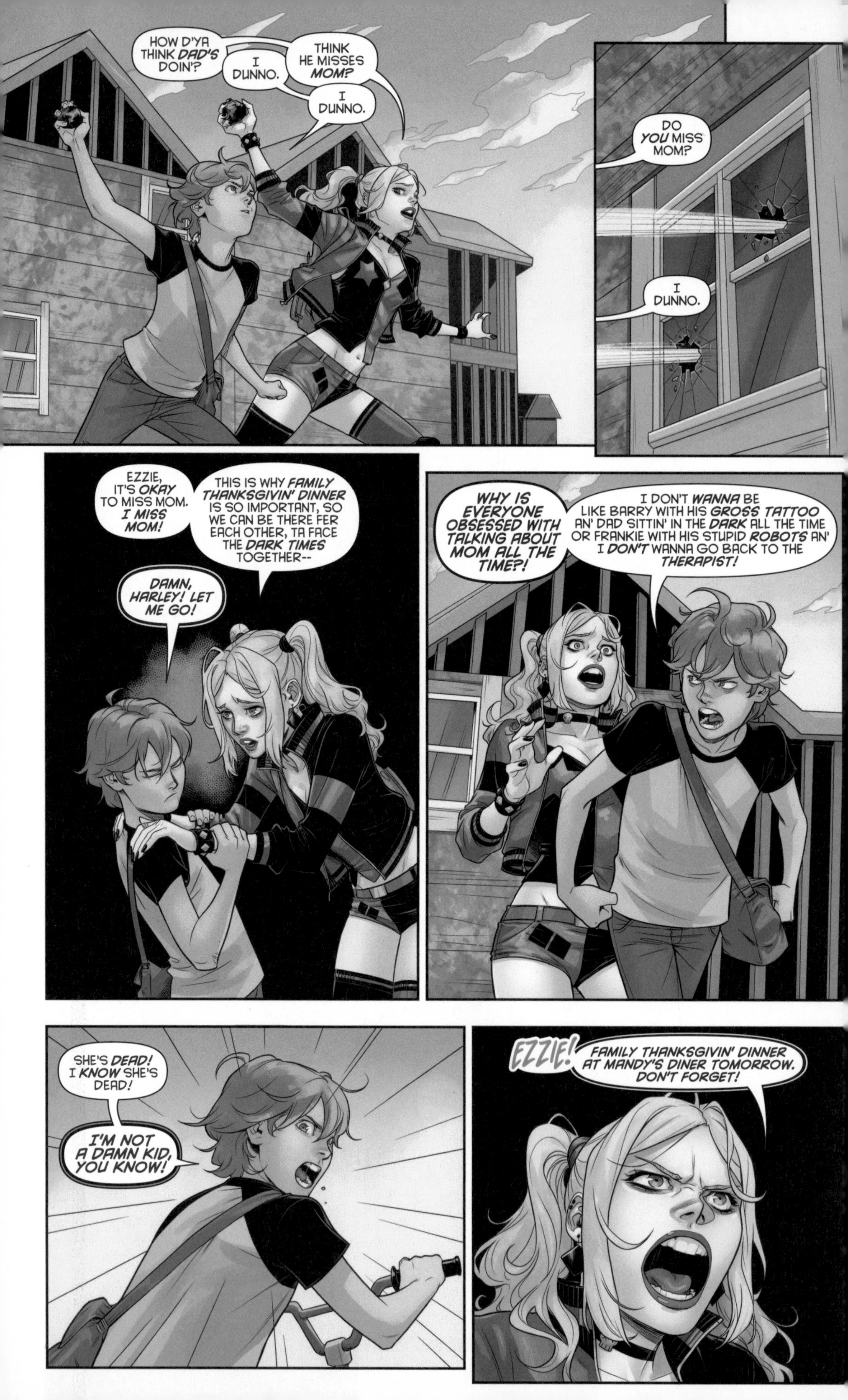
HOW D'YA THINK DAD'S DOIN'?
I DUNNO.
THINK HE MISSES MOM?
I DUNNO.
DO YOU MISS MOM?
I DUNNO.
EZZIE, IT'S OKAY TO MISS MOM. I MISS MOM!
THIS IS WHY FAMILY THANKSGIVIN' DINNER IS SO IMPORTANT, SO WE CAN BE THERE FER EACH OTHER, TA FACE THE DARK TIMES TOGETHER--
DAMN, HARLEY! LET ME GO!
WHY IS EVERYONE OBSESSED WITH TALKING ABOUT MOM ALL THE TIME?!
I DON'T WANNA BE LIKE BARRY WITH HIS GROSS TATTOO AN' DAD SITTIN' IN THE DARK ALL THE TIME OR FRANKIE WITH HIS STUPID ROBOTS AN' I DON'T WANNA GO BACK TO THE THERAPIST!
SHE'S DEAD! I KNOW SHE'S DEAD!
I'M NOT A DAMN KID, YOU KNOW!
EZZIE!
FAMILY THANKSGIVIN' DINNER AT MANDY'S DINER TOMORROW. DON'T FORGET!

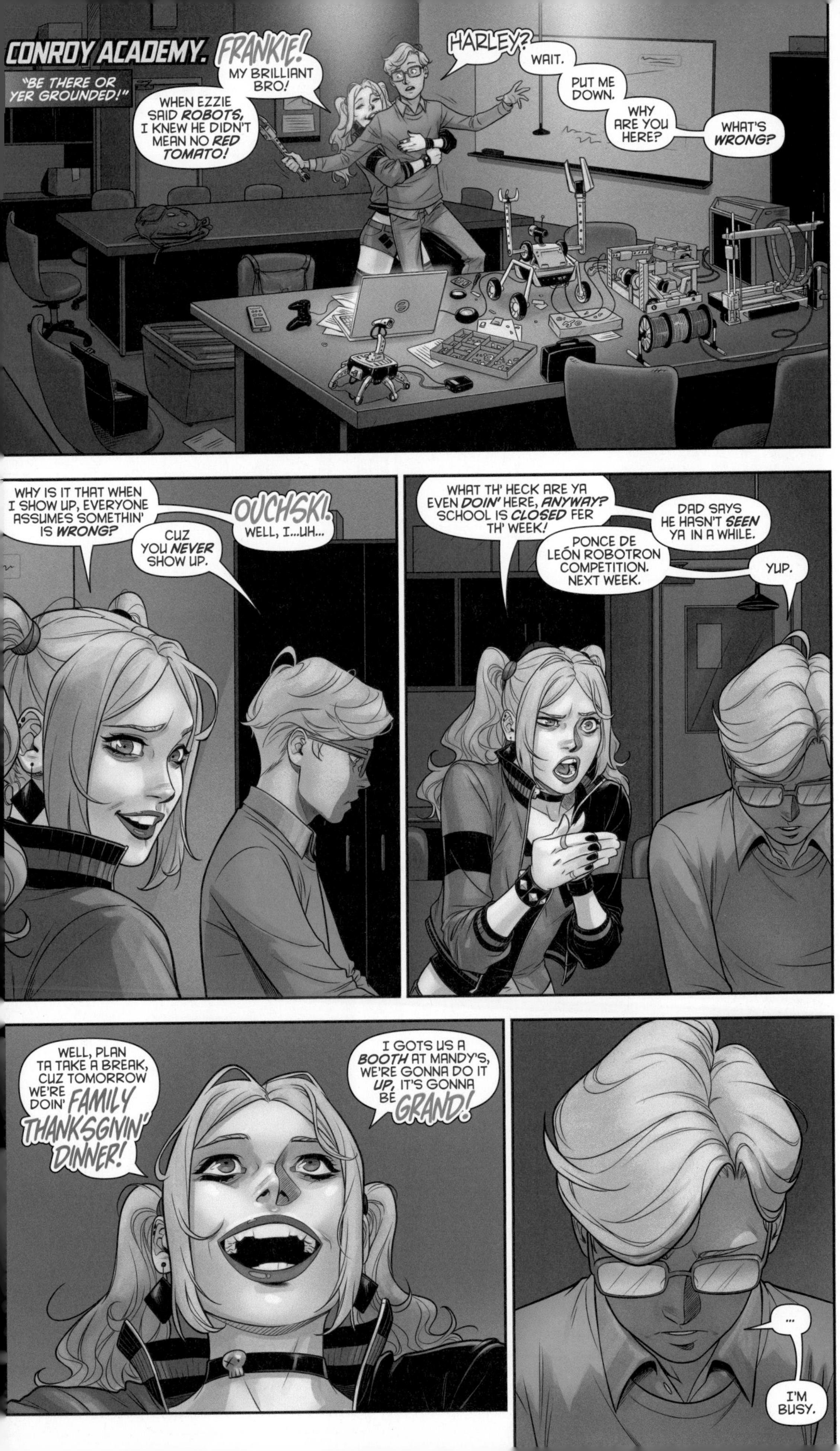

CONROY ACADEMY.
"BE THERE OR YER GROUNDED!"
FRANKIE! MY BRILLIANT BRO!
WHEN EZZIE SAID ROBOTS, I KNEW HE DIDN'T MEAN NO RED TOMATO!
HARLEY?
WAIT.
PUT ME DOWN.
WHY ARE YOU HERE?
WHAT'S WRONG?
WHY IS IT THAT WHEN I SHOW UP, EVERYONE ASSUMES SOMETHIN' IS WRONG?
CUZ YOU NEVER SHOW UP.
OUCHSKI.
WELL, I...UH...
WHAT TH' HECK ARE YA EVEN DOIN' HERE, ANYWAY? SCHOOL IS CLOSED FER TH' WEEK!
PONCE DE LEÓN ROBOTRON COMPETITION. NEXT WEEK.
DAD SAYS HE HASN'T SEEN YA IN A WHILE.
YUP.
WELL, PLAN TA TAKE A BREAK, CUZ TOMORROW WE'RE DOIN' FAMILY THANKSGIVIN' DINNER!
I GOTS US A BOOTH AT MANDY'S, WE'RE GONNA DO IT UP, IT'S GONNA BE GRAND!
...
I'M BUSY.

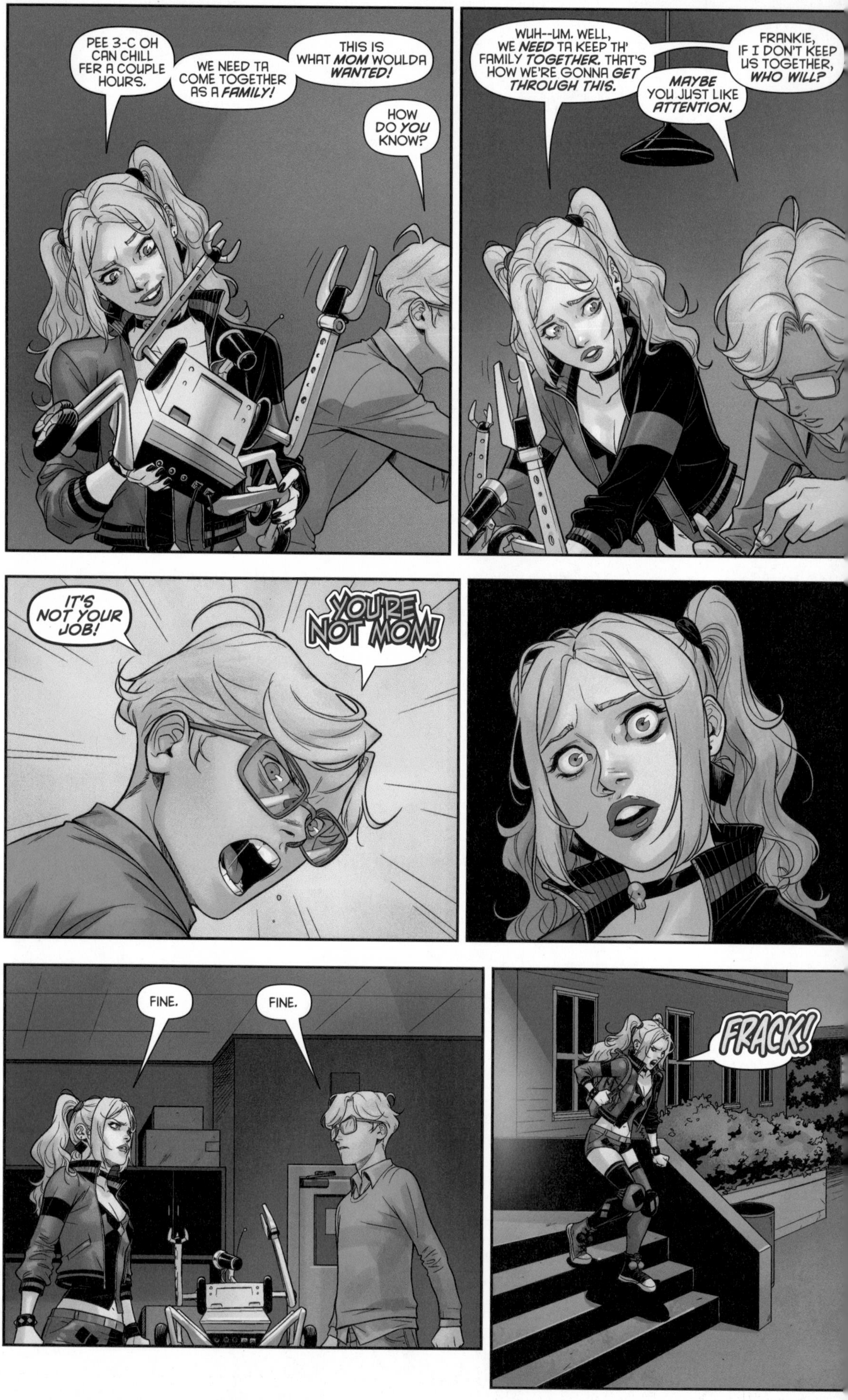
PEE 3-C OH CAN CHILL FER A COUPLE HOURS.
WE NEED TA COME TOGETHER AS A FAMILY!
THIS IS WHAT MOM WOULDA WANTED!
HOW DO YOU KNOW?
WUH--UM. WELL, WE NEED TA KEEP TH' FAMILY TOGETHER. THAT'S HOW WE'RE GONNA GET THROUGH THIS.
MAYBE YOU JUST LIKE ATTENTION.
FRANKIE, IF I DON'T KEEP US TOGETHER, WHO WILL?
IT'S NOT YOUR JOB!
YOU'RE NOT MOM!
FINE.
FINE.
FRACK!

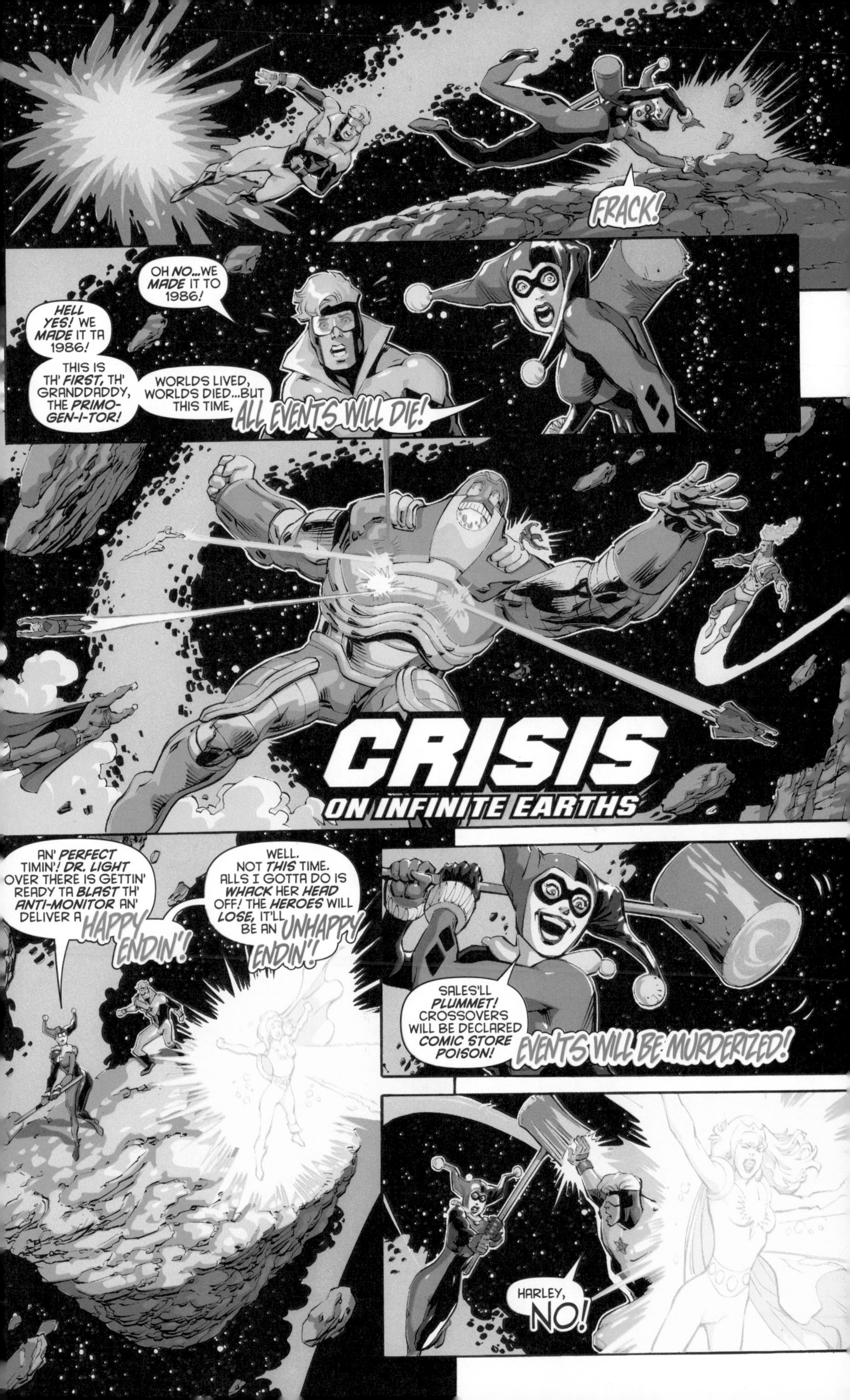
FRACK!
HELL YES! WE MADE IT TA 1986!
OH NO...WE MADE IT TO 1986!
THIS IS TH' FIRST, TH' GRANDDADDY, THE PRIMO-GEN-I-TOR!
WORLDS LIVED, WORLDS DIED...BUT THIS TIME, ALL EVENTS WILL DIE!
CRISIS
ON INFINITE EARTHS
AN' PERFECT TIMIN'! DR. LIGHT OVER THERE IS GETTIN' READY TA BLAST TH' ANTI-MONITOR AN' DELIVER A HAPPY ENDIN'!
WELL. NOT THIS TIME. ALL'S I GOTTA DO IS WHACK HER HEAD OFF! THE HEROES WILL LOSE, IT'LL BE AN UNHAPPY ENDIN'!
SALES'LL PLUMMET! CROSSOVERS WILL BE DECLARED COMIC STORE POISON!
EVENTS WILL BE MURDERIZED!
HARLEY, NO!

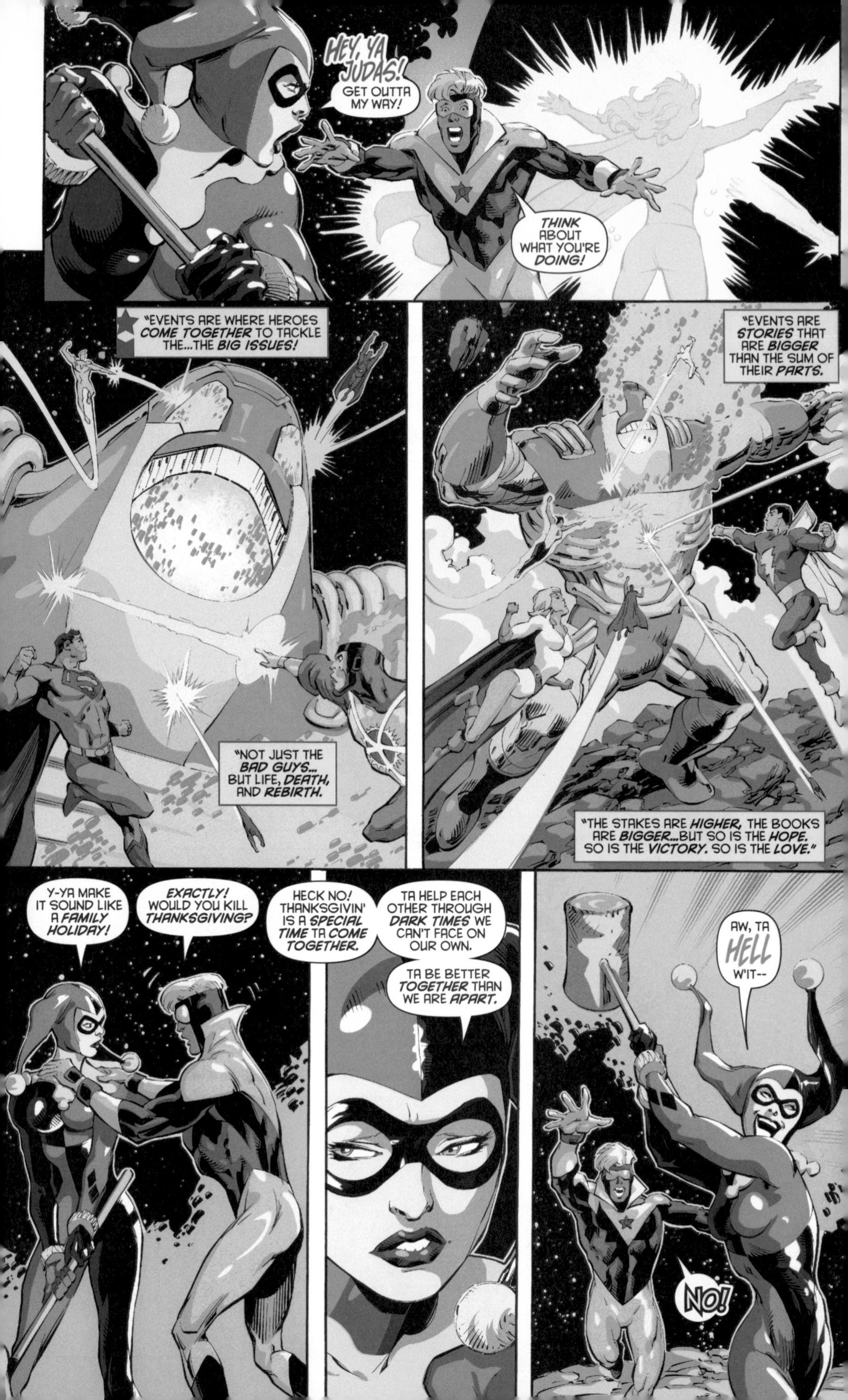
HEY, YA JUDAS!
GET OUTTA MY WAY!
THINK ABOUT WHAT YOU'RE DOING!
"EVENTS ARE WHERE HEROES COME TOGETHER TO TACKLE THE...THE BIG ISSUES!
"NOT JUST THE BAD GUYS... BUT LIFE, DEATH, AND REBIRTH.
"EVENTS ARE STORIES THAT ARE BIGGER THAN THE SUM OF THEIR PARTS.
"THE STAKES ARE HIGHER, THE BOOKS ARE BIGGER...BUT SO IS THE HOPE. SO IS THE VICTORY. SO IS THE LOVE."
Y-YA MAKE IT SOUND LIKE A FAMILY HOLIDAY!
EXACTLY! WOULD YOU KILL THANKSGIVING?
HECK NO! THANKSGIVIN' IS A SPECIAL TIME TA COME TOGETHER.
TA HELP EACH OTHER THROUGH DARK TIMES WE CAN'T FACE ON OUR OWN.
TA BE BETTER TOGETHER THAN WE ARE APART.
AW, TA HELL W'IT--
NO!

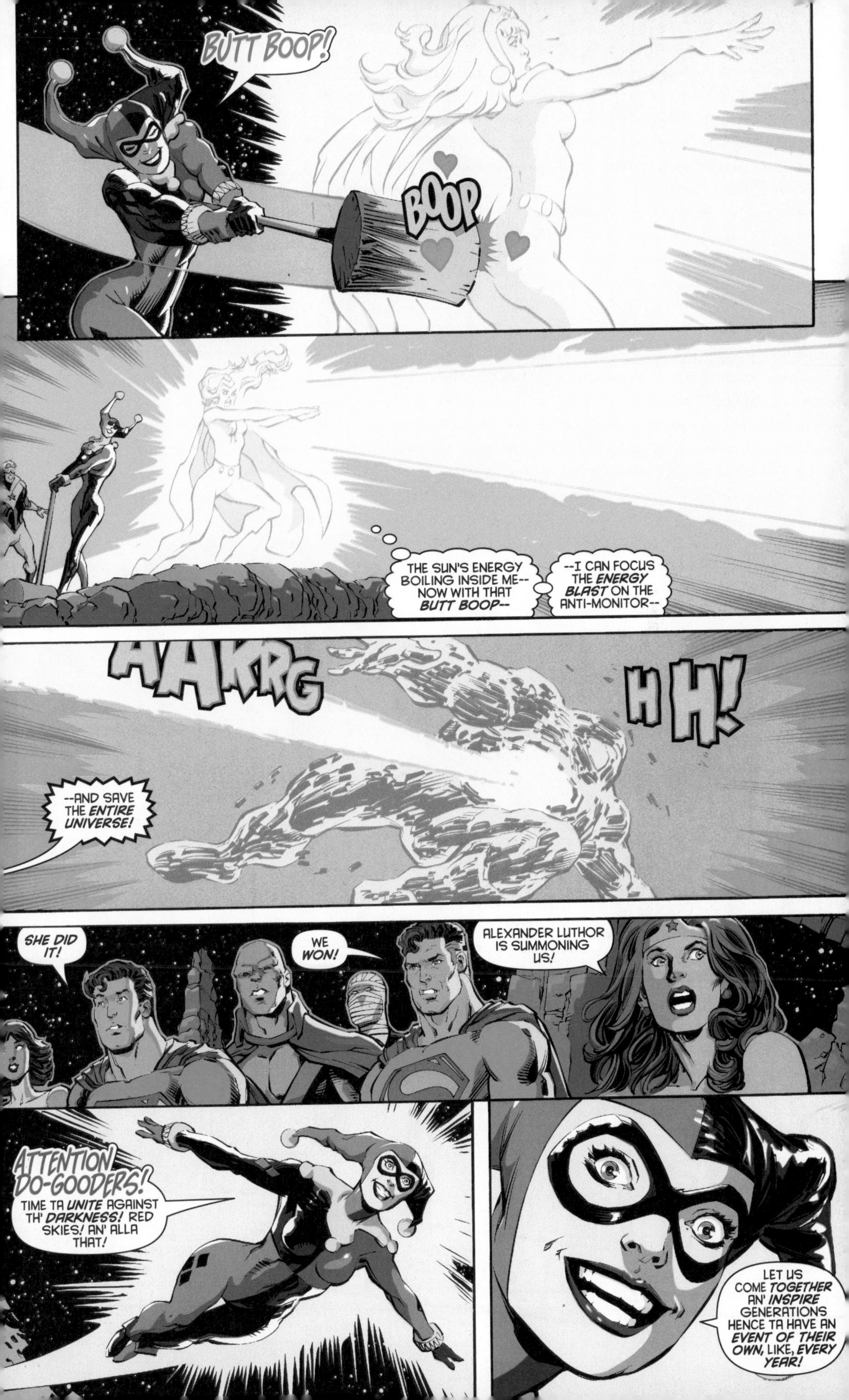
BUTT BOOP!
BOOP
THE SUN'S ENERGY BOILING INSIDE ME-- NOW WITH THAT BUTT BOOP--
--I CAN FOCUS THE ENERGY BLAST ON THE ANTI-MONITOR--
AAKRG
HH!
--AND SAVE THE ENTIRE UNIVERSE!
SHE DID IT!
WE WON!
ALEXANDER LUTHOR IS SUMMONING US!
ATTENTION DO-GOODERS!
TIME TA UNITE AGAINST TH' DARKNESS! RED SKIES! AN' ALLA THAT!
LET US COME TOGETHER AN' INSPIRE GENERATIONS HENCE TA HAVE AN EVENT OF THEIR OWN, LIKE, EVERY YEAR!

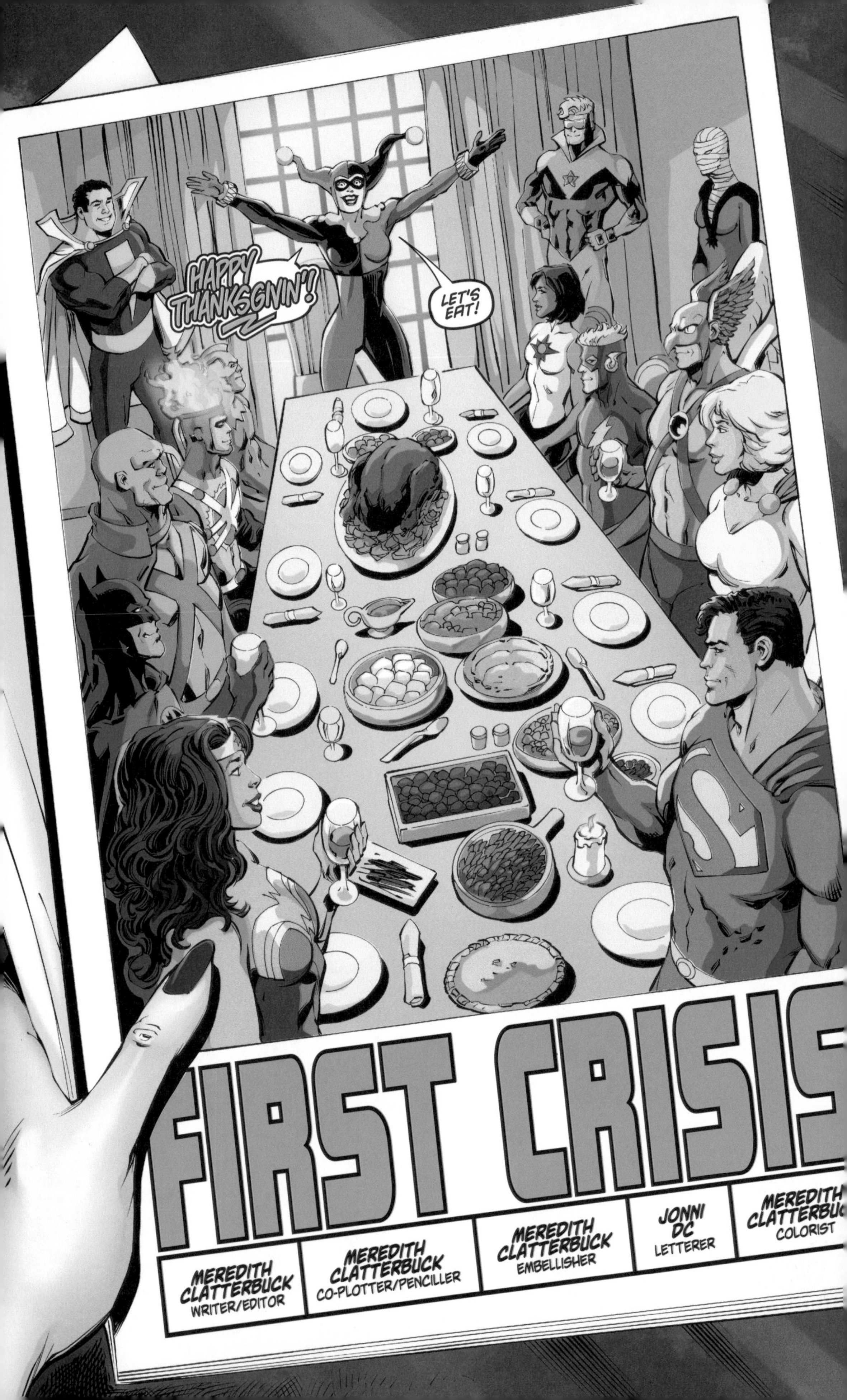

HAPPY THANKSGIVIN'!
LET'S EAT!
FIRST CRISIS
MEREDITH CLATTERBUCK WRITER/EDITOR
MEREDITH CLATTERBUCK CO-PLOTTER/PENCILLER
MEREDITH CLATTERBUCK EMBELLISHER
JONNI DC LETTERER
MEREDITH CLATTERBUC COLORIST

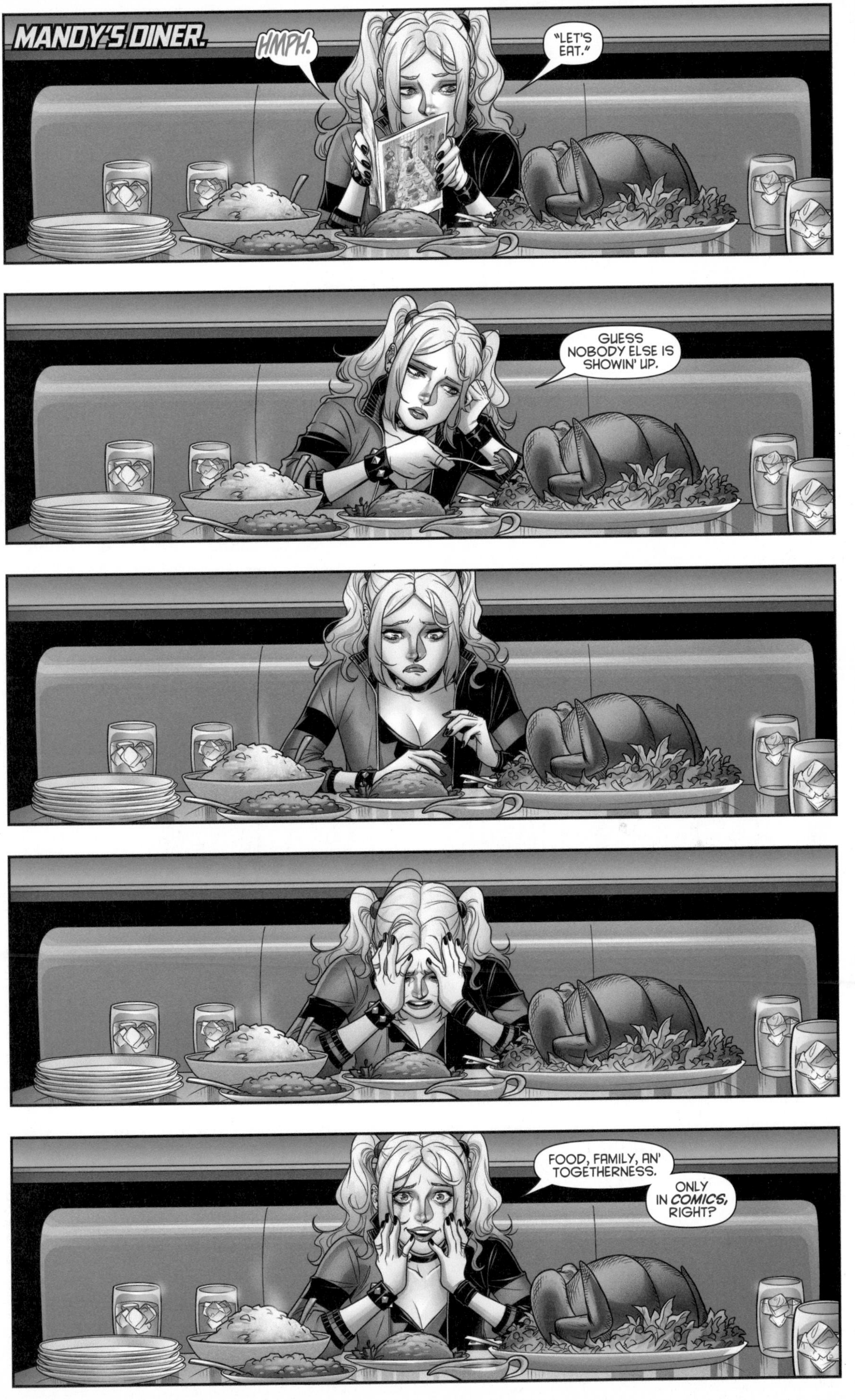
MANDY'S DINER.
HMPH.
"LET'S EAT."
GUESS NOBODY ELSE IS SHOWIN' UP.
FOOD, FAMILY, AN' TOGETHERNESS.
ONLY IN *COMICS*, RIGHT?

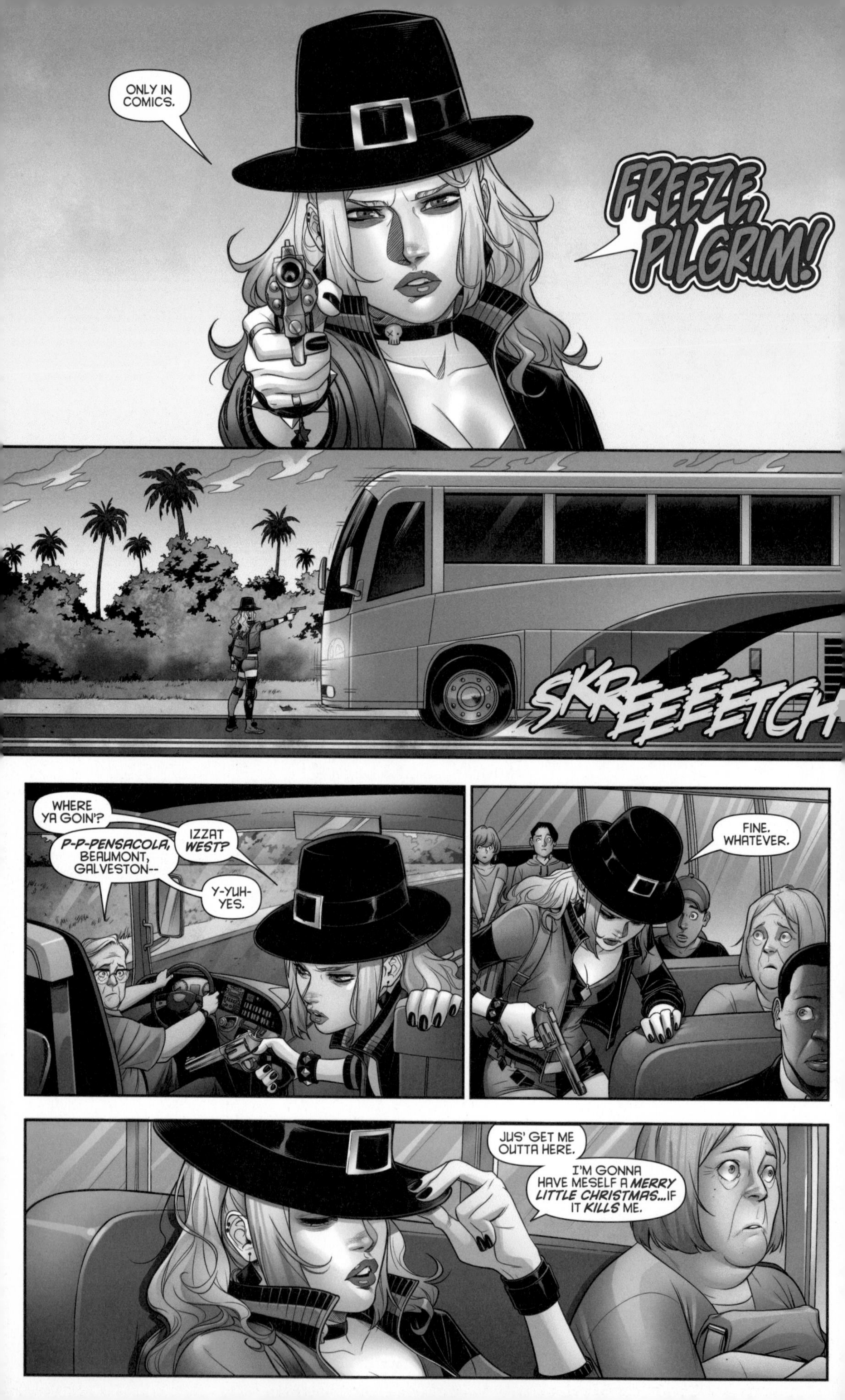

ONLY IN COMICS.
FREEZE, PILGRIM!
SKREEEEETCH
WHERE YA GOIN'?
P-P-PENSACOLA, BEAUMONT, GALVESTON--
IZZAT WEST?
Y-YUH-YES.
FINE. WHATEVER.
JUS' GET ME OUTTA HERE.
I'M GONNA HAVE MESELF A MERRY LITTLE CHRISTMAS...IF IT KILLS ME.

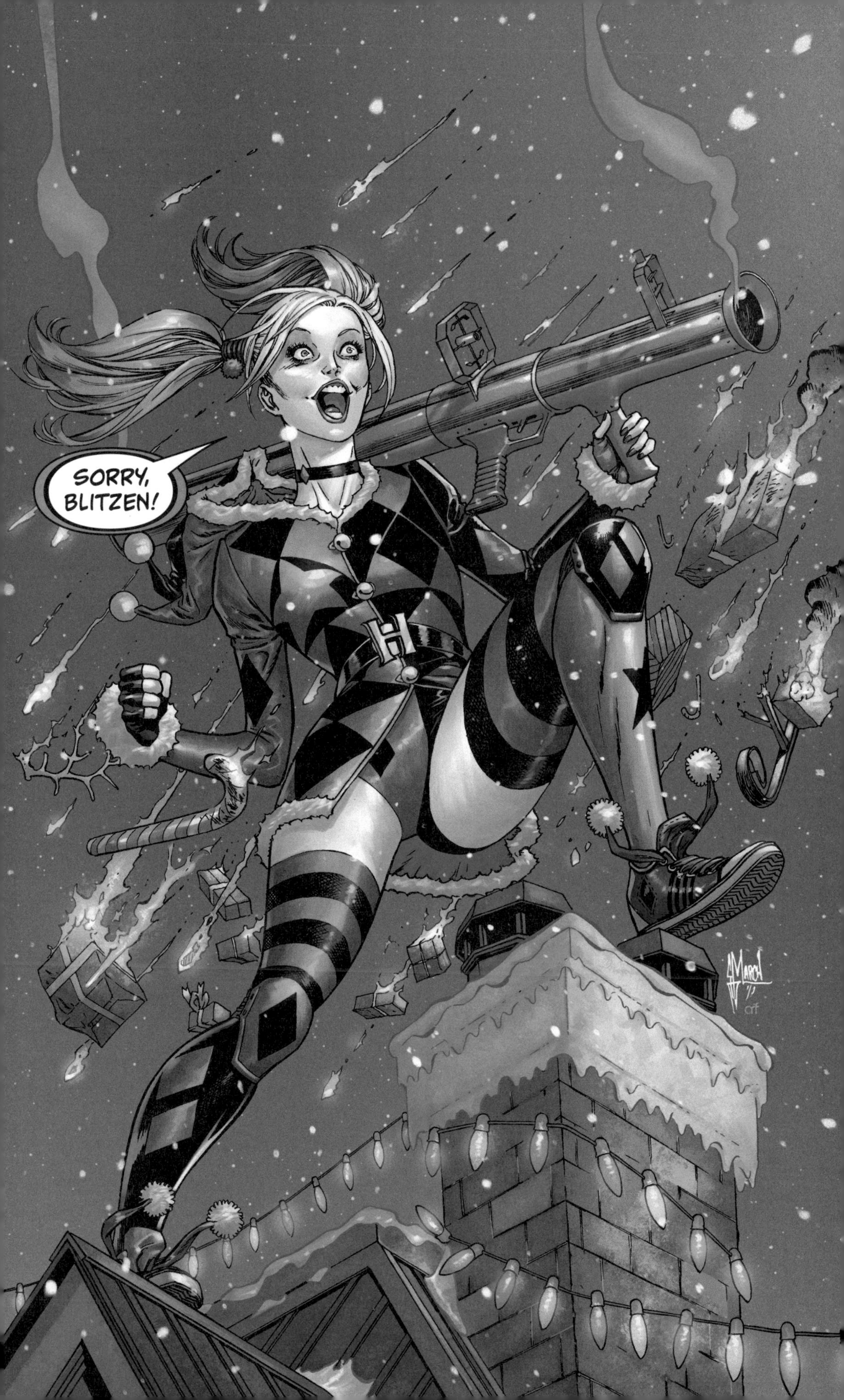
SORRY, BLITZEN!

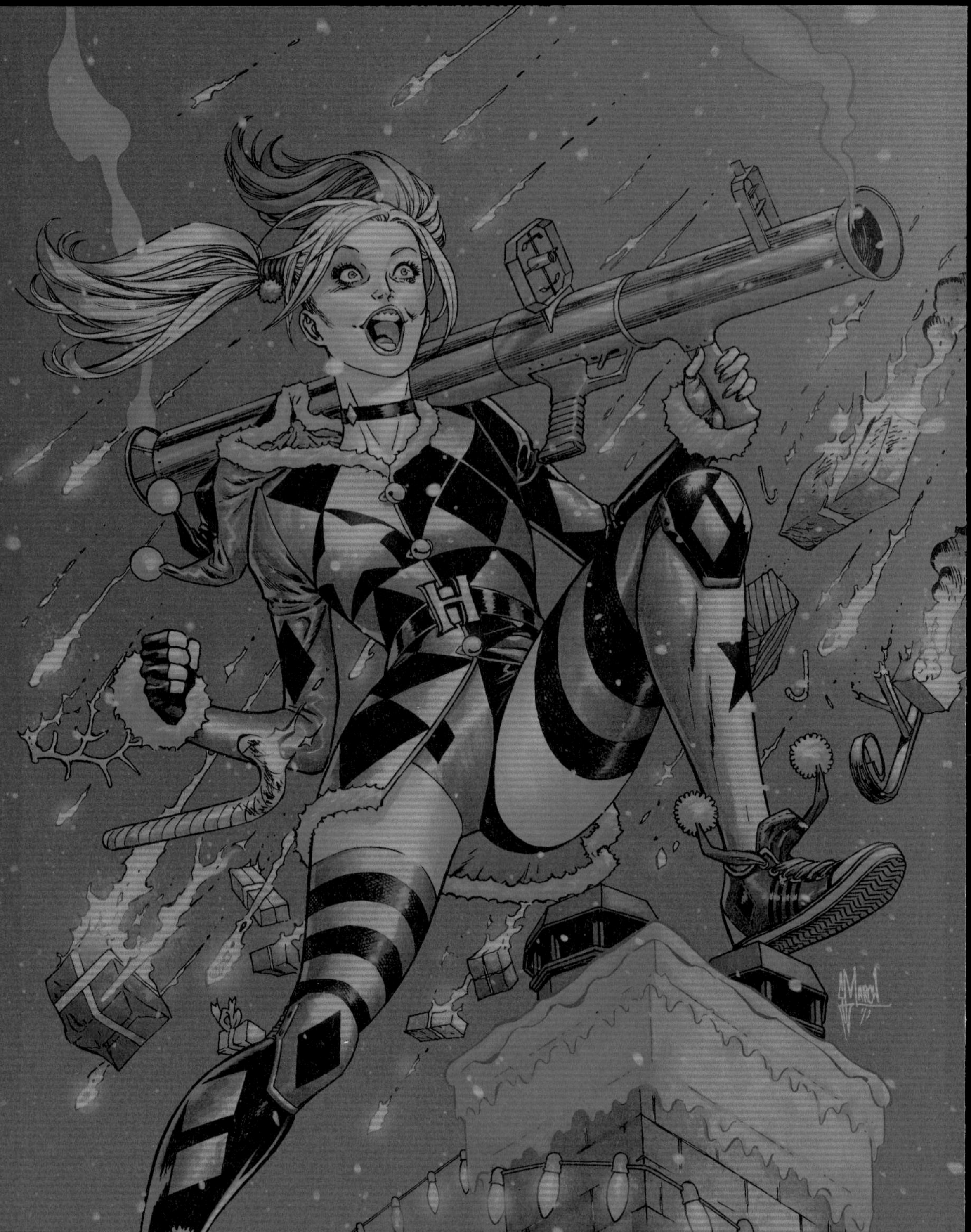

HARLEY QUINN
#68

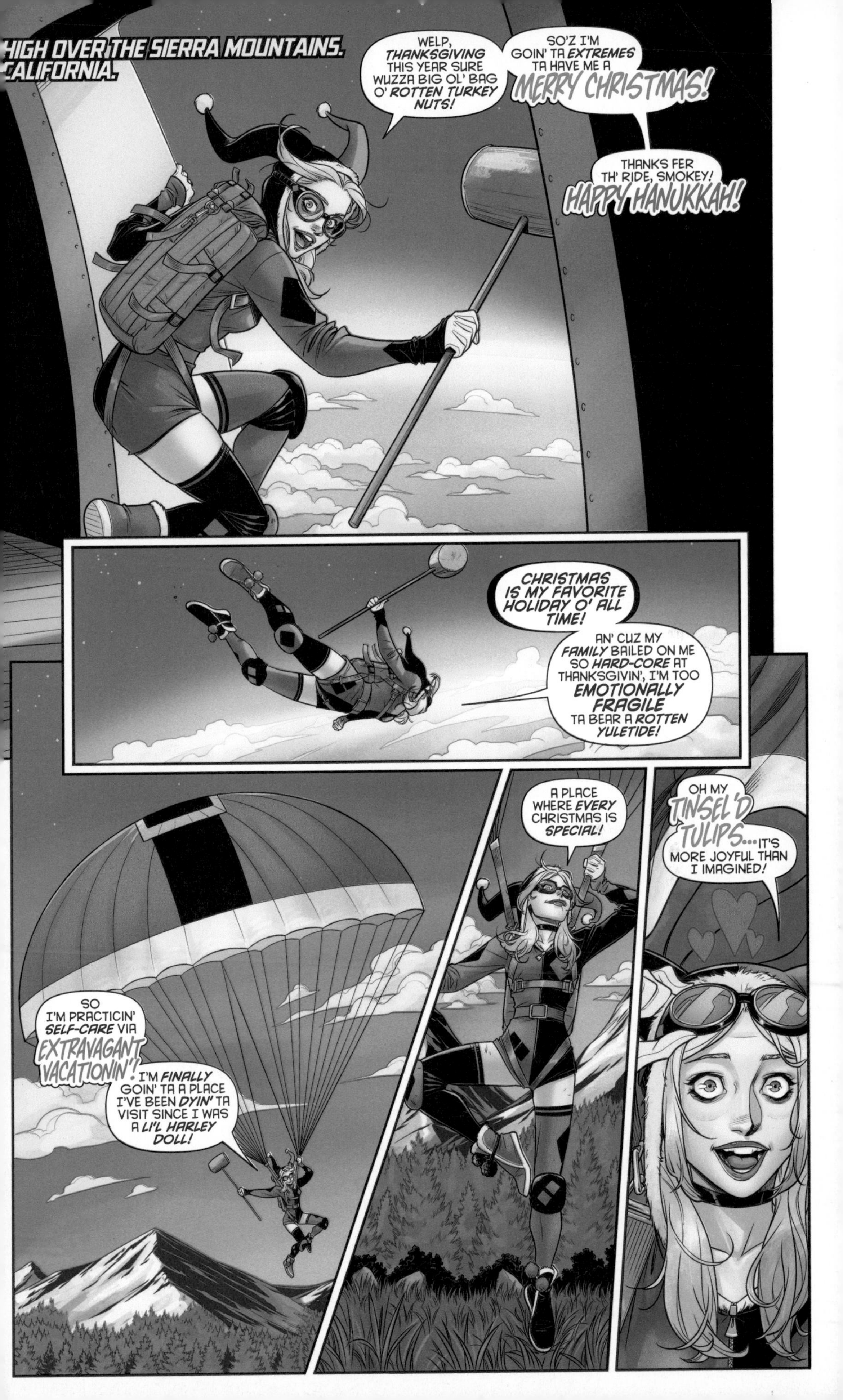

HIGH OVER THE SIERRA MOUNTAINS. CALIFORNIA.
WELP, THANKSGIVING THIS YEAR SURE WUZZA BIG OL' BAG O' ROTTEN TURKEY NUTS!
SO'Z I'M GOIN' TA EXTREMES TA HAVE ME A MERRY CHRISTMAS!
THANKS FER TH' RIDE, SMOKEY! HAPPY HANUKKAH!
CHRISTMAS IS MY FAVORITE HOLIDAY O' ALL TIME!
AN' CUZ MY FAMILY BAILED ON ME SO HARD-CORE AT THANKSGIVIN', I'M TOO EMOTIONALLY FRAGILE TA BEAR A ROTTEN YULETIDE!
SO I'M PRACTICIN' SELF-CARE VIA EXTRAVAGANT VACATIONIN'!
I'M FINALLY GOIN' TA A PLACE I'VE BEEN DYIN' TA VISIT SINCE I WAS A LI'L HARLEY DOLL!
A PLACE WHERE EVERY CHRISTMAS IS SPECIAL!
OH MY TINSEL'D TULIPS... IT'S MORE JOYFUL THAN I IMAGINED!

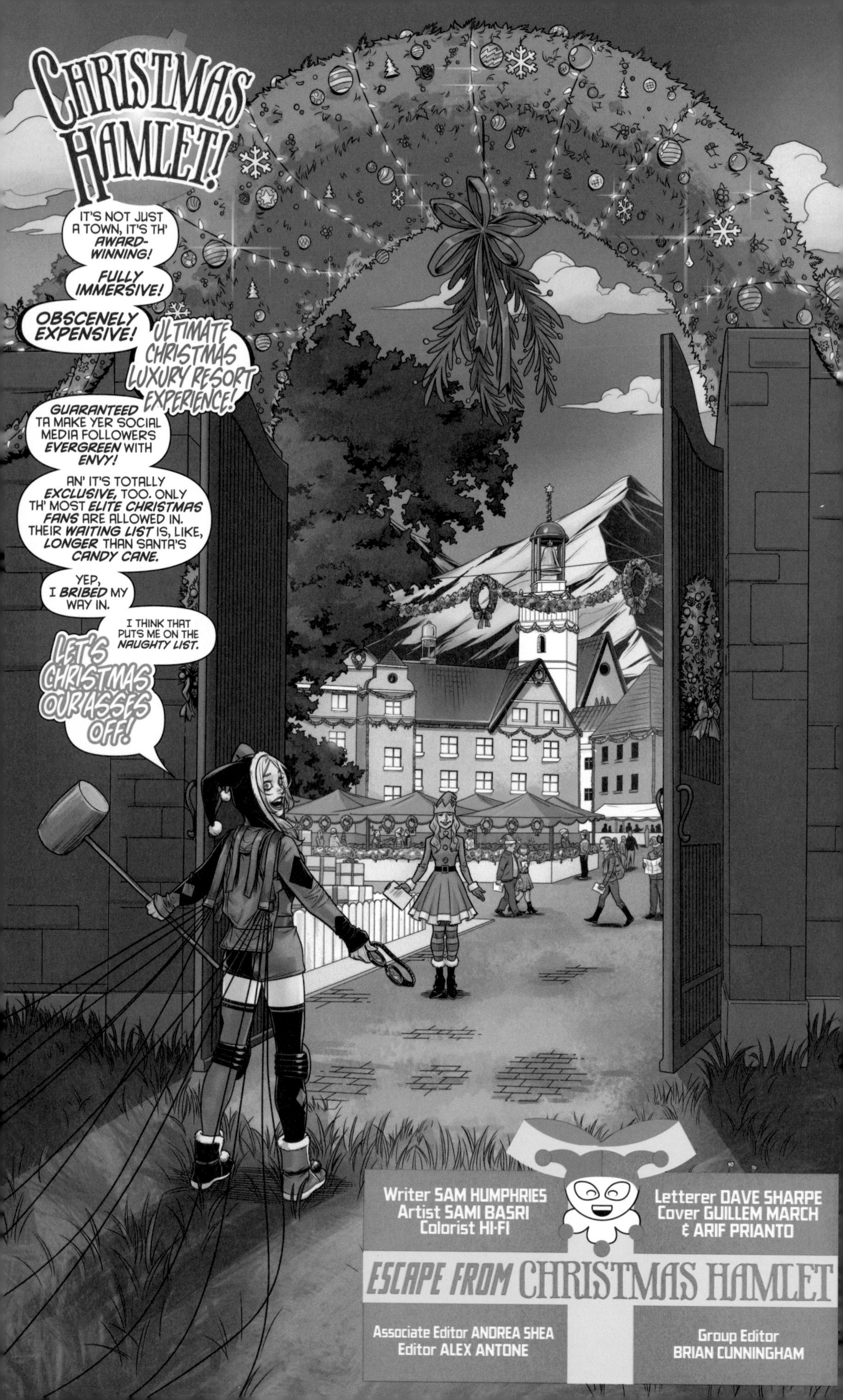
CHRISTMAS HAMLET!
IT'S NOT JUST A TOWN, IT'S TH' AWARD-WINNING!
FULLY IMMERSIVE!
OBSCENELY EXPENSIVE!
ULTIMATE CHRISTMAS LUXURY RESORT EXPERIENCE!
GUARANTEED TA MAKE YER SOCIAL MEDIA FOLLOWERS EVERGREEN WITH ENVY!
AN' IT'S TOTALLY EXCLUSIVE, TOO. ONLY TH' MOST ELITE CHRISTMAS FANS ARE ALLOWED IN. THEIR WAITING LIST IS, LIKE, LONGER THAN SANTA'S CANDY CANE.
YEP, I BRIBED MY WAY IN.
I THINK THAT PUTS ME ON THE NAUGHTY LIST.
LET'S CHRISTMAS OUR ASSES OFF!
Writer SAM HUMPHRIES
Artist SAMI BASRI
Colorist HI-FI
Letterer DAVE SHARPE
Cover GUILLEM MARCH & ARIF PRIANTO
ESCAPE FROM CHRISTMAS HAMLET
Associate Editor ANDREA SHEA
Editor ALEX ANTONE
Group Editor BRIAN CUNNINGHAM

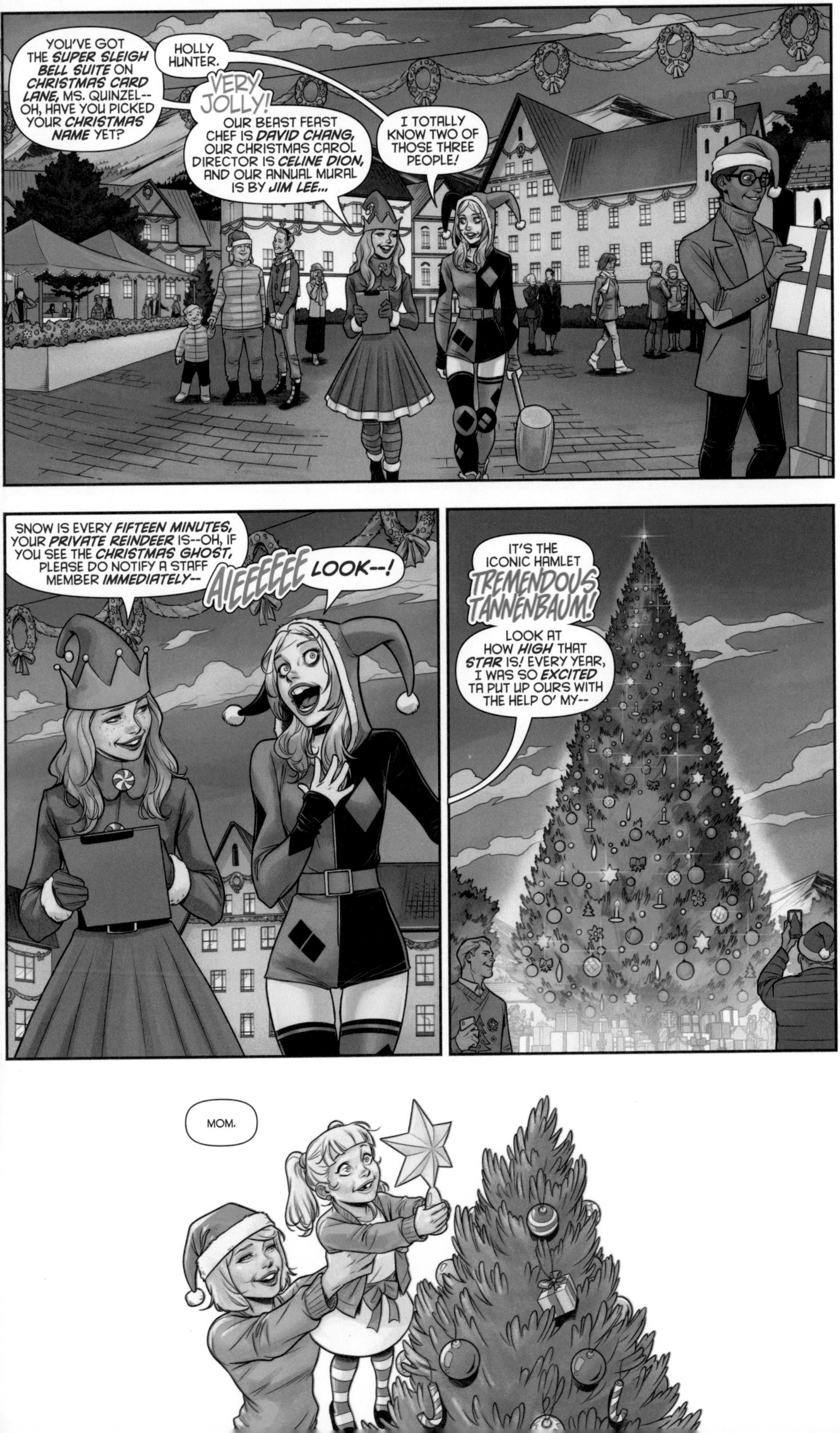

YOU'VE GOT THE SUPER SLEIGH BELL SUITE ON CHRISTMAS CARD LANE, MS. QUINZEL-- OH, HAVE YOU PICKED YOUR CHRISTMAS NAME YET?
HOLLY HUNTER.
VERY JOLLY!
OUR BEAST FEAST CHEF IS DAVID CHANG, OUR CHRISTMAS CAROL DIRECTOR IS CELINE DION, AND OUR ANNUAL MURAL IS BY JIM LEE...
I TOTALLY KNOW TWO OF THOSE THREE PEOPLE!
SNOW IS EVERY FIFTEEN MINUTES, YOUR PRIVATE REINDEER IS--OH, IF YOU SEE THE CHRISTMAS GHOST, PLEASE DO NOTIFY A STAFF MEMBER IMMEDIATELY--
AIEEEEEE
LOOK--!
IT'S THE ICONIC HAMLET
TREMENDOUS TANNENBAUM!
LOOK AT HOW HIGH THAT STAR IS! EVERY YEAR, I WAS SO EXCITED TA PUT UP OURS WITH THE HELP O' MY--
MOM.

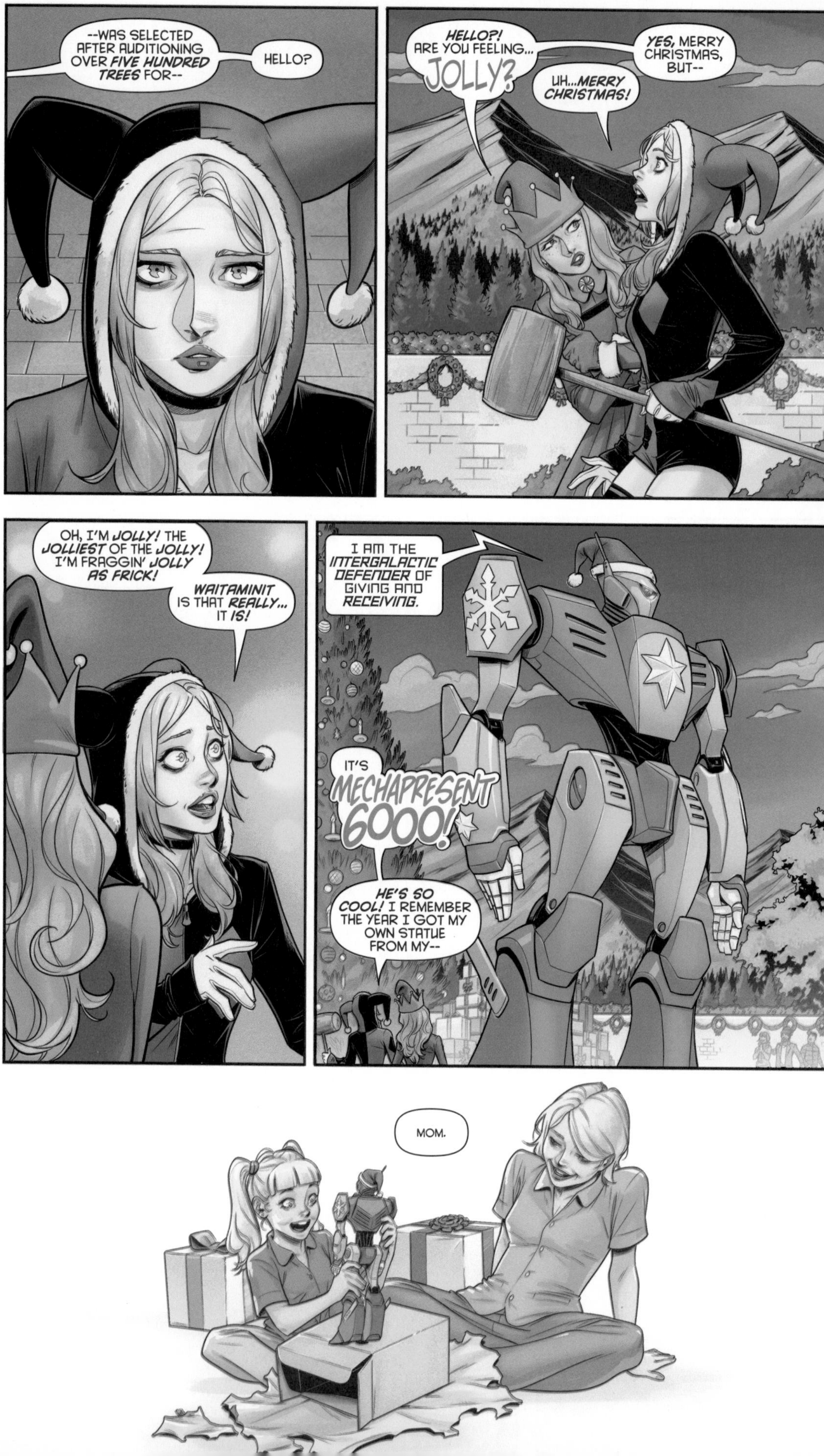
--WAS SELECTED AFTER AUDITIONING OVER FIVE HUNDRED TREES FOR--
HELLO?
HELLO?! ARE YOU FEELING... JOLLY?
UH...MERRY CHRISTMAS!
YES, MERRY CHRISTMAS, BUT--
OH, I'M JOLLY! THE JOLLIEST OF THE JOLLY! I'M FRAGGIN' JOLLY AS FRICK!
WAITAMINIT IS THAT REALLY... IT IS!
I AM THE INTERGALACTIC DEFENDER OF GIVING AND RECEIVING.
IT'S MECHAPRESENT 6000!
HE'S SO COOL! I REMEMBER THE YEAR I GOT MY OWN STATUE FROM MY--
MOM.

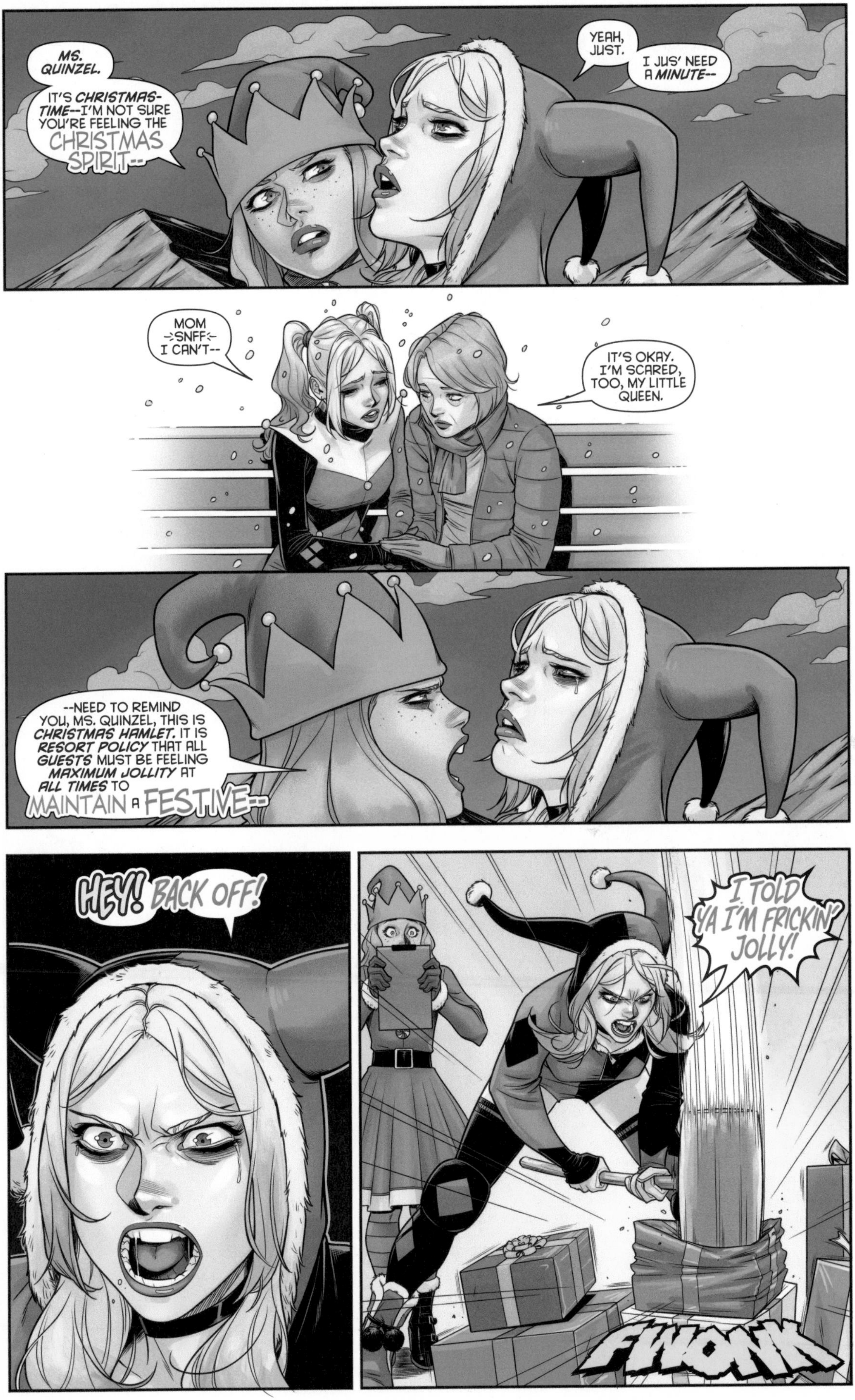
MS. QUINZEL.
IT'S CHRISTMAS-TIME--I'M NOT SURE YOU'RE FEELING THE CHRISTMAS SPIRIT--
YEAH, JUST.
I JUS' NEED A MINUTE--
MOM -SNFF- I CAN'T--
IT'S OKAY. I'M SCARED, TOO, MY LITTLE QUEEN.
--NEED TO REMIND YOU, MS. QUINZEL, THIS IS CHRISTMAS HAMLET. IT IS RESORT POLICY THAT ALL GUESTS MUST BE FEELING MAXIMUM JOLLITY AT ALL TIMES TO MAINTAIN A FESTIVE--
HEY! BACK OFF!
I TOLD YA I'M FRICKIN' JOLLY!
FWONK

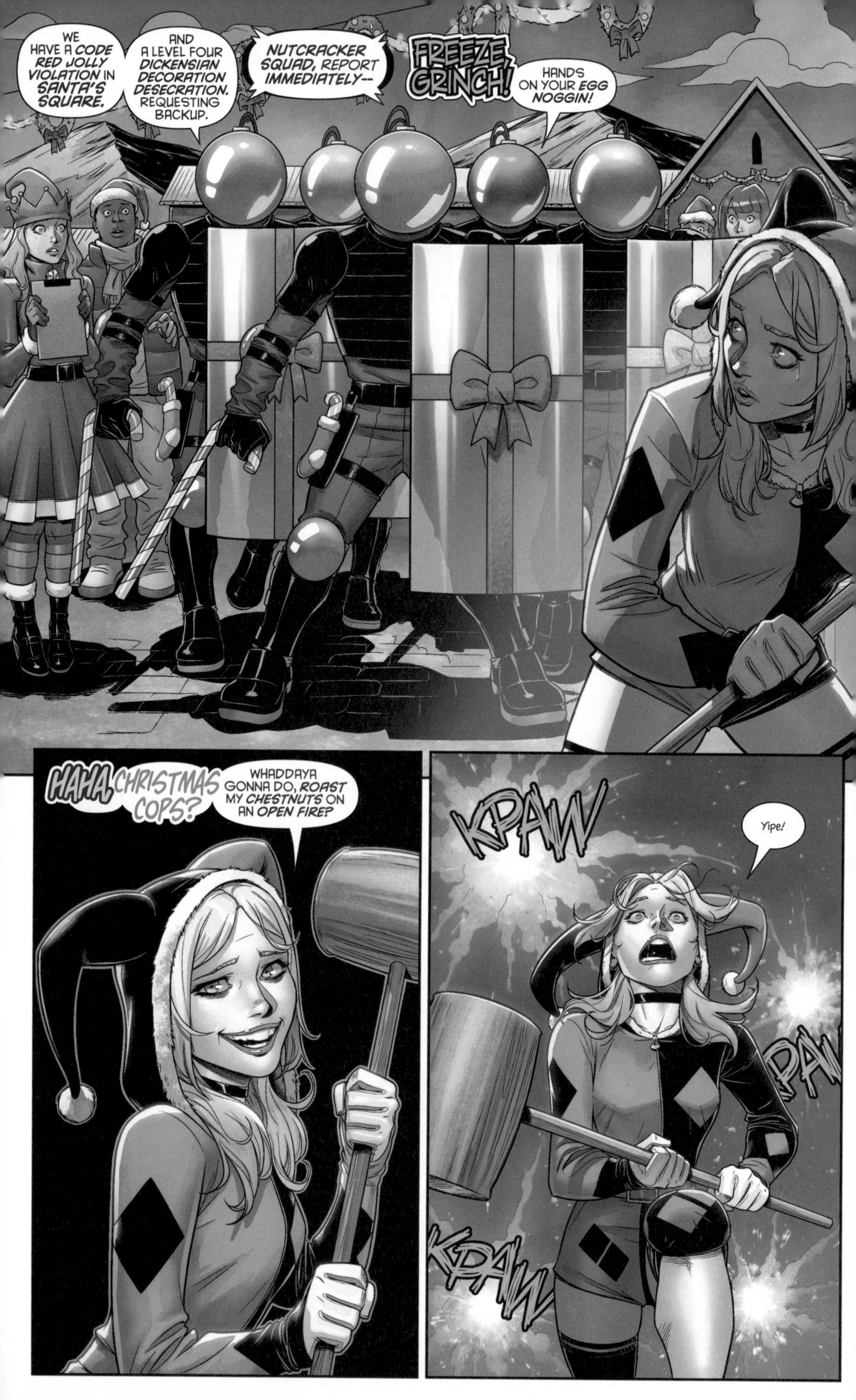
WE HAVE A CODE RED JOLLY VIOLATION IN SANTA'S SQUARE.
AND A LEVEL FOUR DICKENSIAN DECORATION DESECRATION. REQUESTING BACKUP.
NUTCRACKER SQUAD, REPORT IMMEDIATELY--
FREEZE GRINCH!
HANDS ON YOUR EGG NOGGIN!
HAHA, CHRISTMAS COPS?
WHADDAYA GONNA DO, ROAST MY CHESTNUTS ON AN OPEN FIRE?
KPAW
Yipe!
KPAW

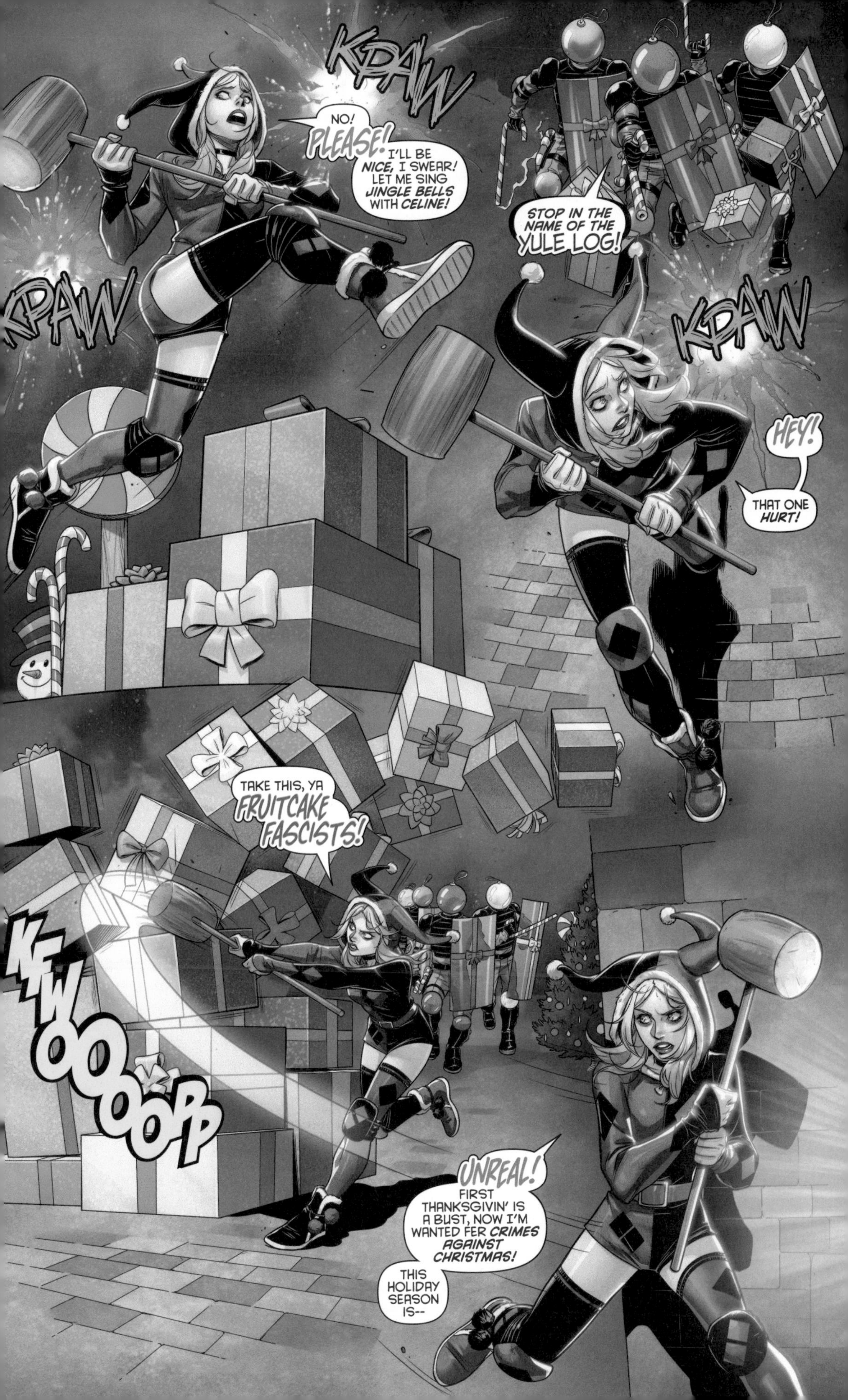
KRAW
NO! PLEASE! I'LL BE NICE, I SWEAR! LET ME SING JINGLE BELLS WITH CELINE!
KRAW
STOP IN THE NAME OF THE YULE LOG!
KRAW
HEY!
THAT ONE HURT!
TAKE THIS, YA FRUITCAKE FASCISTS!
KEWOOOOOP
UNREAL! FIRST THANKSGIVIN' IS A BUST, NOW I'M WANTED FER CRIMES AGAINST CHRISTMAS!
THIS HOLIDAY SEASON IS--

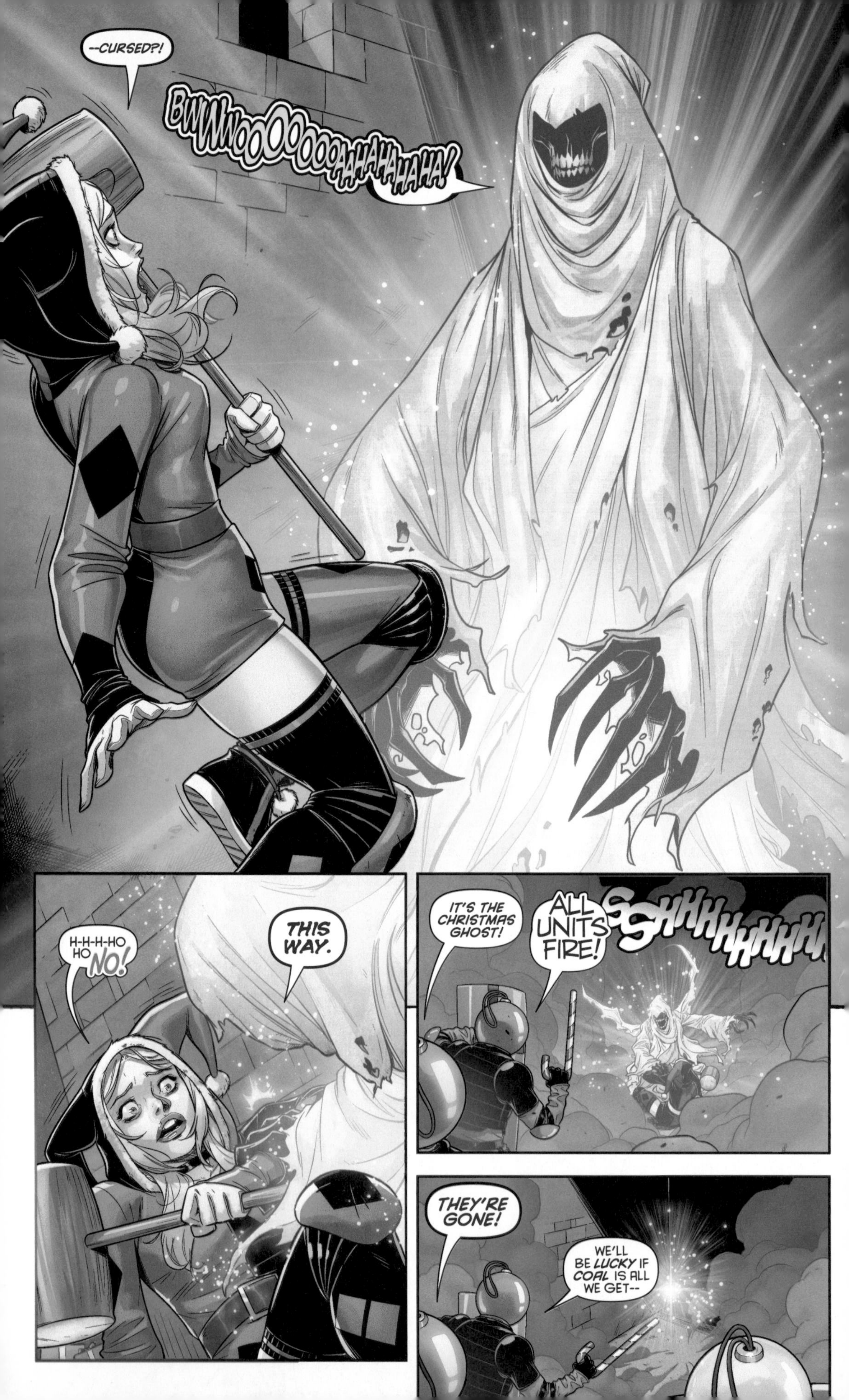

--CURSED?!
BWWWOOOOOOOOAAHAHAHAHA!
H-H-H-HO HO NO!
THIS WAY.
IT'S THE CHRISTMAS GHOST!
ALL UNITS FIRE!
SSHHHHHHHHH
THEY'RE GONE!
WE'LL BE LUCKY IF COAL IS ALL WE GET--

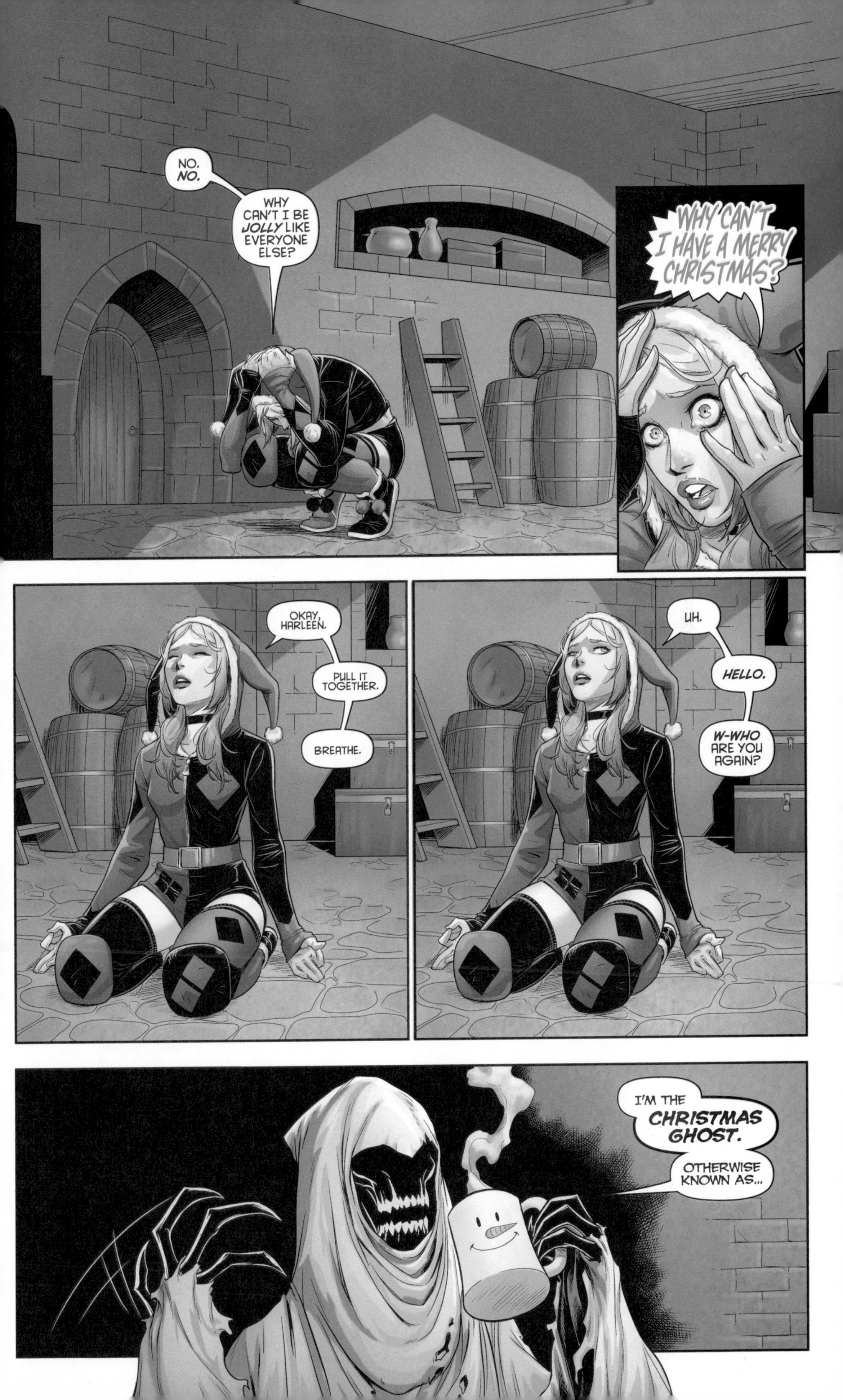

NO. *NO.*
WHY CAN'T I BE *JOLLY* LIKE EVERYONE ELSE?
WHY CAN'T I HAVE A MERRY CHRISTMAS?
OKAY, HARLEEN.
PULL IT TOGETHER.
BREATHE.
UH.
HELLO.
W-WHO ARE YOU AGAIN?
I'M THE **CHRISTMAS GHOST.**
OTHERWISE KNOWN AS...

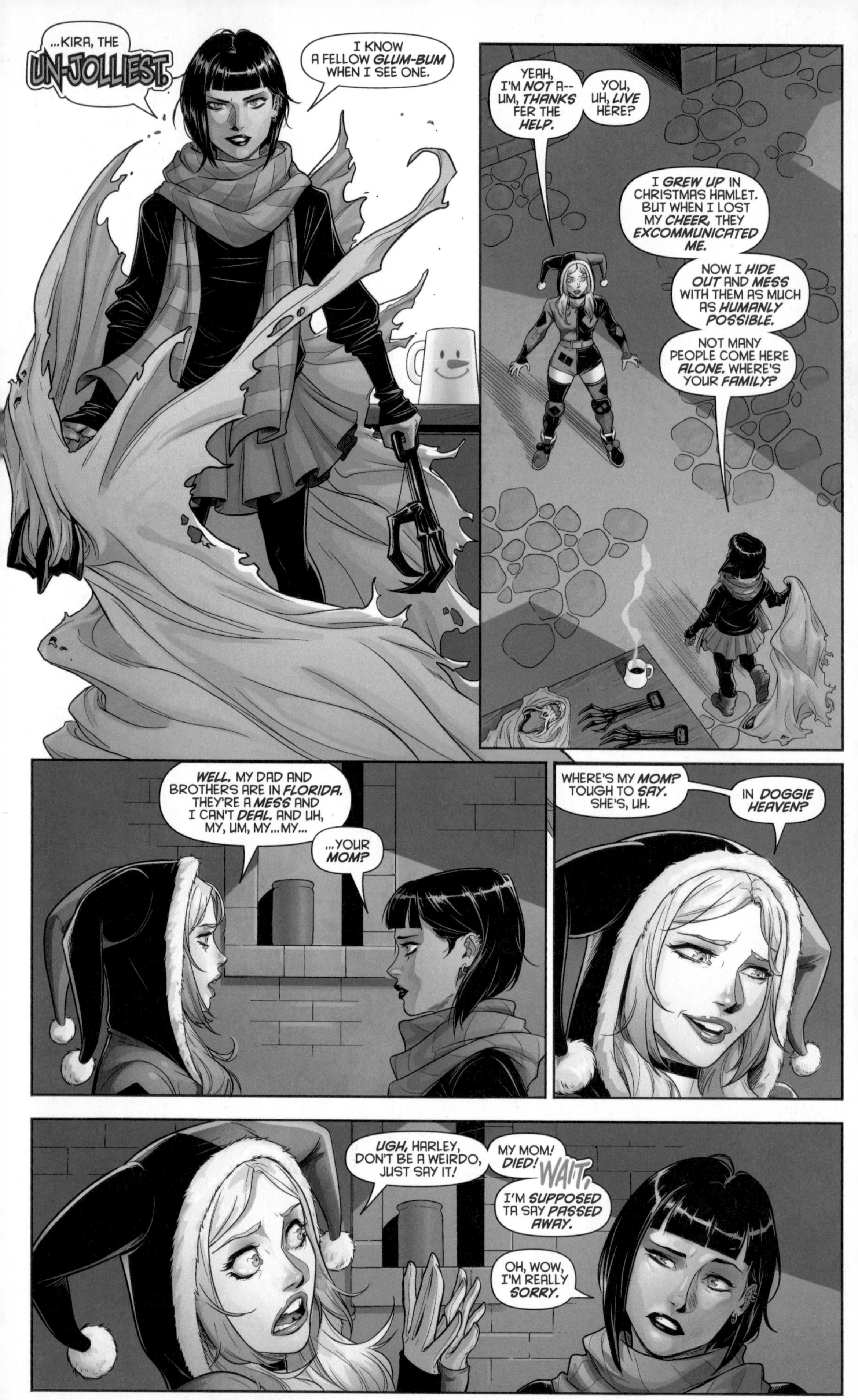

...KIRA, THE
UN-JOLLIEST.
I KNOW A FELLOW GLUM-BUM WHEN I SEE ONE.
YEAH, I'M NOT A-- UM, THANKS FER THE HELP.
YOU, UH, LIVE HERE?
I GREW UP IN CHRISTMAS HAMLET. BUT WHEN I LOST MY CHEER, THEY EXCOMMUNICATED ME.
NOW I HIDE OUT AND MESS WITH THEM AS MUCH AS HUMANLY POSSIBLE.
NOT MANY PEOPLE COME HERE ALONE. WHERE'S YOUR FAMILY?
WELL. MY DAD AND BROTHERS ARE IN FLORIDA. THEY'RE A MESS AND I CAN'T DEAL. AND UH, MY, UM, MY...MY...
...YOUR MOM?
WHERE'S MY MOM? TOUGH TO SAY. SHE'S, UH.
IN DOGGIE HEAVEN?
UGH, HARLEY, DON'T BE A WEIRDO, JUST SAY IT!
MY MOM! DIED!
WAIT,
I'M SUPPOSED TA SAY PASSED AWAY.
OH, WOW, I'M REALLY SORRY.

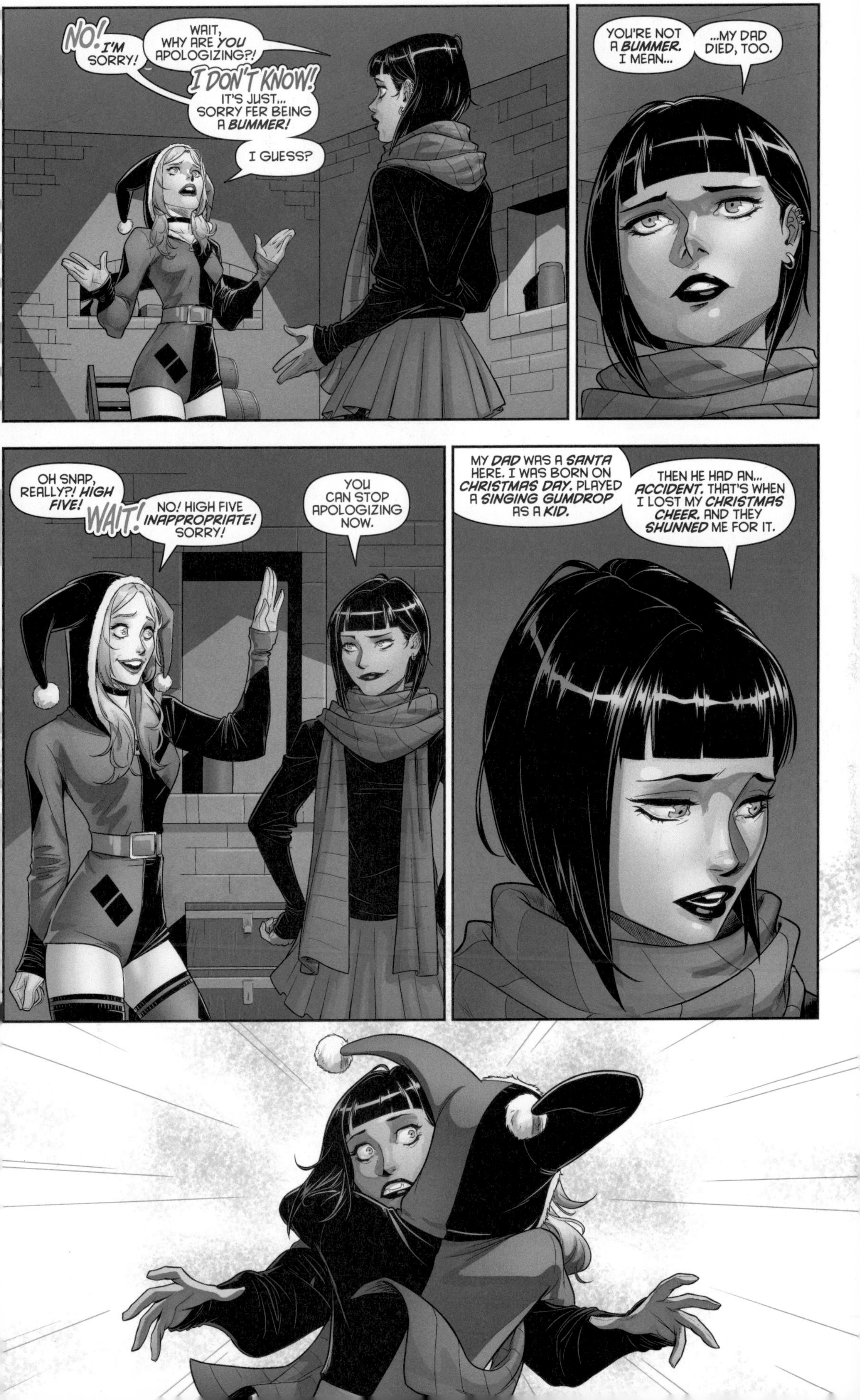
NO! I'M SORRY!
WAIT, WHY ARE YOU APOLOGIZING?!
I DON'T KNOW! IT'S JUST... SORRY FER BEING A BUMMER!
I GUESS?
YOU'RE NOT A BUMMER. I MEAN...
...MY DAD DIED, TOO.
OH SNAP, REALLY?! HIGH FIVE!
WAIT! NO! HIGH FIVE INAPPROPRIATE! SORRY!
YOU CAN STOP APOLOGIZING NOW.
MY DAD WAS A SANTA HERE. I WAS BORN ON CHRISTMAS DAY. PLAYED A SINGING GUMDROP AS A KID.
THEN HE HAD AN... ACCIDENT. THAT'S WHEN I LOST MY CHRISTMAS CHEER. AND THEY SHUNNED ME FOR IT.

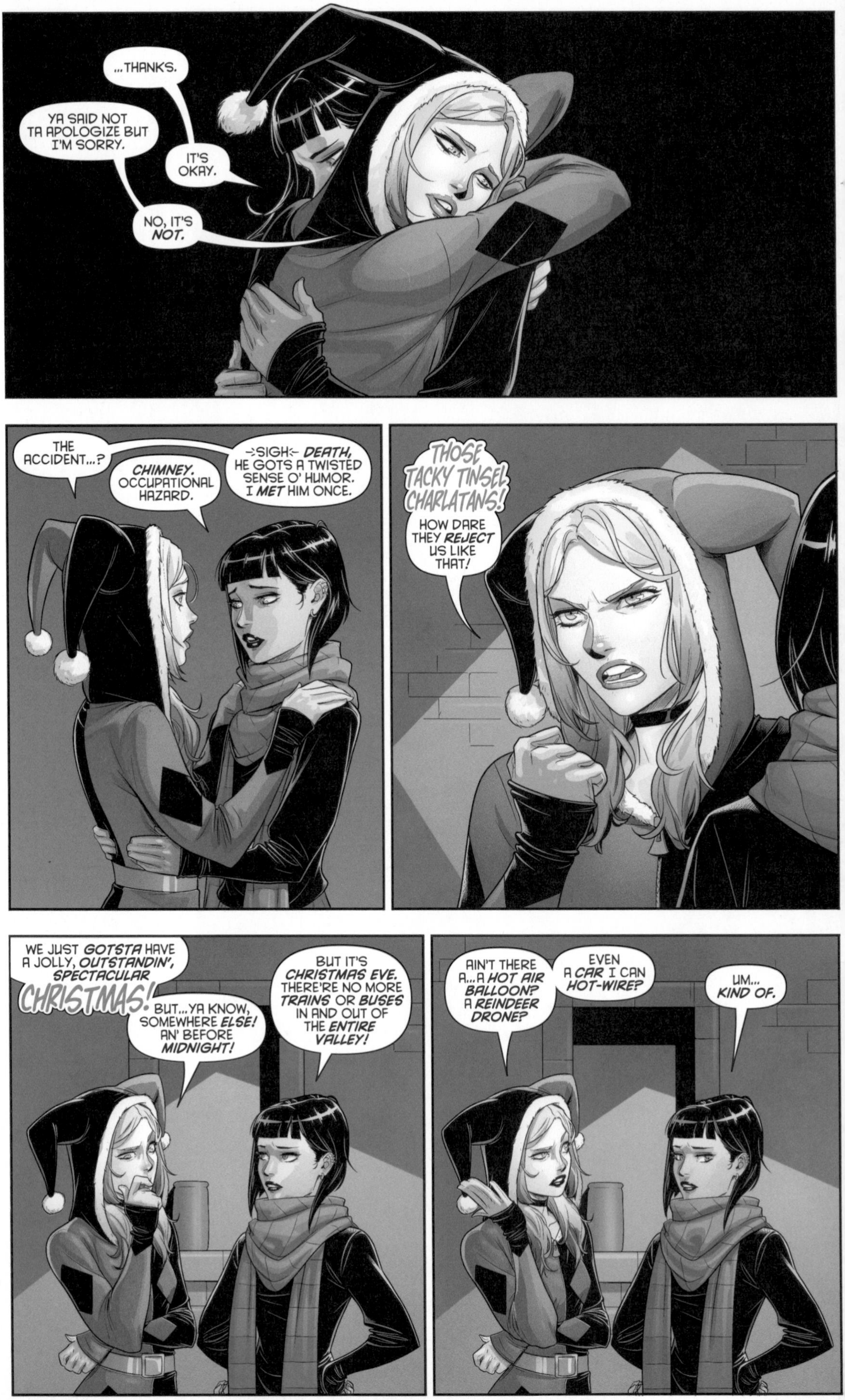

...THANKS.
YA SAID NOT TA APOLOGIZE BUT I'M SORRY.
IT'S OKAY.
NO, IT'S *NOT.*
THE ACCIDENT...?
CHIMNEY. OCCUPATIONAL HAZARD.
-SIGH- *DEATH,* HE GOTS A TWISTED SENSE O' HUMOR. I *MET* HIM ONCE.
THOSE TACKY TINSEL CHARLATANS!
HOW DARE THEY *REJECT* US LIKE THAT!
WE JUST *GOTSTA* HAVE A JOLLY, *OUTSTANDIN',* *SPECTACULAR* CHRISTMAS!
BUT...YA KNOW, SOMEWHERE *ELSE!* AN' BEFORE *MIDNIGHT!*
BUT IT'S *CHRISTMAS EVE.* THERE'RE NO MORE *TRAINS* OR *BUSES* IN AND OUT OF THE *ENTIRE VALLEY!*
AIN'T THERE A...A *HOT AIR BALLOON?* A *REINDEER DRONE?*
EVEN A *CAR* I CAN *HOT-WIRE?*
UM... *KIND OF.*

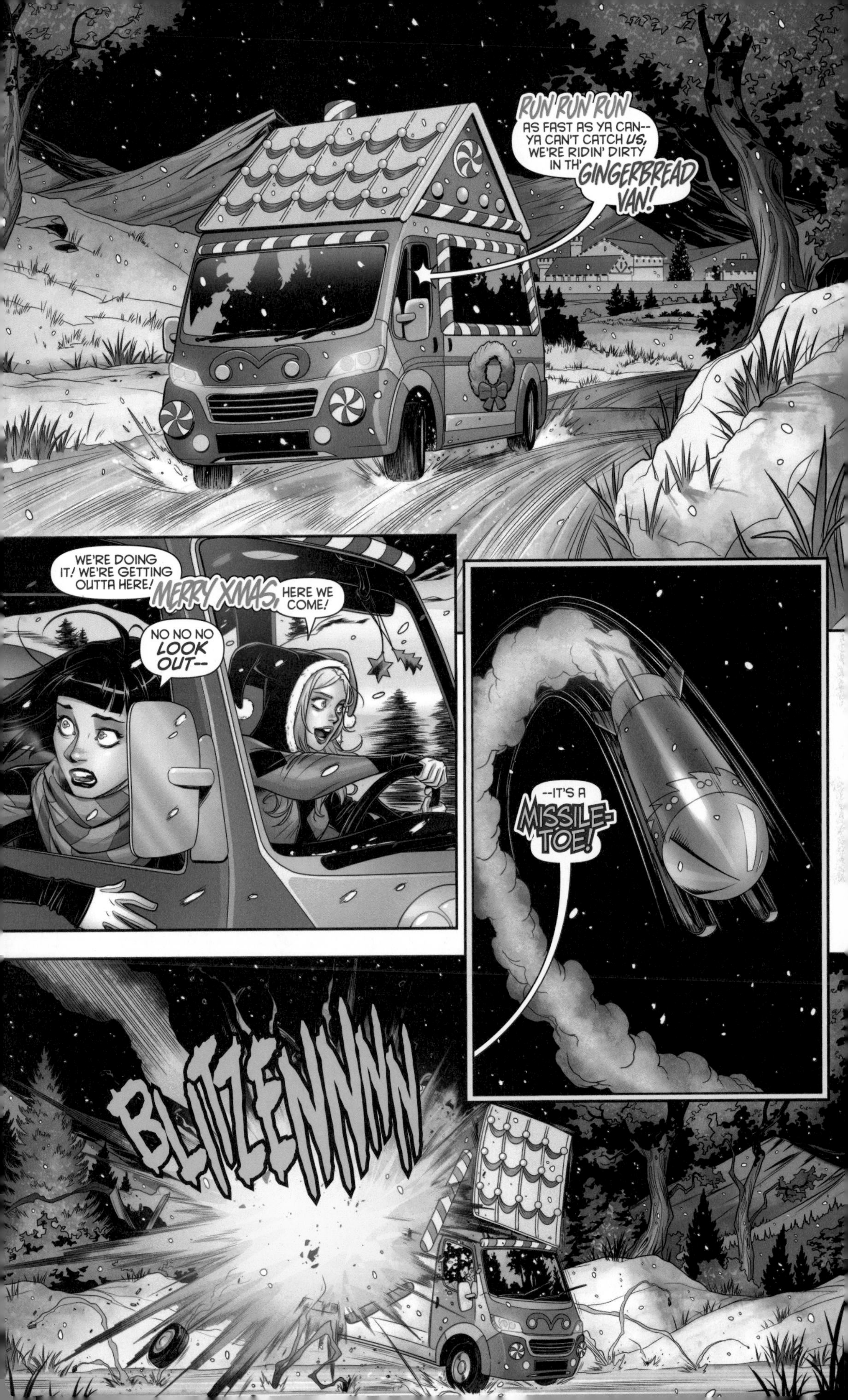
RUN RUN RUN
AS FAST AS YA CAN--
YA CAN'T CATCH US,
WE'RE RIDIN' DIRTY
IN TH' GINGERBREAD VAN!
WE'RE DOING IT! WE'RE GETTING OUTTA HERE!
MERRY XMAS, HERE WE COME!
NO NO NO LOOK OUT--
--IT'S A MISSILE-TOE!
BLITZENNNNN

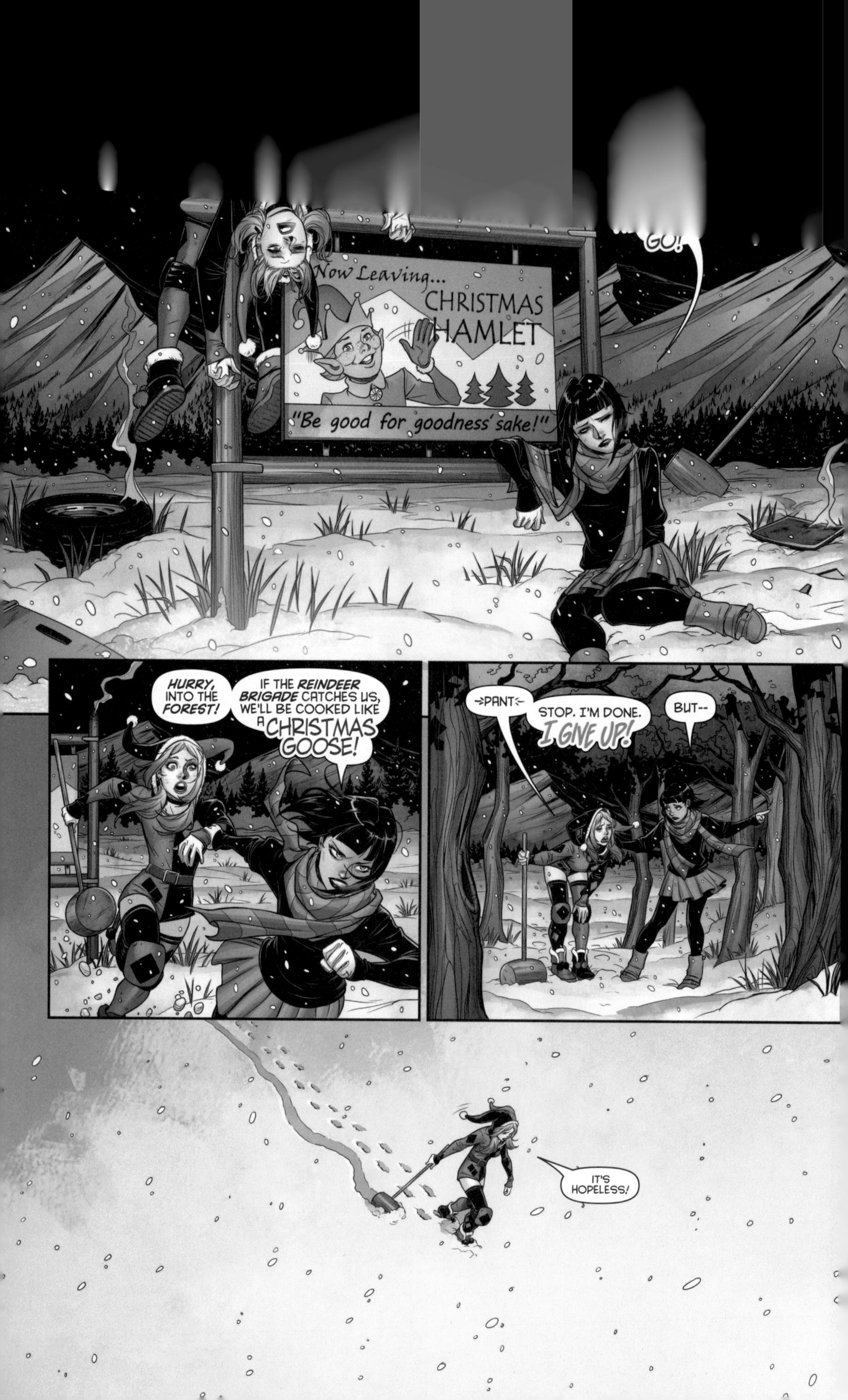
GO!
Now Leaving...
CHRISTMAS HAMLET
"Be good for goodness' sake!"
HURRY, INTO THE FOREST!
IF THE REINDEER BRIGADE CATCHES US, WE'LL BE COOKED LIKE A CHRISTMAS GOOSE!
PANT
STOP. I'M DONE. I GIVE UP!
BUT--
IT'S HOPELESS!

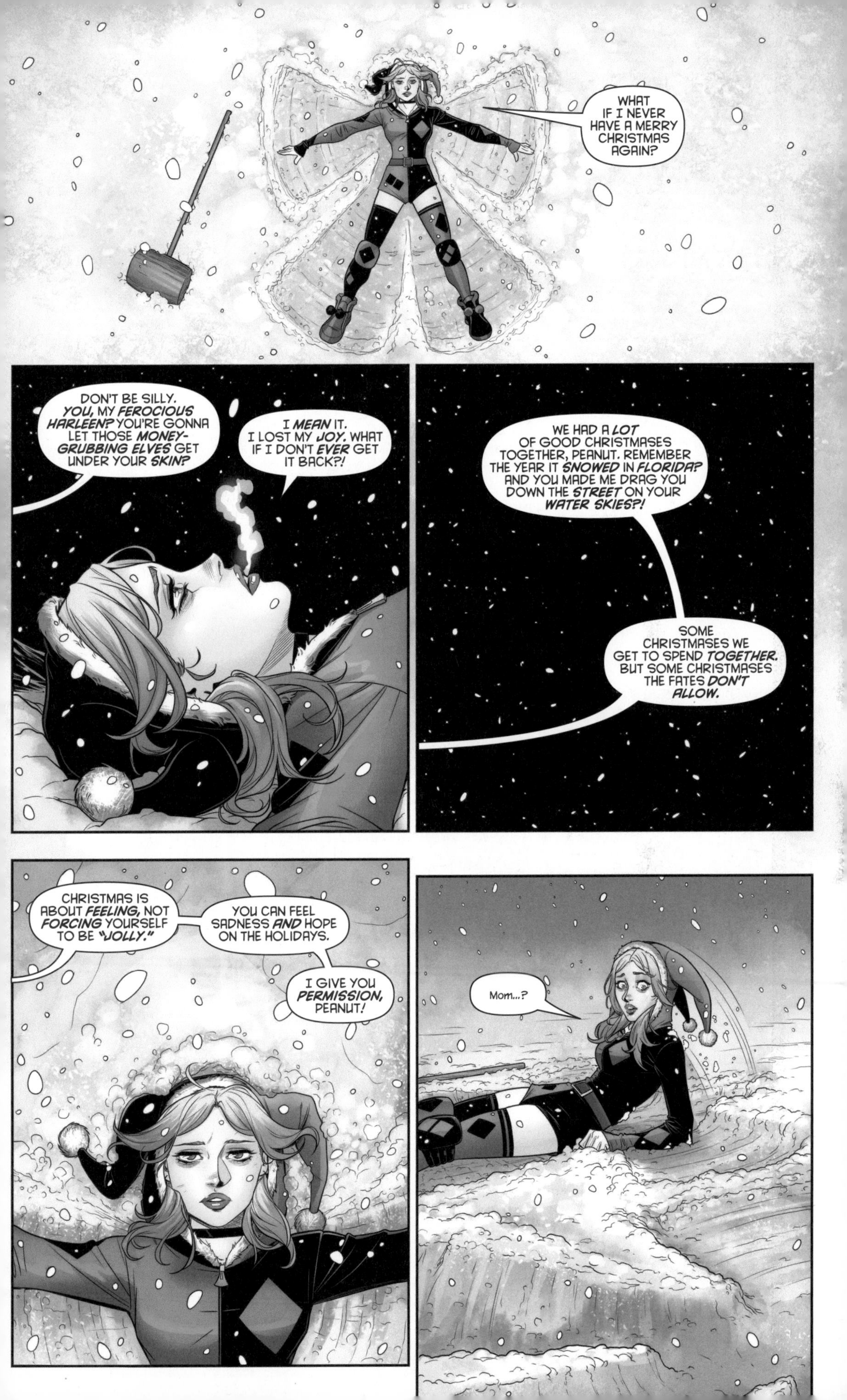
WHAT IF I NEVER HAVE A MERRY CHRISTMAS AGAIN?
DON'T BE SILLY. YOU, MY FEROCIOUS HARLEEN? YOU'RE GONNA LET THOSE MONEY-GRUBBING ELVES GET UNDER YOUR SKIN?
I MEAN IT. I LOST MY JOY. WHAT IF I DON'T EVER GET IT BACK?!
WE HAD A LOT OF GOOD CHRISTMASES TOGETHER, PEANUT. REMEMBER THE YEAR IT SNOWED IN FLORIDA? AND YOU MADE ME DRAG YOU DOWN THE STREET ON YOUR WATER SKIES?!
SOME CHRISTMASES WE GET TO SPEND TOGETHER. BUT SOME CHRISTMASES THE FATES DON'T ALLOW.
CHRISTMAS IS ABOUT FEELING, NOT FORCING YOURSELF TO BE "JOLLY."
YOU CAN FEEL SADNESS AND HOPE ON THE HOLIDAYS.
I GIVE YOU PERMISSION, PEANUT!
Mom...?

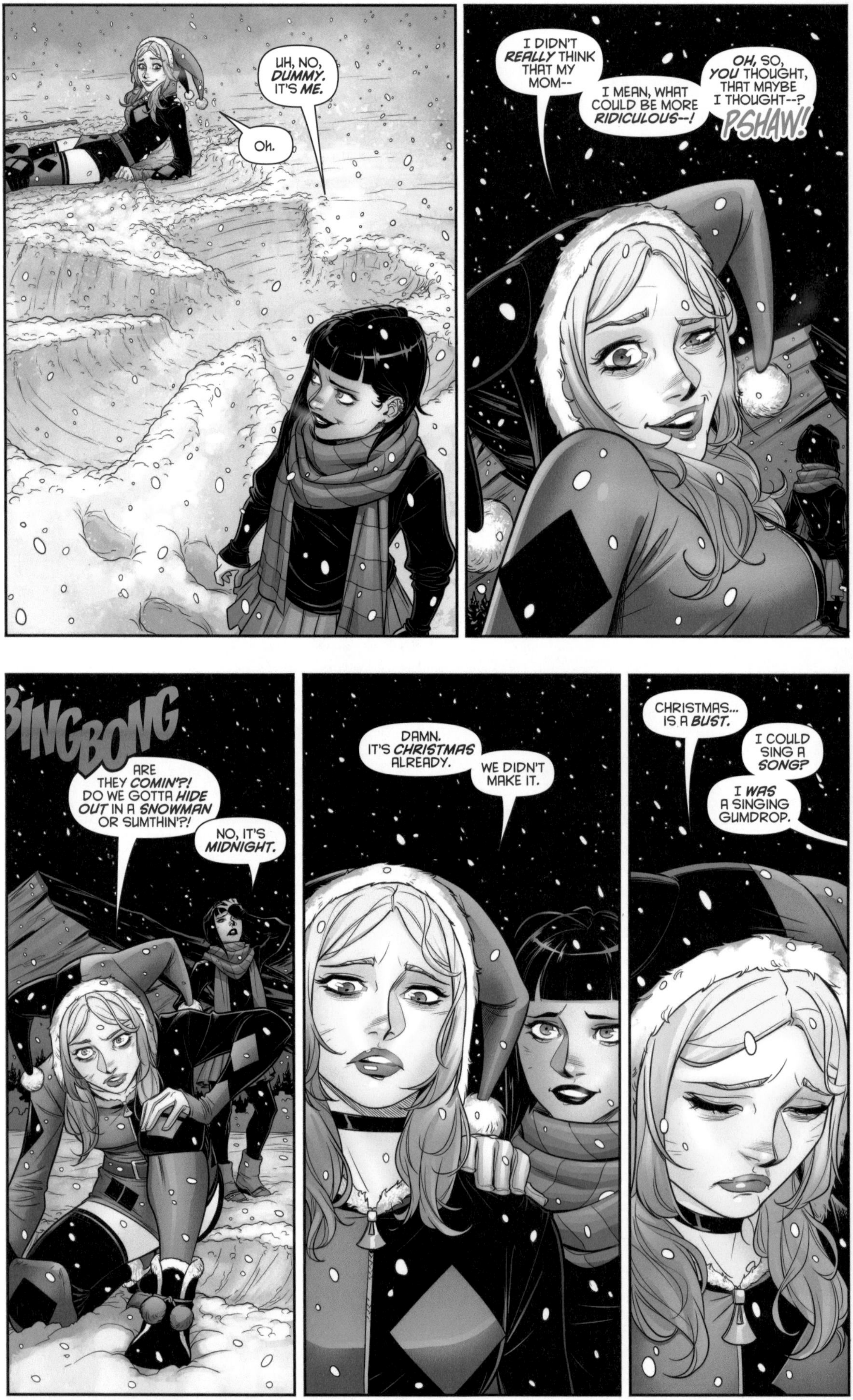
UH, NO, DUMMY. IT'S ME.
Oh.
I DIDN'T REALLY THINK THAT MY MOM--
I MEAN, WHAT COULD BE MORE RIDICULOUS--!
OH, SO, YOU THOUGHT, THAT MAYBE I THOUGHT--?
PSHAW!
BINGBONG
ARE THEY COMIN'?! DO WE GOTTA HIDE OUT IN A SNOWMAN OR SUMTHIN'?!
NO, IT'S MIDNIGHT.
DAMN. IT'S CHRISTMAS ALREADY.
WE DIDN'T MAKE IT.
CHRISTMAS... IS A BUST.
I COULD SING A SONG?
I WAS A SINGING GUMDROP.

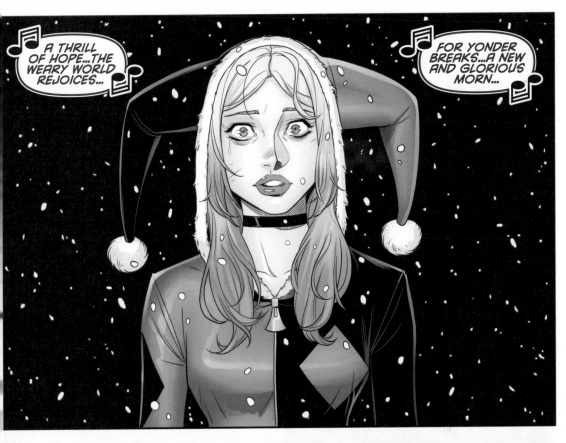

♪ A THRILL OF HOPE...THE WEARY WORLD REJOICES...

♪ FOR YONDER BREAKS...A NEW AND GLORIOUS MORN...

‡SNIFF‡

HARLEY? YOU OKAY?

HM, *ME*? SURE. I'M FINE. JUST *FINE*.

WHAT? DON'T LOOK AT ME LIKE THAT. IT'S A BEAUTIFUL SONG. *SUE* ME.

THAP

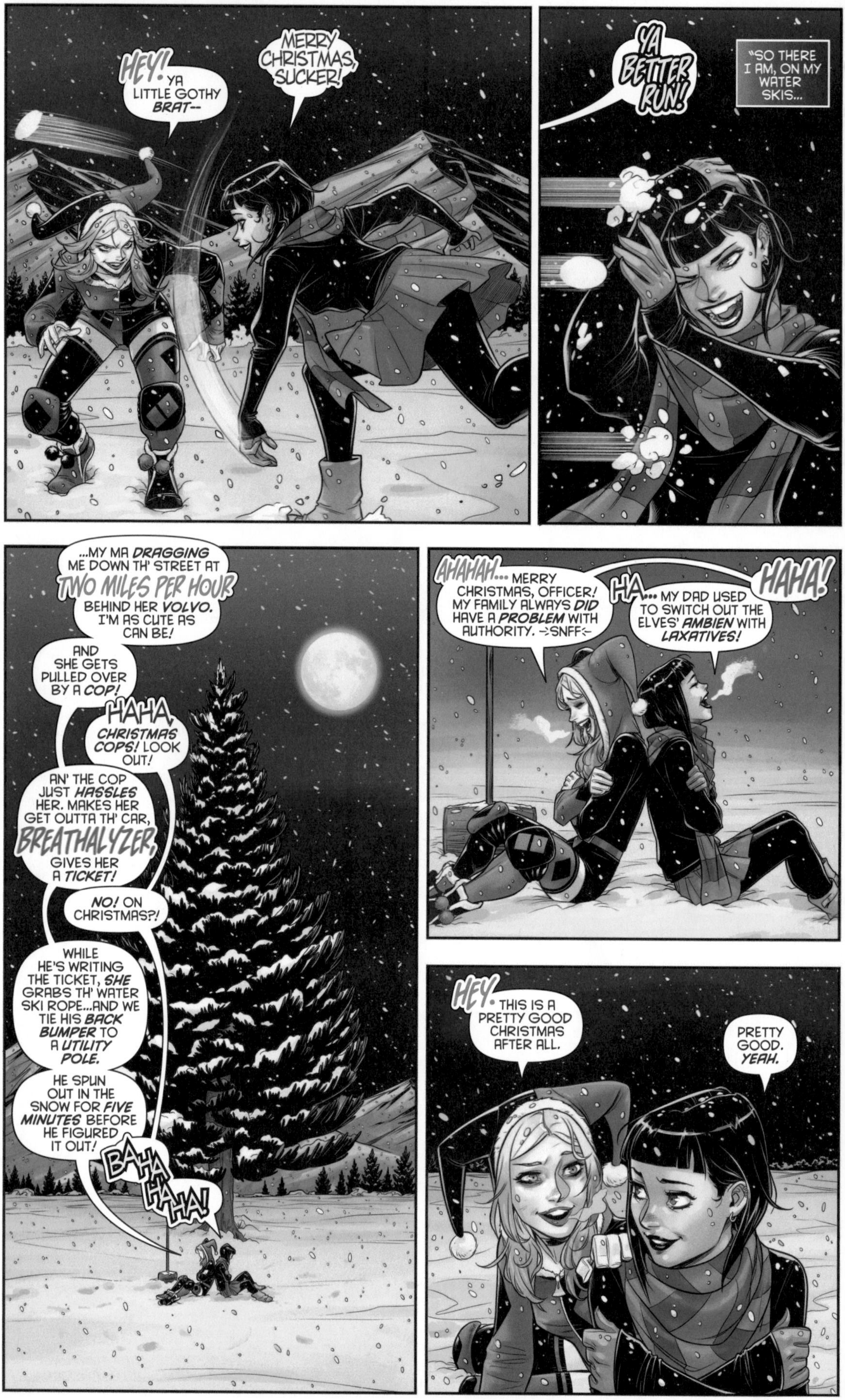
HEY! YA LITTLE GOTHY BRAT--
MERRY CHRISTMAS, SUCKER!
YA BETTER RUN!
"SO THERE I AM, ON MY WATER SKIS...
...MY MA DRAGGING ME DOWN TH' STREET AT TWO MILES PER HOUR BEHIND HER VOLVO. I'M AS CUTE AS CAN BE!
AND SHE GETS PULLED OVER BY A COP!
HAHA, CHRISTMAS COPS! LOOK OUT!
AN' THE COP JUST HASSLES HER. MAKES HER GET OUTTA TH' CAR, BREATHALYZER, GIVES HER A TICKET!
NO! ON CHRISTMAS?!
WHILE HE'S WRITING THE TICKET, SHE GRABS TH' WATER SKI ROPE...AND WE TIE HIS BACK BUMPER TO A UTILITY POLE.
HE SPUN OUT IN THE SNOW FOR FIVE MINUTES BEFORE HE FIGURED IT OUT!
BAHAHAHA!
AHAHAH... MERRY CHRISTMAS, OFFICER! MY FAMILY ALWAYS DID HAVE A PROBLEM WITH AUTHORITY. -SNFF-
HA... MY DAD USED TO SWITCH OUT THE ELVES' AMBIEN WITH LAXATIVES!
HAHA!
HEY. THIS IS A PRETTY GOOD CHRISTMAS AFTER ALL.
PRETTY GOOD. YEAH.

EXCEPT I AM A *TEENSY BIT* FREEZING MY COCKLES OFF.

I GOTCHU. I'VE SPENT A LOT OF NIGHTS OUT HERE...

KLIK KLIK

ALLEY OOP!

FWOOOOOSH!!

YER A *DEMENTED GIRL SCOUT FROM HELL*...AND I LOVE IT.

RIGHT? NOW YOU SEE WHY THEY CAN'T STAND ME AT THE *HAMLET.*

Hm.

HOW FAR DO YOU THINK I COULD HIT ONE O' THEM PINE CONES WITH THIS *SANTA'S LITTLE HELPER?*

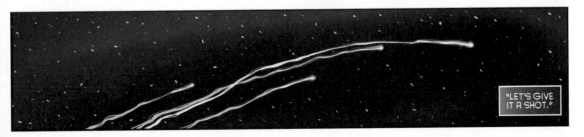

"LET'S GIVE IT A SHOT."

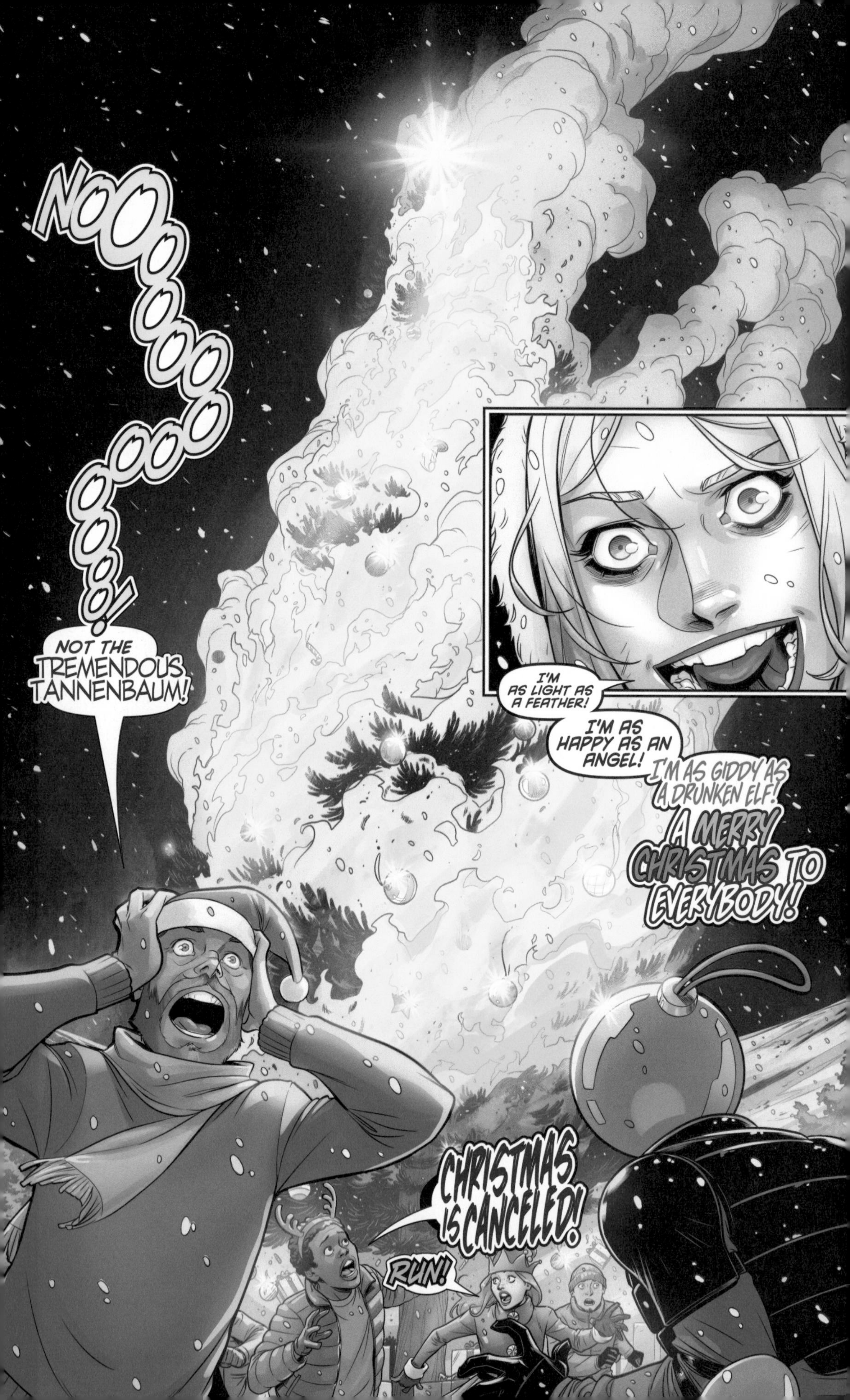
NOOOOOOOOOOOOOO!
NOT THE TREMENDOUS TANNENBAUM!
I'M AS LIGHT AS A FEATHER!
I'M AS HAPPY AS AN ANGEL!
I'M AS GIDDY AS A DRUNKEN ELF!
A MERRY CHRISTMAS TO EVERYBODY!
CHRISTMAS IS CANCELED!
RUN!

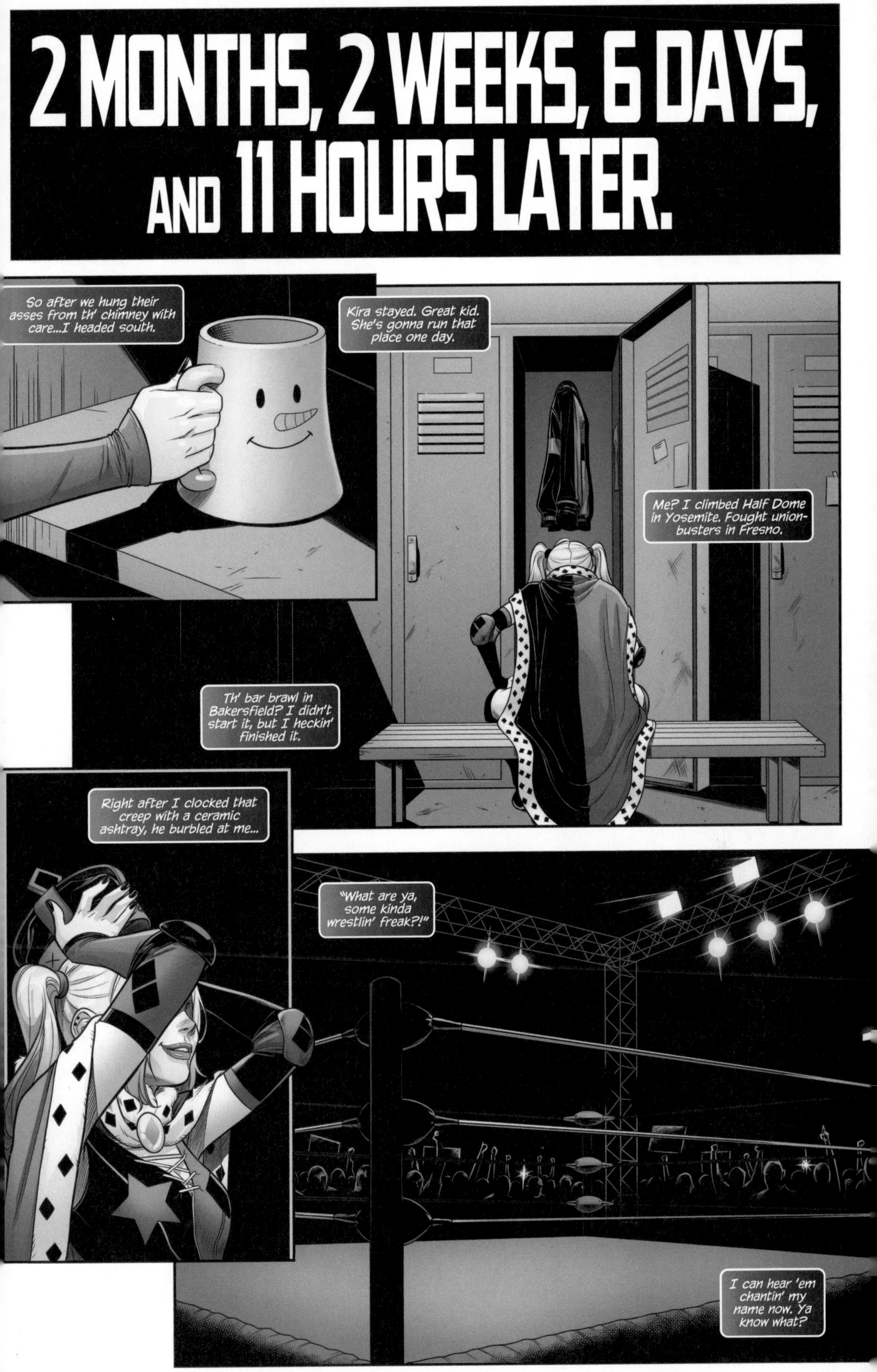
2 MONTHS, 2 WEEKS, 6 DAYS, AND 11 HOURS LATER.
So after we hung their asses from th' chimney with care...I headed south.
Kira stayed. Great kid. She's gonna run that place one day.
Me? I climbed Half Dome in Yosemite. Fought union-busters in Fresno.
Th' bar brawl in Bakersfield? I didn't start it, but I heckin' finished it.
Right after I clocked that creep with a ceramic ashtray, he burbled at me...
"What are ya, some kinda wrestlin' freak?!"
I can hear 'em chantin' my name now. Ya know what?

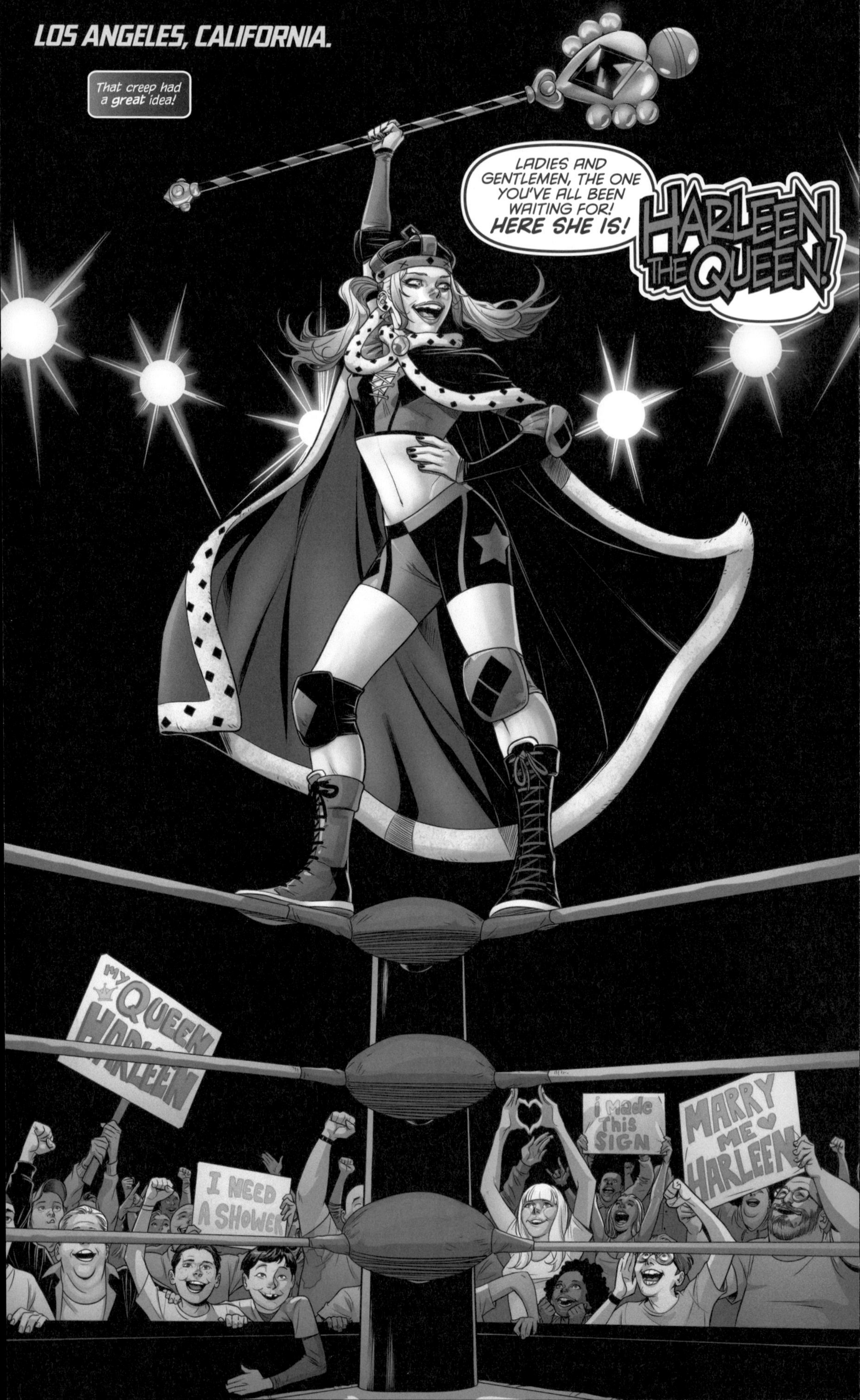

LOS ANGELES, CALIFORNIA.
That creep had a **great** idea!
LADIES AND GENTLEMEN, THE ONE YOU'VE ALL BEEN WAITING FOR! **HERE SHE IS!**
HARLEEN THE QUEEN!
MY QUEEN HARLEEN
I NEED A SHOWER
i Made This SIGN
MARRY ME HARLEEN

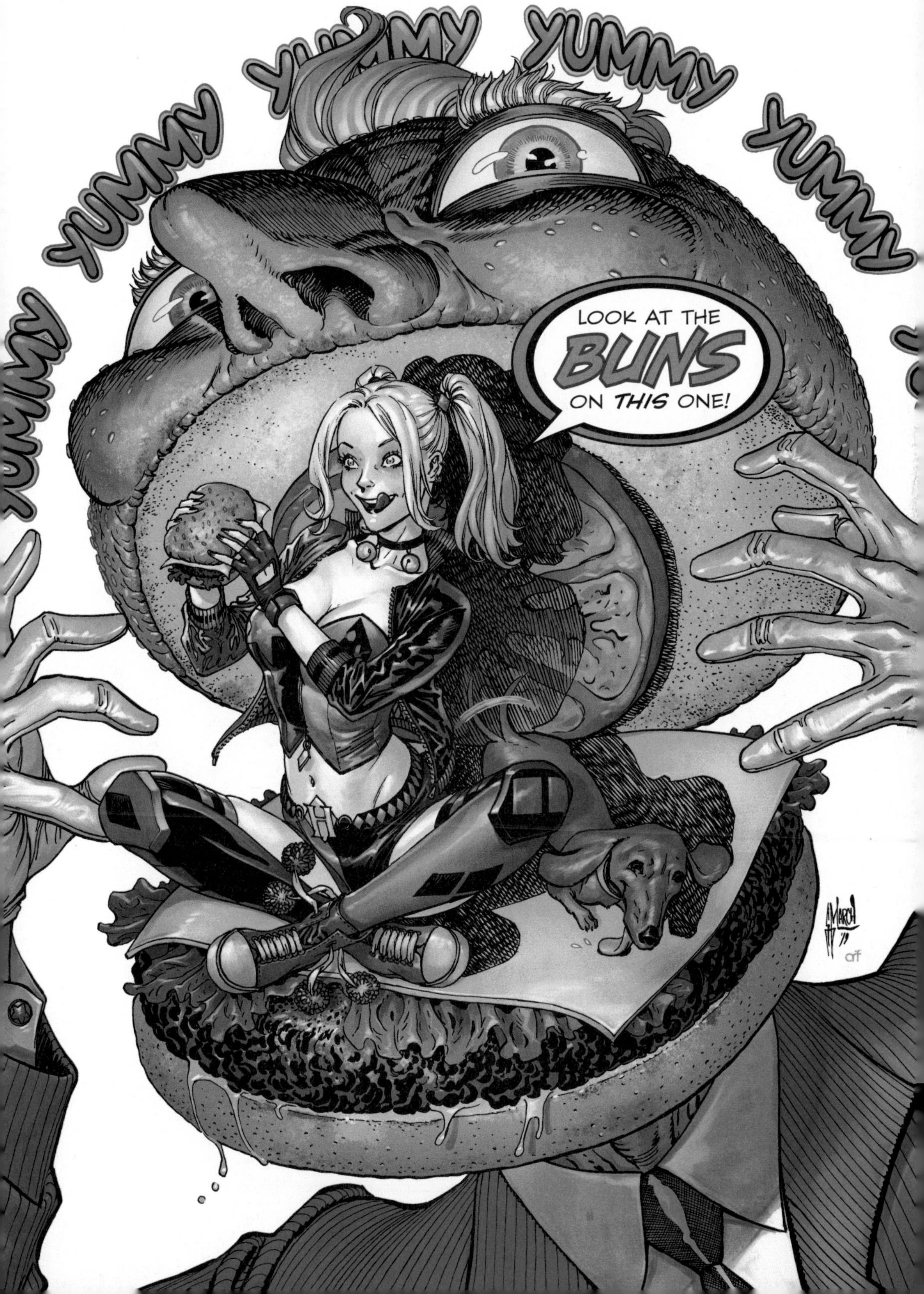
YUMMY YUMMY YUMMY YUMMY YUMMY YUMMY
LOOK AT THE BUNS ON THIS ONE!

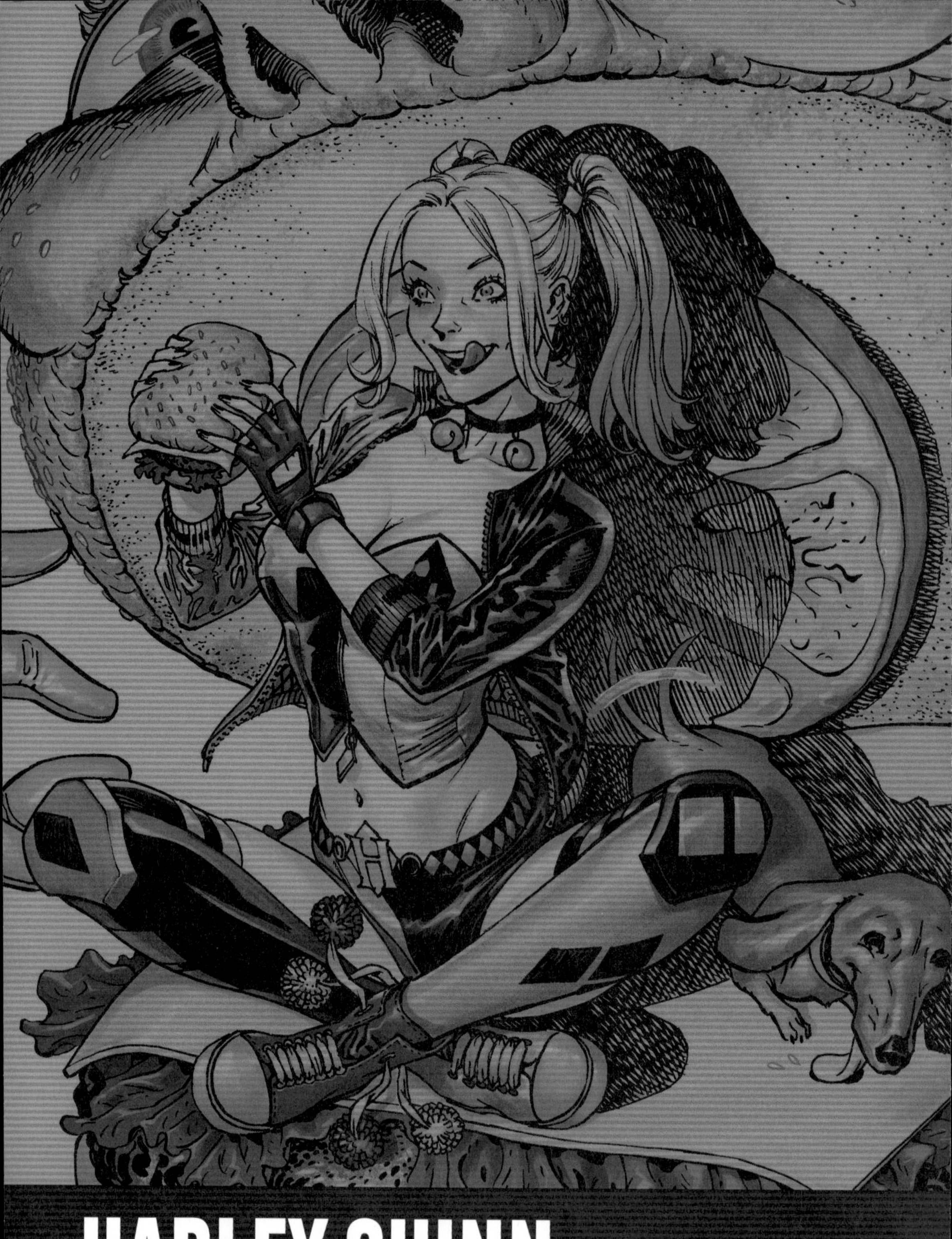

HARLEY QUINN
#69

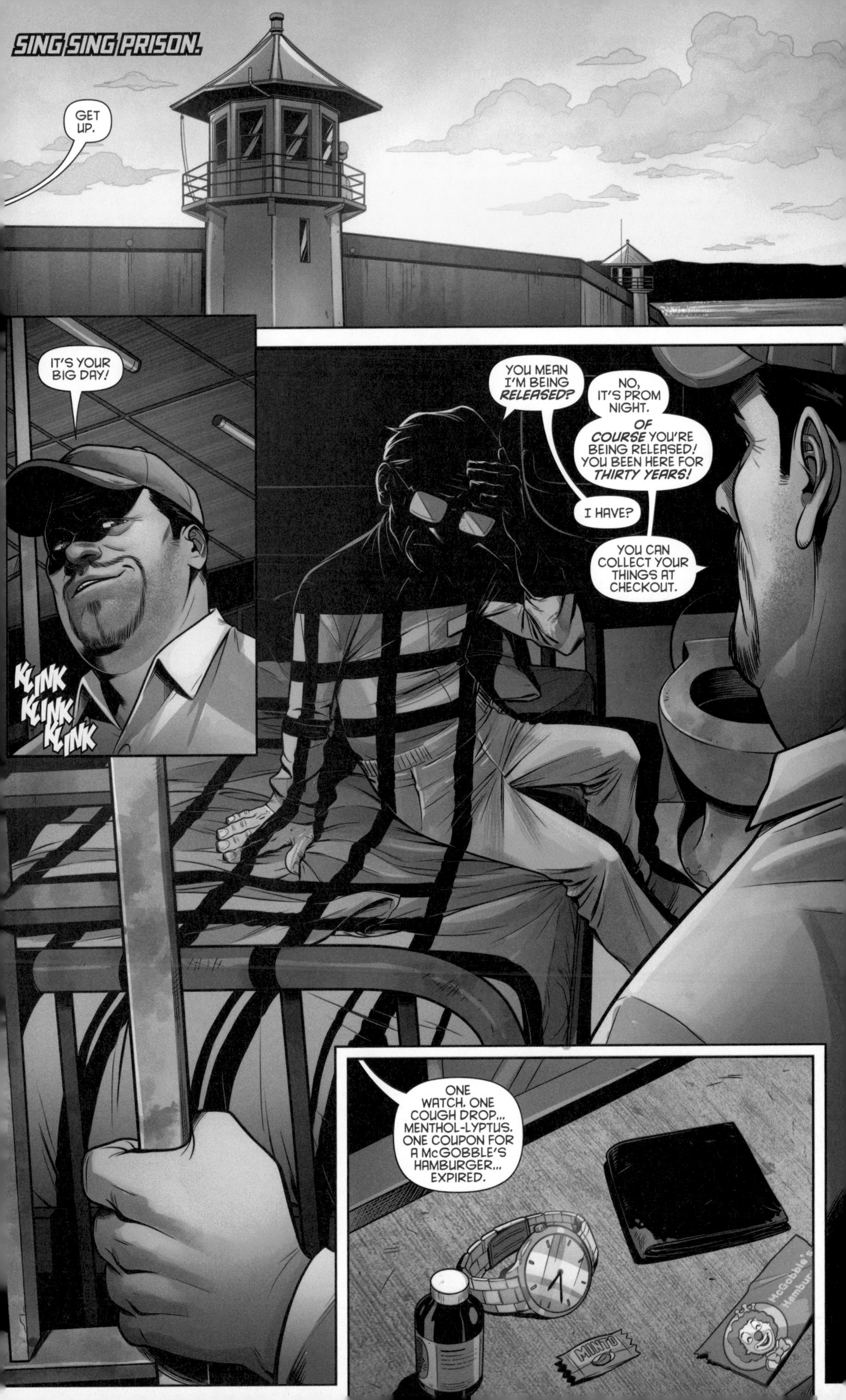
SING SING PRISON.
GET UP.
IT'S YOUR BIG DAY!
KLINK KLINK KLINK
YOU MEAN I'M BEING RELEASED?
NO, IT'S PROM NIGHT.
OF COURSE YOU'RE BEING RELEASED! YOU BEEN HERE FOR THIRTY YEARS!
I HAVE?
YOU CAN COLLECT YOUR THINGS AT CHECKOUT.
ONE WATCH. ONE COUGH DROP... MENTHOL-LYPTUS. ONE COUPON FOR A McGOBBLE'S HAMBURGER... EXPIRED.
MINTO

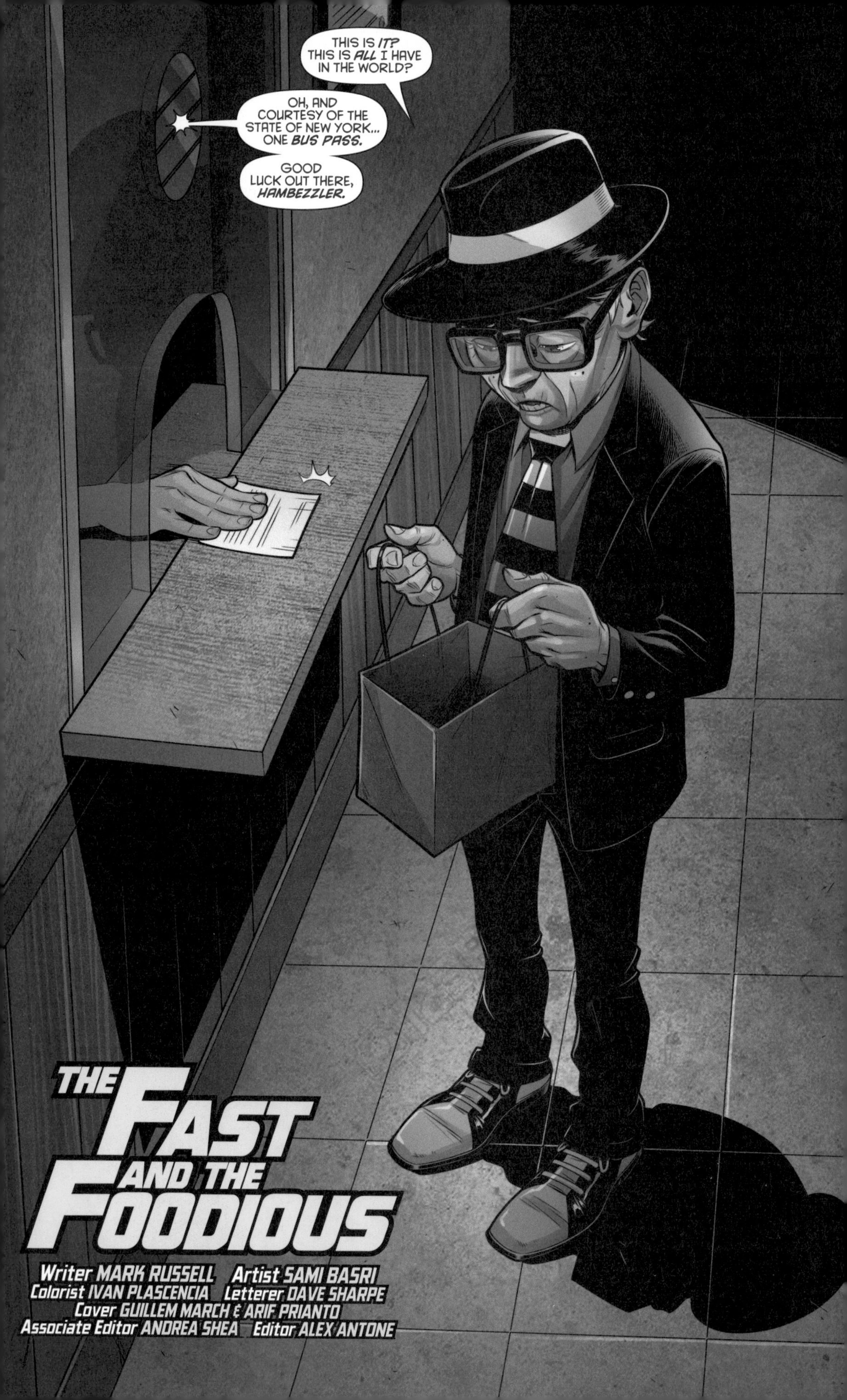
THIS IS IT? THIS IS ALL I HAVE IN THE WORLD?
OH, AND COURTESY OF THE STATE OF NEW YORK... ONE BUS PASS.
GOOD LUCK OUT THERE, HAMBEZZLER.
THE FAST AND THE FOODIOUS
Writer MARK RUSSELL Artist SAMI BASRI
Colorist IVAN PLASCENCIA Letterer DAVE SHARPE
Cover GUILLEM MARCH & ARIF PRIANTO
Associate Editor ANDREA SHEA Editor ALEX ANTONE

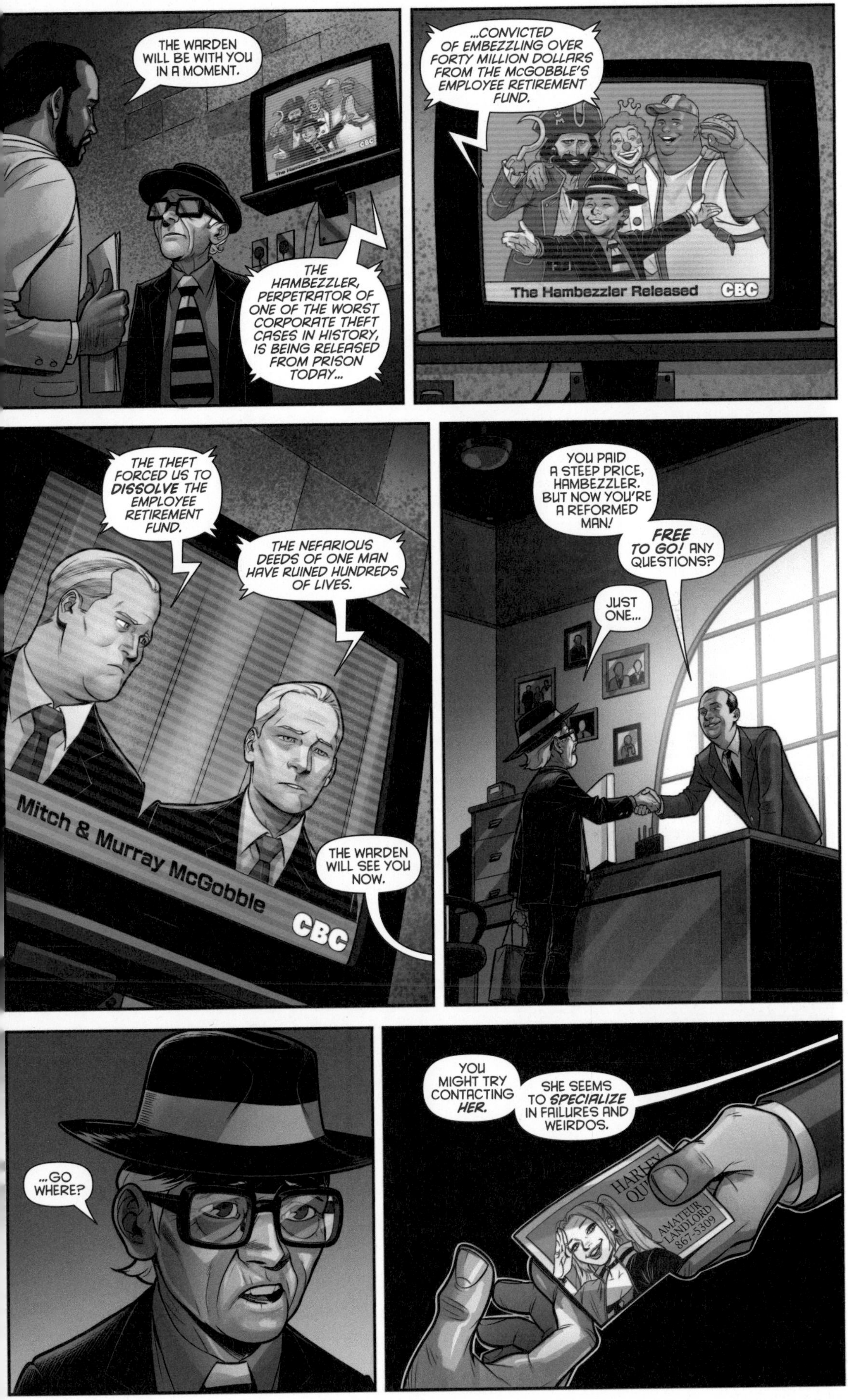
THE WARDEN WILL BE WITH YOU IN A MOMENT.
THE HAMBEZZLER, PERPETRATOR OF ONE OF THE WORST CORPORATE THEFT CASES IN HISTORY, IS BEING RELEASED FROM PRISON TODAY...
...CONVICTED OF EMBEZZLING OVER FORTY MILLION DOLLARS FROM THE McGOBBLE'S EMPLOYEE RETIREMENT FUND.
The Hambezzler Released
CBC
THE THEFT FORCED US TO DISSOLVE THE EMPLOYEE RETIREMENT FUND.
THE NEFARIOUS DEEDS OF ONE MAN HAVE RUINED HUNDREDS OF LIVES.
Mitch & Murray McGobble
CBC
THE WARDEN WILL SEE YOU NOW.
YOU PAID A STEEP PRICE, HAMBEZZLER. BUT NOW YOU'RE A REFORMED MAN!
FREE TO GO! ANY QUESTIONS?
JUST ONE...
...GO WHERE?
YOU MIGHT TRY CONTACTING HER.
SHE SEEMS TO SPECIALIZE IN FAILURES AND WEIRDOS.
AMATEUR LANDLORD
867-5309

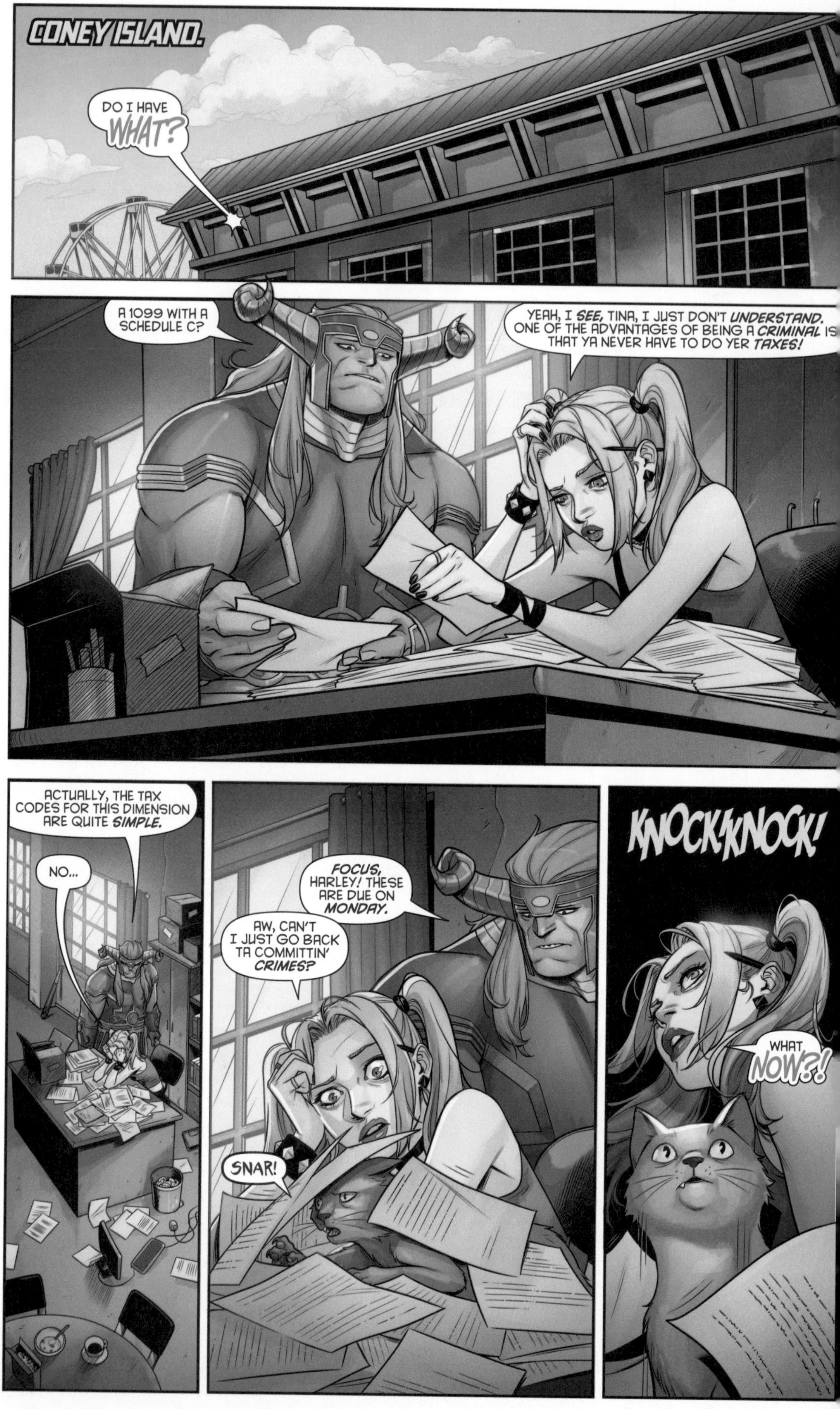
CONEY ISLAND.
DO I HAVE WHAT?
A 1099 WITH A SCHEDULE C?
YEAH, I *SEE*, TINA, I JUST DON'T *UNDERSTAND*. ONE OF THE ADVANTAGES OF BEING A *CRIMINAL* IS THAT YA NEVER HAVE TO DO YER *TAXES!*
ACTUALLY, THE TAX CODES FOR THIS DIMENSION ARE QUITE *SIMPLE*.
NO...
FOCUS, HARLEY! THESE ARE DUE ON *MONDAY*.
AW, CAN'T I JUST GO BACK TA COMMITTIN' *CRIMES?*
SNAR!
KNOCK KNOCK!
WHAT NOW?!

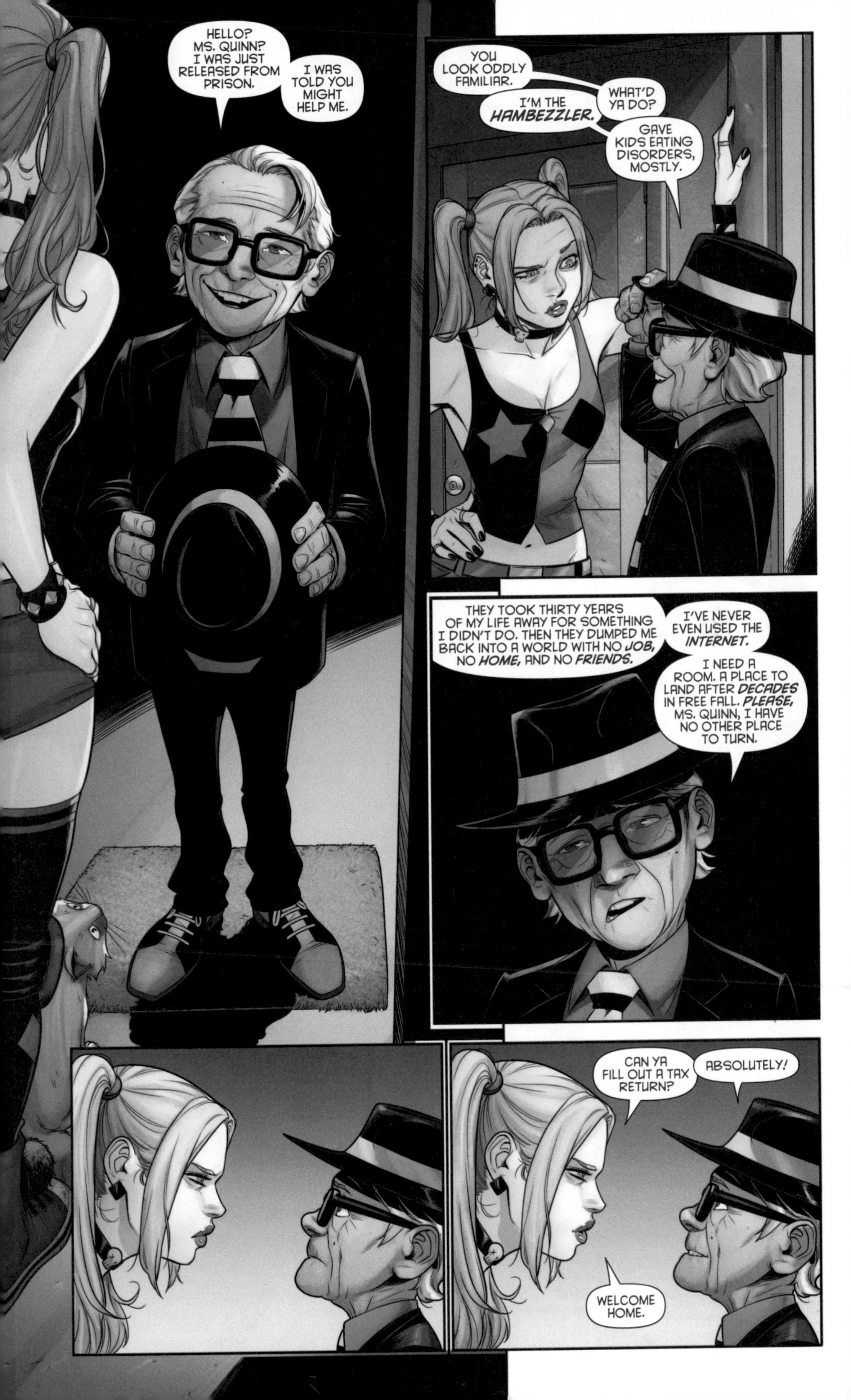
HELLO? MS. QUINN? I WAS JUST RELEASED FROM PRISON.
I WAS TOLD YOU MIGHT HELP ME.
YOU LOOK ODDLY FAMILIAR.
WHAT'D YA DO?
I'M THE HAMBEZZLER.
GAVE KIDS EATING DISORDERS, MOSTLY.
THEY TOOK THIRTY YEARS OF MY LIFE AWAY FOR SOMETHING I DIDN'T DO. THEN THEY DUMPED ME BACK INTO A WORLD WITH NO JOB, NO HOME, AND NO FRIENDS.
I'VE NEVER EVEN USED THE INTERNET.
I NEED A ROOM. A PLACE TO LAND AFTER DECADES IN FREE FALL. PLEASE, MS. QUINN, I HAVE NO OTHER PLACE TO TURN.
CAN YA FILL OUT A TAX RETURN?
ABSOLUTELY!
WELCOME HOME.

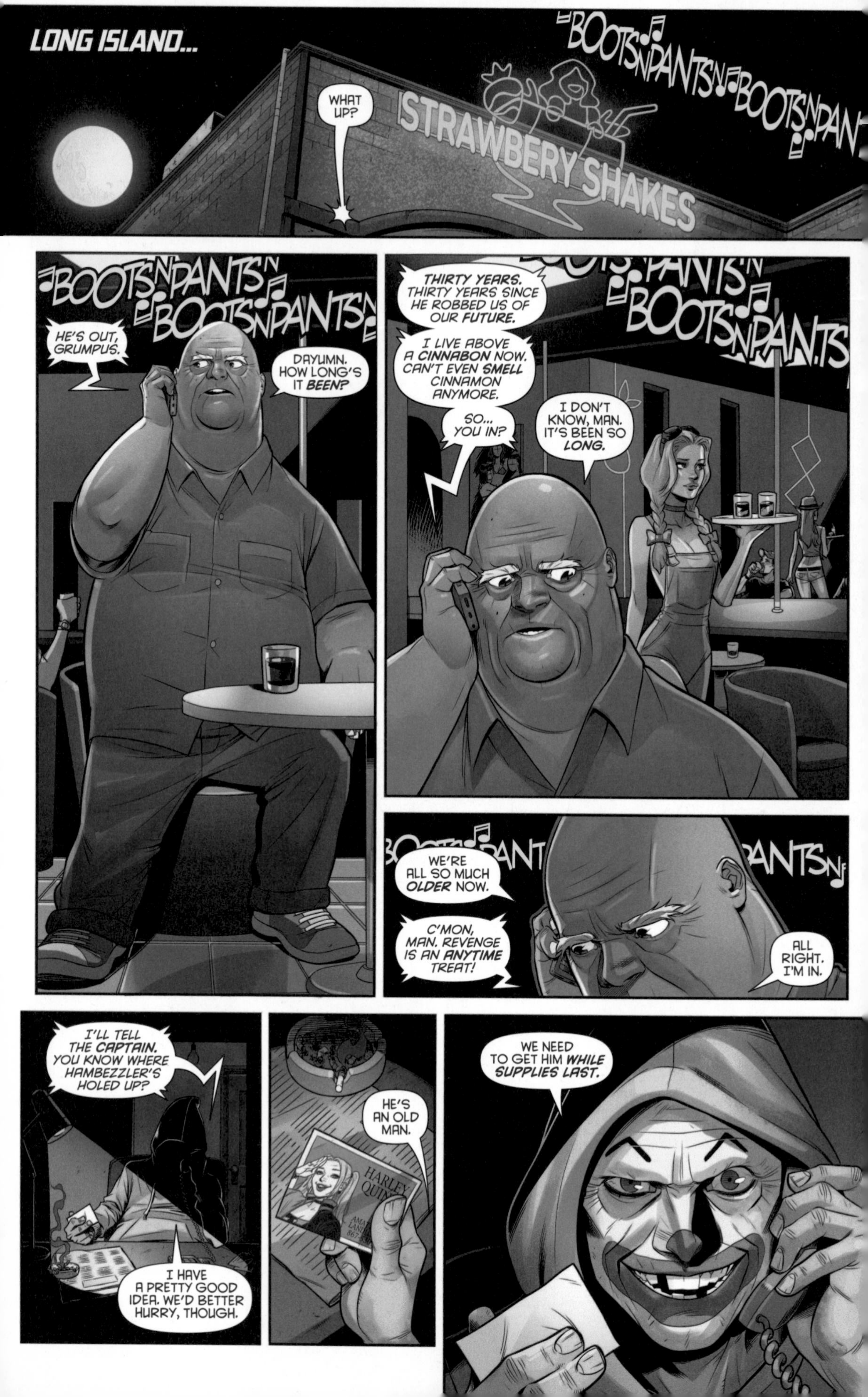
LONG ISLAND...
BOOTS N PANTS N BOOTS N PAN
WHAT UP?
STRAWBERY SHAKES
BOOTS N PANTS N BOOTS N PANTS N
HE'S OUT, GRUMPUS.
DAYUMN. HOW LONG'S IT BEEN?
THIRTY YEARS. THIRTY YEARS SINCE HE ROBBED US OF OUR FUTURE.
I LIVE ABOVE A CINNABON NOW. CAN'T EVEN SMELL CINNAMON ANYMORE.
SO... YOU IN?
I DON'T KNOW, MAN. IT'S BEEN SO LONG.
WE'RE ALL SO MUCH OLDER NOW.
C'MON, MAN. REVENGE IS AN ANYTIME TREAT!
ALL RIGHT. I'M IN.
I'LL TELL THE CAPTAIN. YOU KNOW WHERE HAMBEZZLER'S HOLED UP?
I HAVE A PRETTY GOOD IDEA. WE'D BETTER HURRY, THOUGH.
HE'S AN OLD MAN.
HARLEY QUINN
WE NEED TO GET HIM WHILE SUPPLIES LAST.

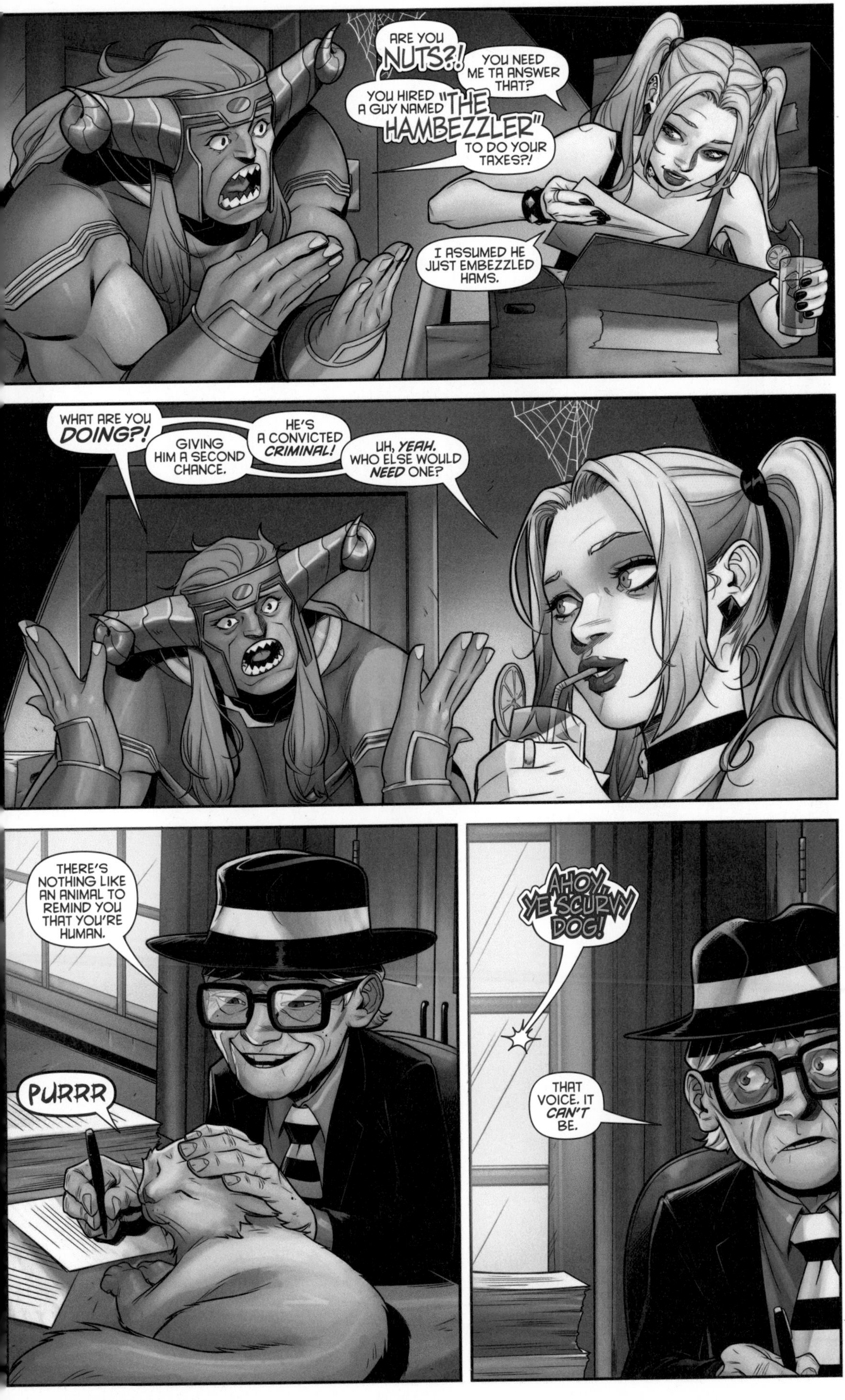
ARE YOU NUTS?!
YOU NEED ME TA ANSWER THAT?
YOU HIRED A GUY NAMED "THE HAMBEZZLER" TO DO YOUR TAXES?!
I ASSUMED HE JUST EMBEZZLED HAMS.
WHAT ARE YOU DOING?!
GIVING HIM A SECOND CHANCE.
HE'S A CONVICTED CRIMINAL!
UH, YEAH. WHO ELSE WOULD NEED ONE?
THERE'S NOTHING LIKE AN ANIMAL TO REMIND YOU THAT YOU'RE HUMAN.
PURRR
AHOY, YE SCURVY DOG!
THAT VOICE. IT CAN'T BE.

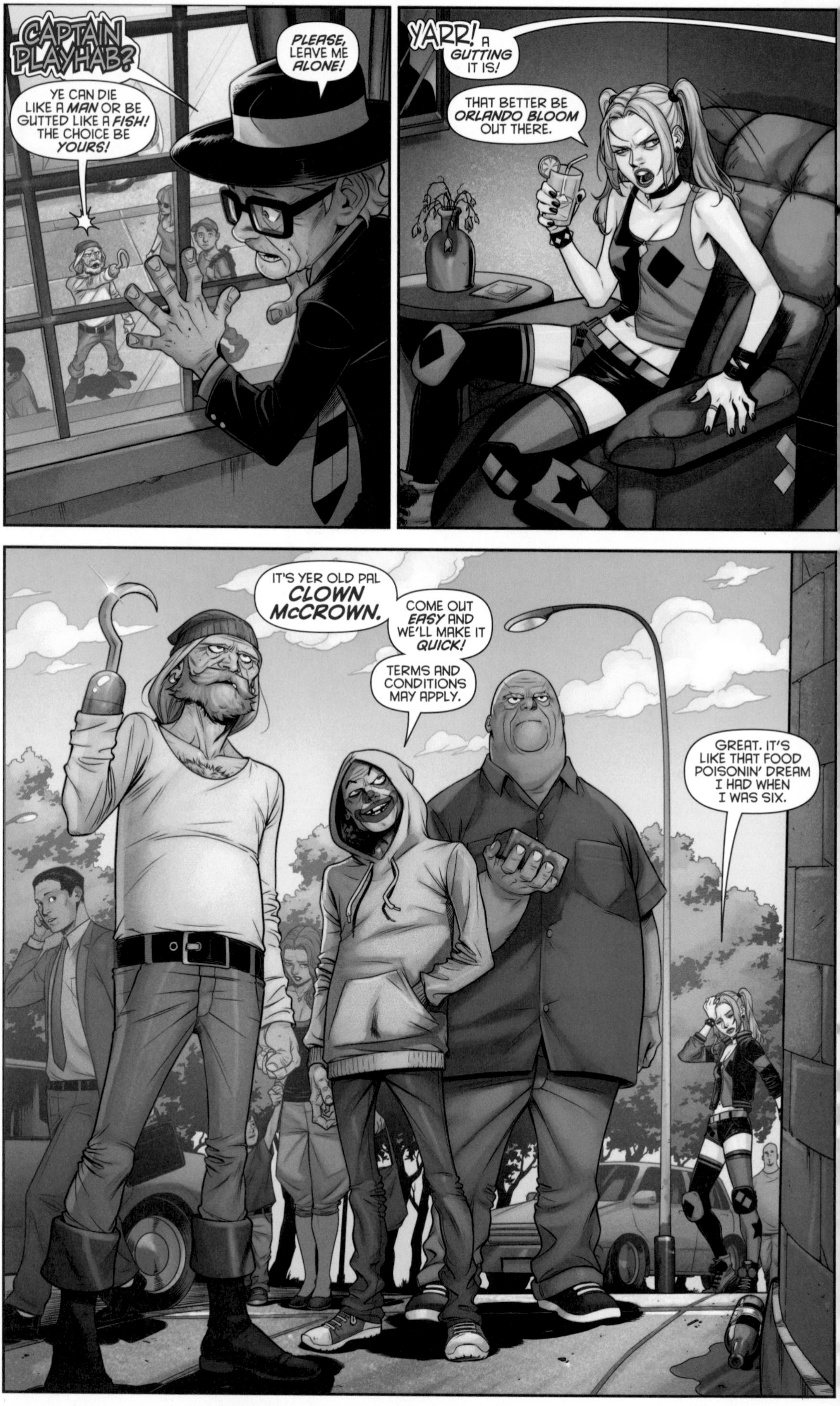
CAPTAIN PLAYHAB?
YE CAN DIE LIKE A MAN OR BE GUTTED LIKE A FISH! THE CHOICE BE YOURS!
PLEASE, LEAVE ME ALONE!
YARR! A GUTTING IT IS!
THAT BETTER BE ORLANDO BLOOM OUT THERE.
IT'S YER OLD PAL CLOWN McCROWN.
COME OUT EASY AND WE'LL MAKE IT QUICK!
TERMS AND CONDITIONS MAY APPLY.
GREAT. IT'S LIKE THAT FOOD POISONIN' DREAM I HAD WHEN I WAS SIX.

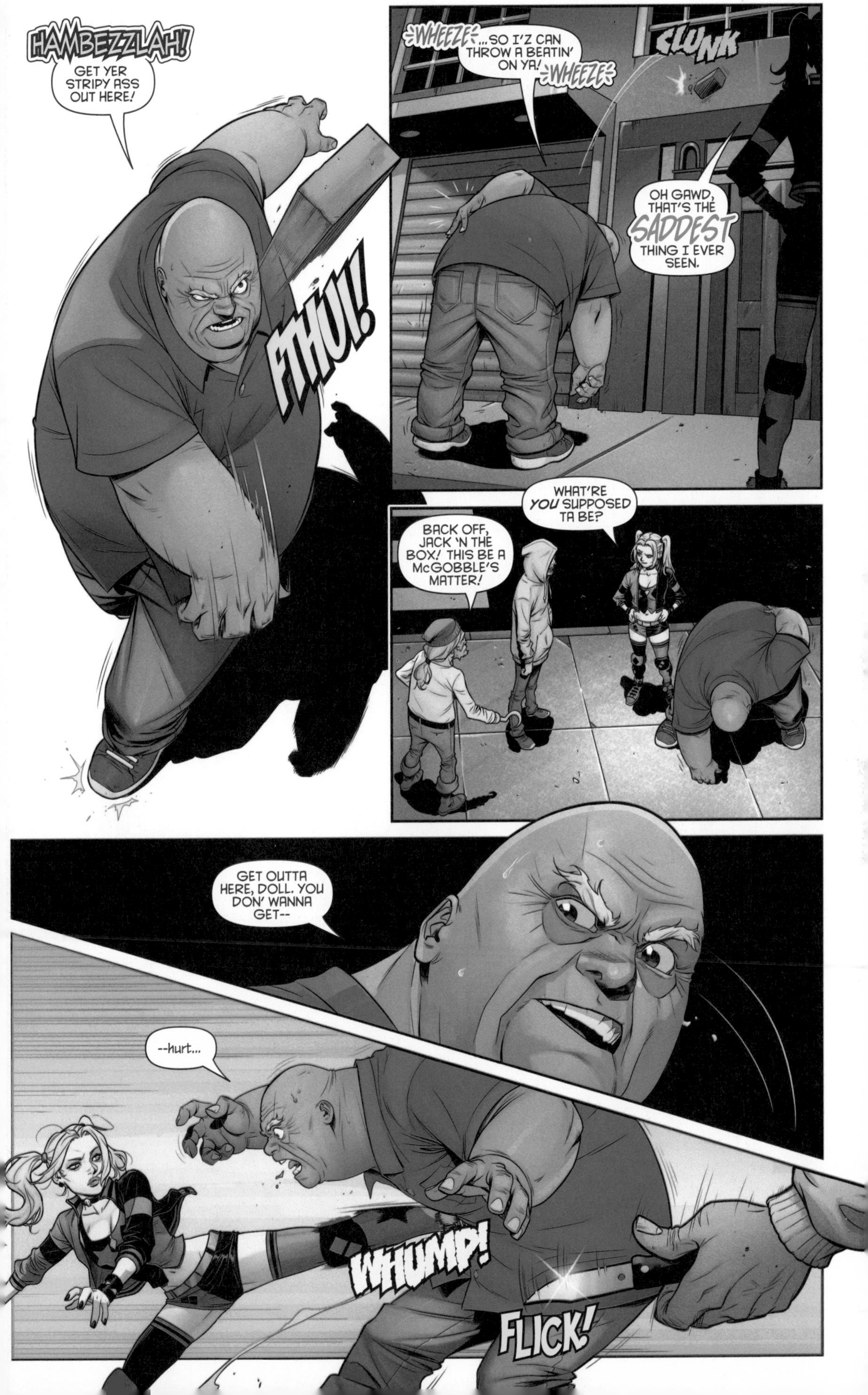
HAMBEZZLAH!
GET YER STRIPY ASS OUT HERE!
FTHUI!
WHEEZE
...SO I'Z CAN THROW A BEATIN' ON YA!
WHEEZE
CLUNK
OH GAWD, THAT'S THE SADDEST THING I EVER SEEN.
WHAT'RE YOU SUPPOSED TA BE?
BACK OFF, JACK 'N THE BOX! THIS BE A McGOBBLE'S MATTER!
GET OUTTA HERE, DOLL. YOU DON' WANNA GET--
--hurt...
WHUMP!
FLICK!

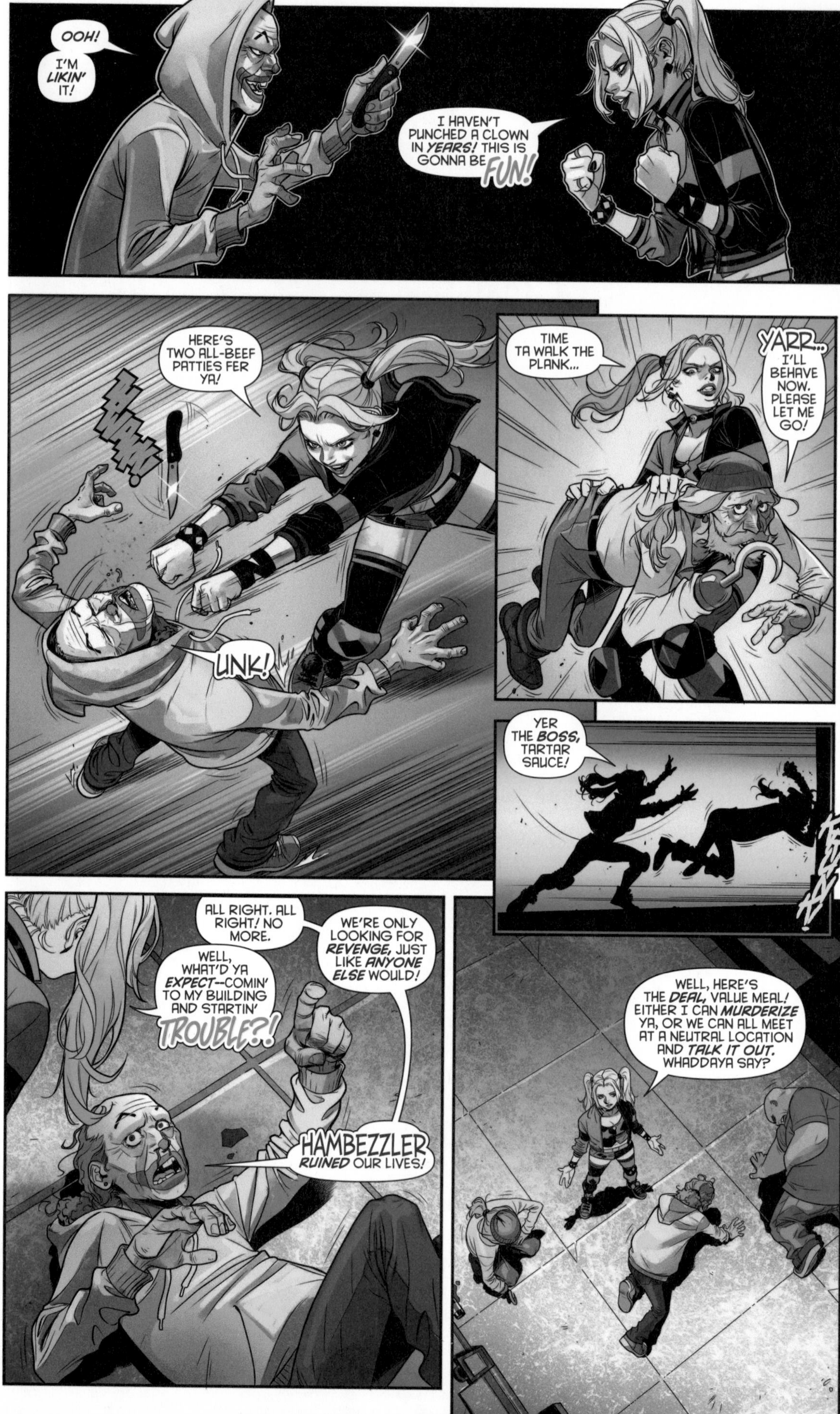
OOH!
I'M LIKIN' IT!
I HAVEN'T PUNCHED A CLOWN IN YEARS! THIS IS GONNA BE FUN!
HERE'S TWO ALL-BEEF PATTIES FER YA!
UNK!
TIME TA WALK THE PLANK...
YARR... I'LL BEHAVE NOW. PLEASE LET ME GO!
YER THE BOSS, TARTAR SAUCE!
ALL RIGHT. ALL RIGHT! NO MORE.
WELL, WHAT'D YA EXPECT--COMIN' TO MY BUILDING AND STARTIN' TROUBLE?!
WE'RE ONLY LOOKING FOR REVENGE, JUST LIKE ANYONE ELSE WOULD!
HAMBEZZLER RUINED OUR LIVES!
WELL, HERE'S THE DEAL, VALUE MEAL! EITHER I CAN MURDERIZE YA, OR WE CAN ALL MEET AT A NEUTRAL LOCATION AND TALK IT OUT. WHADDAYA SAY?

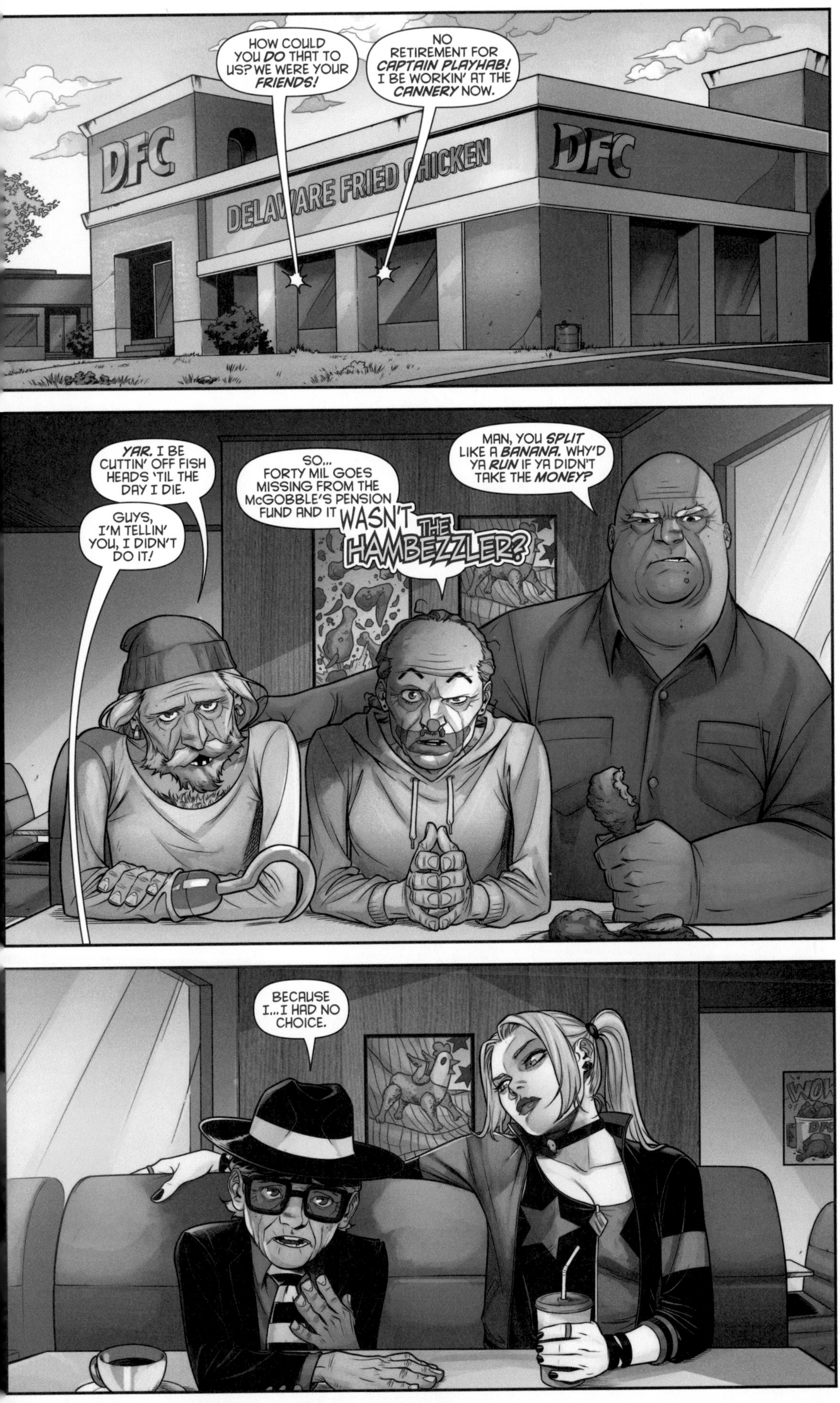
HOW COULD YOU DO THAT TO US? WE WERE YOUR FRIENDS!
NO RETIREMENT FOR CAPTAIN PLAYHAB! I BE WORKIN' AT THE CANNERY NOW.
DFC
DELAWARE FRIED CHICKEN
DFC
YAR. I BE CUTTIN' OFF FISH HEADS 'TIL THE DAY I DIE.
GUYS, I'M TELLIN' YOU, I DIDN'T DO IT!
SO... FORTY MIL GOES MISSING FROM THE McGOBBLE'S PENSION FUND AND IT WASN'T THE HAMBEZZLER?
MAN, YOU SPLIT LIKE A BANANA. WHY'D YA RUN IF YA DIDN'T TAKE THE MONEY?
BECAUSE I...I HAD NO CHOICE.
WOW
DFC

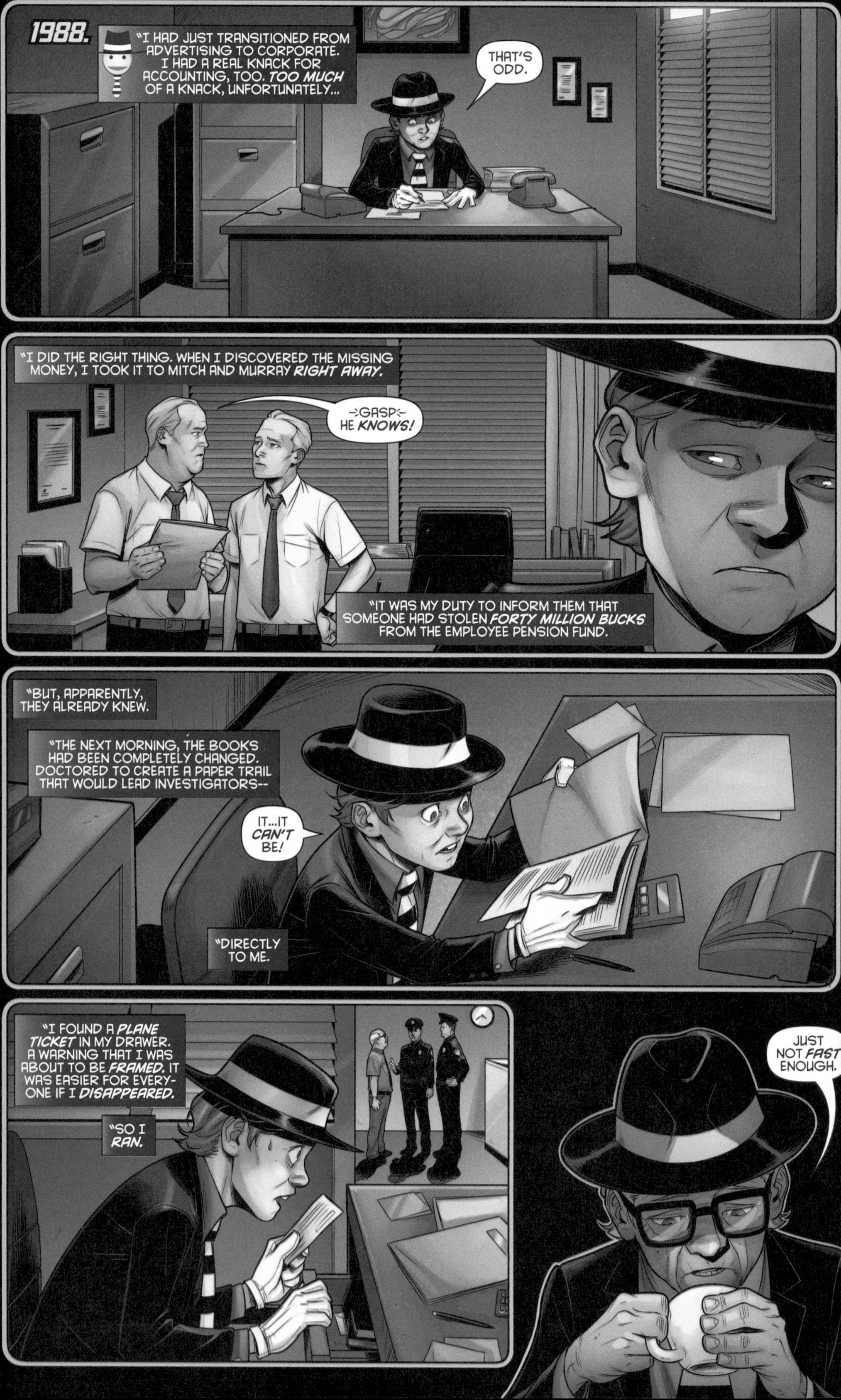
1988.
"I HAD JUST TRANSITIONED FROM ADVERTISING TO CORPORATE. I HAD A REAL KNACK FOR ACCOUNTING, TOO. TOO MUCH OF A KNACK, UNFORTUNATELY...
THAT'S ODD.
"I DID THE RIGHT THING. WHEN I DISCOVERED THE MISSING MONEY, I TOOK IT TO MITCH AND MURRAY RIGHT AWAY.
GASP HE KNOWS!
"IT WAS MY DUTY TO INFORM THEM THAT SOMEONE HAD STOLEN FORTY MILLION BUCKS FROM THE EMPLOYEE PENSION FUND.
"BUT, APPARENTLY, THEY ALREADY KNEW.
"THE NEXT MORNING, THE BOOKS HAD BEEN COMPLETELY CHANGED. DOCTORED TO CREATE A PAPER TRAIL THAT WOULD LEAD INVESTIGATORS--
IT...IT CAN'T BE!
"DIRECTLY TO ME.
"I FOUND A PLANE TICKET IN MY DRAWER. A WARNING THAT I WAS ABOUT TO BE FRAMED. IT WAS EASIER FOR EVERYONE IF I DISAPPEARED.
"SO I RAN.
JUST NOT FAST ENOUGH.

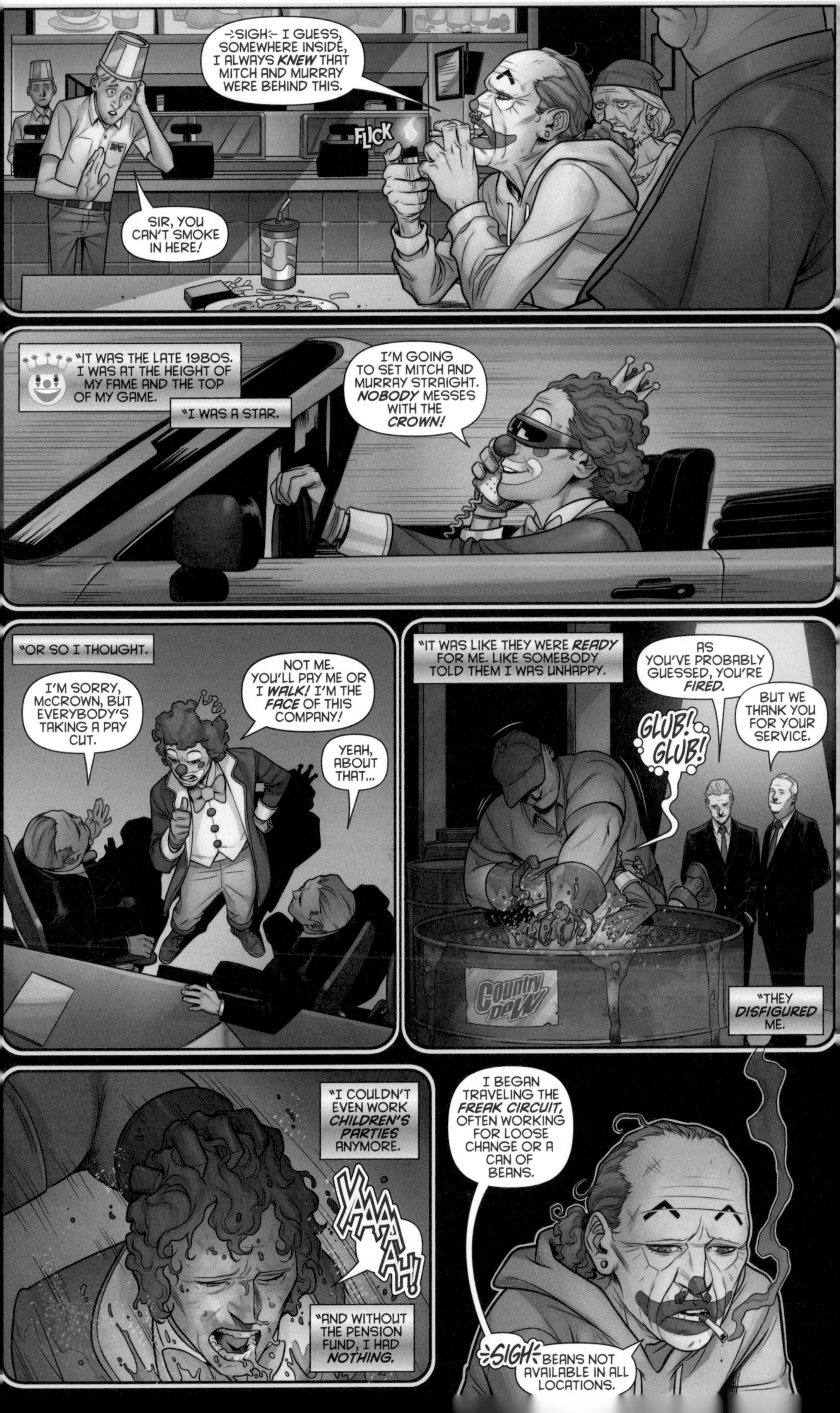

-SIGH- I GUESS, SOMEWHERE INSIDE, I ALWAYS KNEW THAT MITCH AND MURRAY WERE BEHIND THIS.
FLICK
SIR, YOU CAN'T SMOKE IN HERE!
"IT WAS THE LATE 1980S. I WAS AT THE HEIGHT OF MY FAME AND THE TOP OF MY GAME.
"I WAS A STAR.
I'M GOING TO SET MITCH AND MURRAY STRAIGHT. NOBODY MESSES WITH THE CROWN!
"OR SO I THOUGHT.
I'M SORRY, McCROWN, BUT EVERYBODY'S TAKING A PAY CUT.
NOT ME. YOU'LL PAY ME OR I WALK! I'M THE FACE OF THIS COMPANY!
YEAH, ABOUT THAT...
"IT WAS LIKE THEY WERE READY FOR ME. LIKE SOMEBODY TOLD THEM I WAS UNHAPPY.
AS YOU'VE PROBABLY GUESSED, YOU'RE FIRED.
BUT WE THANK YOU FOR YOUR SERVICE.
GLUB! GLUB!
Country Dew
"THEY DISFIGURED ME.
"I COULDN'T EVEN WORK CHILDREN'S PARTIES ANYMORE.
YAAAAAH!
"AND WITHOUT THE PENSION FUND, I HAD NOTHING.
I BEGAN TRAVELING THE FREAK CIRCUIT, OFTEN WORKING FOR LOOSE CHANGE OR A CAN OF BEANS.
-SIGH- BEANS NOT AVAILABLE IN ALL LOCATIONS.

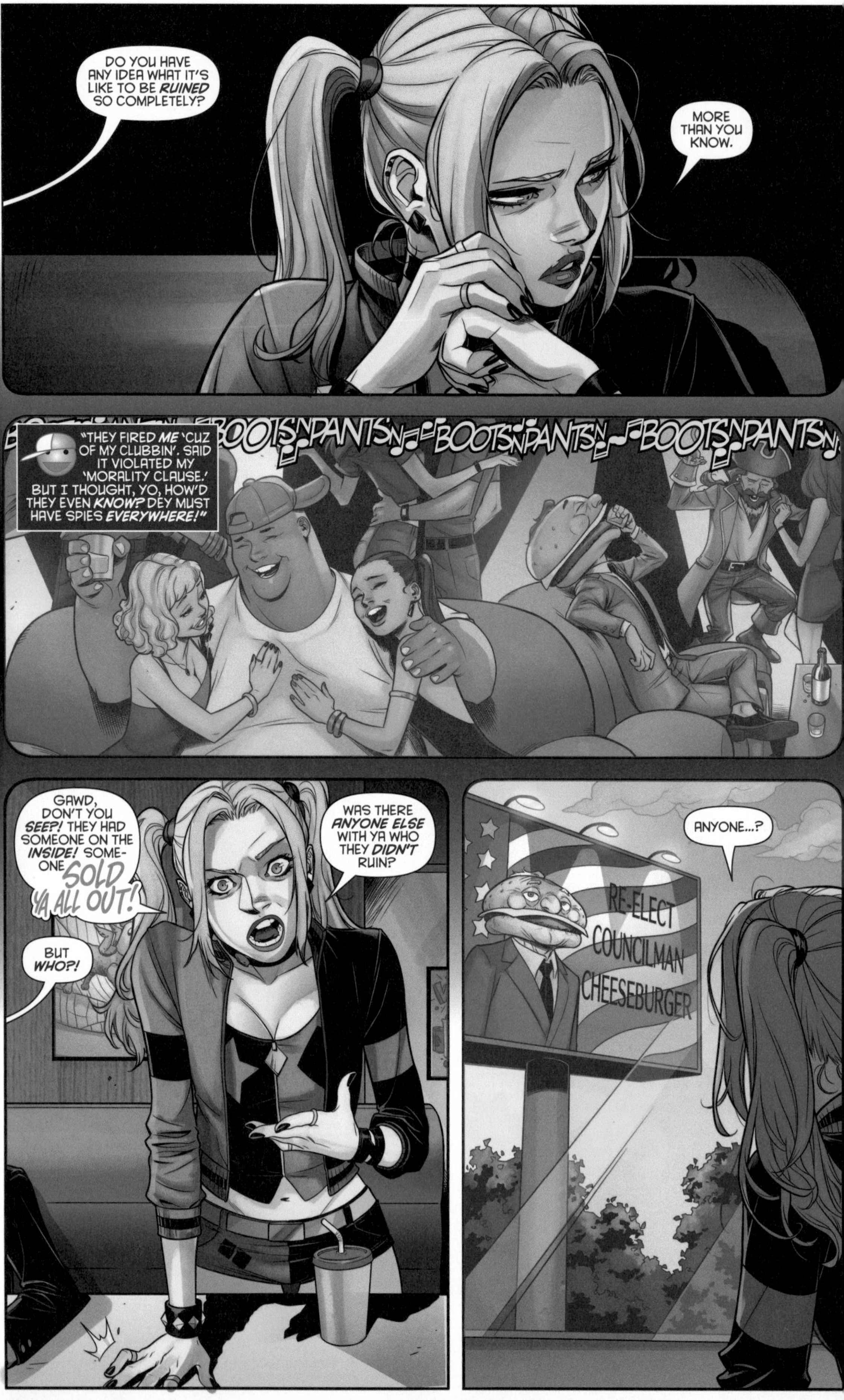
DO YOU HAVE ANY IDEA WHAT IT'S LIKE TO BE *RUINED* SO COMPLETELY?
MORE THAN YOU KNOW.
BOOTS N PANTS N BOOTS N PANTS N BOOTS N PANTS N
"THEY FIRED *ME* 'CUZ OF MY CLUBBIN'. SAID IT VIOLATED MY 'MORALITY CLAUSE.' BUT I THOUGHT, YO, HOW'D THEY EVEN *KNOW?* DEY MUST HAVE SPIES *EVERYWHERE!*"
GAWD, DON'T YOU *SEE?!* THEY HAD SOMEONE ON THE *INSIDE!* SOME-ONE SOLD YA ALL OUT!
BUT *WHO?!*
WAS THERE *ANYONE ELSE* WITH YA WHO THEY *DIDN'T* RUIN?
ANYONE...?
RE-ELECT COUNCILMAN CHEESEBURGER

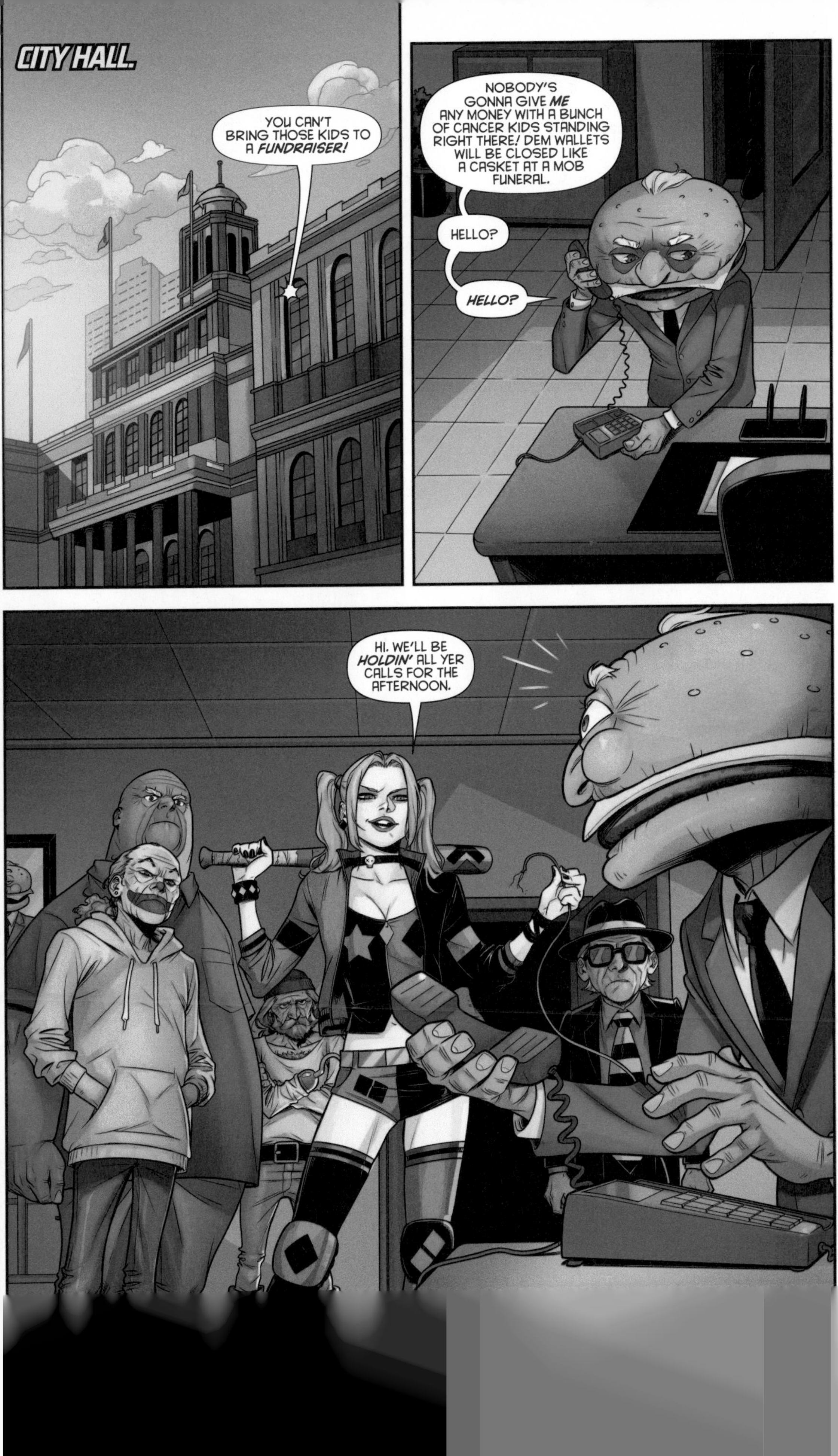
CITY HALL.
YOU CAN'T BRING THOSE KIDS TO A FUNDRAISER!
NOBODY'S GONNA GIVE ME ANY MONEY WITH A BUNCH OF CANCER KIDS STANDING RIGHT THERE! DEM WALLETS WILL BE CLOSED LIKE A CASKET AT A MOB FUNERAL.
HELLO?
HELLO?
HI. WE'LL BE HOLDIN' ALL YER CALLS FOR THE AFTERNOON.

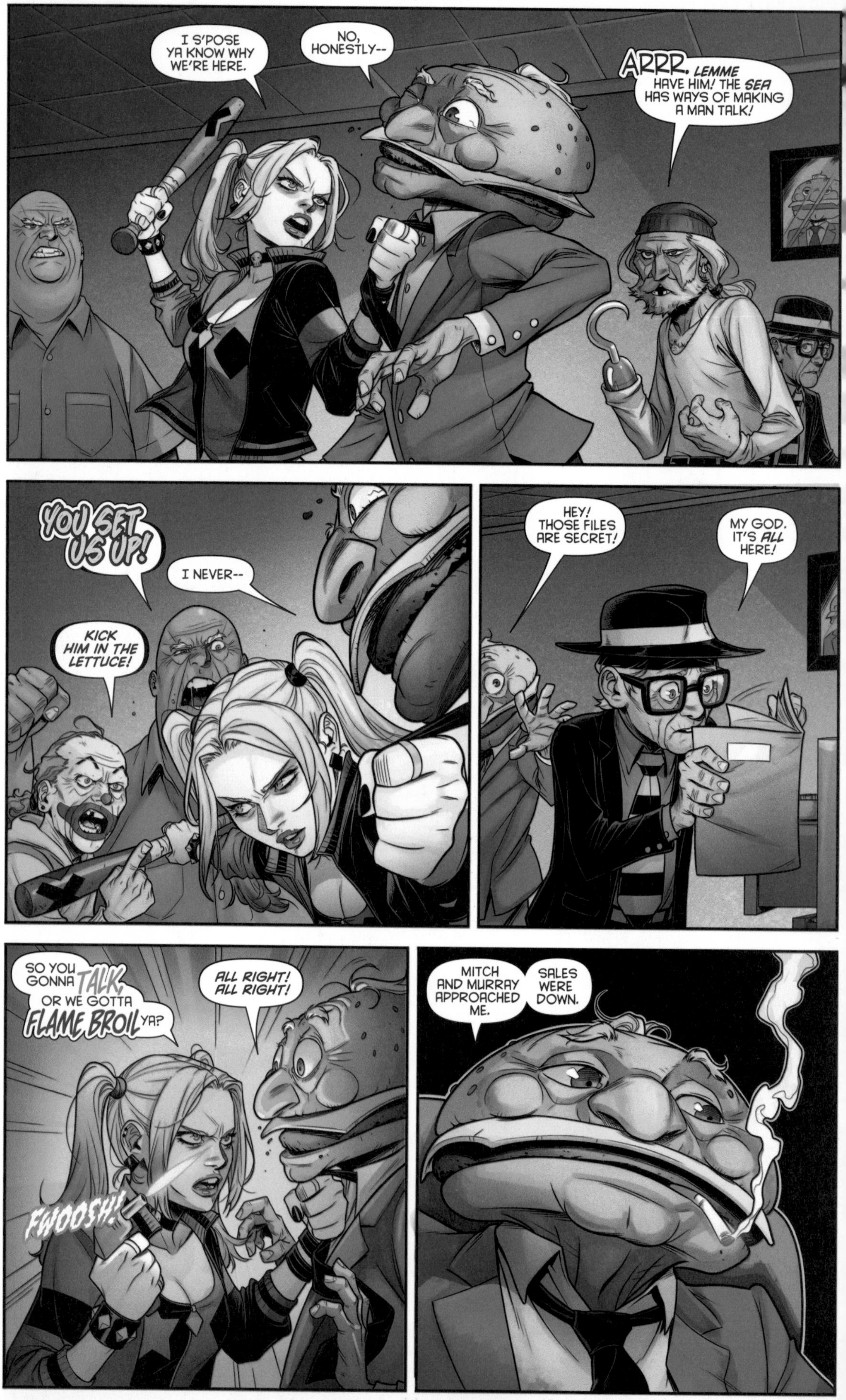

I S'POSE YA KNOW WHY WE'RE HERE.
NO, HONESTLY--
ARRR. LEMME HAVE HIM! THE SEA HAS WAYS OF MAKING A MAN TALK!
YOU SET US UP!
I NEVER--
KICK HIM IN THE LETTUCE!
HEY! THOSE FILES ARE SECRET!
MY GOD. IT'S ALL HERE!
SO YOU GONNA TALK, OR WE GOTTA FLAME BROIL YA?
ALL RIGHT! ALL RIGHT!
FWOOSH!
MITCH AND MURRAY APPROACHED ME.
SALES WERE DOWN.

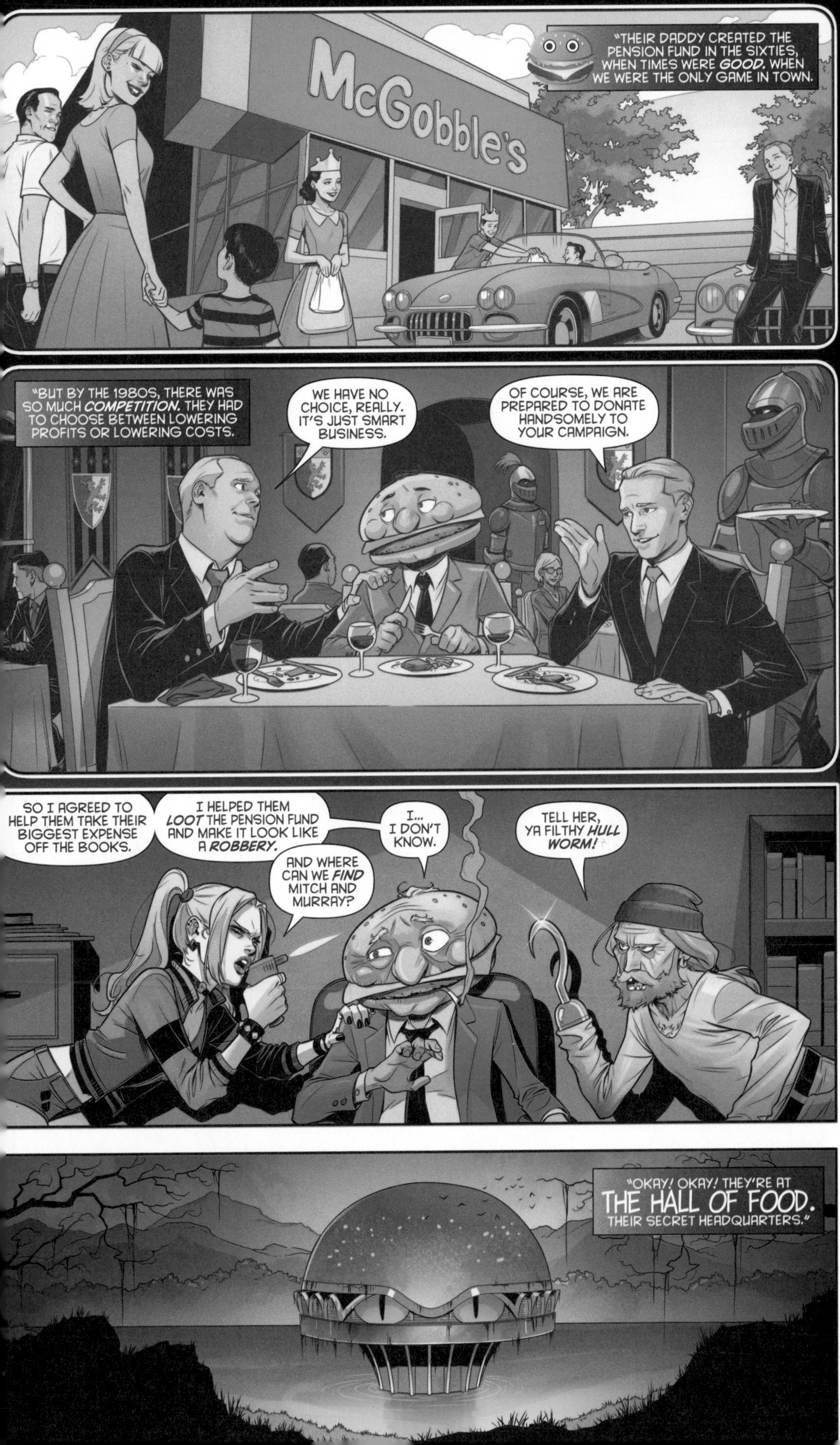

"THEIR DADDY CREATED THE PENSION FUND IN THE SIXTIES, WHEN TIMES WERE *GOOD*, WHEN WE WERE THE ONLY GAME IN TOWN.
McGobble's
"BUT BY THE 1980S, THERE WAS SO MUCH *COMPETITION*. THEY HAD TO CHOOSE BETWEEN LOWERING PROFITS OR LOWERING COSTS.
WE HAVE NO CHOICE, REALLY. IT'S JUST SMART BUSINESS.
OF COURSE, WE ARE PREPARED TO DONATE HANDSOMELY TO YOUR CAMPAIGN.
SO I AGREED TO HELP THEM TAKE THEIR BIGGEST EXPENSE OFF THE BOOKS.
I HELPED THEM *LOOT* THE PENSION FUND AND MAKE IT LOOK LIKE A *ROBBERY*.
AND WHERE CAN WE *FIND* MITCH AND MURRAY?
I... I DON'T KNOW.
TELL HER, YA FILTHY *HULL WORM!*
"OKAY! OKAY! THEY'RE AT THE HALL OF FOOD. THEIR SECRET HEADQUARTERS."

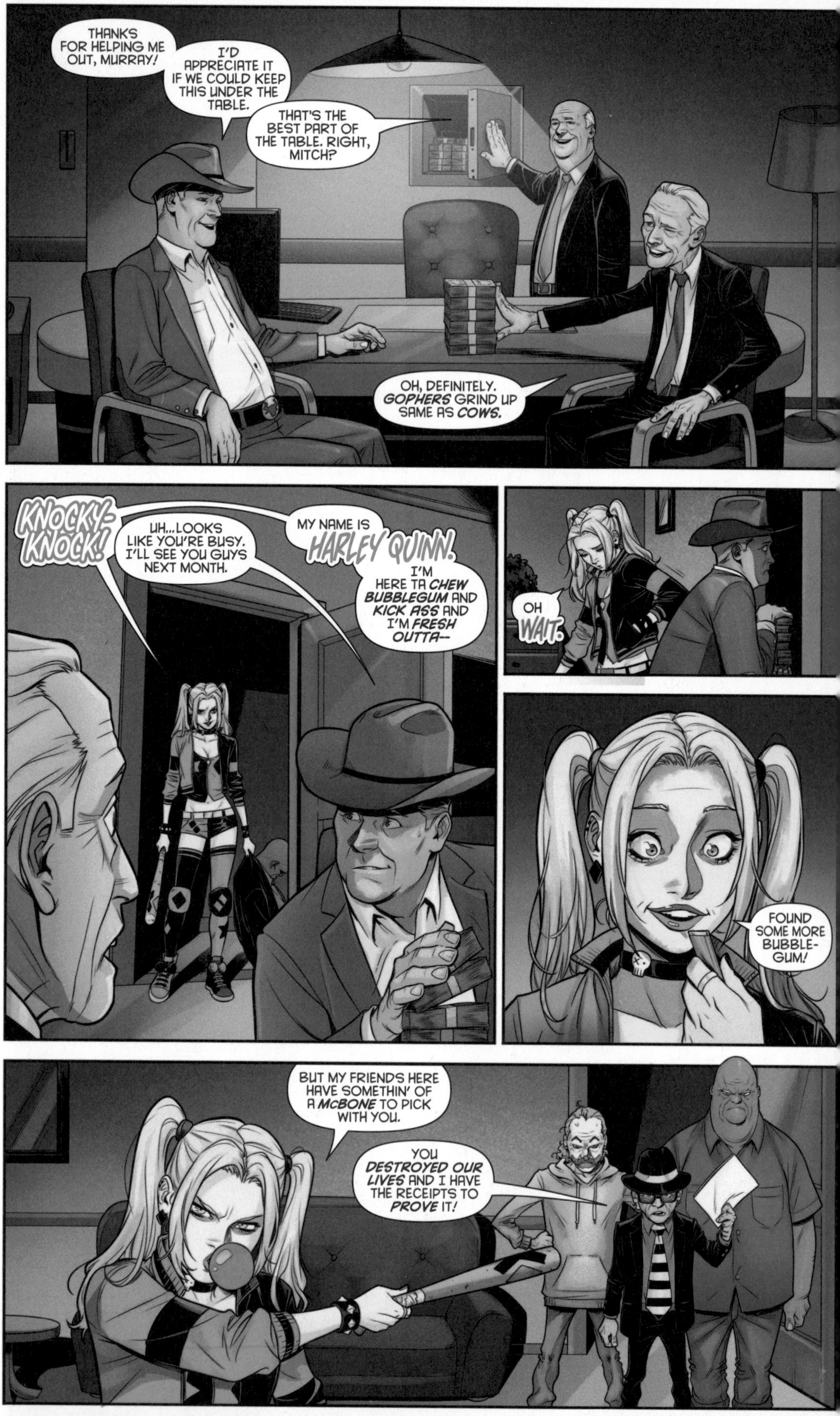
THANKS FOR HELPING ME OUT, MURRAY!
I'D APPRECIATE IT IF WE COULD KEEP THIS UNDER THE TABLE.
THAT'S THE BEST PART OF THE TABLE. RIGHT, MITCH?
OH, DEFINITELY. GOPHERS GRIND UP SAME AS COWS.
KNOCKY-KNOCK!
UH...LOOKS LIKE YOU'RE BUSY. I'LL SEE YOU GUYS NEXT MONTH.
MY NAME IS HARLEY QUINN.
I'M HERE TA CHEW BUBBLEGUM AND KICK ASS AND I'M FRESH OUTTA--
OH WAIT.
FOUND SOME MORE BUBBLE-GUM!
BUT MY FRIENDS HERE HAVE SOMETHIN' OF A McBONE TO PICK WITH YOU.
YOU DESTROYED OUR LIVES AND I HAVE THE RECEIPTS TO PROVE IT!

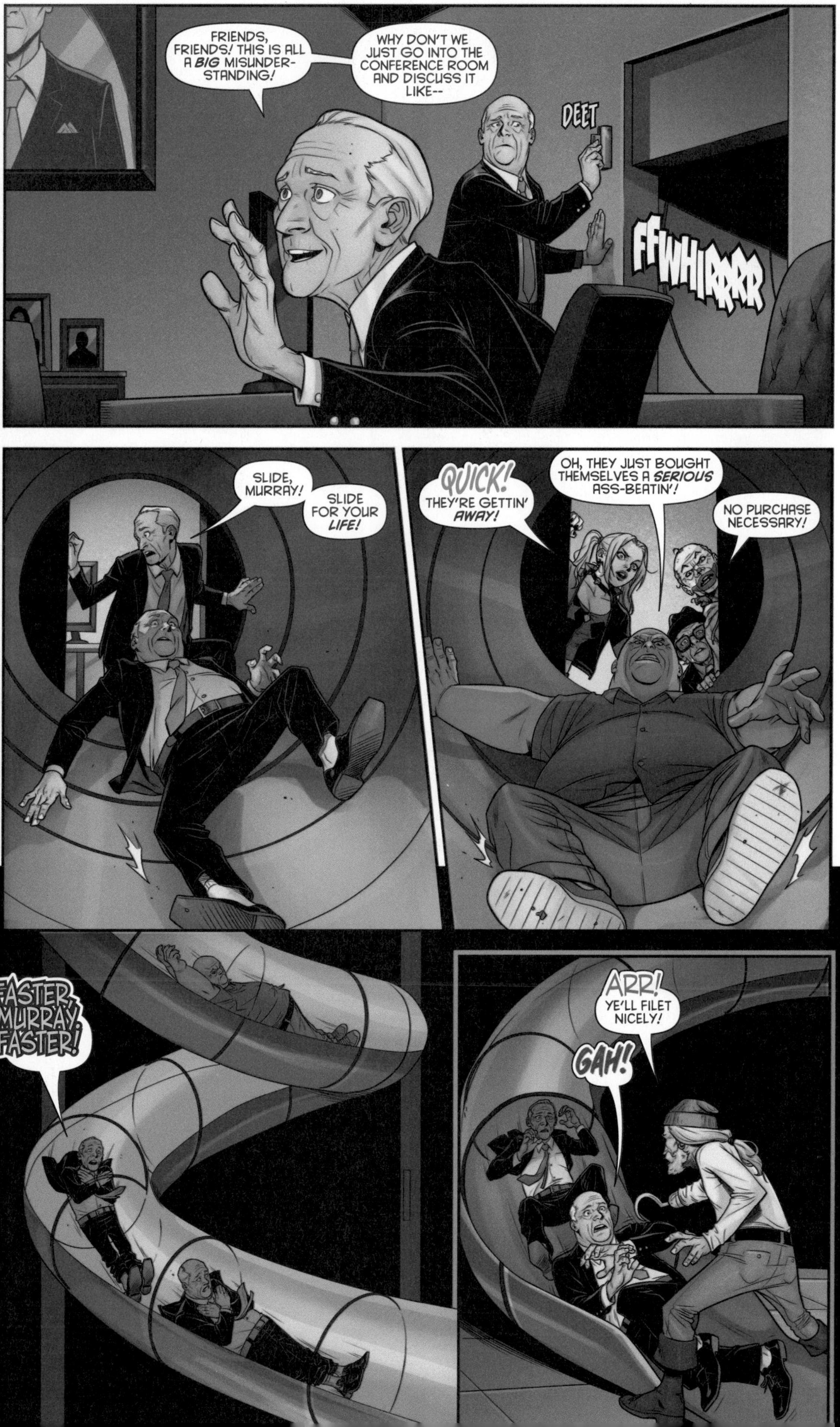
FRIENDS, FRIENDS! THIS IS ALL A BIG MISUNDER-STANDING!
WHY DON'T WE JUST GO INTO THE CONFERENCE ROOM AND DISCUSS IT LIKE--
DEET
FFWHIRRRR
SLIDE, MURRAY!
SLIDE FOR YOUR LIFE!
QUICK! THEY'RE GETTIN' AWAY!
OH, THEY JUST BOUGHT THEMSELVES A SERIOUS ASS-BEATIN'!
NO PURCHASE NECESSARY!
FASTER, MURRAY, FASTER!
ARR! YE'LL FILET NICELY!
GAH!

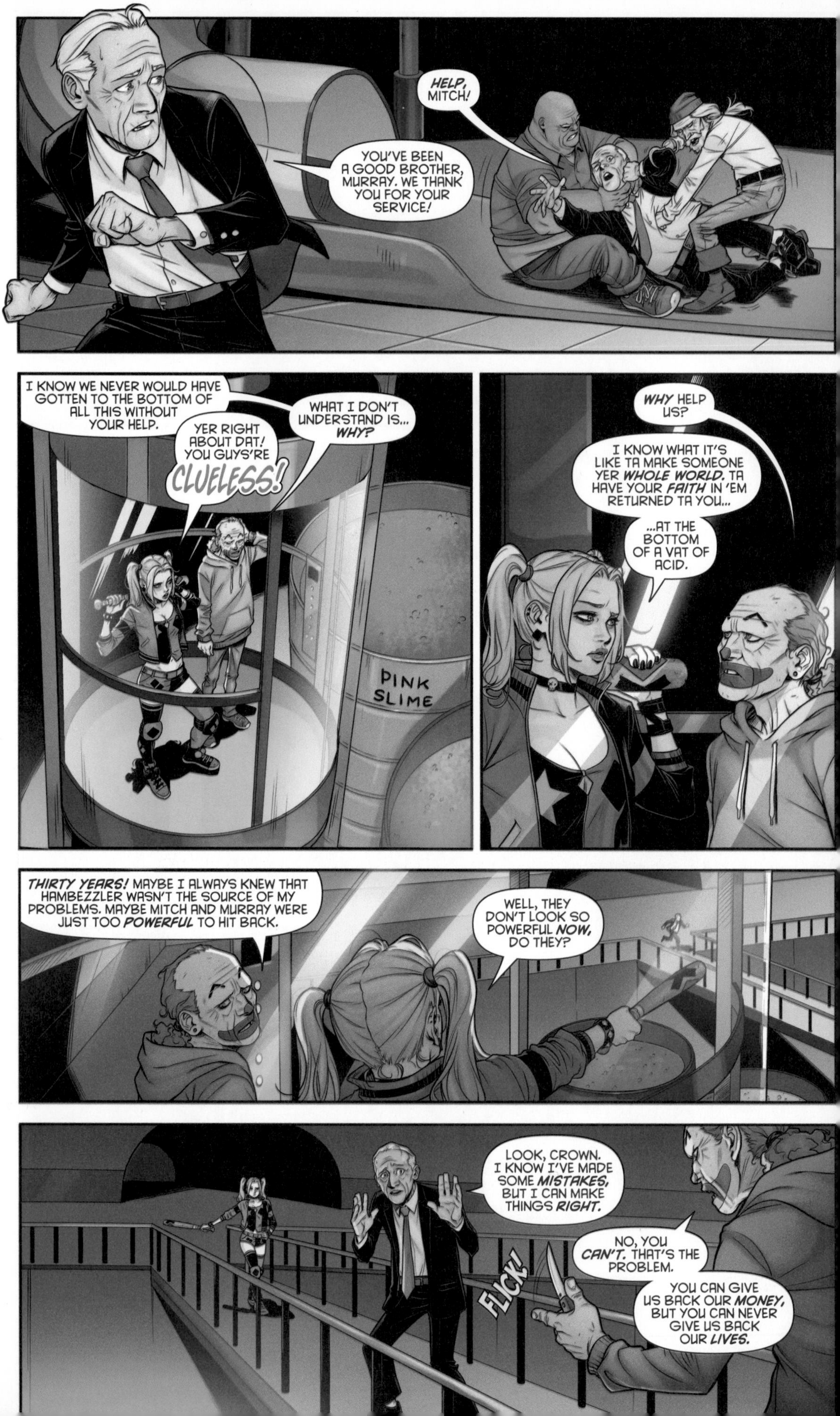
HELP, MITCH!
YOU'VE BEEN A GOOD BROTHER, MURRAY. WE THANK YOU FOR YOUR SERVICE!
I KNOW WE NEVER WOULD HAVE GOTTEN TO THE BOTTOM OF ALL THIS WITHOUT YOUR HELP.
YER RIGHT ABOUT DAT! YOU GUYS'RE CLUELESS!
WHAT I DON'T UNDERSTAND IS... WHY?
PINK SLIME
WHY HELP US?
I KNOW WHAT IT'S LIKE TA MAKE SOMEONE YER WHOLE WORLD. TA HAVE YOUR FAITH IN 'EM RETURNED TA YOU...
...AT THE BOTTOM OF A VAT OF ACID.
THIRTY YEARS! MAYBE I ALWAYS KNEW THAT HAMBEZZLER WASN'T THE SOURCE OF MY PROBLEMS. MAYBE MITCH AND MURRAY WERE JUST TOO POWERFUL TO HIT BACK.
WELL, THEY DON'T LOOK SO POWERFUL NOW, DO THEY?
LOOK, CROWN. I KNOW I'VE MADE SOME MISTAKES, BUT I CAN MAKE THINGS RIGHT.
NO, YOU CAN'T. THAT'S THE PROBLEM.
FLICK!
YOU CAN GIVE US BACK OUR MONEY, BUT YOU CAN NEVER GIVE US BACK OUR LIVES.

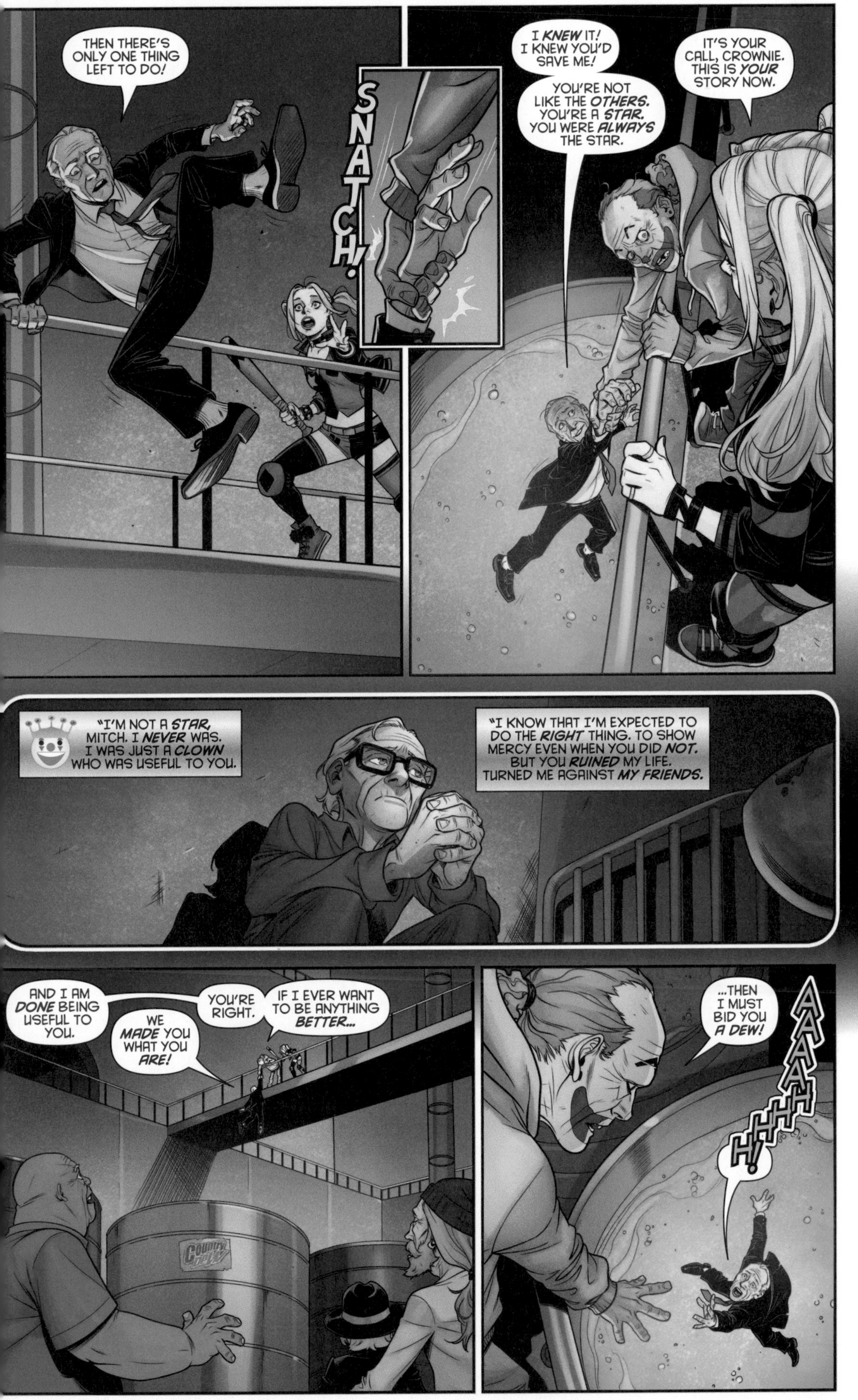
THEN THERE'S ONLY ONE THING LEFT TO DO!
SNATCH!
I KNEW IT! I KNEW YOU'D SAVE ME!
YOU'RE NOT LIKE THE OTHERS. YOU'RE A STAR. YOU WERE ALWAYS THE STAR.
IT'S YOUR CALL, CROWNIE. THIS IS YOUR STORY NOW.
"I'M NOT A STAR, MITCH. I NEVER WAS. I WAS JUST A CLOWN WHO WAS USEFUL TO YOU.
"I KNOW THAT I'M EXPECTED TO DO THE RIGHT THING. TO SHOW MERCY EVEN WHEN YOU DID NOT. BUT YOU RUINED MY LIFE. TURNED ME AGAINST MY FRIENDS.
AND I AM DONE BEING USEFUL TO YOU.
WE MADE YOU WHAT YOU ARE!
YOU'RE RIGHT.
IF I EVER WANT TO BE ANYTHING BETTER...
...THEN I MUST BID YOU A DEW!
AAAAHHHH!

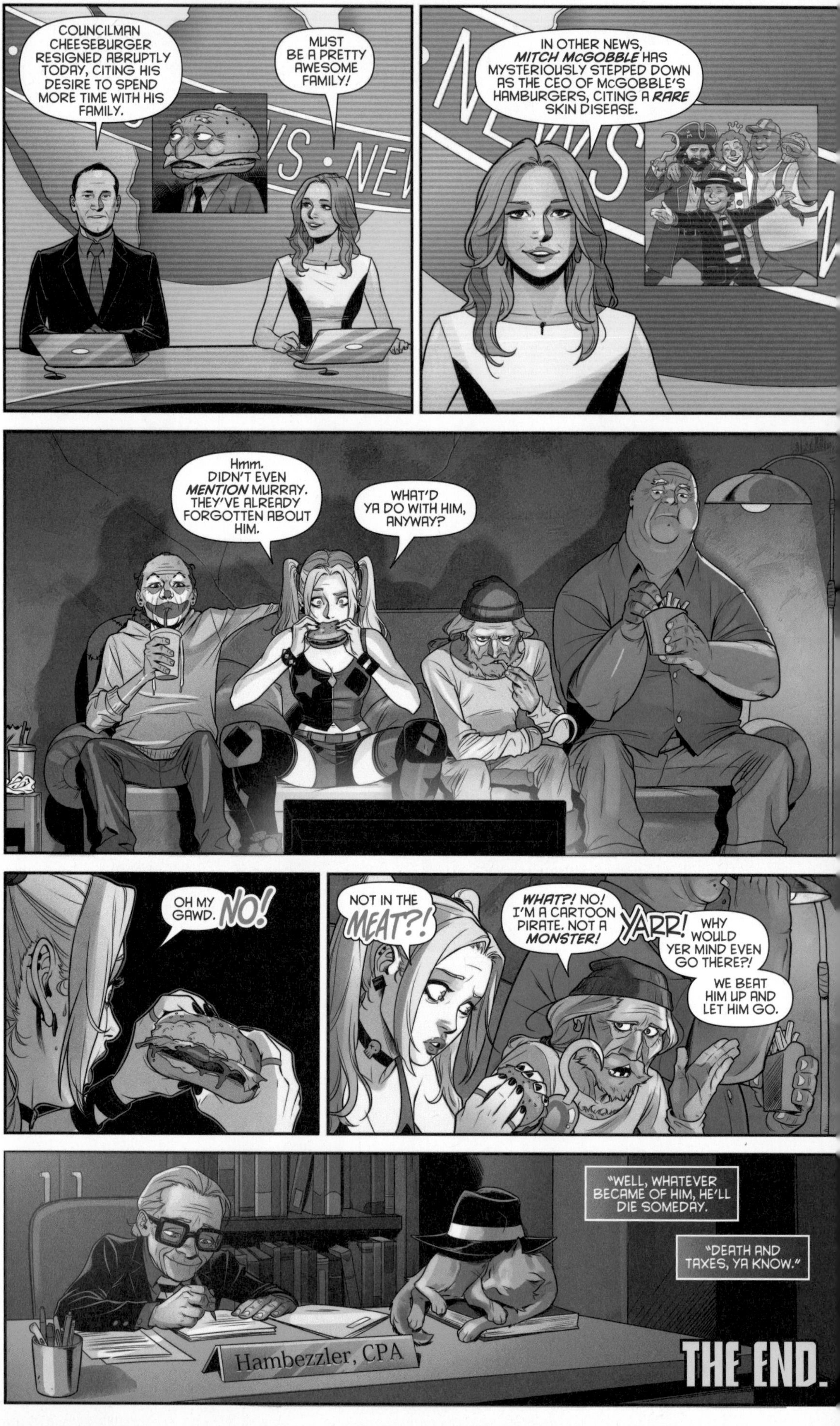
COUNCILMAN CHEESEBURGER RESIGNED ABRUPTLY TODAY, CITING HIS DESIRE TO SPEND MORE TIME WITH HIS FAMILY.
MUST BE A PRETTY AWESOME FAMILY!
IN OTHER NEWS, MITCH McGOBBLE HAS MYSTERIOUSLY STEPPED DOWN AS THE CEO OF McGOBBLE'S HAMBURGERS, CITING A RARE SKIN DISEASE.
Hmm. DIDN'T EVEN MENTION MURRAY. THEY'VE ALREADY FORGOTTEN ABOUT HIM.
WHAT'D YA DO WITH HIM, ANYWAY?
OH MY GAWD. NO!
NOT IN THE MEAT?!
WHAT?! NO! I'M A CARTOON PIRATE. NOT A MONSTER!
YARR!
WHY WOULD YER MIND EVEN GO THERE?!
WE BEAT HIM UP AND LET HIM GO.
"WELL, WHATEVER BECAME OF HIM, HE'LL DIE SOMEDAY.
"DEATH AND TAXES, YA KNOW."
Hambezzler, CPA
THE END.

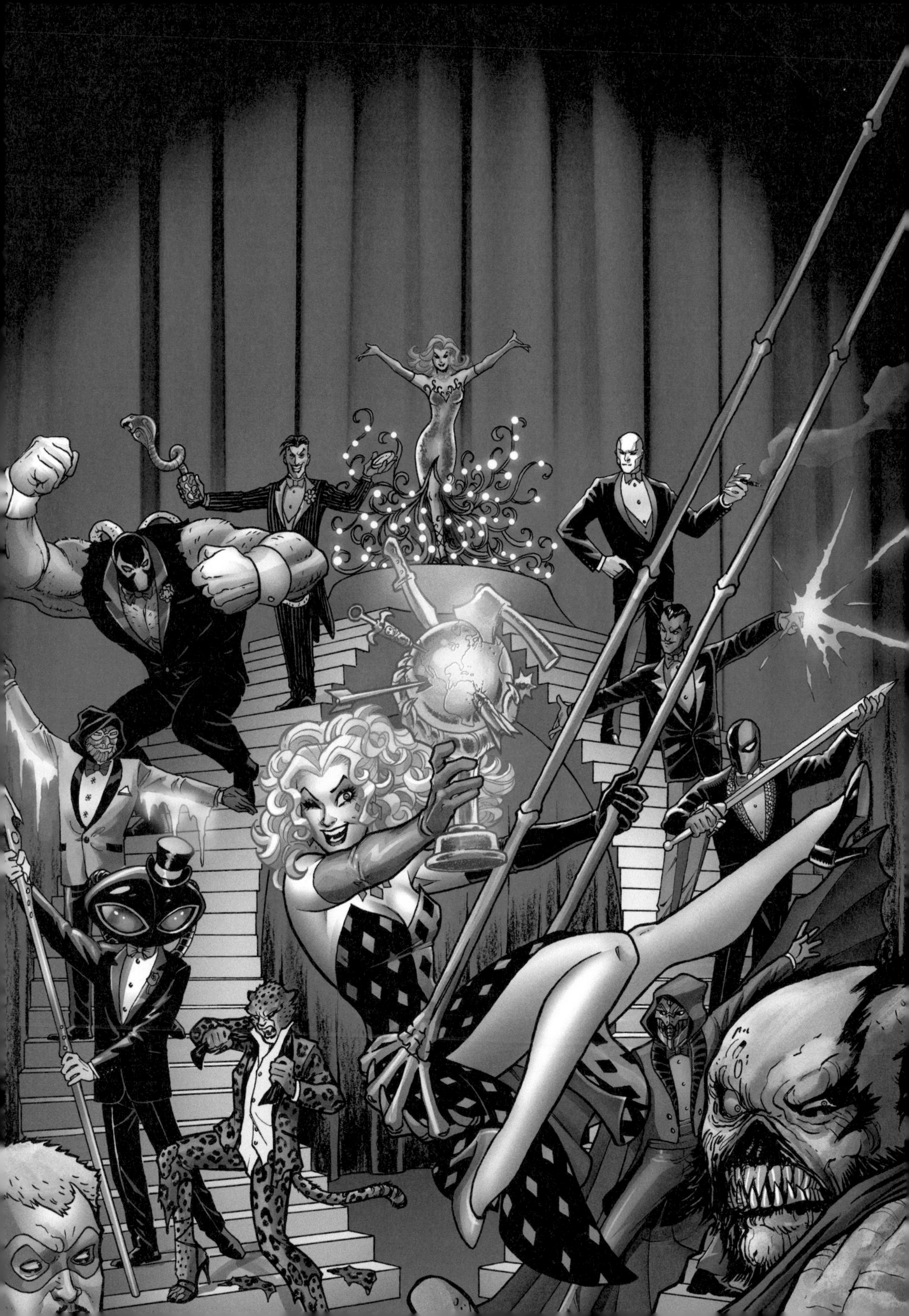

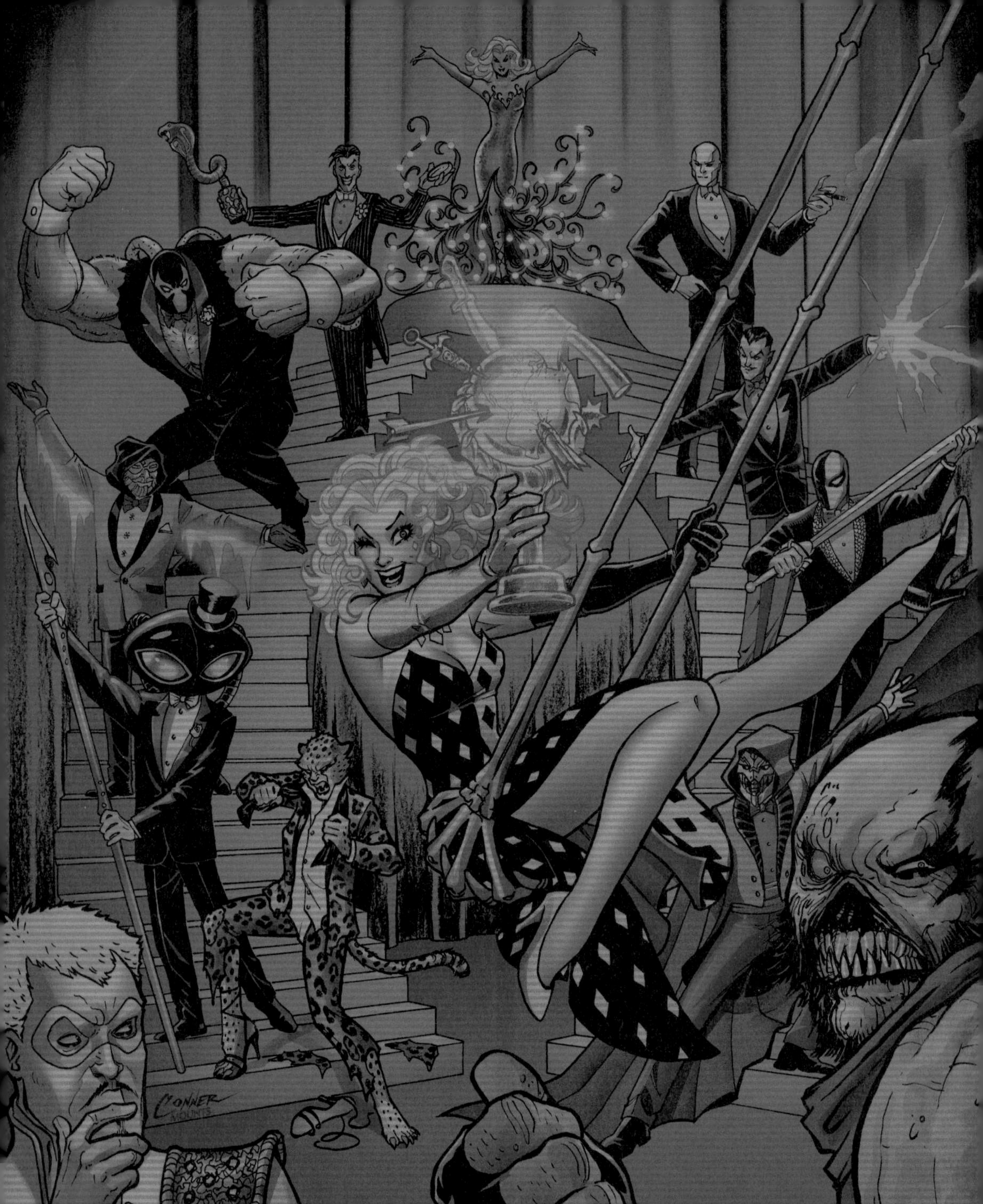

HARLEY QUINN'S
VILLAIN OF THE YEAR #1

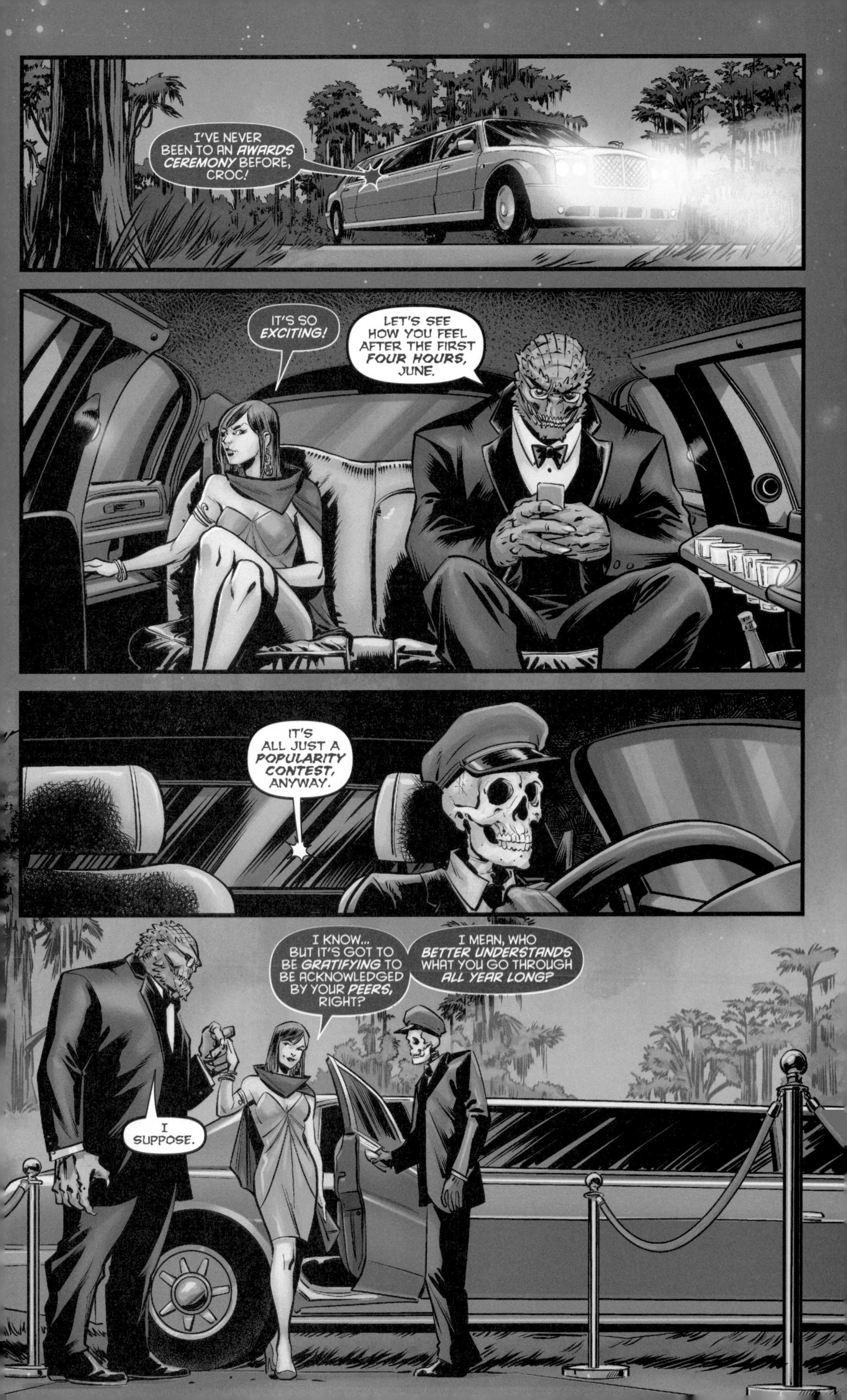

I'VE NEVER BEEN TO AN *AWARDS CEREMONY* BEFORE, CROC!
IT'S SO *EXCITING!*
LET'S SEE HOW YOU FEEL AFTER THE FIRST *FOUR HOURS,* JUNE.
IT'S ALL JUST A *POPULARITY CONTEST,* ANYWAY.
I KNOW... BUT IT'S GOT TO BE *GRATIFYING* TO BE ACKNOWLEDGED BY YOUR *PEERS,* RIGHT?
I MEAN, WHO *BETTER UNDERSTANDS* WHAT YOU GO THROUGH *ALL YEAR LONG?*
I SUPPOSE.

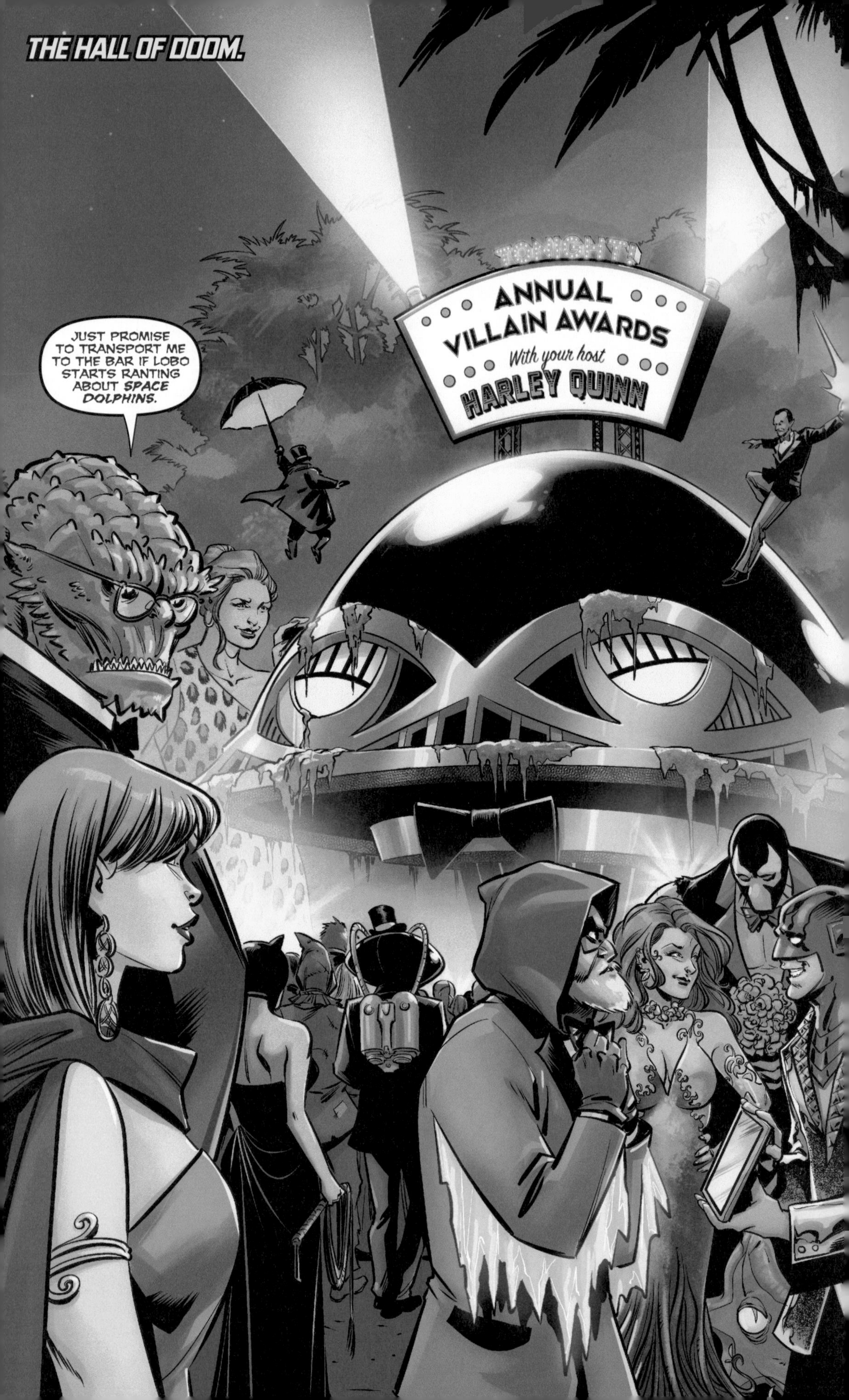

THE HALL OF DOOM.
TONIGHT!
ANNUAL VILLAIN AWARDS
With your host
HARLEY QUINN
JUST PROMISE TO TRANSPORT ME TO THE BAR IF LOBO STARTS RANTING ABOUT SPACE DOLPHINS.

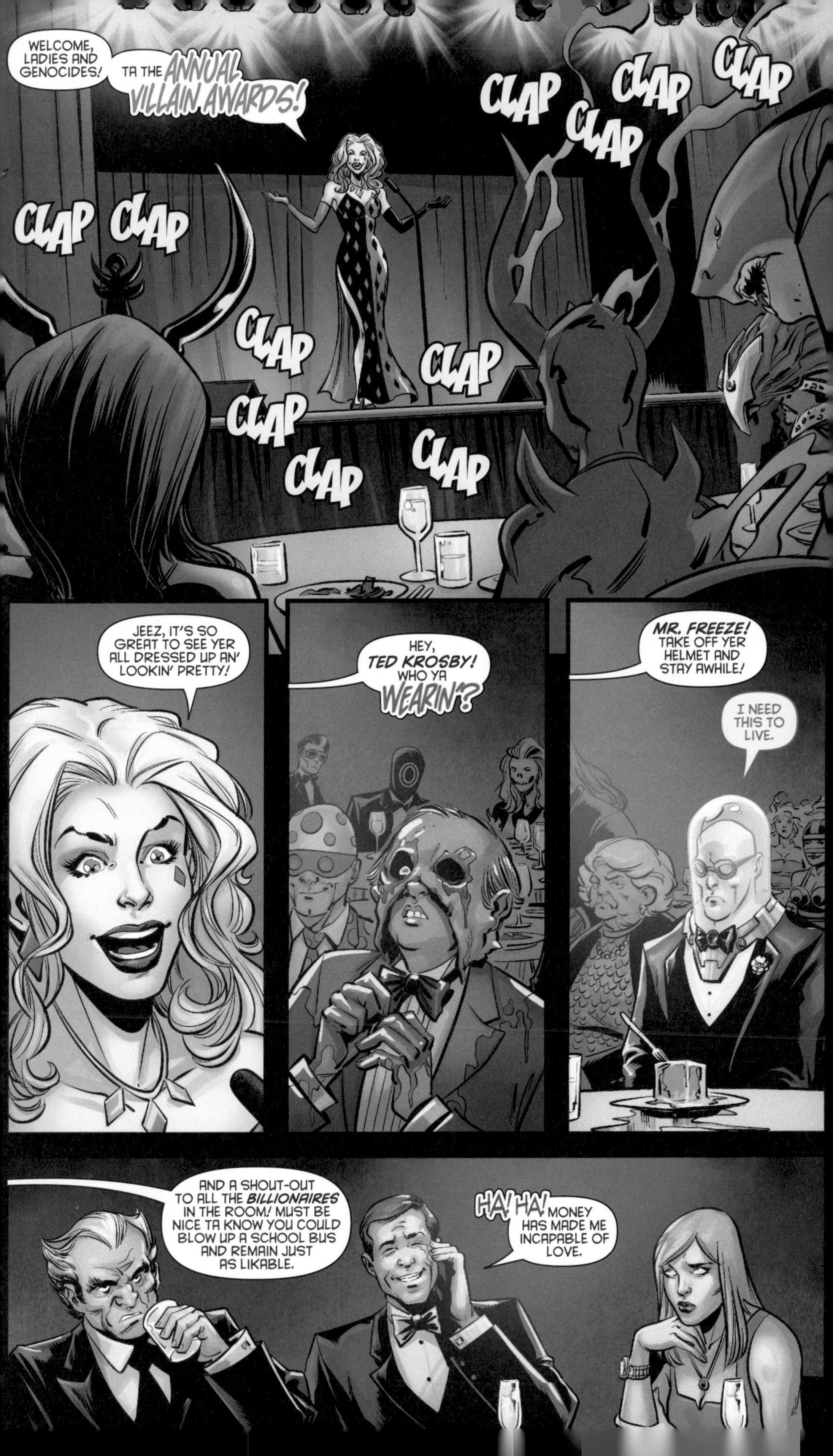
WELCOME, LADIES AND GENOCIDES!
TA THE ANNUAL VILLAIN AWARDS!
CLAP CLAP CLAP CLAP
CLAP CLAP
CLAP CLAP CLAP CLAP CLAP
JEEZ, IT'S SO GREAT TO SEE YER ALL DRESSED UP AN' LOOKIN' PRETTY!
HEY, TED KROSBY! WHO YA WEARIN'?
MR. FREEZE! TAKE OFF YER HELMET AND STAY AWHILE!
I NEED THIS TO LIVE.
AND A SHOUT-OUT TO ALL THE BILLIONAIRES IN THE ROOM! MUST BE NICE TA KNOW YOU COULD BLOW UP A SCHOOL BUS AND REMAIN JUST AS LIKABLE.
HA! HA! MONEY HAS MADE ME INCAPABLE OF LOVE.

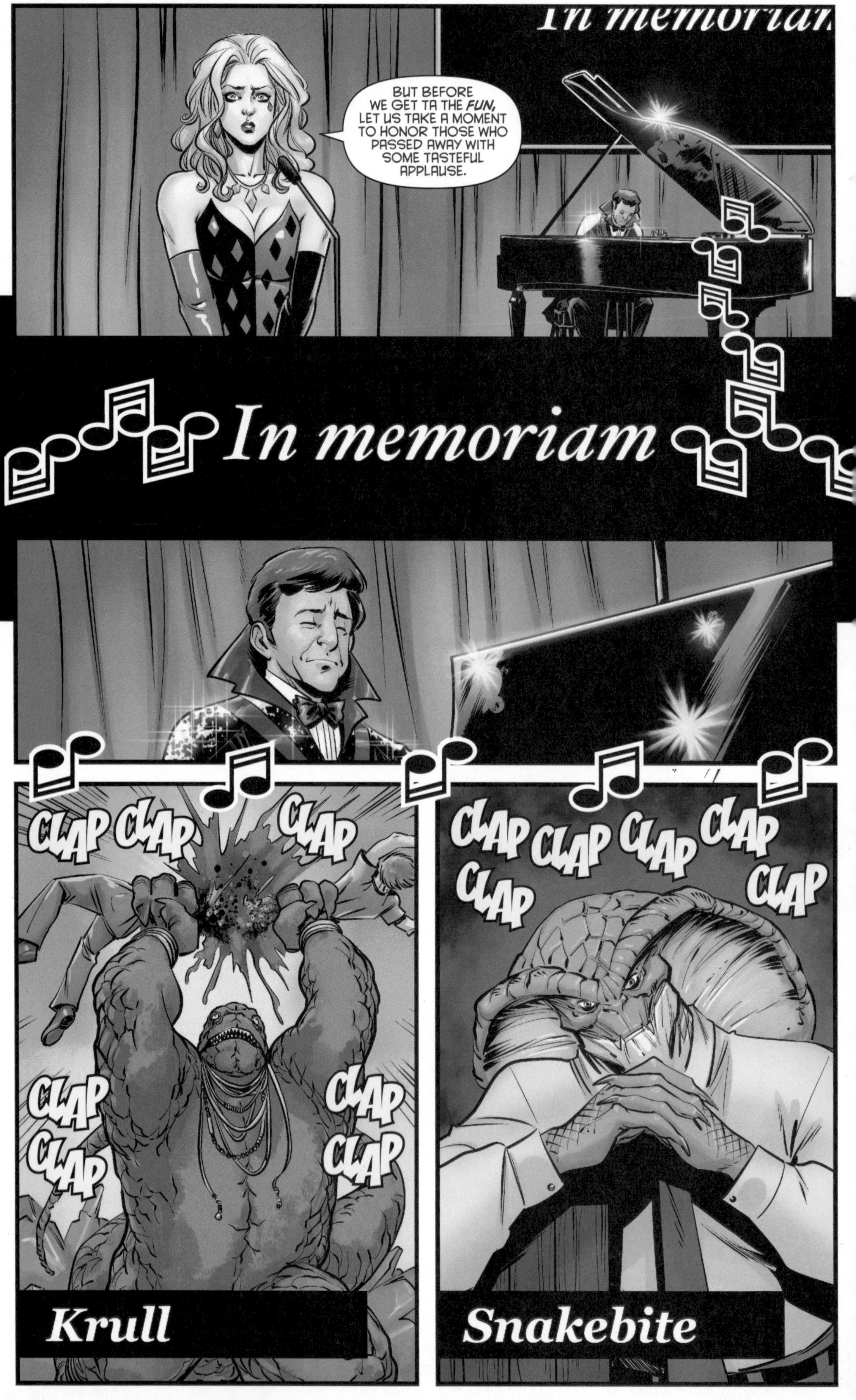
In memoriam
BUT BEFORE WE GET TA THE *FUN,* LET US TAKE A MOMENT TO HONOR THOSE WHO PASSED AWAY WITH SOME TASTEFUL APPLAUSE.
In memoriam
CLAP CLAP CLAP
CLAP CLAP
CLAP CLAP
Krull
CLAP CLAP CLAP CLAP
CLAP CLAP
Snakebite

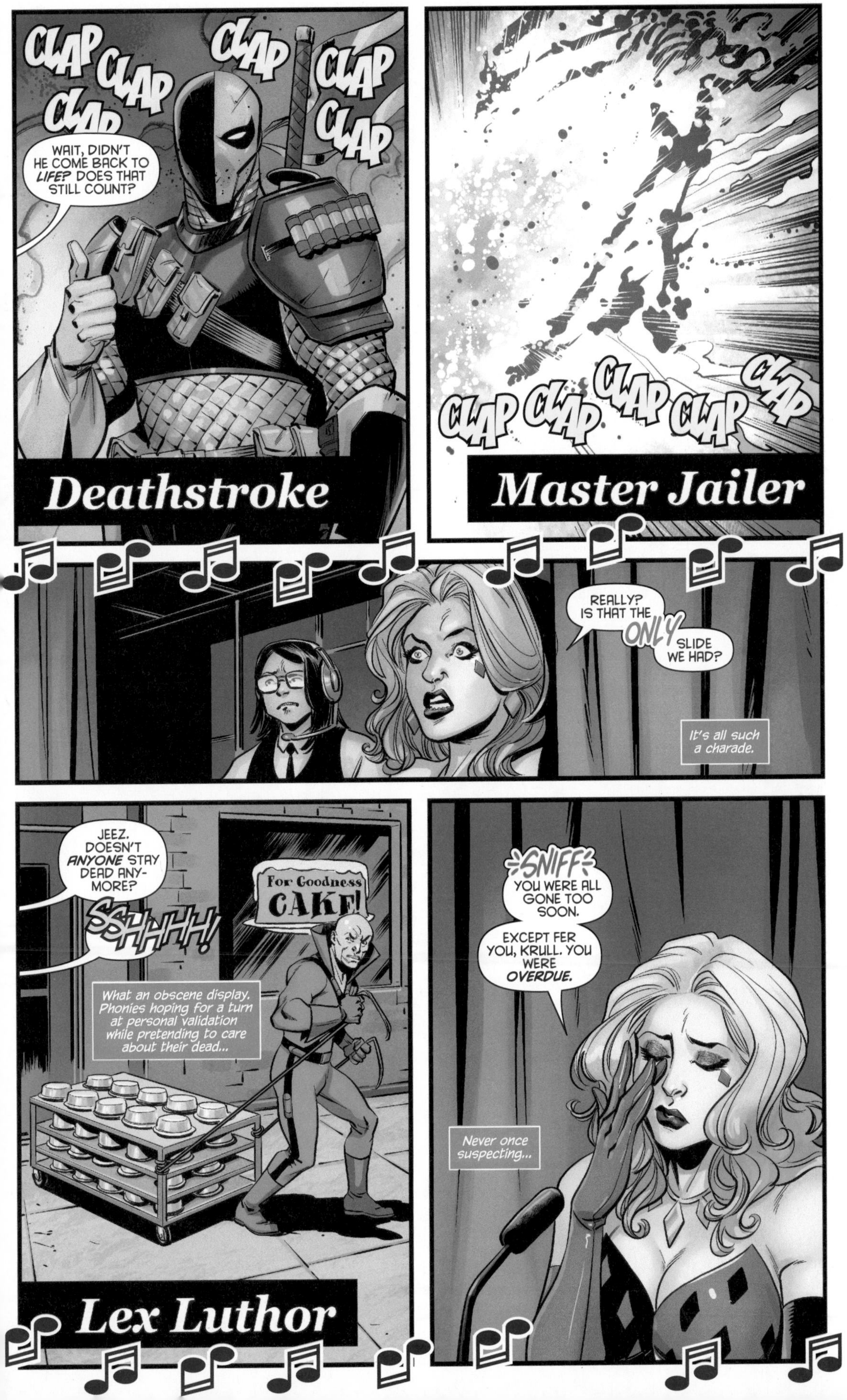
CLAP CLAP CLAP CLAP CLAP CLAP
WAIT, DIDN'T HE COME BACK TO LIFE? DOES THAT STILL COUNT?
Deathstroke
CLAP CLAP CLAP CLAP CLAP
Master Jailer
REALLY? IS THAT THE ONLY SLIDE WE HAD?
It's all such a charade.
JEEZ. DOESN'T ANYONE STAY DEAD ANY-MORE?
SSHHHH!
For Goodness CAKE!
What an obscene display. Phonies hoping for a turn at personal validation while pretending to care about their dead...
Lex Luthor
SNIFF
YOU WERE ALL GONE TOO SOON.
EXCEPT FER YOU, KRULL. YOU WERE OVERDUE.
Never once suspecting...

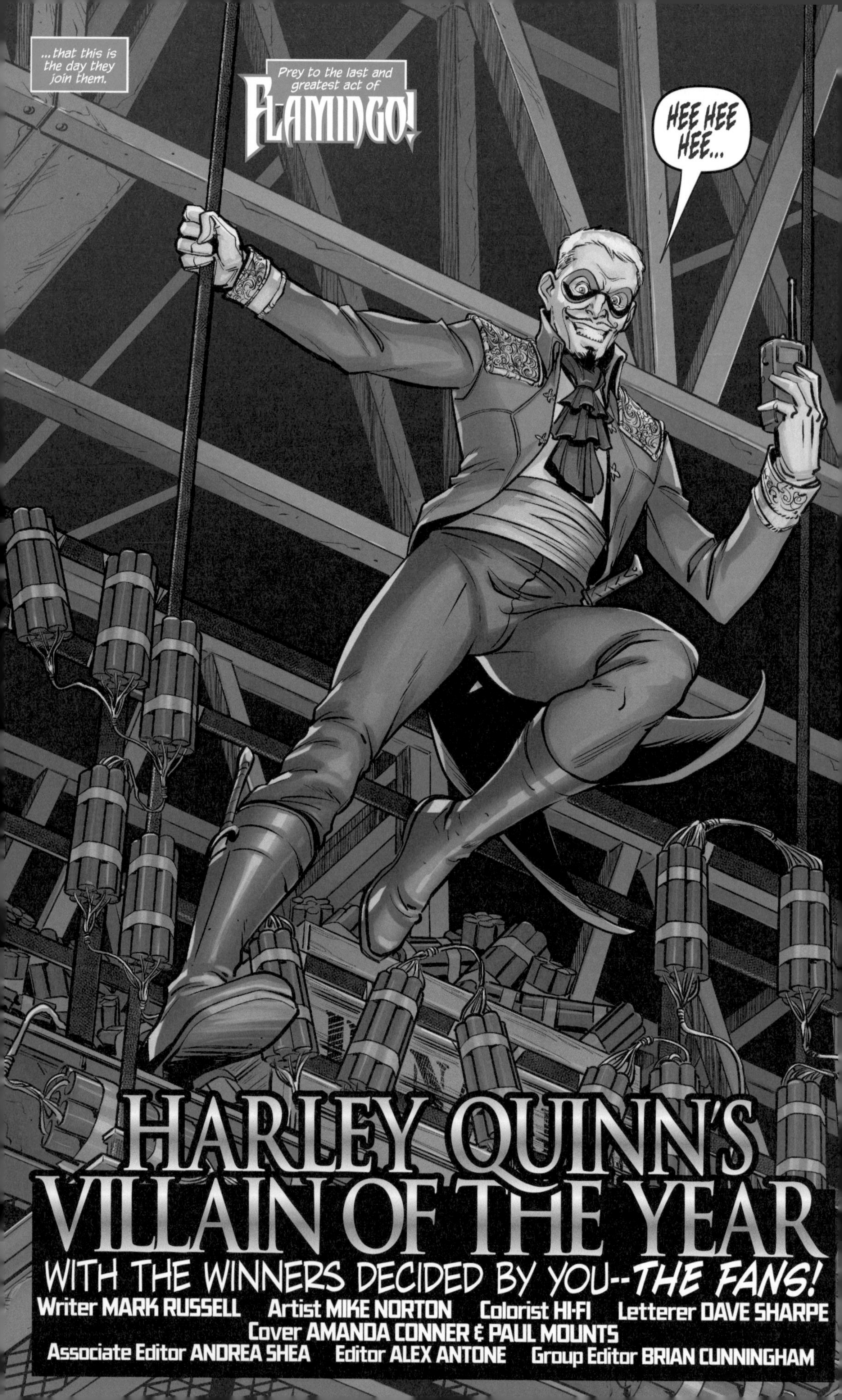
...that this is the day they join them.
Prey to the last and greatest act of
FLAMINGO!
HEE HEE HEE...
HARLEY QUINN'S VILLAIN OF THE YEAR
WITH THE WINNERS DECIDED BY YOU--THE FANS!
Writer MARK RUSSELL Artist MIKE NORTON Colorist HI-FI Letterer DAVE SHARPE
Cover AMANDA CONNER & PAUL MOUNTS
Associate Editor ANDREA SHEA Editor ALEX ANTONE Group Editor BRIAN CUNNINGHAM

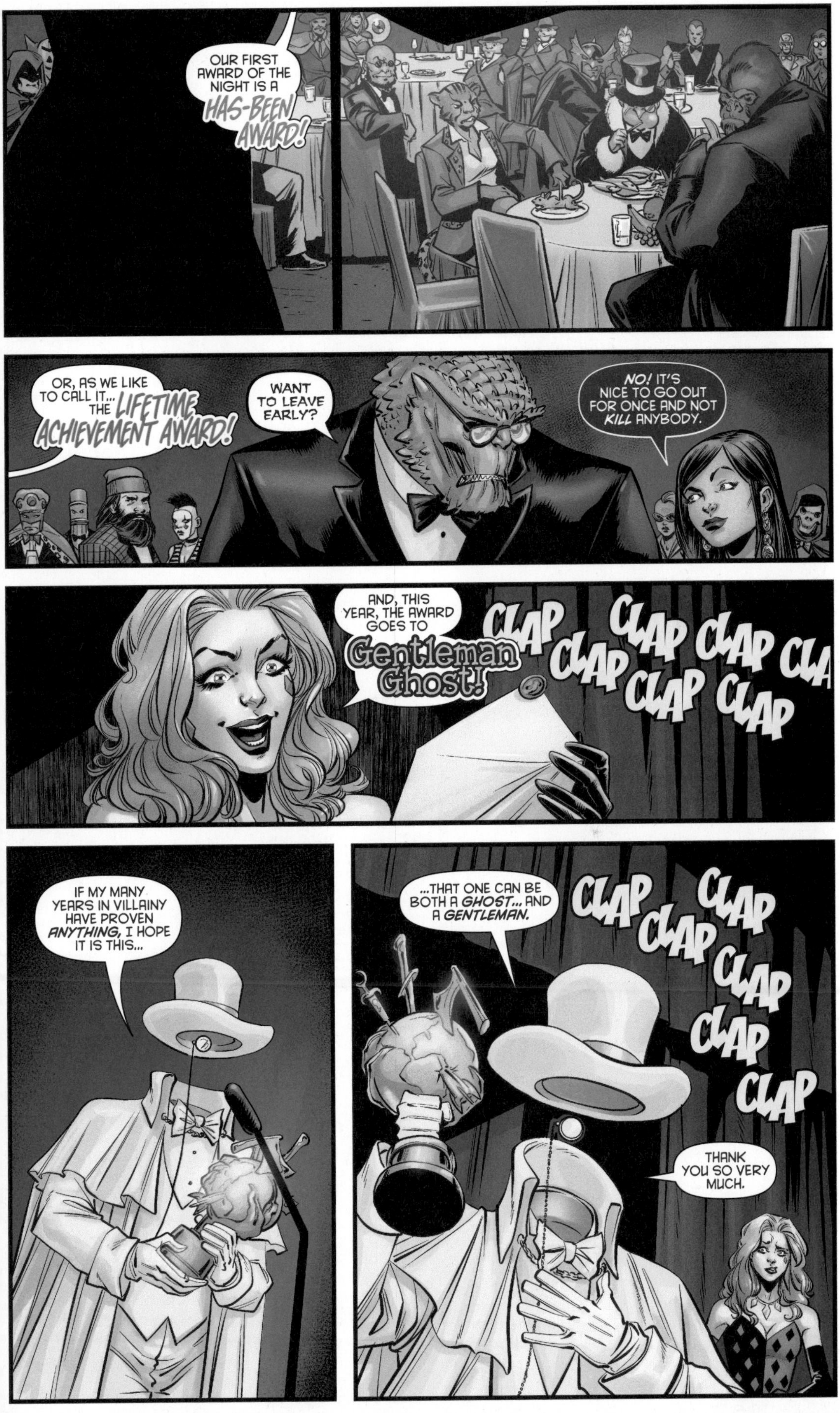

OUR FIRST AWARD OF THE NIGHT IS A HAS-BEEN AWARD!
OR, AS WE LIKE TO CALL IT... THE LIFETIME ACHIEVEMENT AWARD!
WANT TO LEAVE EARLY?
NO! IT'S NICE TO GO OUT FOR ONCE AND NOT KILL ANYBODY.
AND, THIS YEAR, THE AWARD GOES TO Gentleman Ghost!
CLAP CLAP CLAP CLAP CLAP CLAP CLAP CLA
IF MY MANY YEARS IN VILLAINY HAVE PROVEN ANYTHING, I HOPE IT IS THIS...
...THAT ONE CAN BE BOTH A GHOST... AND A GENTLEMAN.
CLAP CLAP CLAP CLAP CLAP CLAP
THANK YOU SO VERY MUCH.

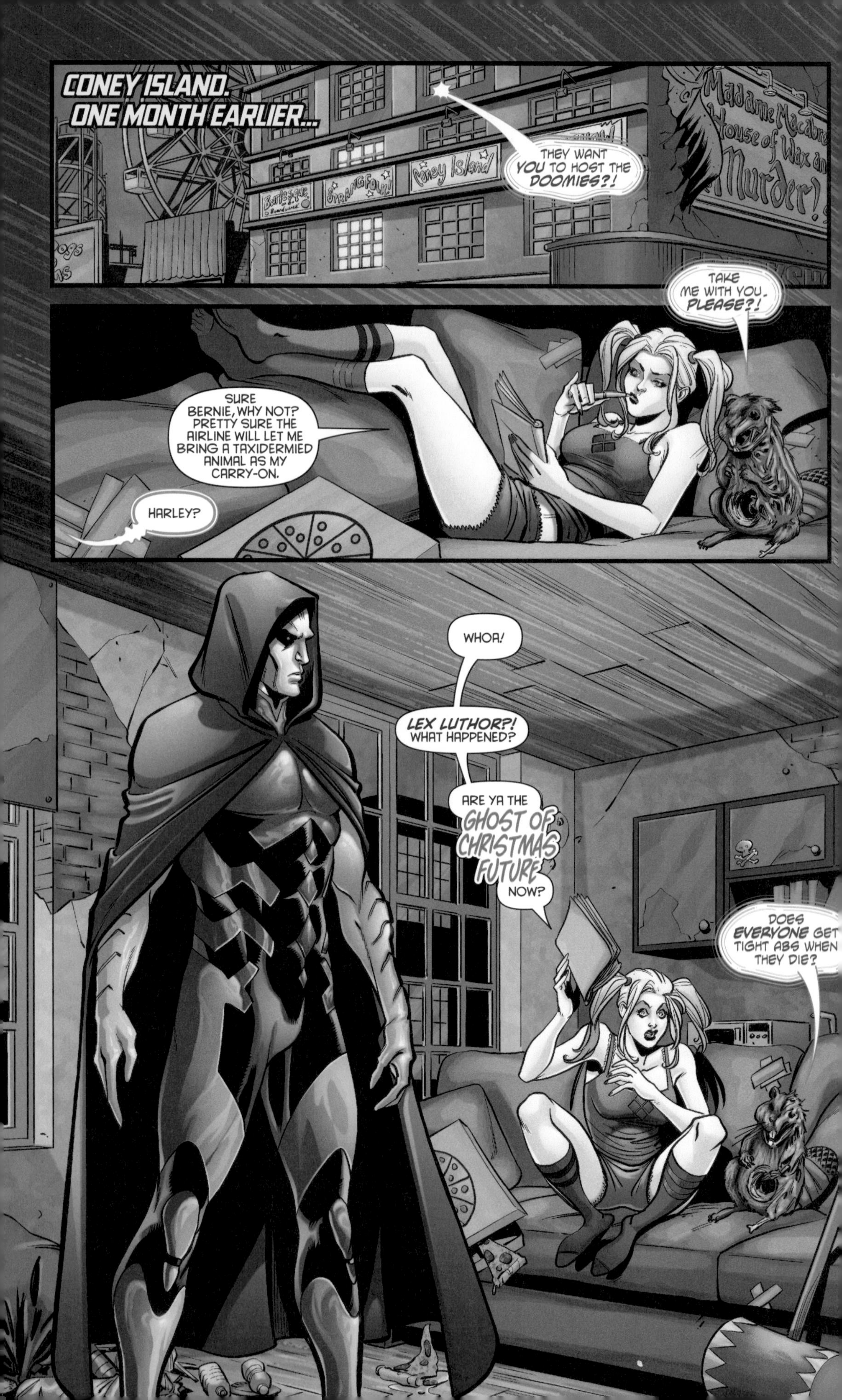
CONEY ISLAND. ONE MONTH EARLIER...
Madame Macabre's House of Wax and Murder!
Burlesque
STRANGE FOLK!
Coney Island
THEY WANT YOU TO HOST THE DOOMIES?!
TAKE ME WITH YOU, PLEASE?!
SURE BERNIE, WHY NOT? PRETTY SURE THE AIRLINE WILL LET ME BRING A TAXIDERMIED ANIMAL AS MY CARRY-ON.
HARLEY?
WHOA!
LEX LUTHOR?! WHAT HAPPENED?
ARE YA THE GHOST OF CHRISTMAS FUTURE NOW?
DOES EVERYONE GET TIGHT ABS WHEN THEY DIE?

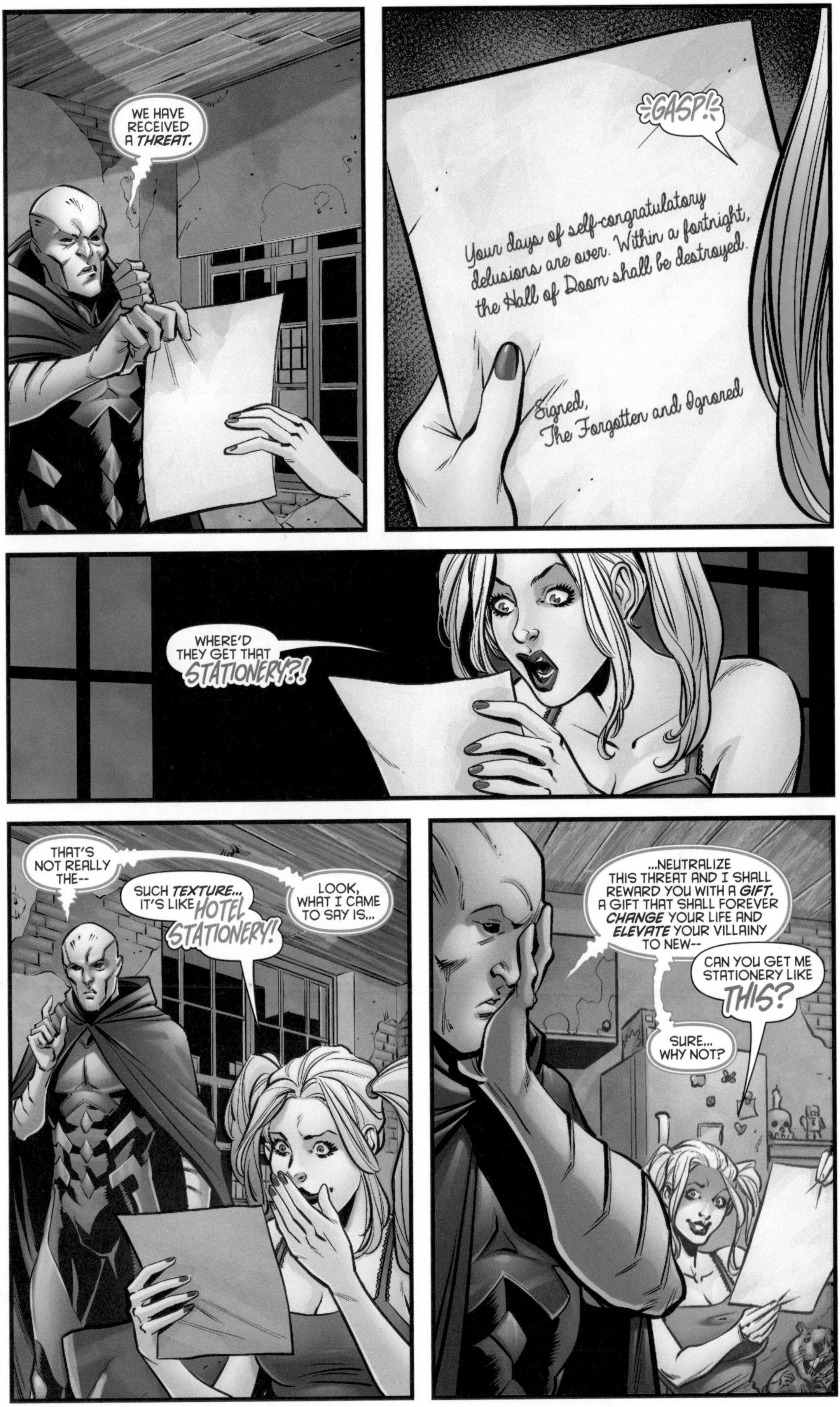
WE HAVE RECEIVED A *THREAT.*
GASP!
Your days of self-congratulatory delusions are over. Within a fortnight, the Hall of Doom shall be destroyed.
Signed, The Forgotten and Ignored
WHERE'D THEY GET THAT STATIONERY?!
THAT'S NOT REALLY THE--
SUCH *TEXTURE...* IT'S LIKE HOTEL STATIONERY!
LOOK, WHAT I CAME TO SAY IS...
...NEUTRALIZE THIS THREAT AND I SHALL REWARD YOU WITH A *GIFT.* A GIFT THAT SHALL FOREVER *CHANGE* YOUR LIFE AND *ELEVATE* YOUR VILLAINY TO NEW--
CAN YOU GET ME STATIONERY LIKE THIS?
SURE... WHY NOT?

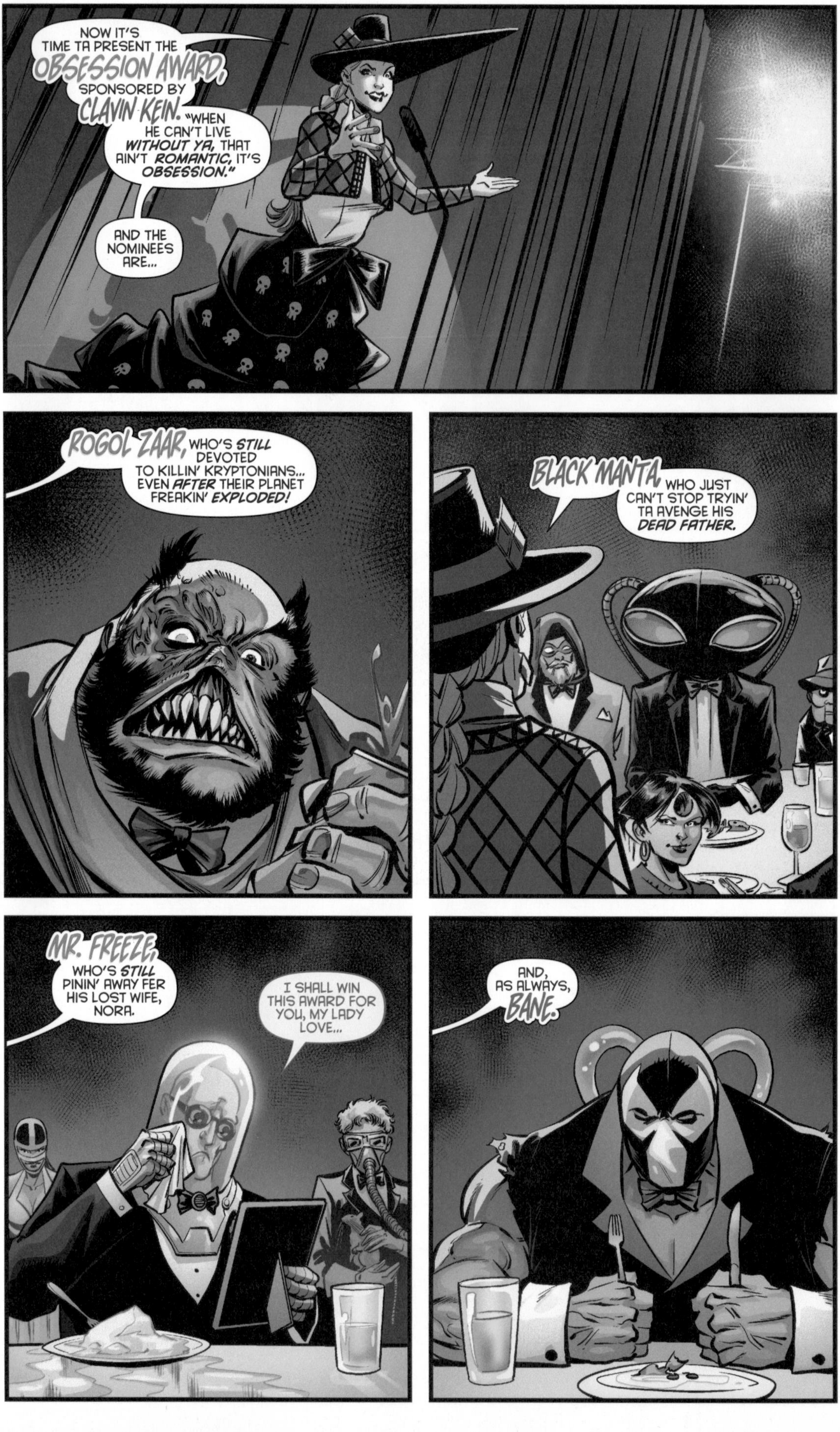
NOW IT'S TIME TA PRESENT THE OBSESSION AWARD, SPONSORED BY CLAVIN KEIN. "WHEN HE CAN'T LIVE WITHOUT YA, THAT AIN'T ROMANTIC, IT'S OBSESSION."
AND THE NOMINEES ARE...
ROGOL ZAAR, WHO'S STILL DEVOTED TO KILLIN' KRYPTONIANS... EVEN AFTER THEIR PLANET FREAKIN' EXPLODED!
BLACK MANTA, WHO JUST CAN'T STOP TRYIN' TA AVENGE HIS DEAD FATHER.
MR. FREEZE, WHO'S STILL PININ' AWAY FER HIS LOST WIFE, NORA.
I SHALL WIN THIS AWARD FOR YOU, MY LADY LOVE...
AND, AS ALWAYS, BANE.

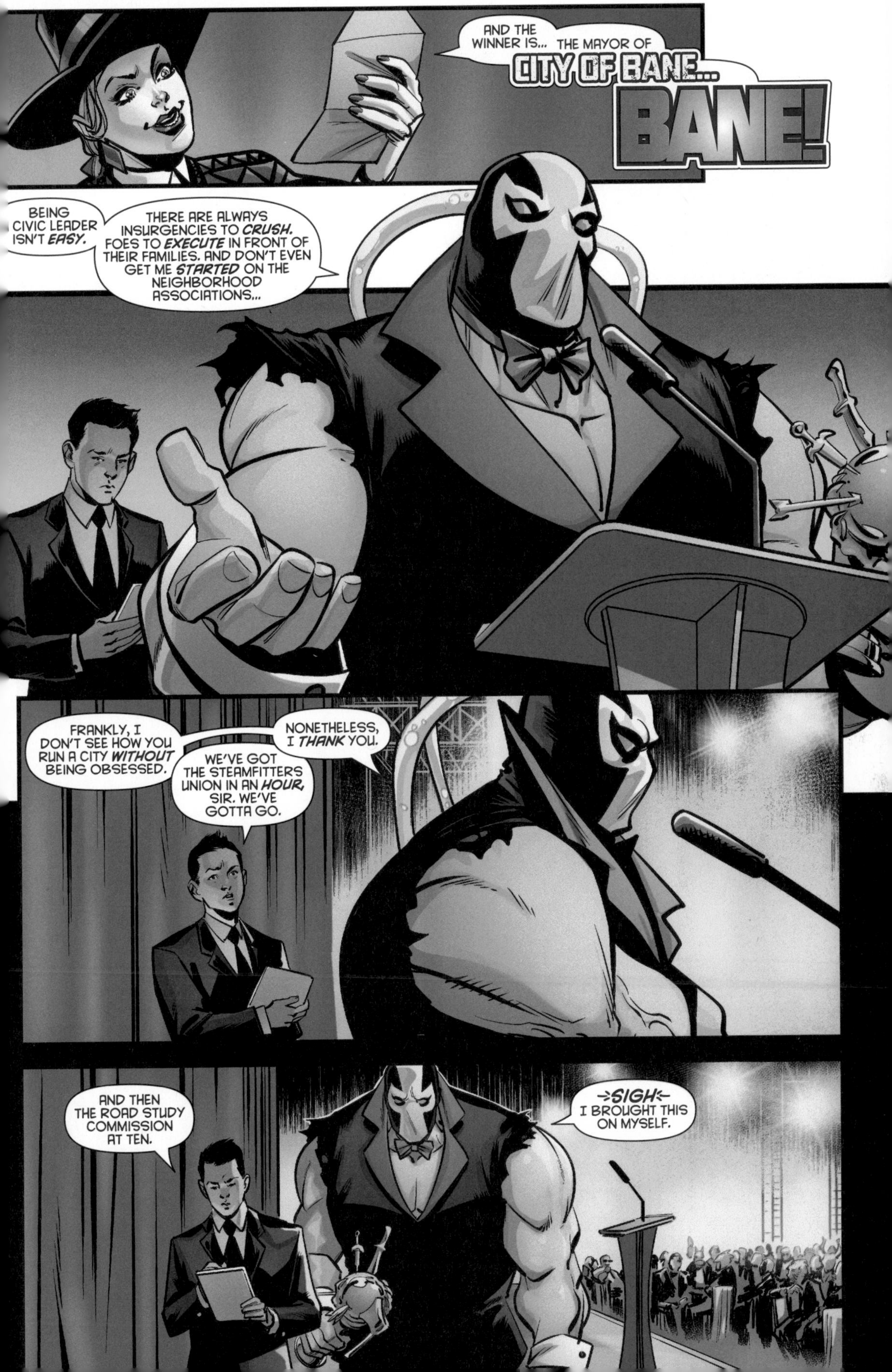
AND THE WINNER IS... THE MAYOR OF
CITY OF BANE...
BANE!
BEING CIVIC LEADER ISN'T EASY.
THERE ARE ALWAYS INSURGENCIES TO CRUSH. FOES TO EXECUTE IN FRONT OF THEIR FAMILIES. AND DON'T EVEN GET ME STARTED ON THE NEIGHBORHOOD ASSOCIATIONS...
FRANKLY, I DON'T SEE HOW YOU RUN A CITY WITHOUT BEING OBSESSED.
NONETHELESS, I THANK YOU.
WE'VE GOT THE STEAMFITTERS UNION IN AN HOUR, SIR. WE'VE GOTTA GO.
AND THEN THE ROAD STUDY COMMISSION AT TEN.
SIGH
I BROUGHT THIS ON MYSELF.

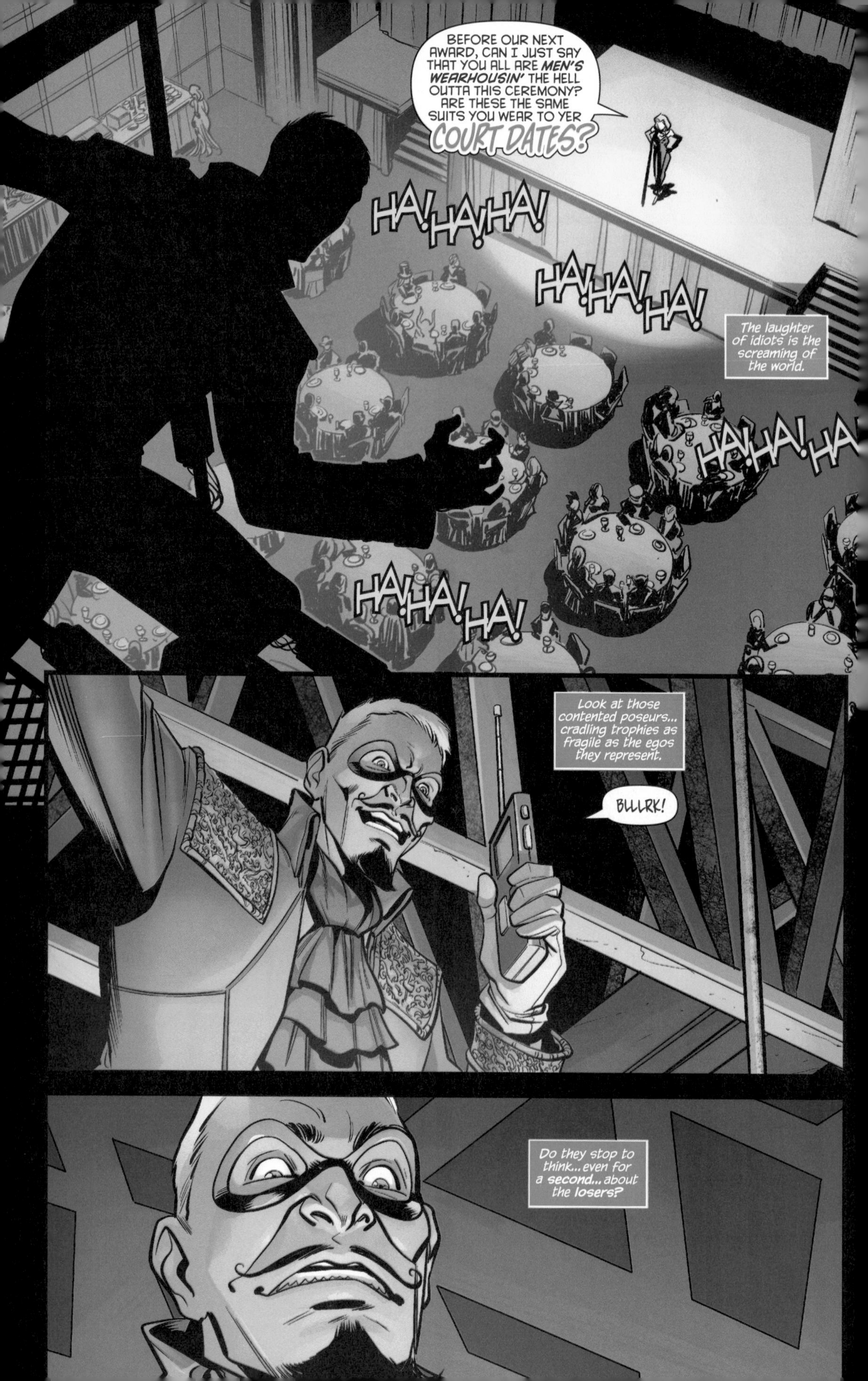

BEFORE OUR NEXT AWARD, CAN I JUST SAY THAT YOU ALL ARE ***MEN'S WEARHOUSIN'*** THE HELL OUTTA THIS CEREMONY? ARE THESE THE SAME SUITS YOU WEAR TO YER COURT DATES?
HA! HA! HA!
HA! HA! HA!
The laughter of idiots is the screaming of the world.
HA! HA! HA
HA! HA! HA!
Look at those contented poseurs... cradling trophies as fragile as the egos they represent.
BLLLRK!
*Do they stop to think... even for a **second**... about the **losers**?*

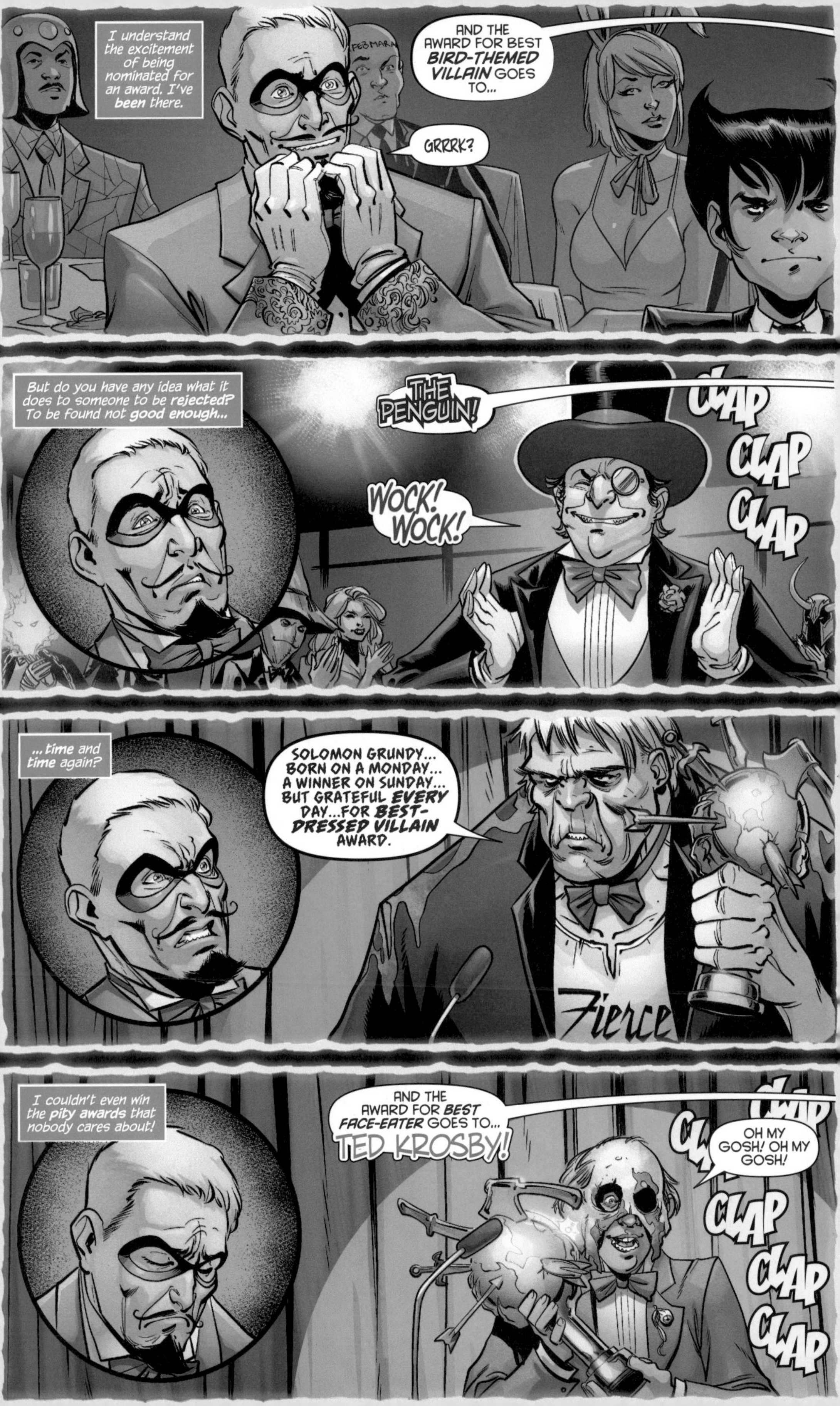
I understand the excitement of being nominated for an award. I've been there.
AND THE AWARD FOR BEST BIRD-THEMED VILLAIN GOES TO...
GRRRK?
But do you have any idea what it does to someone to be rejected? To be found not good enough...
THE PENGUIN!
CLAP CLAP CLAP
WOCK! WOCK!
...time and time again?
SOLOMON GRUNDY... BORN ON A MONDAY... A WINNER ON SUNDAY... BUT GRATEFUL EVERY DAY...FOR BEST-DRESSED VILLAIN AWARD.
Fierce
I couldn't even win the pity awards that nobody cares about!
AND THE AWARD FOR BEST FACE-EATER GOES TO... TED KROSBY!
OH MY GOSH! OH MY GOSH!
CLAP CLAP CLAP

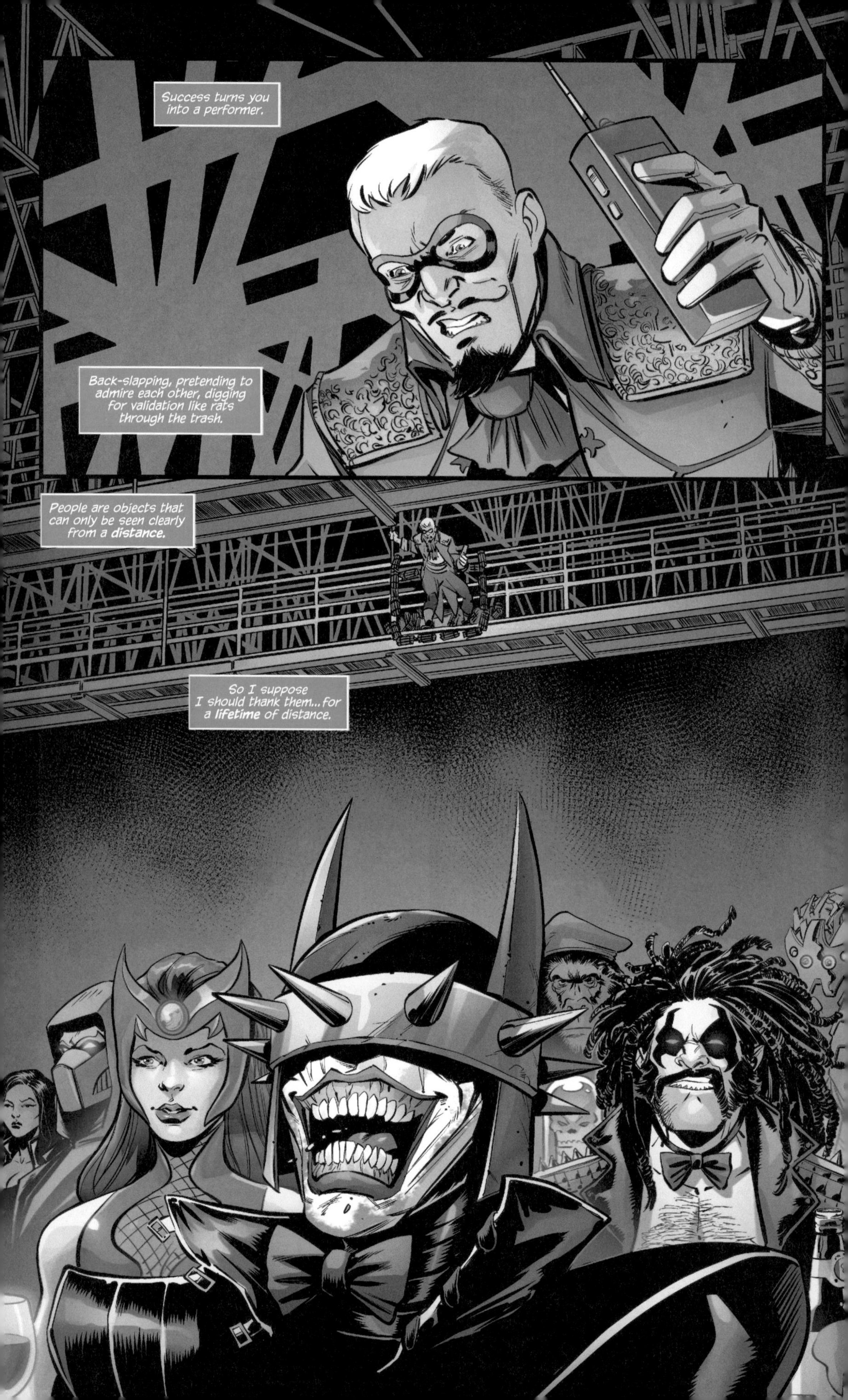
Success turns you into a performer.
Back-slapping, pretending to admire each other, digging for validation like rats through the trash.
People are objects that can only be seen clearly from a **distance.**
So I suppose I should thank them...for a ***lifetime*** of distance.

OUR NEXT AWARD IS THE "WE'RE NOT SO DIFFERENT, YOU AND I" AWARD FOR *BEST MORAL JUSTIFICATION!*

AND THE NOMINEES ARE...

"...LEX LUTHOR!"

AND THEN IT OCCURRED TO ME...THAT *EVIL* IS SIMPLY THE NAME WE GIVE TO THE *WORK* OTHERS ARE TOO WEAK TO *DO.*

SURE, I'LL *BUY* THAT!

"MIRROR MASTER!"

BEFORE YOU CALL *ME* EVIL, CONSIDER... WHAT WOULD *YOU* DO TO BRING BACK THE WOMAN *YOU* LOVE?! IS THERE EVEN SUCH A THING AS *EVIL,* WHEN COMMITTED OUT OF *LOVE?*

UH...I'M PRETTY SURE EVERYONE YOU JUST *KILLED* WAS LOVED BY *SOMEBODY.*

SHUT UP.

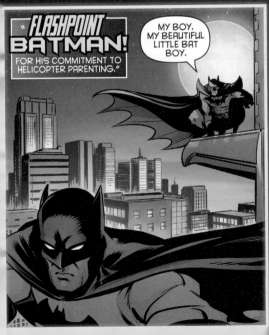

"*FLASHPOINT* BATMAN! FOR HIS COMMITMENT TO HELICOPTER PARENTING."

MY BOY. MY BEAUTIFUL LITTLE BAT BOY.

"...AND *LEVIATHAN.*"

YOU'VE DESTROYED *A.R.G.U.S.,* THE *D.E.O.,* AND *S.H.A.D.E.*

WHY?!

JUST NOT A BIG FAN OF *ACRONYMS.*

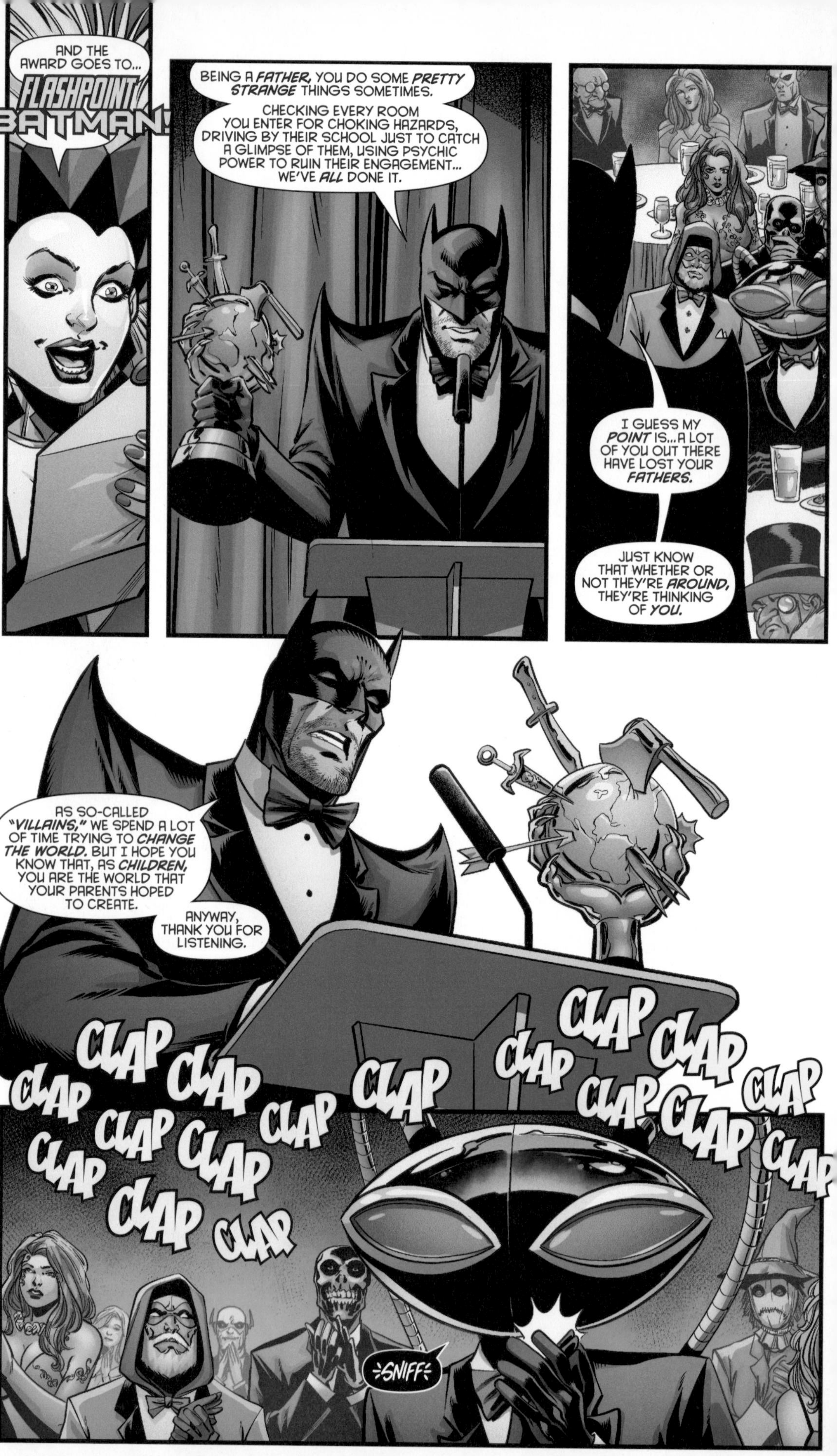
AND THE AWARD GOES TO...
FLASHPOINT BATMAN!
BEING A FATHER, YOU DO SOME PRETTY STRANGE THINGS SOMETIMES.
CHECKING EVERY ROOM YOU ENTER FOR CHOKING HAZARDS, DRIVING BY THEIR SCHOOL JUST TO CATCH A GLIMPSE OF THEM, USING PSYCHIC POWER TO RUIN THEIR ENGAGEMENT... WE'VE ALL DONE IT.
I GUESS MY POINT IS...A LOT OF YOU OUT THERE HAVE LOST YOUR FATHERS.
JUST KNOW THAT WHETHER OR NOT THEY'RE AROUND, THEY'RE THINKING OF YOU.
AS SO-CALLED "VILLAINS," WE SPEND A LOT OF TIME TRYING TO CHANGE THE WORLD. BUT I HOPE YOU KNOW THAT, AS CHILDREN, YOU ARE THE WORLD THAT YOUR PARENTS HOPED TO CREATE.
ANYWAY, THANK YOU FOR LISTENING.
CLAP CLAP CLAP CLAP CLAP CLAP CLAP CLAP CLAP CLAP CLAP CLAP CLAP CLAP CLAP CLAP CLAP CLAP
SNIFF

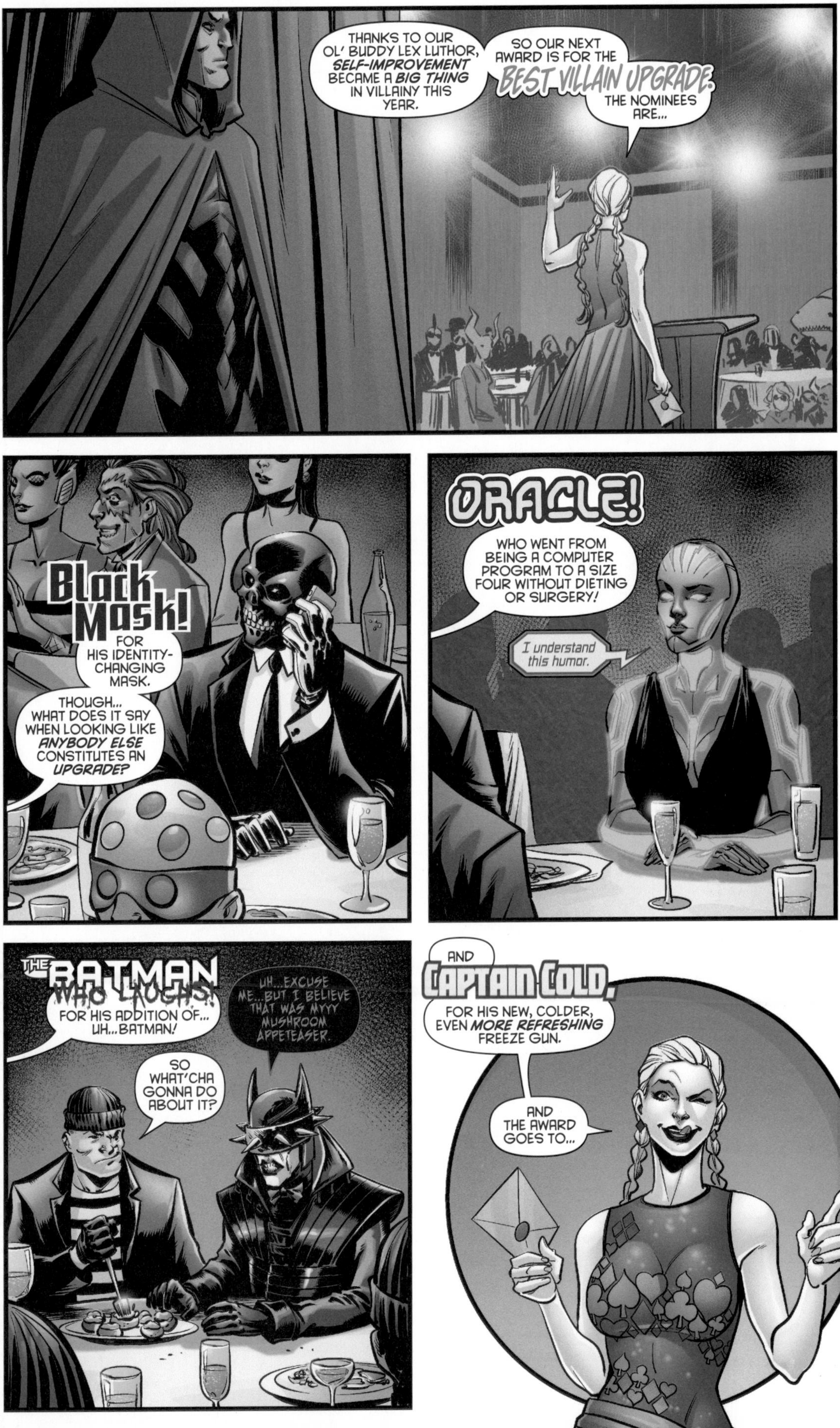
THANKS TO OUR OL' BUDDY LEX LUTHOR, SELF-IMPROVEMENT BECAME A BIG THING IN VILLAINY THIS YEAR.
SO OUR NEXT AWARD IS FOR THE BEST VILLAIN UPGRADE.
THE NOMINEES ARE...
BLACK MASK!
FOR HIS IDENTITY-CHANGING MASK.
THOUGH... WHAT DOES IT SAY WHEN LOOKING LIKE ANYBODY ELSE CONSTITUTES AN UPGRADE?
ORACLE!
WHO WENT FROM BEING A COMPUTER PROGRAM TO A SIZE FOUR WITHOUT DIETING OR SURGERY!
I understand this humor.
THE BATMAN WHO LAUGHS!
FOR HIS ADDITION OF... UH...BATMAN!
UH...EXCUSE ME...BUT I BELIEVE THAT WAS MYYY MUSHROOM APPETEASER.
SO WHAT'CHA GONNA DO ABOUT IT?
AND
CAPTAIN COLD,
FOR HIS NEW, COLDER, EVEN MORE REFRESHING FREEZE GUN.
AND THE AWARD GOES TO...

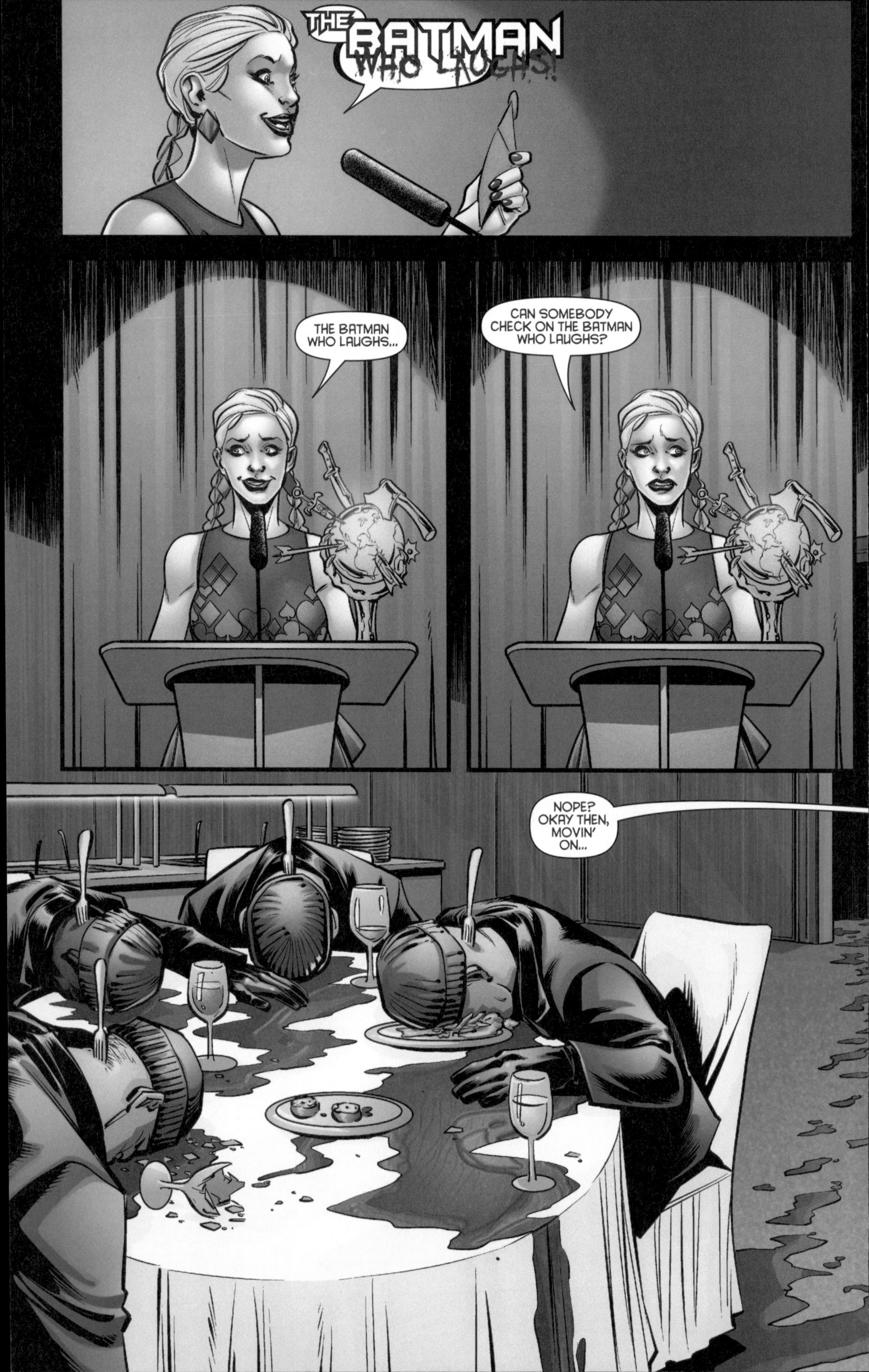
THE BATMAN WHO LAUGHS!
THE BATMAN WHO LAUGHS...
CAN SOMEBODY CHECK ON THE BATMAN WHO LAUGHS?
NOPE? OKAY THEN, MOVIN' ON...

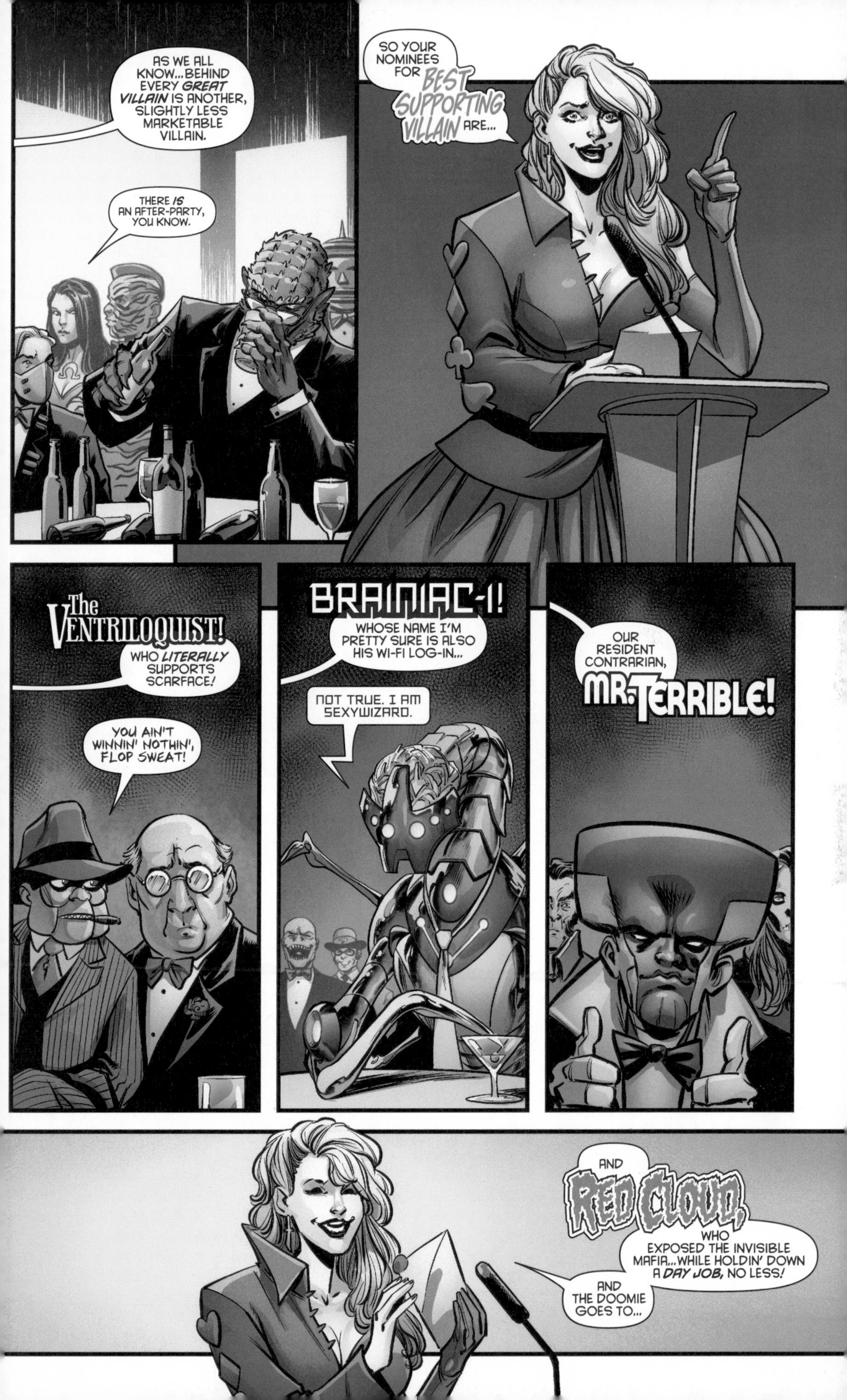

AS WE ALL KNOW...BEHIND EVERY GREAT VILLAIN IS ANOTHER, SLIGHTLY LESS MARKETABLE VILLAIN.
SO YOUR NOMINEES FOR BEST SUPPORTING VILLAIN ARE...
THERE IS AN AFTER-PARTY, YOU KNOW.
The VENTRILOQUIST!
WHO LITERALLY SUPPORTS SCARFACE!
YOU AIN'T WINNIN' NOTHIN', FLOP SWEAT!
BRAINIAC-1!
WHOSE NAME I'M PRETTY SURE IS ALSO HIS WI-FI LOG-IN...
NOT TRUE. I AM SEXYWIZARD.
OUR RESIDENT CONTRARIAN,
MR. TERRIBLE!
AND
RED CLOUD,
WHO EXPOSED THE INVISIBLE MAFIA...WHILE HOLDIN' DOWN A DAY JOB, NO LESS!
AND THE DOOMIE GOES TO...

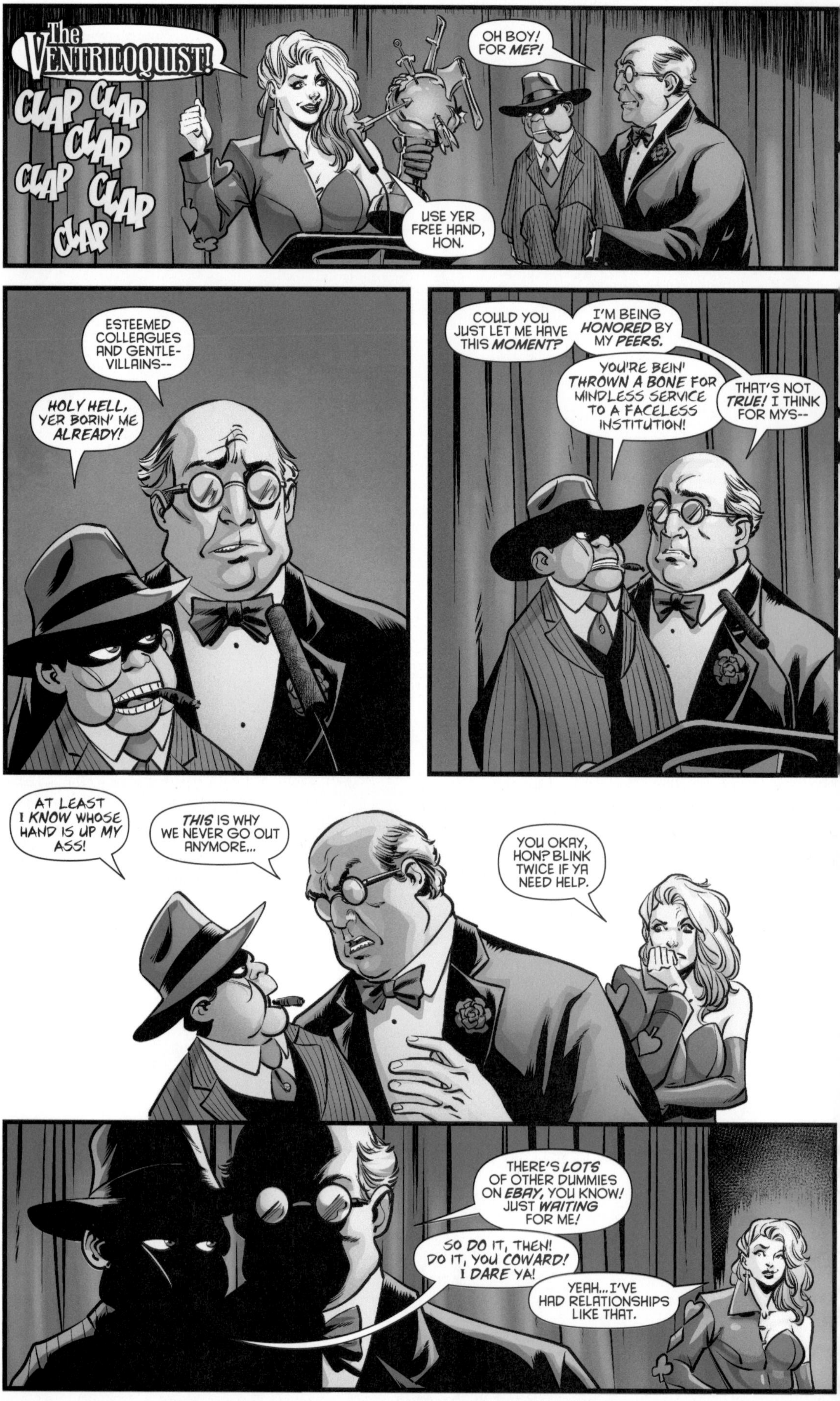
The VENTRILOQUIST!
CLAP CLAP CLAP CLAP CLAP CLAP
OH BOY! FOR ME?!
USE YER FREE HAND, HON.
ESTEEMED COLLEAGUES AND GENTLE-VILLAINS--
HOLY HELL, YER BORIN' ME ALREADY!
COULD YOU JUST LET ME HAVE THIS MOMENT?
I'M BEING HONORED BY MY PEERS.
YOU'RE BEIN' THROWN A BONE FOR MINDLESS SERVICE TO A FACELESS INSTITUTION!
THAT'S NOT TRUE! I THINK FOR MYS--
AT LEAST I KNOW WHOSE HAND IS UP MY ASS!
THIS IS WHY WE NEVER GO OUT ANYMORE...
YOU OKAY, HON? BLINK TWICE IF YA NEED HELP.
THERE'S LOTS OF OTHER DUMMIES ON EBAY, YOU KNOW! JUST WAITING FOR ME!
SO DO IT, THEN! DO IT, YOU COWARD! I DARE YA!
YEAH...I'VE HAD RELATIONSHIPS LIKE THAT.

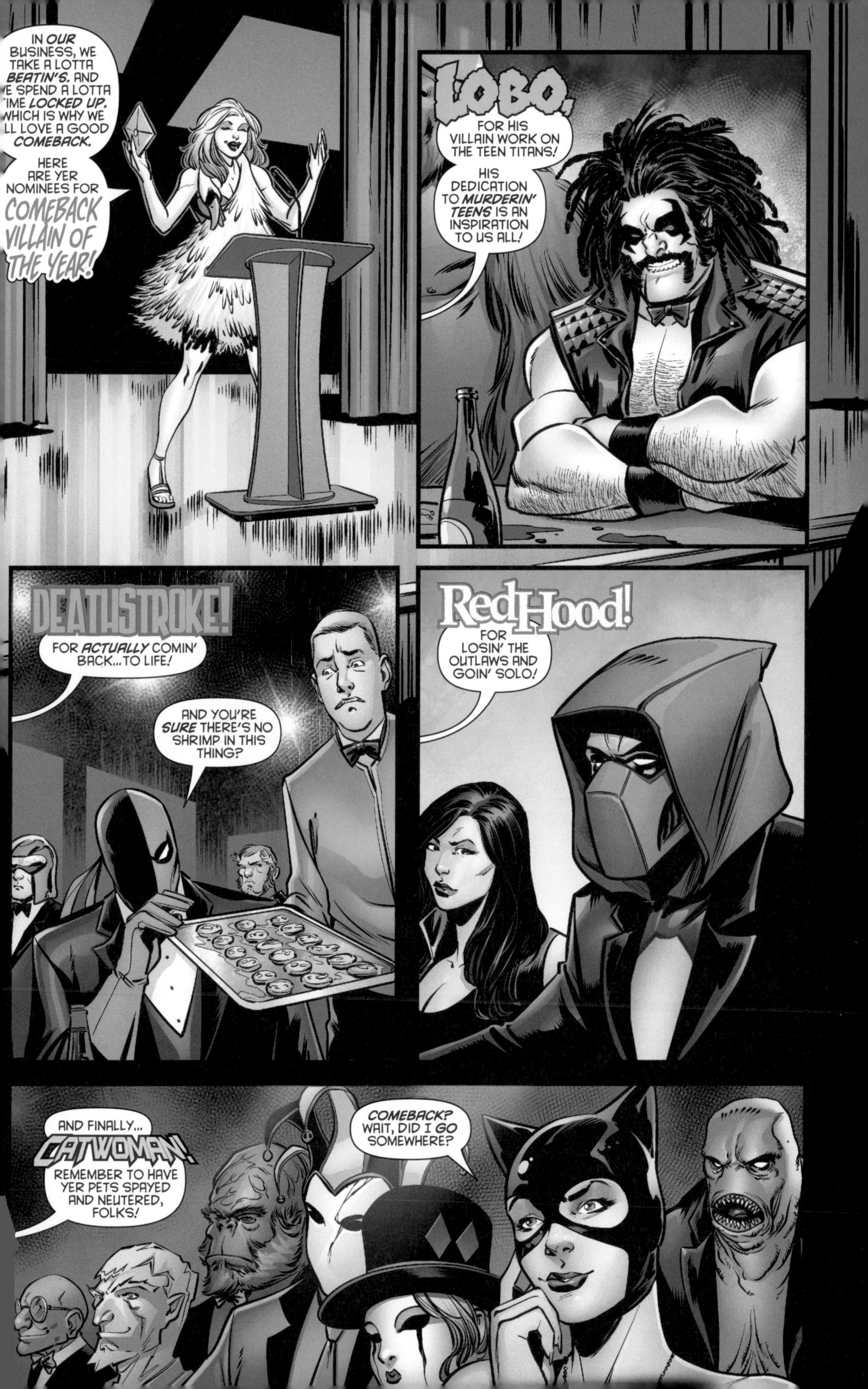
IN OUR BUSINESS, WE TAKE A LOTTA BEATIN'S. AND WE SPEND A LOTTA TIME LOCKED UP. WHICH IS WHY WE ALL LOVE A GOOD COMEBACK.
HERE ARE YER NOMINEES FOR
COMEBACK VILLAIN OF THE YEAR!
LOBO.
FOR HIS VILLAIN WORK ON THE TEEN TITANS!
HIS DEDICATION TO MURDERIN' TEENS IS AN INSPIRATION TO US ALL!
DEATHSTROKE!
FOR ACTUALLY COMIN' BACK...TO LIFE!
AND YOU'RE SURE THERE'S NO SHRIMP IN THIS THING?
RedHood!
FOR LOSIN' THE OUTLAWS AND GOIN' SOLO!
AND FINALLY...
CATWOMAN!
REMEMBER TO HAVE YER PETS SPAYED AND NEUTERED, FOLKS!
COMEBACK? WAIT, DID I GO SOMEWHERE?

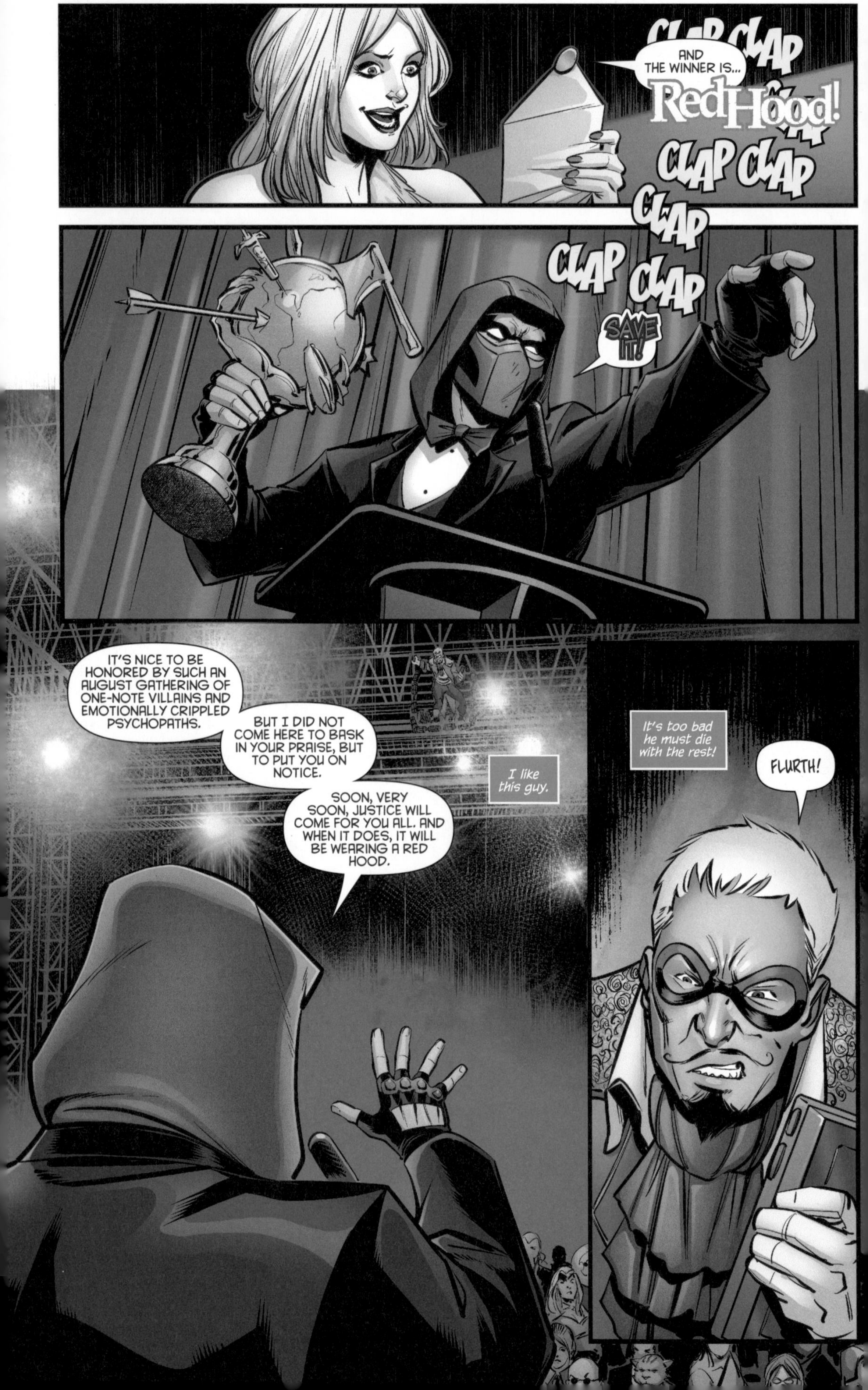
CLAP CLAP
AND THE WINNER IS...
Red Hood!
CLAP CLAP
CLAP
CLAP CLAP
SAVE IT!
IT'S NICE TO BE HONORED BY SUCH AN AUGUST GATHERING OF ONE-NOTE VILLAINS AND EMOTIONALLY CRIPPLED PSYCHOPATHS.
BUT I DID NOT COME HERE TO BASK IN YOUR PRAISE, BUT TO PUT YOU ON NOTICE.
SOON, VERY SOON, JUSTICE WILL COME FOR YOU ALL. AND WHEN IT DOES, IT WILL BE WEARING A RED HOOD.
I like this guy.
It's too bad he must die with the rest!
FLURTH!

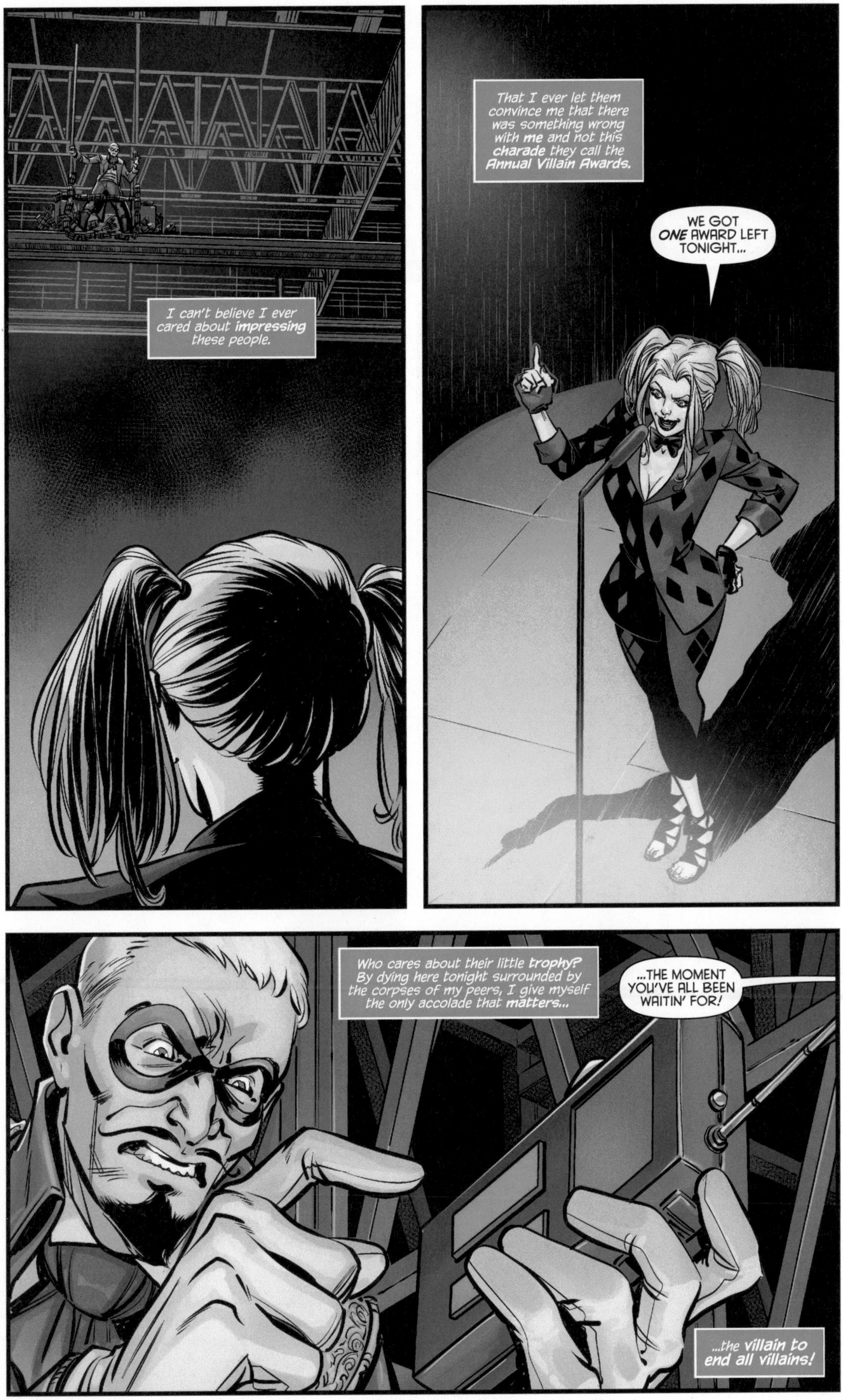
I can't believe I ever cared about impressing these people.
That I ever let them convince me that there was something wrong with me and not this charade they call the Annual Villain Awards.
WE GOT ONE AWARD LEFT TONIGHT...
Who cares about their little trophy? By dying here tonight surrounded by the corpses of my peers, I give myself the only accolade that matters...
...THE MOMENT YOU'VE ALL BEEN WAITIN' FOR!
...the villain to end all villains!

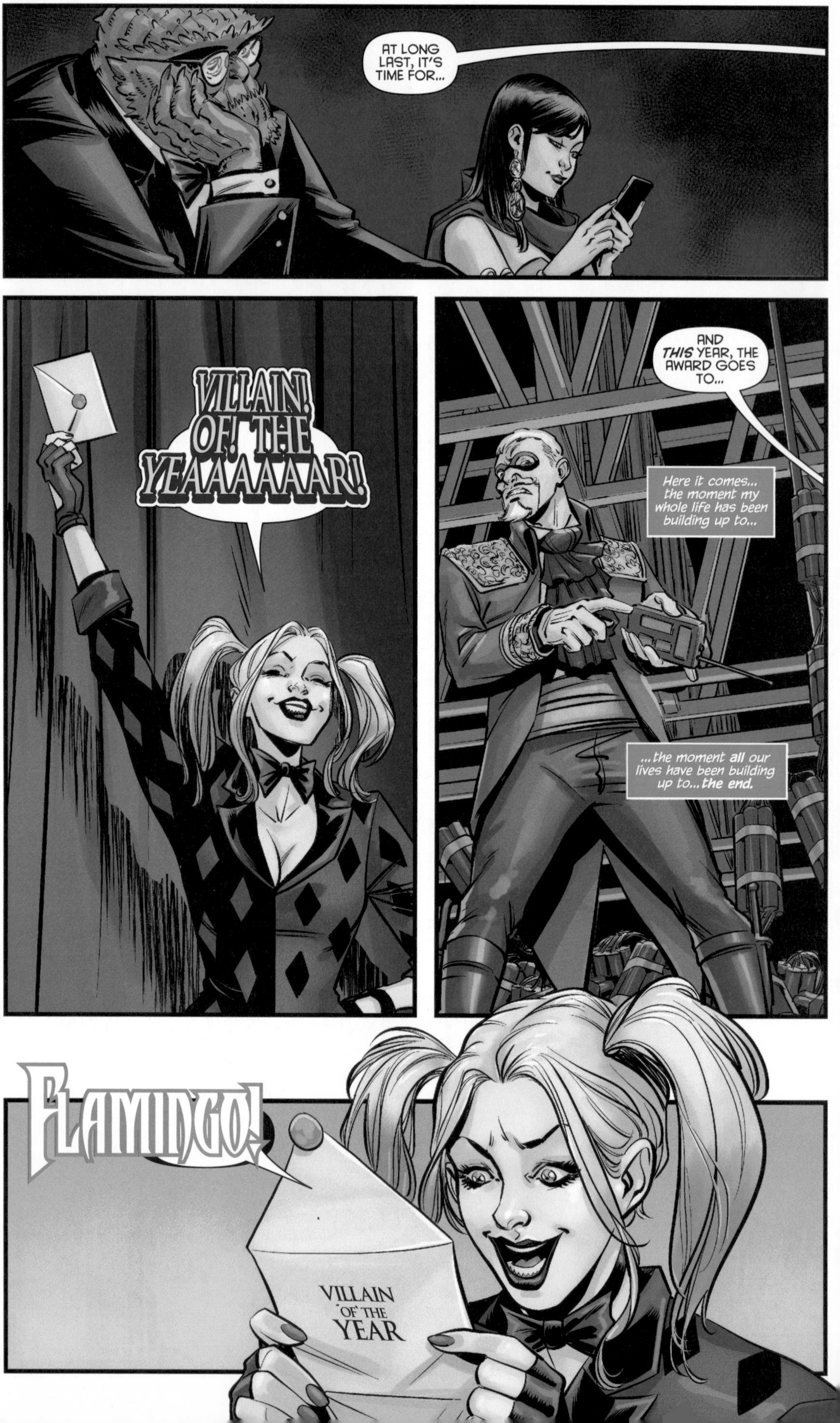

AT LONG LAST, IT'S TIME FOR...
VILLAIN! OF! THE YEAAAAAAAR!
AND *THIS* YEAR, THE AWARD GOES TO...
Here it comes... the moment my whole life has been building up to...
*...the moment **all** our lives have been building up to... **the end.***
FLAMINGO!
VILLAIN OF THE YEAR

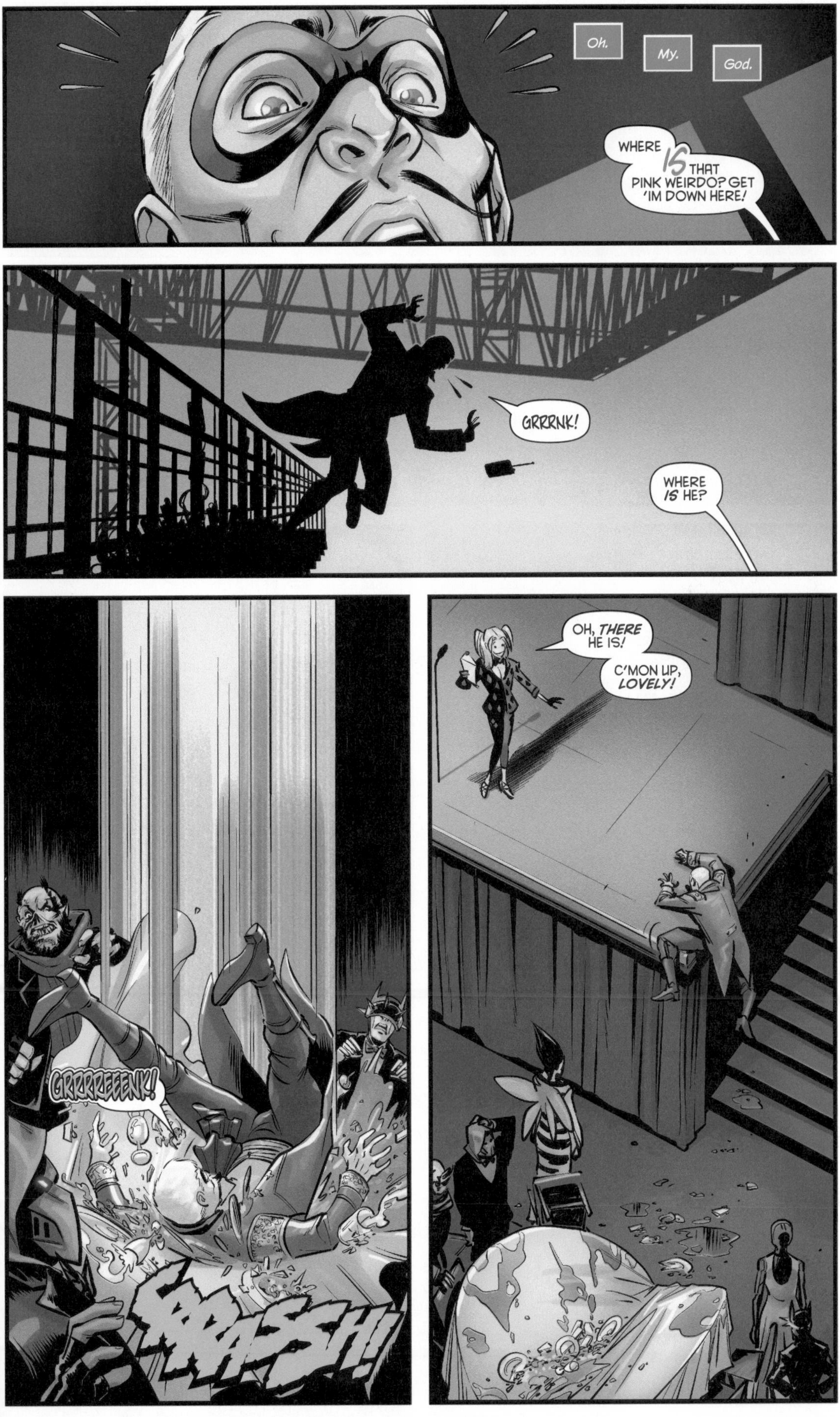
Oh.
My.
God.
WHERE IS THAT PINK WEIRDO? GET 'IM DOWN HERE!
GRRRNK!
WHERE IS HE?
GRRRREEEENK!
SPLASH!
OH, THERE HE IS!
C'MON UP, LOVELY!

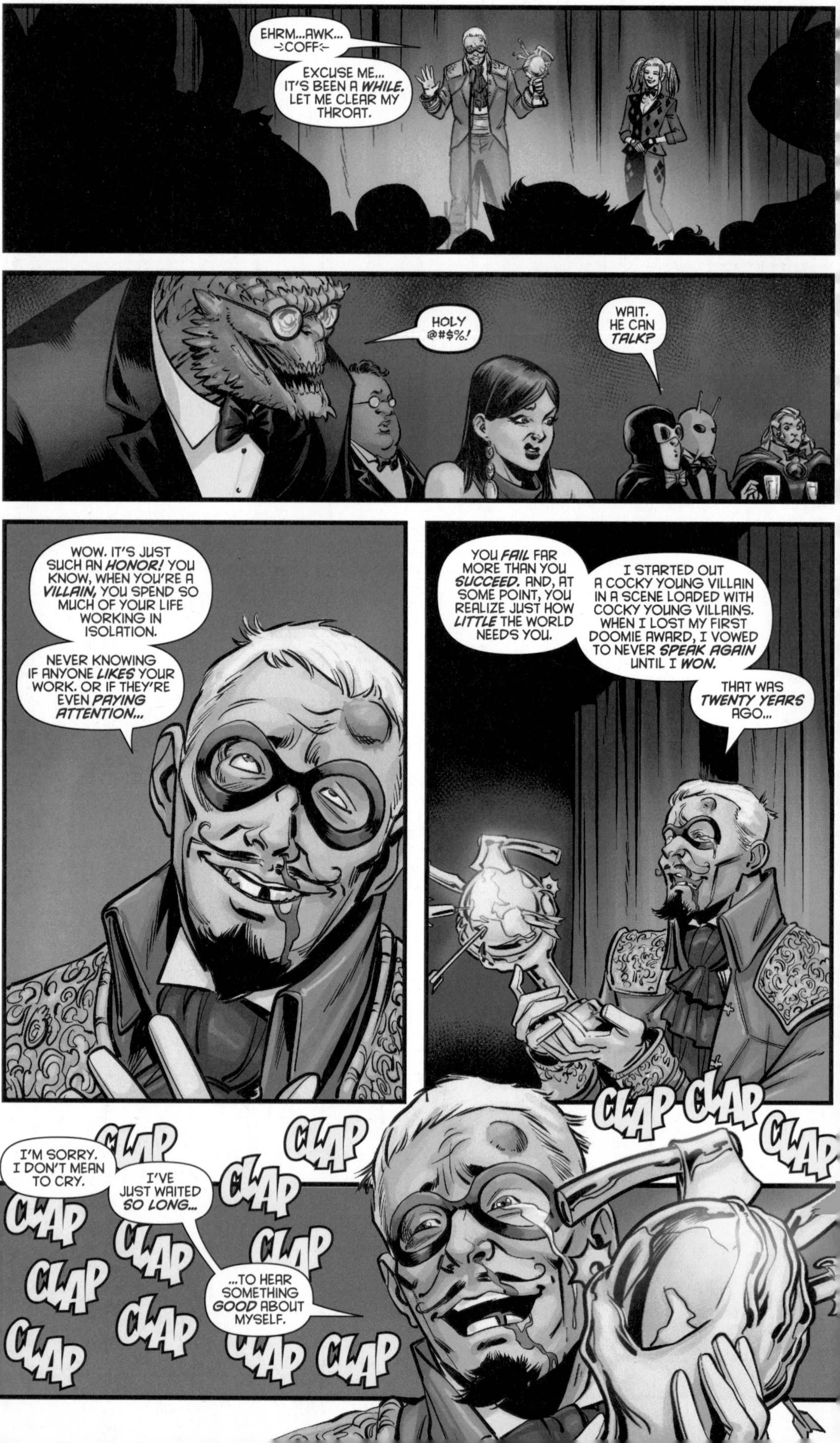

EHRM...AWK... -COFF-
EXCUSE ME... IT'S BEEN A WHILE. LET ME CLEAR MY THROAT.
HOLY @#$%!
WAIT. HE CAN TALK?
WOW. IT'S JUST SUCH AN HONOR! YOU KNOW, WHEN YOU'RE A VILLAIN, YOU SPEND SO MUCH OF YOUR LIFE WORKING IN ISOLATION.
NEVER KNOWING IF ANYONE LIKES YOUR WORK. OR IF THEY'RE EVEN PAYING ATTENTION...
YOU FAIL FAR MORE THAN YOU SUCCEED. AND, AT SOME POINT, YOU REALIZE JUST HOW LITTLE THE WORLD NEEDS YOU.
I STARTED OUT A COCKY YOUNG VILLAIN IN A SCENE LOADED WITH COCKY YOUNG VILLAINS. WHEN I LOST MY FIRST DOOMIE AWARD, I VOWED TO NEVER SPEAK AGAIN UNTIL I WON.
THAT WAS TWENTY YEARS AGO...
CLAP CLAP CLAP
I'M SORRY. I DON'T MEAN TO CRY.
I'VE JUST WAITED SO LONG...
...TO HEAR SOMETHING GOOD ABOUT MYSELF.
CLAP CLAP CLAP CLAP CLAP CLAP CLAP CLAP CLAP CLAP CLAP

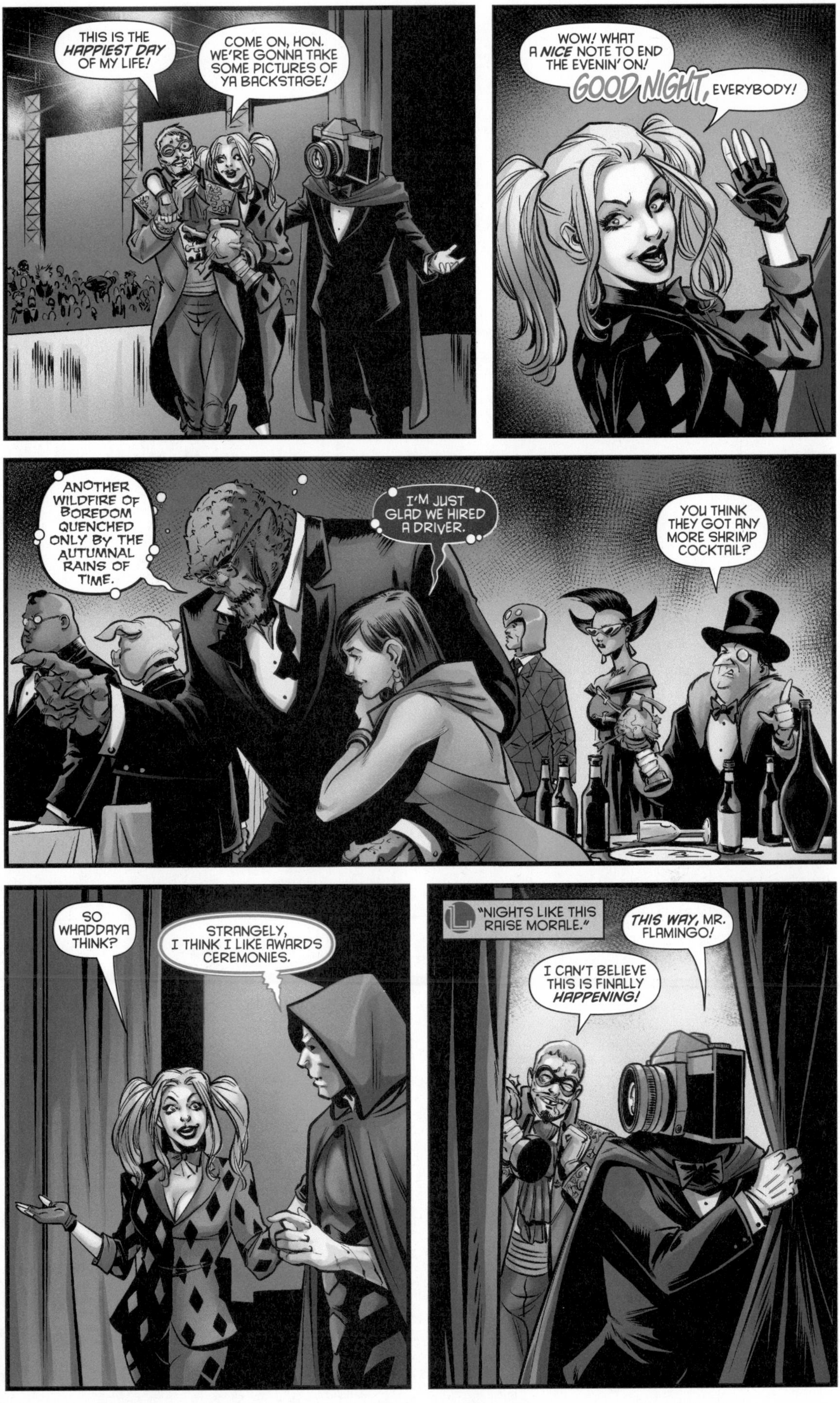
THIS IS THE HAPPIEST DAY OF MY LIFE!
COME ON, HON. WE'RE GONNA TAKE SOME PICTURES OF YA BACKSTAGE!
WOW! WHAT A NICE NOTE TO END THE EVENIN' ON! GOOD NIGHT, EVERYBODY!
ANOTHER WILDFIRE OF BOREDOM QUENCHED ONLY BY THE AUTUMNAL RAINS OF TIME.
I'M JUST GLAD WE HIRED A DRIVER.
YOU THINK THEY GOT ANY MORE SHRIMP COCKTAIL?
SO WHADDAYA THINK?
STRANGELY, I THINK I LIKE AWARDS CEREMONIES.
"NIGHTS LIKE THIS RAISE MORALE."
THIS WAY, MR. FLAMINGO!
I CAN'T BELIEVE THIS IS FINALLY HAPPENING!

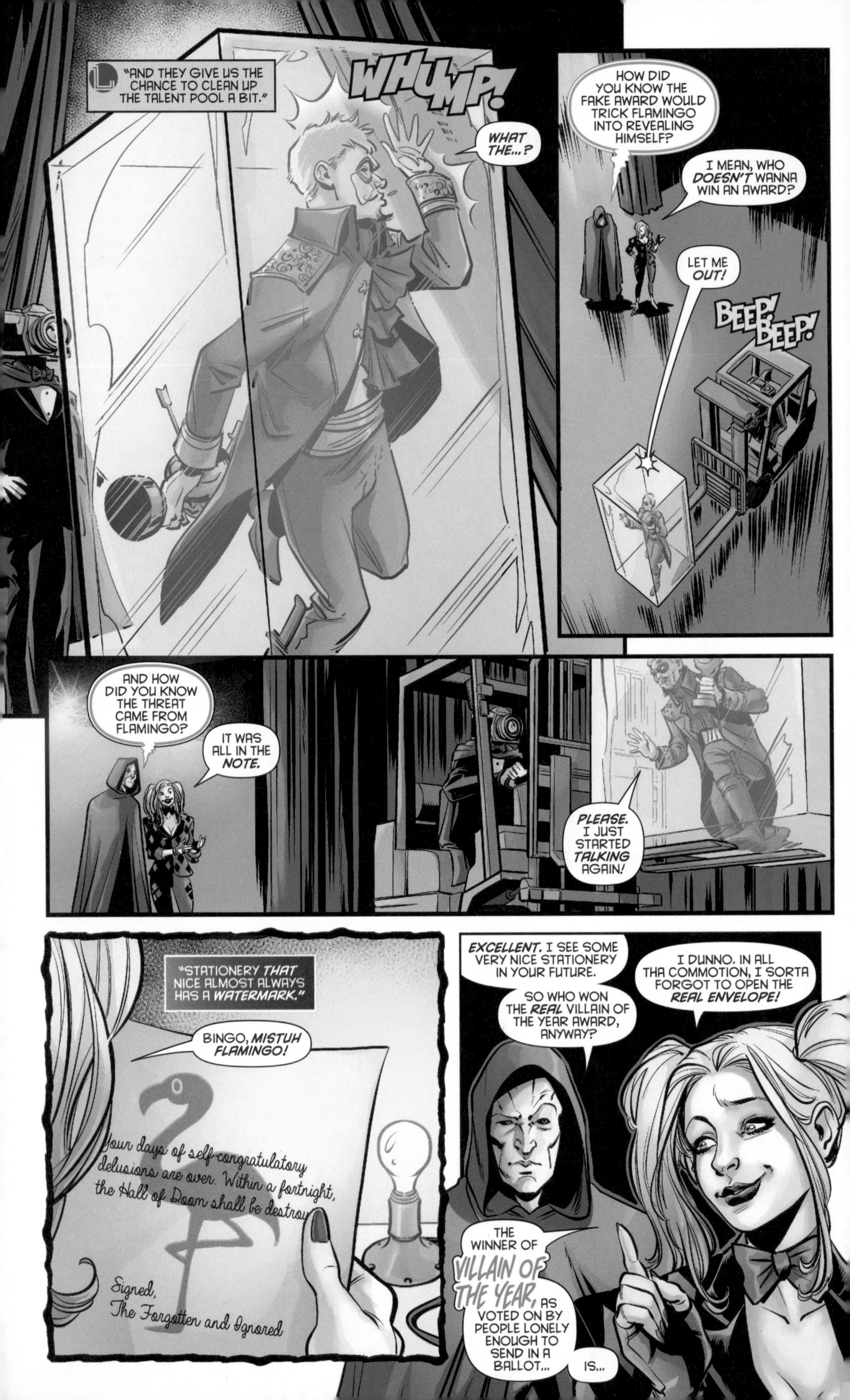
"AND THEY GIVE US THE CHANCE TO CLEAN UP THE TALENT POOL A BIT."
WHUMP!
WHAT THE...?
HOW DID YOU KNOW THE FAKE AWARD WOULD TRICK FLAMINGO INTO REVEALING HIMSELF?
I MEAN, WHO DOESN'T WANNA WIN AN AWARD?
LET ME OUT!
BEEP! BEEP!
AND HOW DID YOU KNOW THE THREAT CAME FROM FLAMINGO?
IT WAS ALL IN THE NOTE.
PLEASE. I JUST STARTED TALKING AGAIN!
"STATIONERY THAT NICE ALMOST ALWAYS HAS A WATERMARK."
BINGO, MISTUH FLAMINGO!
Your days of self-congratulatory delusions are over. Within a fortnight, the Hall of Doom shall be destro
Signed, The Forgotten and Ignored
EXCELLENT. I SEE SOME VERY NICE STATIONERY IN YOUR FUTURE.
SO WHO WON THE REAL VILLAIN OF THE YEAR AWARD, ANYWAY?
I DUNNO. IN ALL THA COMMOTION, I SORTA FORGOT TO OPEN THE REAL ENVELOPE!
THE WINNER OF VILLAIN OF THE YEAR, AS VOTED ON BY PEOPLE LONELY ENOUGH TO SEND IN A BALLOT...
IS...

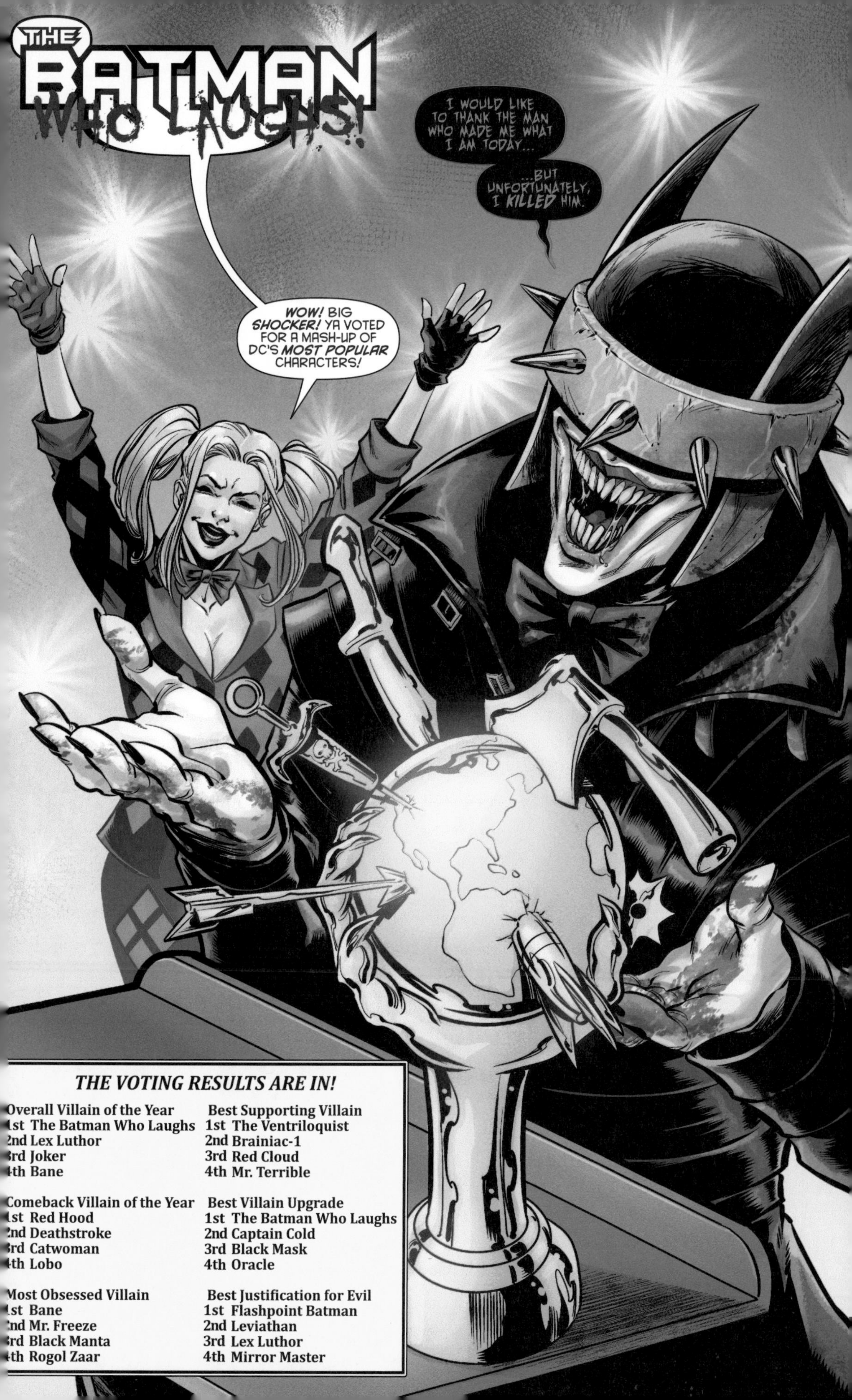
THE BATMAN WHO LAUGHS!
I WOULD LIKE TO THANK THE MAN WHO MADE ME WHAT I AM TODAY...
...BUT UNFORTUNATELY, I KILLED HIM.
WOW! BIG SHOCKER! YA VOTED FOR A MASH-UP OF DC'S MOST POPULAR CHARACTERS!

THE VOTING RESULTS ARE IN!

Overall Villain of the Year
1st The Batman Who Laughs
2nd Lex Luthor
3rd Joker
4th Bane

Best Supporting Villain
1st The Ventriloquist
2nd Brainiac-1
3rd Red Cloud
4th Mr. Terrible

Comeback Villain of the Year
1st Red Hood
2nd Deathstroke
3rd Catwoman
4th Lobo

Best Villain Upgrade
1st The Batman Who Laughs
2nd Captain Cold
3rd Black Mask
4th Oracle

Most Obsessed Villain
1st Bane
2nd Mr. Freeze
3rd Black Manta
4th Rogol Zaar

Best Justification for Evil
1st Flashpoint Batman
2nd Leviathan
3rd Lex Luthor
4th Mirror Master

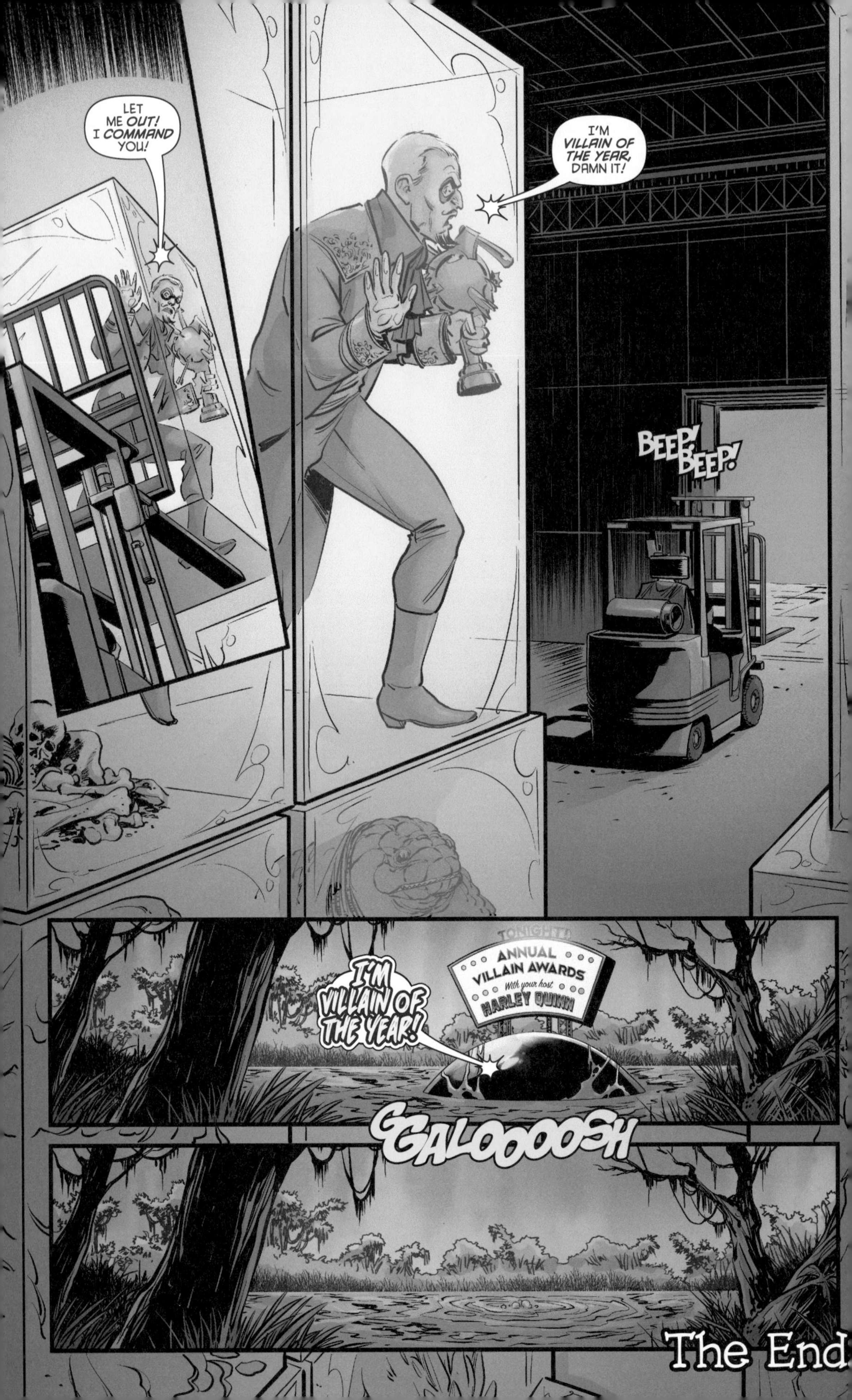
LET ME OUT! I COMMAND YOU!
I'M VILLAIN OF THE YEAR, DAMN IT!
BEEP! BEEP!
TONIGHT!
ANNUAL VILLAIN AWARDS
With your host HARLEY QUINN
I'M VILLAIN OF THE YEAR!
GGALOOOOSH
The End.

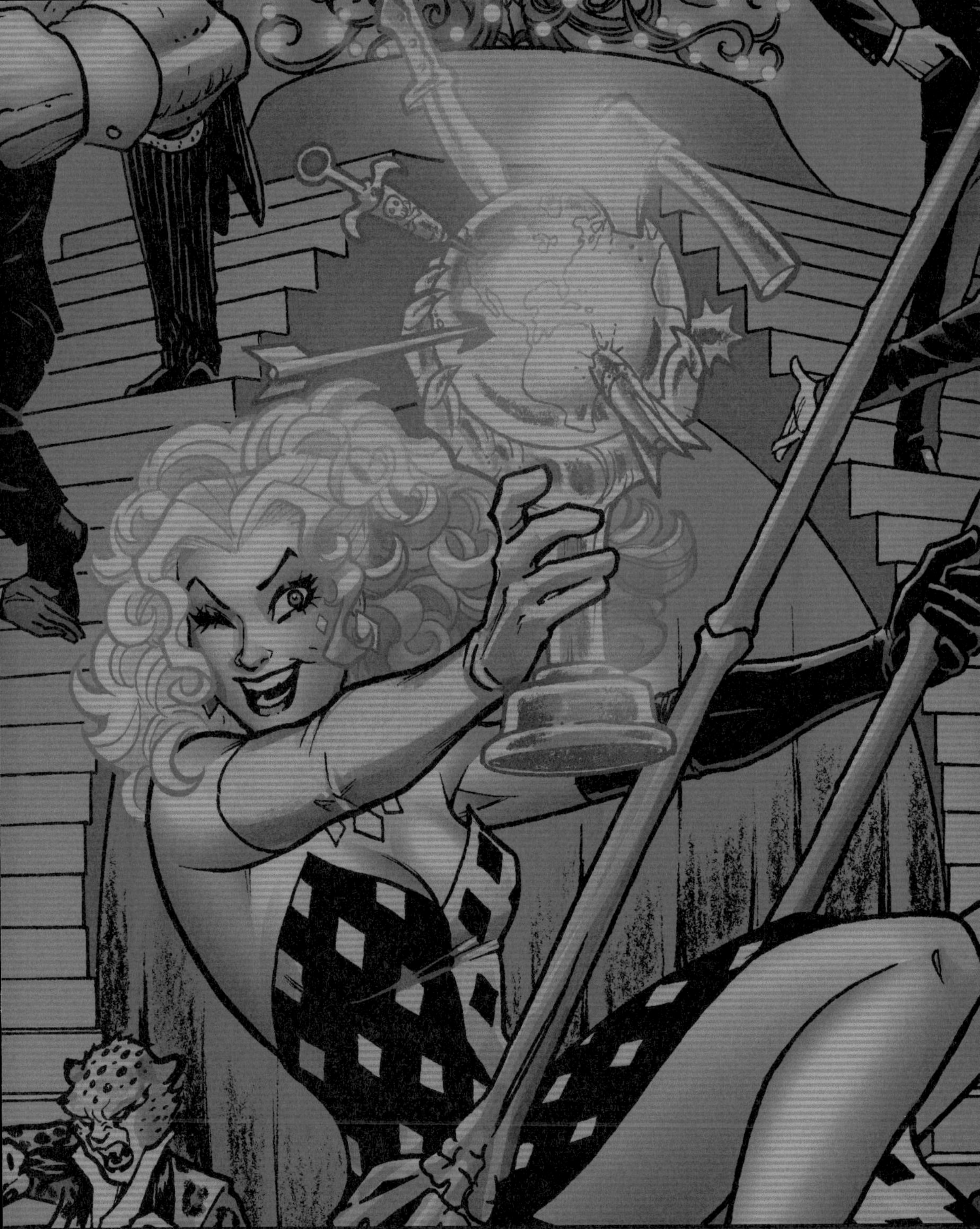

That's a wrap on villainy's biggest night! But it could have gone differently. The winner of each category was selected by fan vote, but alternate scenes were scripted and drawn for each nominee.

In the next few pages, check out the outcomes you didn't see as well as the final vote tally!

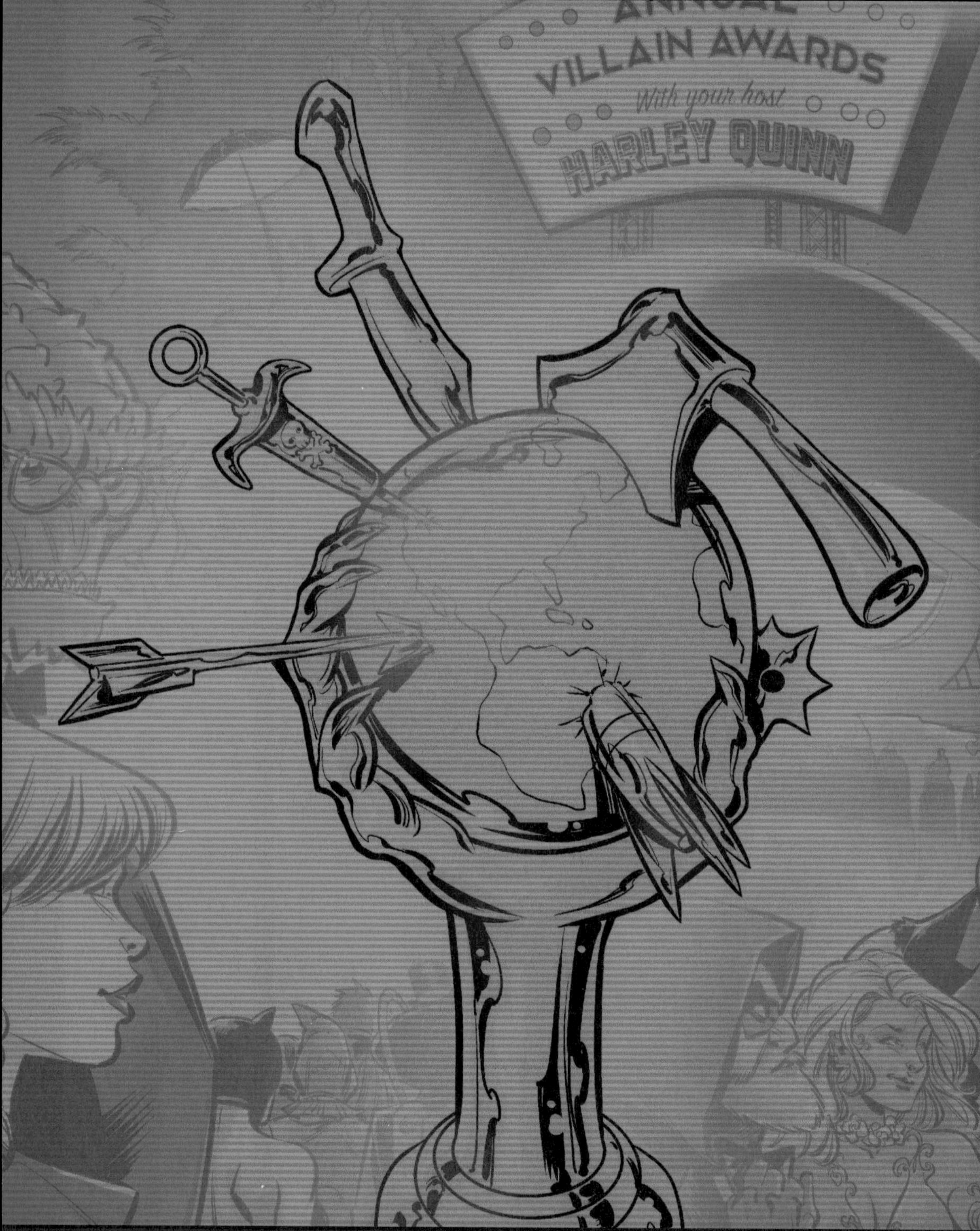
VILLAIN AWARDS
With your host
HARLEY QUINN

MOST OBSESSED VILLAIN

BANE 1ST PLACE

MR. FREEZE 2ND PLACE

BLACK MANTA 3RD PLACE

ROGOL ZAAR 4TH PLACE

"AND THE AWARD FOR MOST OBSESSED VILLAIN GOES TO...
"MR. FREEZE!"
AS YOU ALL KNOW, I'VE DEVOTED MY LIFE TO *COLD.*
BUT IN ALL MY YEARS OF STUDY, I'VE *NEVER* FOUND COLD LIKE THAT OF A HEART BEREFT OF LOVE.
I SUPPOSE THAT'S WHY I STILL CARRY A TORCH FOR NORA.
NOT THAT I EXPECT HER TO EVER *COME BACK.*
BUT BECAUSE THAT *LOVE* IS THE LAST SMOLDERING EMBER OF WARMTH IN MY LIFE.
I GUESS I'M JUST NOT READY TO EXTINGUISH IT YET.
BUT STILL, IT'S NICE TO BE RECOGNIZED.
CLAP CLAP CLAP CLAP CLAP CLAP
CLAP CLAP CLAP CLAP CLAP

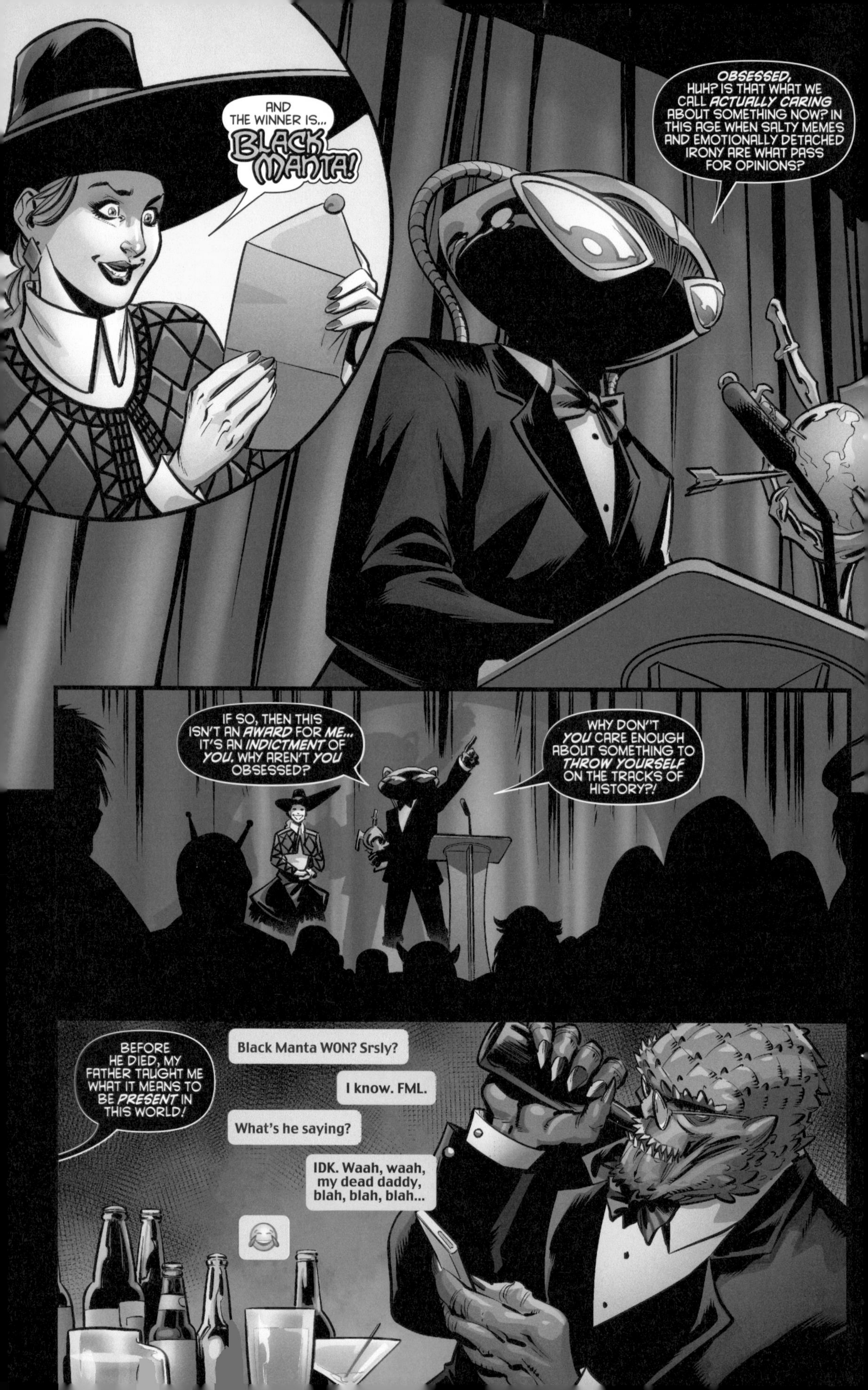
AND THE WINNER IS... BLACK MANTA!
OBSESSED, HUH? IS THAT WHAT WE CALL ACTUALLY CARING ABOUT SOMETHING NOW? IN THIS AGE WHEN SALTY MEMES AND EMOTIONALLY DETACHED IRONY ARE WHAT PASS FOR OPINIONS?
IF SO, THEN THIS ISN'T AN AWARD FOR ME... IT'S AN INDICTMENT OF YOU. WHY AREN'T YOU OBSESSED?
WHY DON'T YOU CARE ENOUGH ABOUT SOMETHING TO THROW YOURSELF ON THE TRACKS OF HISTORY?!
BEFORE HE DIED, MY FATHER TAUGHT ME WHAT IT MEANS TO BE PRESENT IN THIS WORLD!
Black Manta WON? Srsly?
I know. FML.
What's he saying?
IDK. Waah, waah, my dead daddy, blah, blah, blah...

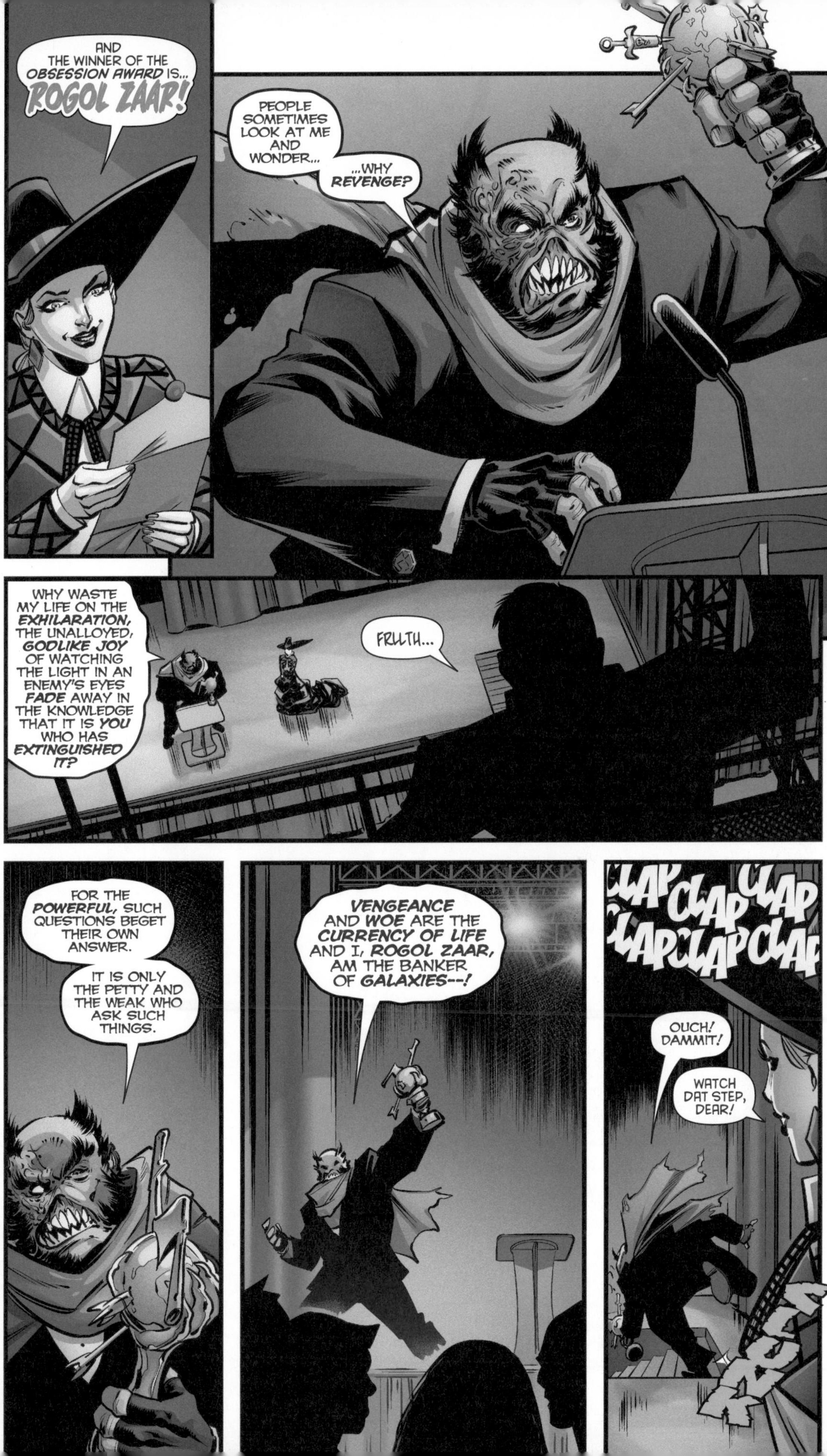
AND THE WINNER OF THE OBSESSION AWARD IS... ROGOL ZAAR!
PEOPLE SOMETIMES LOOK AT ME AND WONDER...
...WHY REVENGE?
WHY WASTE MY LIFE ON THE EXHILARATION, THE UNALLOYED, GODLIKE JOY OF WATCHING THE LIGHT IN AN ENEMY'S EYES FADE AWAY IN THE KNOWLEDGE THAT IT IS YOU WHO HAS EXTINGUISHED IT?
FRLLTH...
FOR THE POWERFUL, SUCH QUESTIONS BEGET THEIR OWN ANSWER.
IT IS ONLY THE PETTY AND THE WEAK WHO ASK SUCH THINGS.
VENGEANCE AND WOE ARE THE CURRENCY OF LIFE AND I, ROGOL ZAAR, AM THE BANKER OF GALAXIES--!
CLAP CLAP CLAP CLAP CLAP CLAP
OUCH! DAMMIT!
WATCH DAT STEP, DEAR!

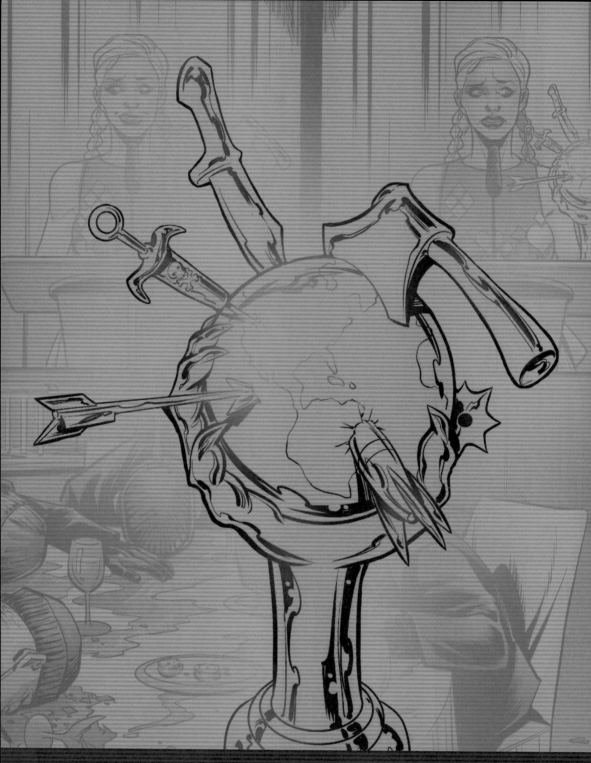

BEST JUSTIFICATION FOR EVIL

FLASHPOINT BATMAN 1ST PLACE

LEVIATHAN 2ND PLACE

LEX LUTHOR 3RD PLACE

MIRROR MASTER 4TH PLACE

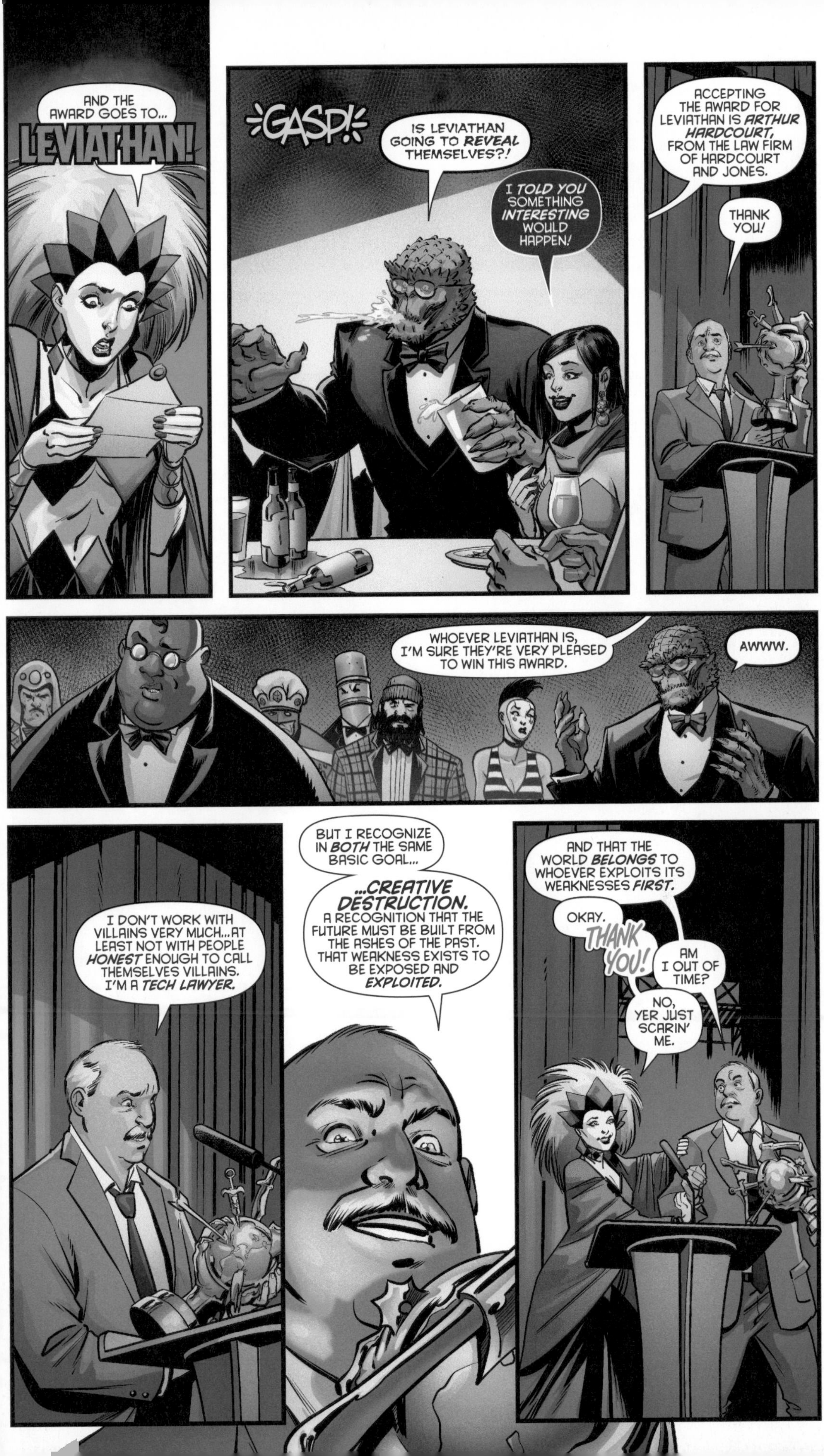

AND THE AWARD GOES TO...
LEVIATHAN!
GASP!
IS LEVIATHAN GOING TO REVEAL THEMSELVES?!
I TOLD YOU SOMETHING INTERESTING WOULD HAPPEN!
ACCEPTING THE AWARD FOR LEVIATHAN IS ARTHUR HARDCOURT, FROM THE LAW FIRM OF HARDCOURT AND JONES.
THANK YOU!
WHOEVER LEVIATHAN IS, I'M SURE THEY'RE VERY PLEASED TO WIN THIS AWARD.
AWWW.
I DON'T WORK WITH VILLAINS VERY MUCH...AT LEAST NOT WITH PEOPLE HONEST ENOUGH TO CALL THEMSELVES VILLAINS. I'M A TECH LAWYER.
BUT I RECOGNIZE IN BOTH THE SAME BASIC GOAL...
...CREATIVE DESTRUCTION. A RECOGNITION THAT THE FUTURE MUST BE BUILT FROM THE ASHES OF THE PAST. THAT WEAKNESS EXISTS TO BE EXPOSED AND EXPLOITED.
AND THAT THE WORLD BELONGS TO WHOEVER EXPLOITS ITS WEAKNESSES FIRST.
OKAY.
THANK YOU!
AM I OUT OF TIME?
NO, YER JUST SCARIN' ME.

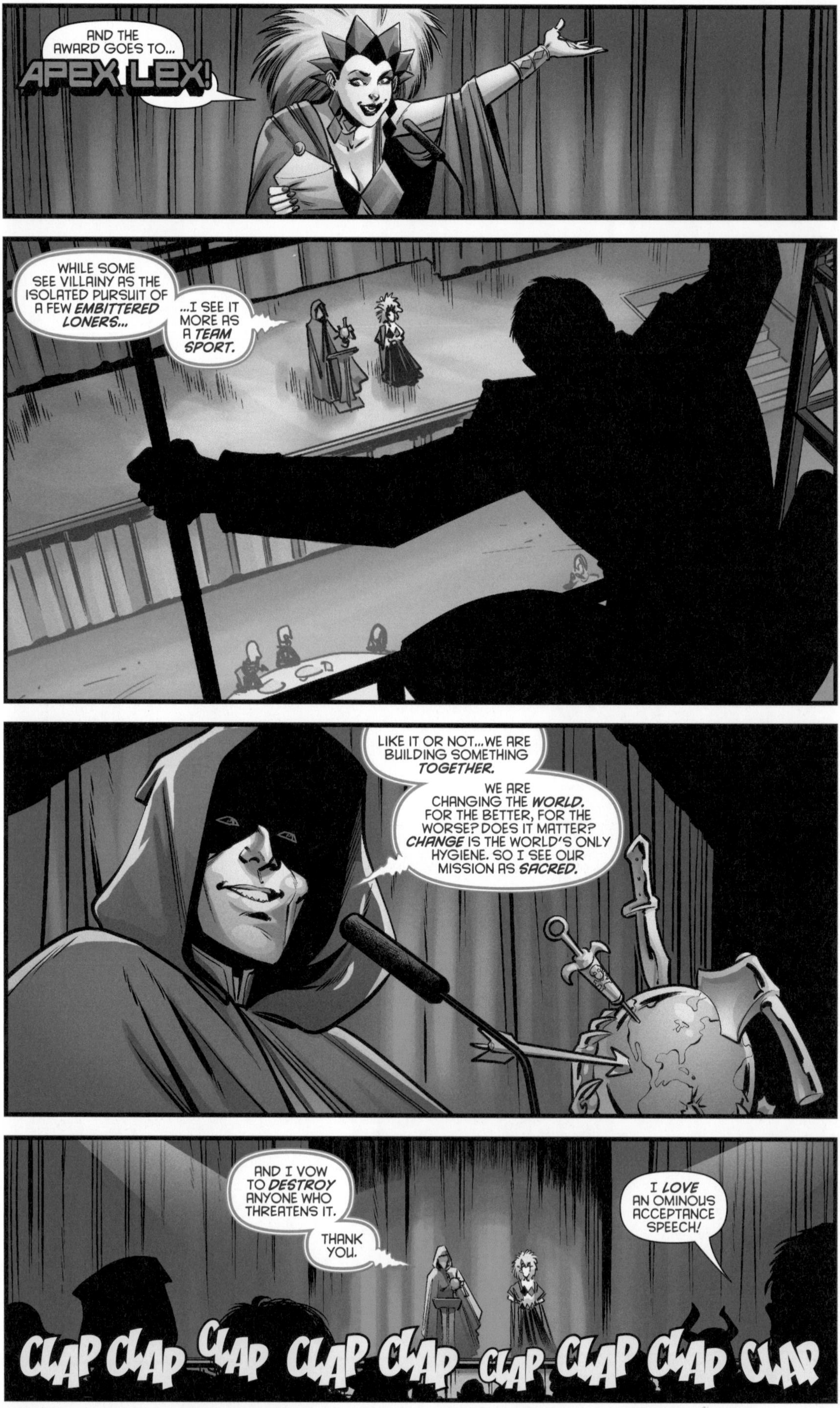
AND THE AWARD GOES TO...
APEX LEX!
WHILE SOME SEE VILLAINY AS THE ISOLATED PURSUIT OF A FEW EMBITTERED LONERS...
...I SEE IT MORE AS A TEAM SPORT.
LIKE IT OR NOT...WE ARE BUILDING SOMETHING TOGETHER.
WE ARE CHANGING THE WORLD. FOR THE BETTER, FOR THE WORSE? DOES IT MATTER? CHANGE IS THE WORLD'S ONLY HYGIENE. SO I SEE OUR MISSION AS SACRED.
AND I VOW TO DESTROY ANYONE WHO THREATENS IT.
THANK YOU.
I LOVE AN OMINOUS ACCEPTANCE SPEECH!
CLAP CLAP CLAP CLAP CLAP CLAP CLAP CLAP CLAP

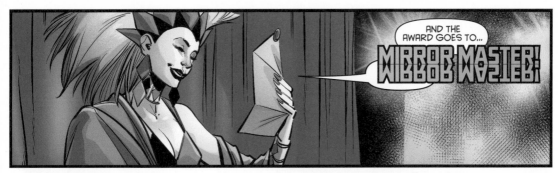

AND THE AWARD GOES TO...

MIRROR MASTER!

CONGRATULATIONS ON THA *DOOMIE!*

I HAD HOPED WE'D BE BEYOND SUCH TRITE CONCEPTS AS "EVIL" BY NOW.

BUT THEN, HERE WE ARE.

NOBODY DOES SOMETHING BECAUSE IT'S *EVIL.* THEY DO IT BECAUSE IT MATTERS MORE TO THEM THAN ITS CONSEQUENCES TO *OTHER PEOPLE.* WHICH IS TRUE OF VIRTUALLY *EVERYTHING* WE DO.

AS MEL BROOKS ONCE SAID, "TRAGEDY IS WHEN *I* CUT MY FINGER. COMEDY IS WHEN *YOU* FALL INTO A SEWER AND *DIE.*"

BUT WHATEVER. ON BEHALF OF MYSELF AND THE OTHER EIGHT BILLION "EVIL" PEOPLE ON THIS PLANET, I ACCEPT THIS AWARD.

CLAP

CLAP

CLAP

CLAP

CLAP

CLAP

CLAP

CLAP

CLAP

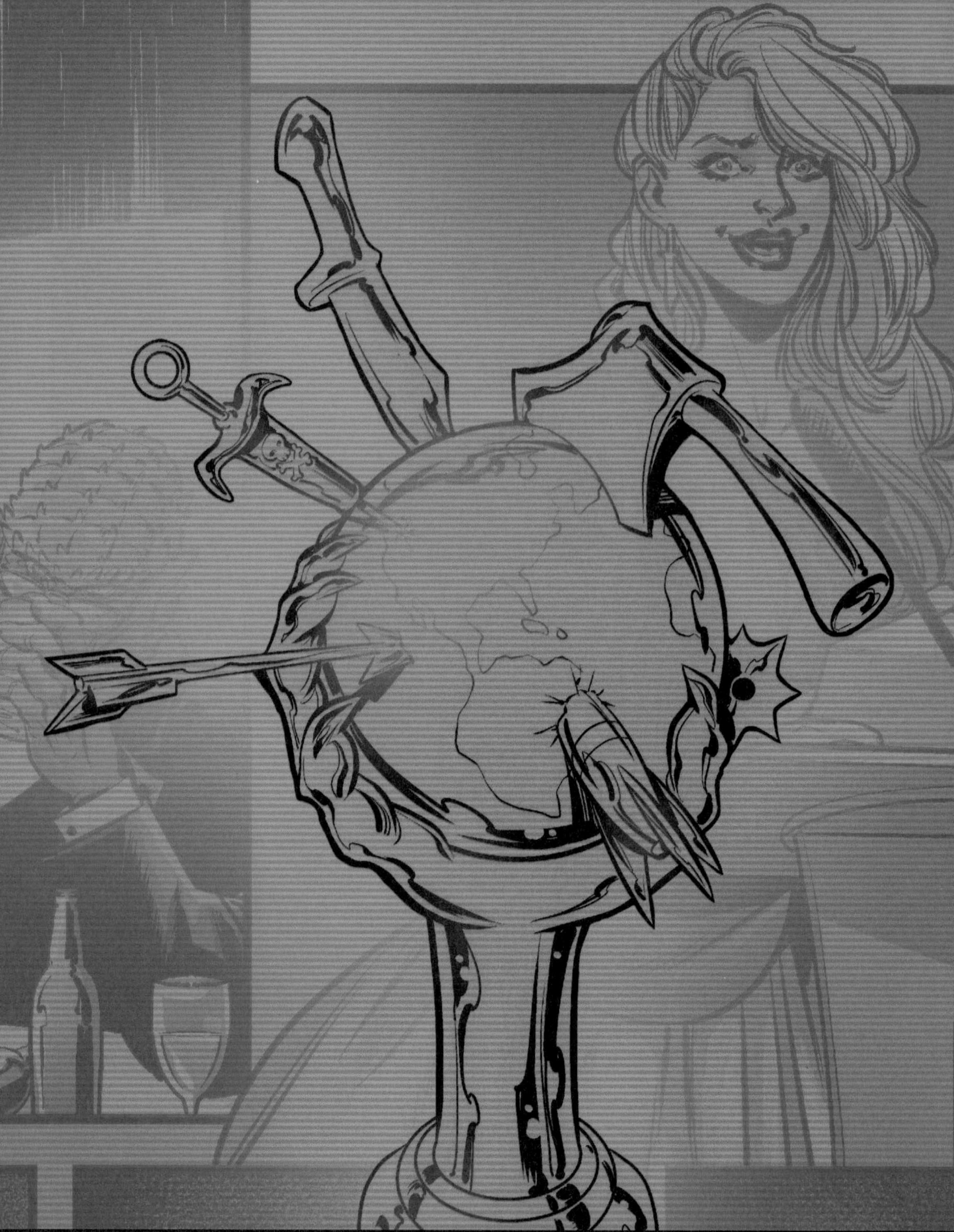

BEST VILLAIN UPGRADE

THE BATMAN WHO LAUGHS 1ST PLACE

CAPTAIN COLD 2ND PLACE

BLACK MASK 3RD PLACE

ORACLE 4TH PLACE

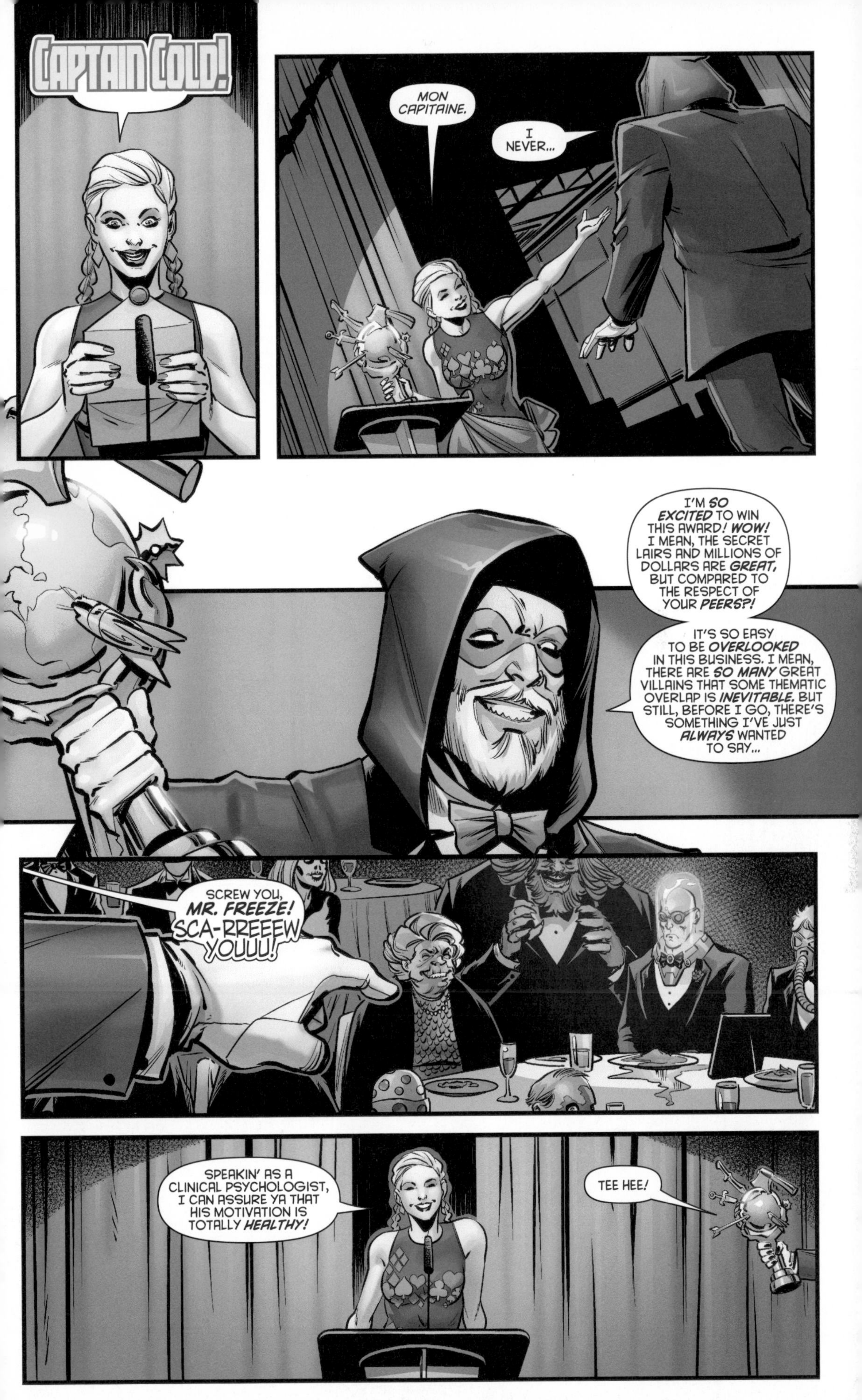
CAPTAIN COLD!
MON CAPITAINE.
I NEVER...
I'M SO EXCITED TO WIN THIS AWARD! WOW! I MEAN, THE SECRET LAIRS AND MILLIONS OF DOLLARS ARE GREAT, BUT COMPARED TO THE RESPECT OF YOUR PEERS?!
IT'S SO EASY TO BE OVERLOOKED IN THIS BUSINESS. I MEAN, THERE ARE SO MANY GREAT VILLAINS THAT SOME THEMATIC OVERLAP IS INEVITABLE. BUT STILL, BEFORE I GO, THERE'S SOMETHING I'VE JUST ALWAYS WANTED TO SAY...
SCREW YOU, MR. FREEZE! SCA-RREEEW YOUUU!
SPEAKIN' AS A CLINICAL PSYCHOLOGIST, I CAN ASSURE YA THAT HIS MOTIVATION IS TOTALLY HEALTHY!
TEE HEE!

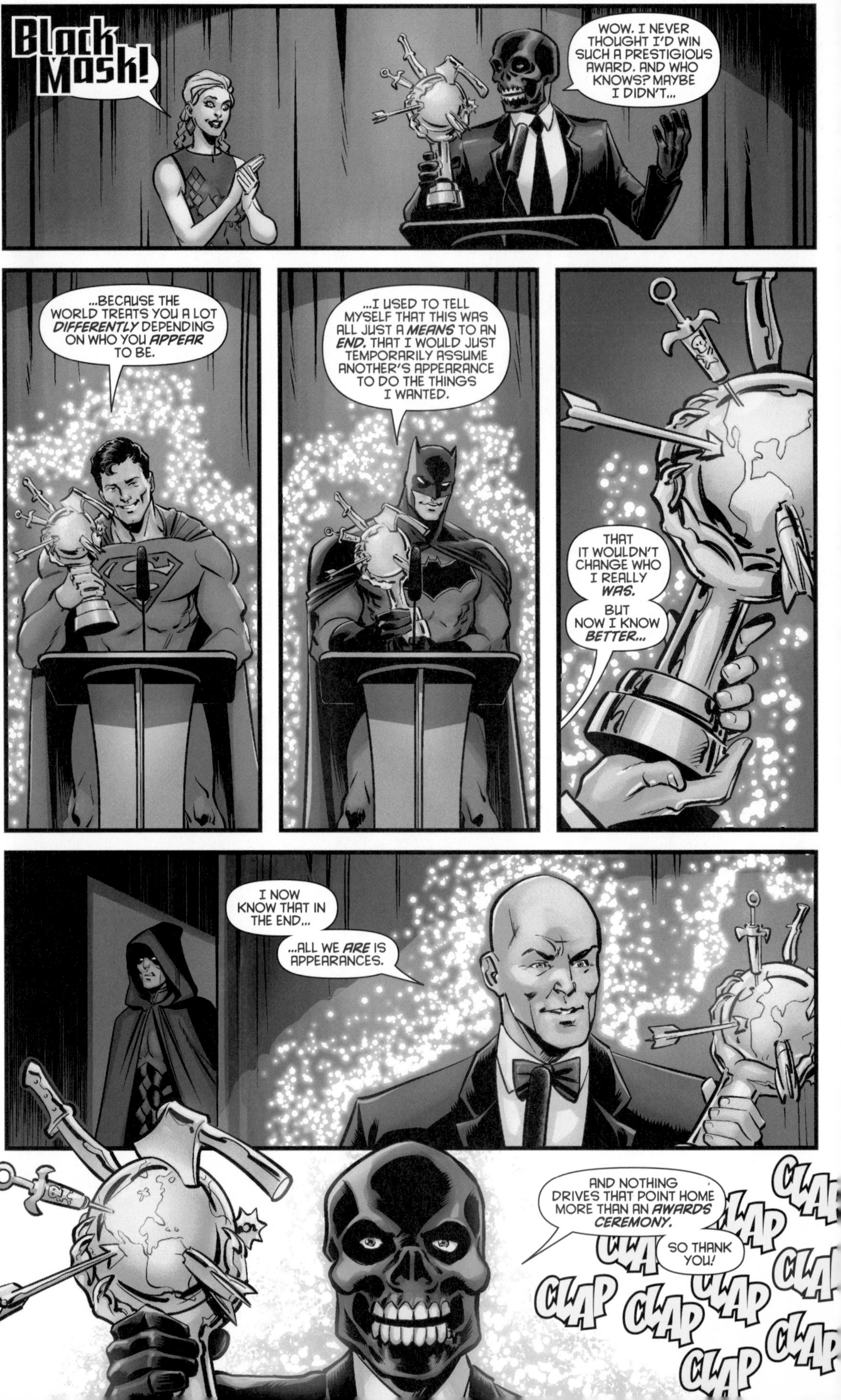
Black Mask!
WOW. I NEVER THOUGHT I'D WIN SUCH A PRESTIGIOUS AWARD. AND WHO KNOWS? MAYBE I DIDN'T...
...BECAUSE THE WORLD TREATS YOU A LOT DIFFERENTLY DEPENDING ON WHO YOU APPEAR TO BE.
...I USED TO TELL MYSELF THAT THIS WAS ALL JUST A MEANS TO AN END. THAT I WOULD JUST TEMPORARILY ASSUME ANOTHER'S APPEARANCE TO DO THE THINGS I WANTED.
THAT IT WOULDN'T CHANGE WHO I REALLY WAS.
BUT NOW I KNOW BETTER...
I NOW KNOW THAT IN THE END...
...ALL WE ARE IS APPEARANCES.
AND NOTHING DRIVES THAT POINT HOME MORE THAN AN AWARDS CEREMONY.
SO THANK YOU!
CLAP CLAP CLAP CLAP CLAP CLAP CLAP CLAP CLAP CLAP

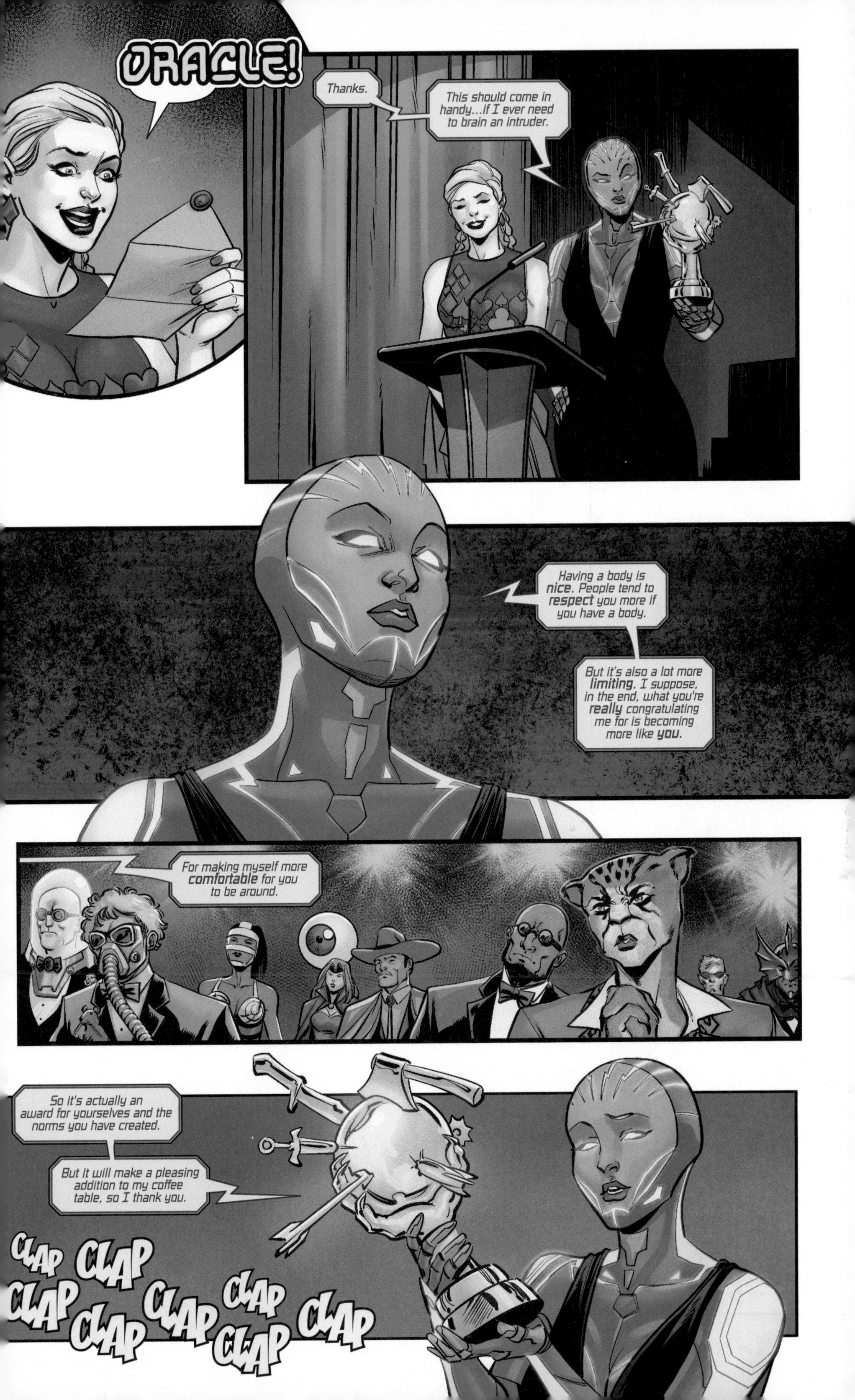
ORACLE!
Thanks.
This should come in handy...if I ever need to brain an intruder.
Having a body is nice. People tend to respect you more if you have a body.
But it's also a lot more limiting. I suppose, in the end, what you're really congratulating me for is becoming more like you.
For making myself more comfortable for you to be around.
So it's actually an award for yourselves and the norms you have created.
But it will make a pleasing addition to my coffee table, so I thank you.
CLAP CLAP CLAP CLAP CLAP CLAP CLAP CLAP

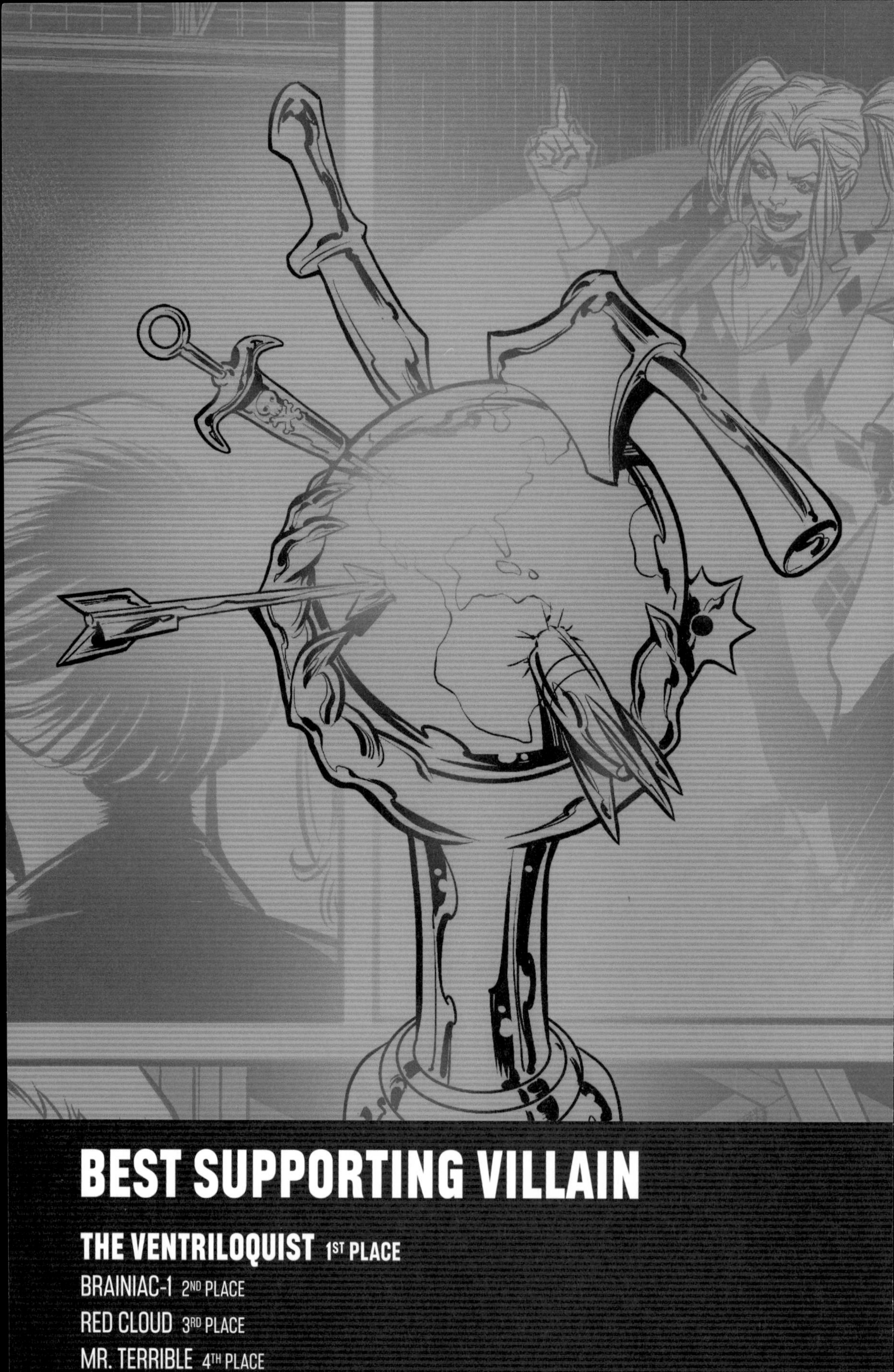

BEST SUPPORTING VILLAIN

THE VENTRILOQUIST 1ST PLACE

BRAINIAC-1 2ND PLACE

RED CLOUD 3RD PLACE

MR. TERRIBLE 4TH PLACE

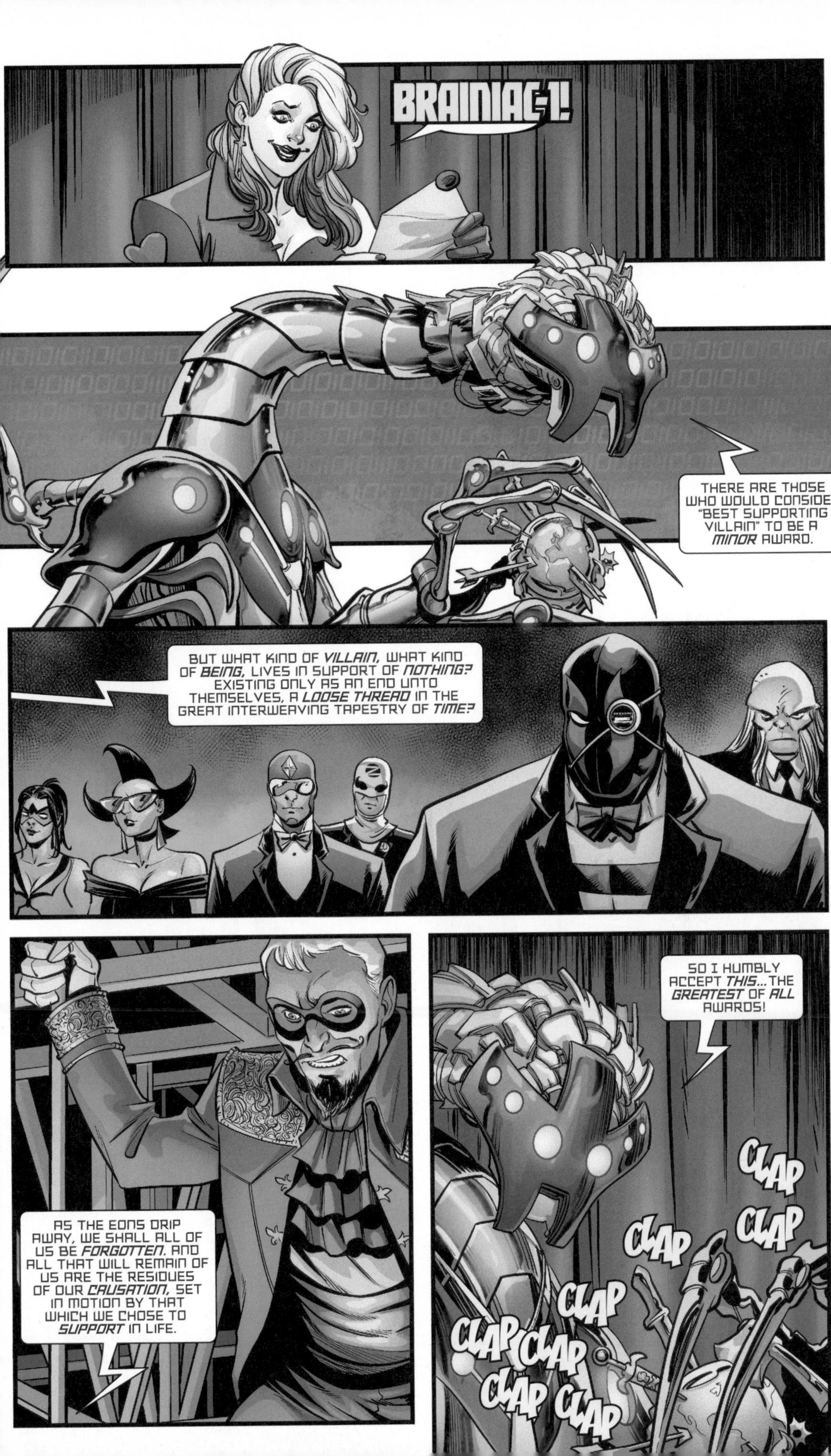
BRAINIAC-1!
THERE ARE THOSE WHO WOULD CONSIDER "BEST SUPPORTING VILLAIN" TO BE A MINOR AWARD.
BUT WHAT KIND OF VILLAIN, WHAT KIND OF BEING, LIVES IN SUPPORT OF NOTHING? EXISTING ONLY AS AN END UNTO THEMSELVES, A LOOSE THREAD IN THE GREAT INTERWEAVING TAPESTRY OF TIME?
AS THE EONS DRIP AWAY, WE SHALL ALL OF US BE FORGOTTEN. AND ALL THAT WILL REMAIN OF US ARE THE RESIDUES OF OUR CAUSATION, SET IN MOTION BY THAT WHICH WE CHOSE TO SUPPORT IN LIFE.
SO I HUMBLY ACCEPT THIS... THE GREATEST OF ALL AWARDS!
CLAP
CLAP
CLAP
CLAP
CLAP
CLAP
CLAP
CLAP

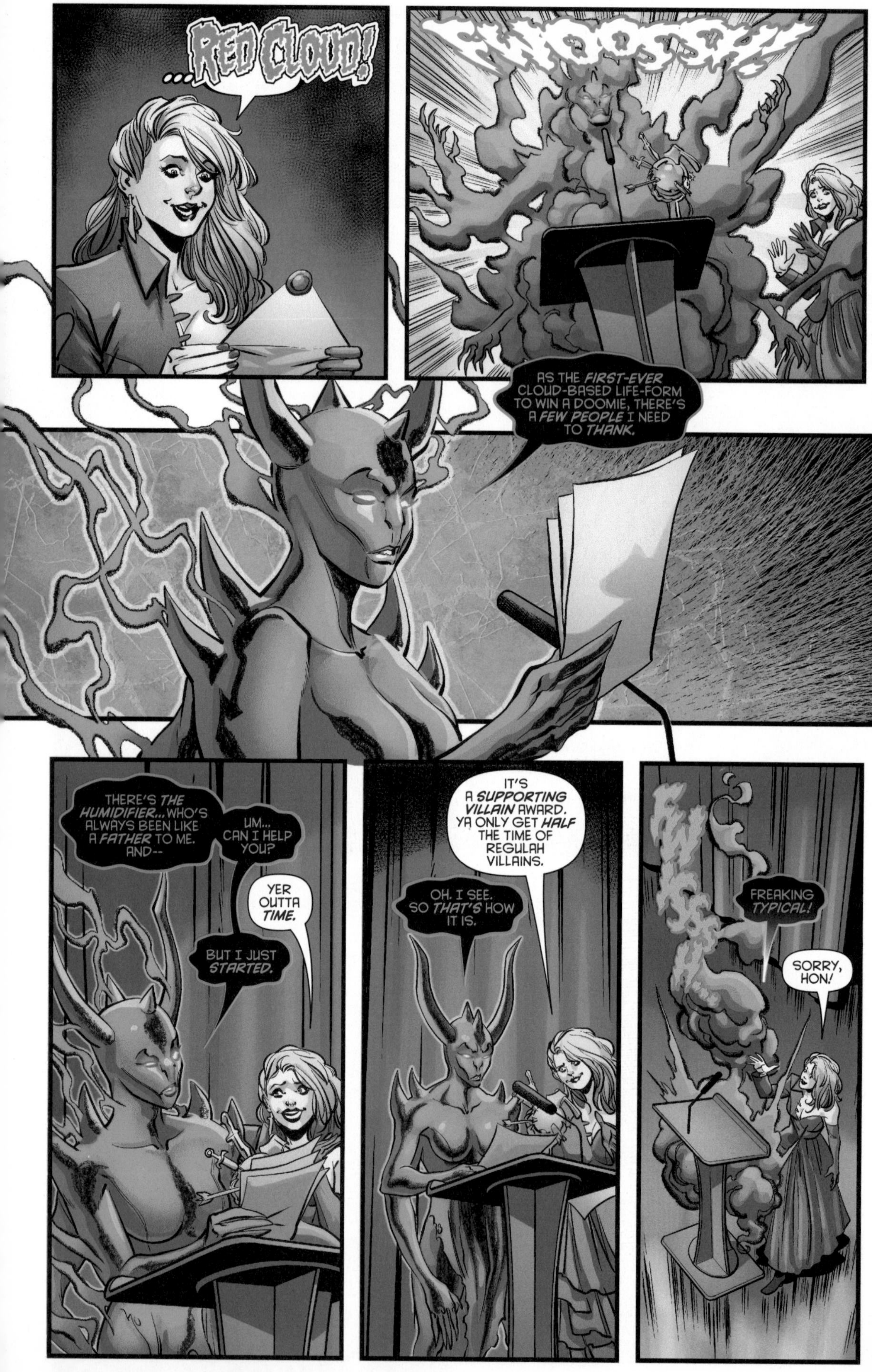
...RED CLOUD!
AS THE *FIRST-EVER* CLOUD-BASED LIFE-FORM TO WIN A DOOMIE, THERE'S A *FEW PEOPLE* I NEED TO *THANK.*
THERE'S *THE HUMIDIFIER*... WHO'S ALWAYS BEEN LIKE A *FATHER* TO ME. AND--
UM... CAN I HELP YOU?
YER OUTTA *TIME.*
BUT I JUST *STARTED.*
IT'S A *SUPPORTING VILLAIN* AWARD. YA ONLY GET *HALF* THE TIME OF REGULAH VILLAINS.
OH. I SEE. SO *THAT'S* HOW IT IS.
FREAKING *TYPICAL!*
SORRY, HON!

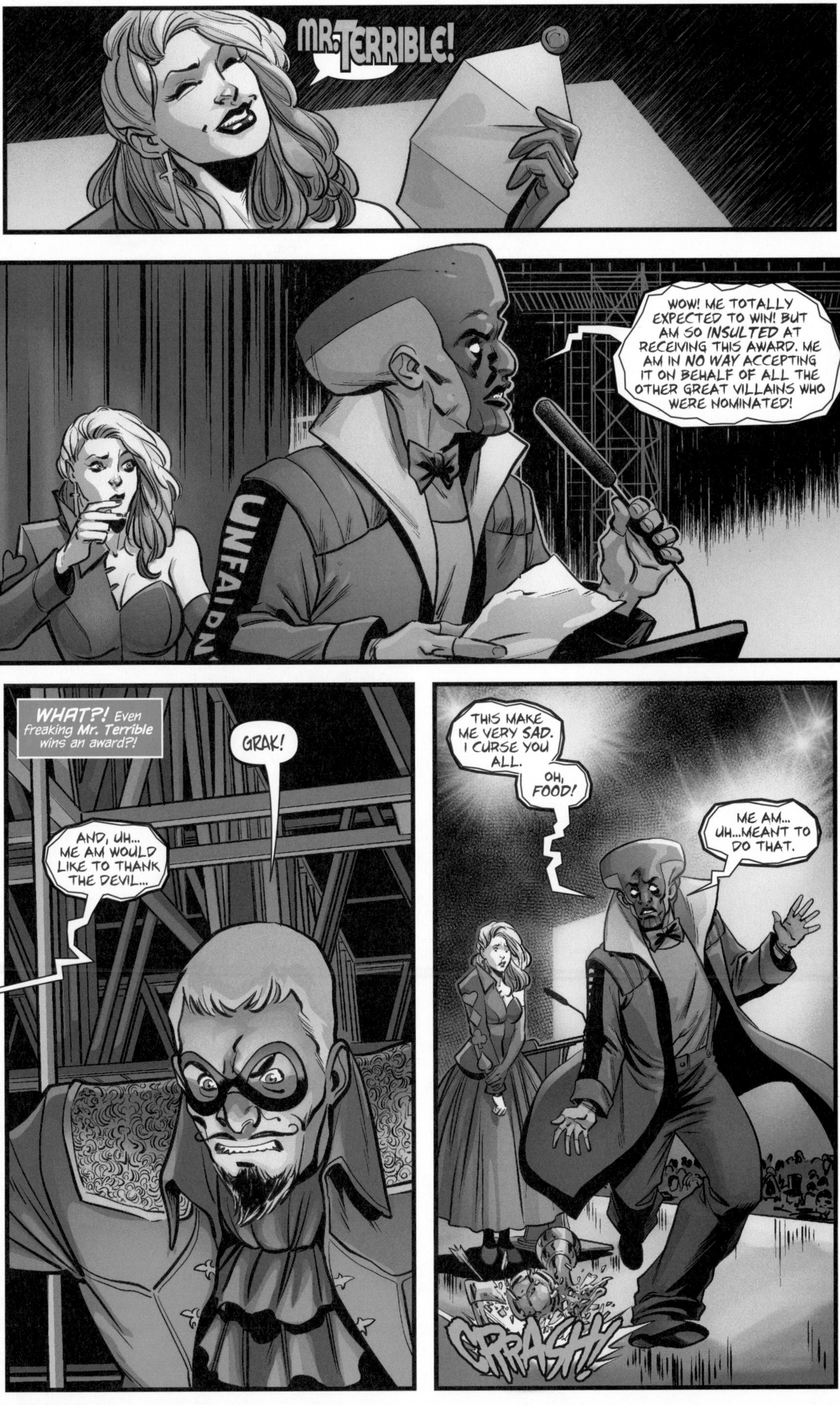
MR. TERRIBLE!
WOW! ME TOTALLY EXPECTED TO WIN! BUT AM SO INSULTED AT RECEIVING THIS AWARD. ME AM IN NO WAY ACCEPTING IT ON BEHALF OF ALL THE OTHER GREAT VILLAINS WHO WERE NOMINATED!
UNFAIRLY
WHAT?! Even freaking Mr. Terrible wins an award?!
GRAK!
AND, UH... ME AM WOULD LIKE TO THANK THE DEVIL...
THIS MAKE ME VERY SAD. I CURSE YOU ALL.
OH, FOOD!
ME AM... UH...MEANT TO DO THAT.
CRASH!

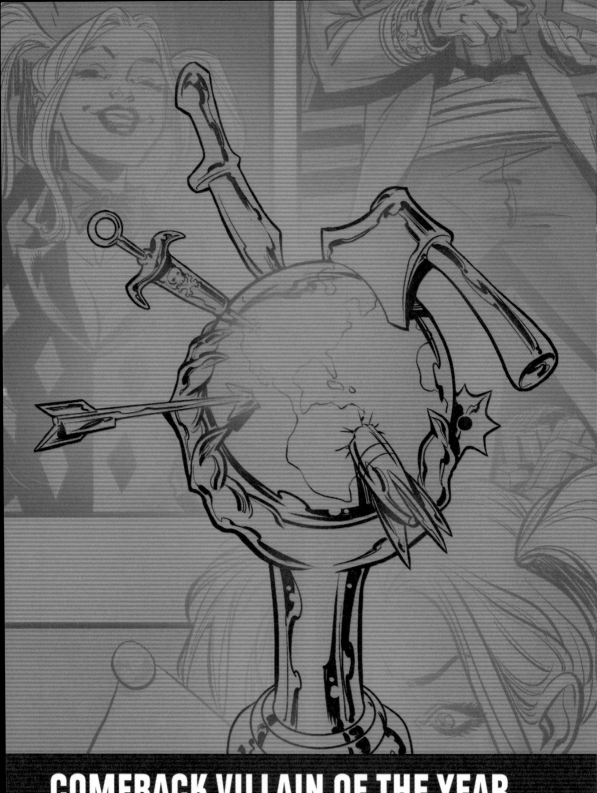

COMEBACK VILLAIN OF THE YEAR

RED HOOD 1ST PLACE

DEATHSTROKE 2ND PLACE

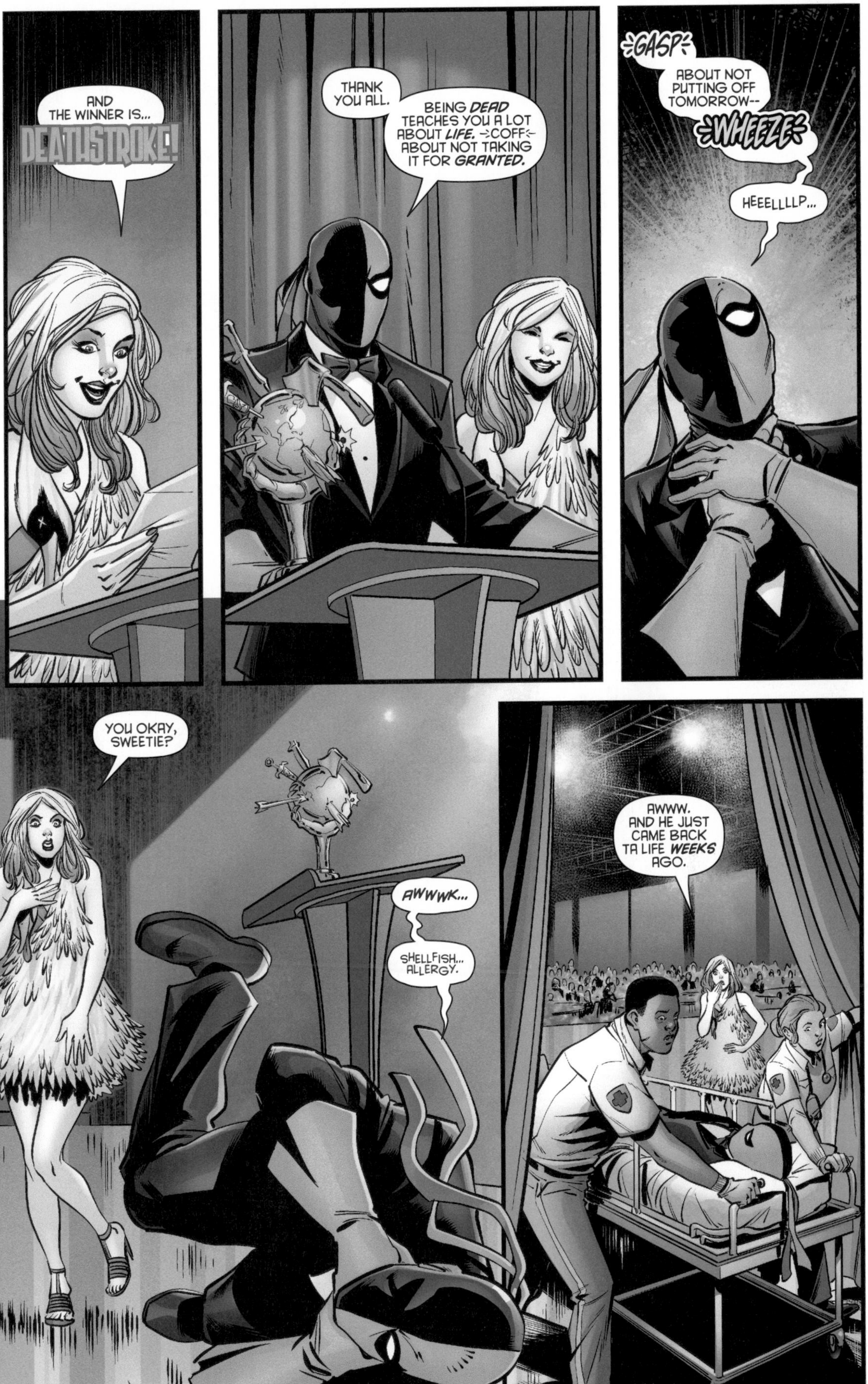

AND THE WINNER IS... DEATHSTROKE!
THANK YOU ALL.
BEING DEAD TEACHES YOU A LOT ABOUT LIFE. COFF ABOUT NOT TAKING IT FOR GRANTED.
GASP
ABOUT NOT PUTTING OFF TOMORROW--
WHEEZE
HEEELLLLP...
YOU OKAY, SWEETIE?
AWWWK...
SHELLFISH... ALLERGY.
AWWW. AND HE JUST CAME BACK TA LIFE WEEKS AGO.

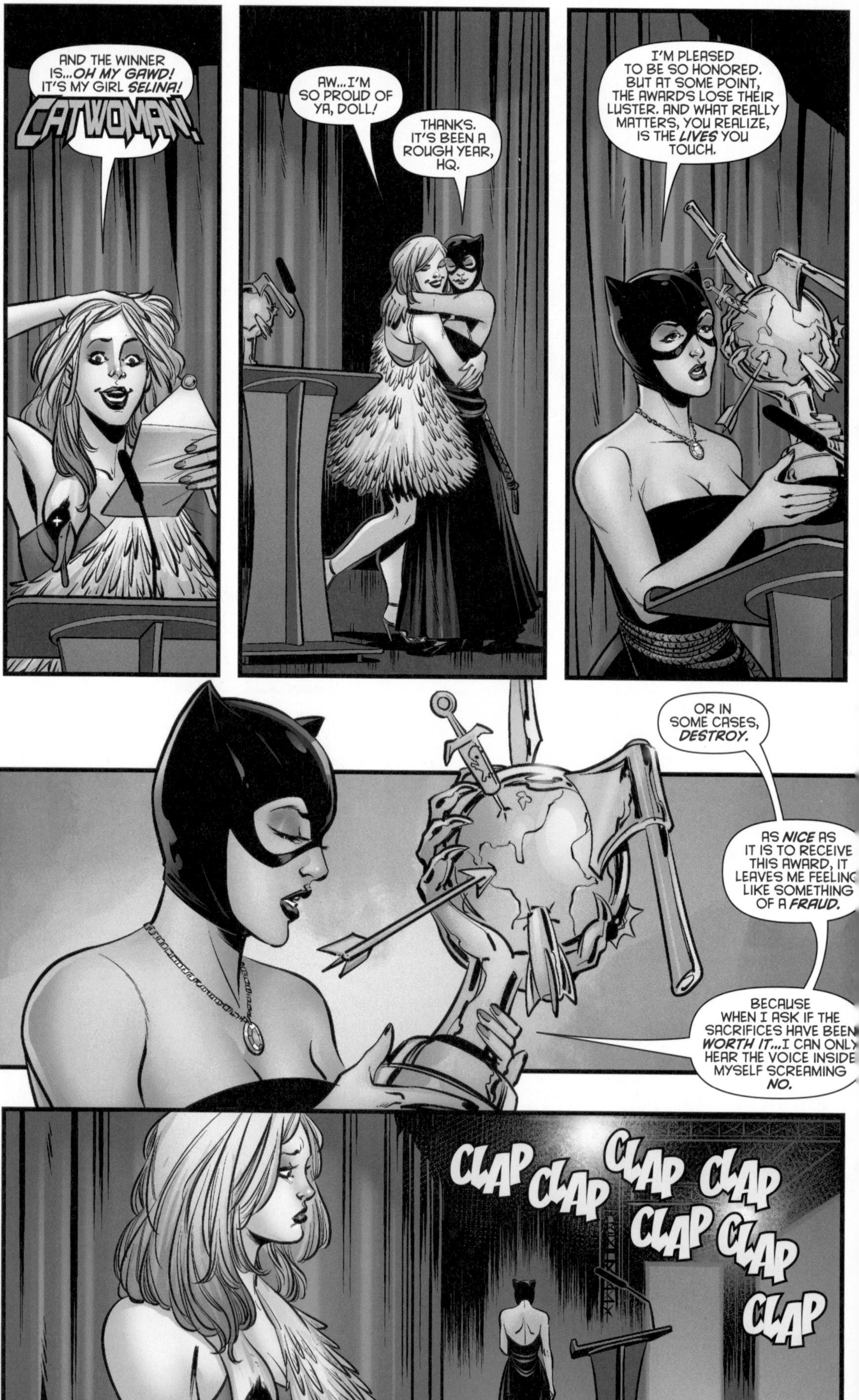
AND THE WINNER IS...OH MY GAWD! IT'S MY GIRL SELINA!
CATWOMAN!
AW...I'M SO PROUD OF YA, DOLL!
THANKS. IT'S BEEN A ROUGH YEAR, HQ.
I'M PLEASED TO BE SO HONORED. BUT AT SOME POINT, THE AWARDS LOSE THEIR LUSTER. AND WHAT REALLY MATTERS, YOU REALIZE, IS THE LIVES YOU TOUCH.
OR IN SOME CASES, DESTROY.
AS NICE AS IT IS TO RECEIVE THIS AWARD, IT LEAVES ME FEELING LIKE SOMETHING OF A FRAUD.
BECAUSE WHEN I ASK IF THE SACRIFICES HAVE BEEN WORTH IT...I CAN ONLY HEAR THE VOICE INSIDE MYSELF SCREAMING NO.
CLAP CLAP CLAP CLAP CLAP CLAP CLAP

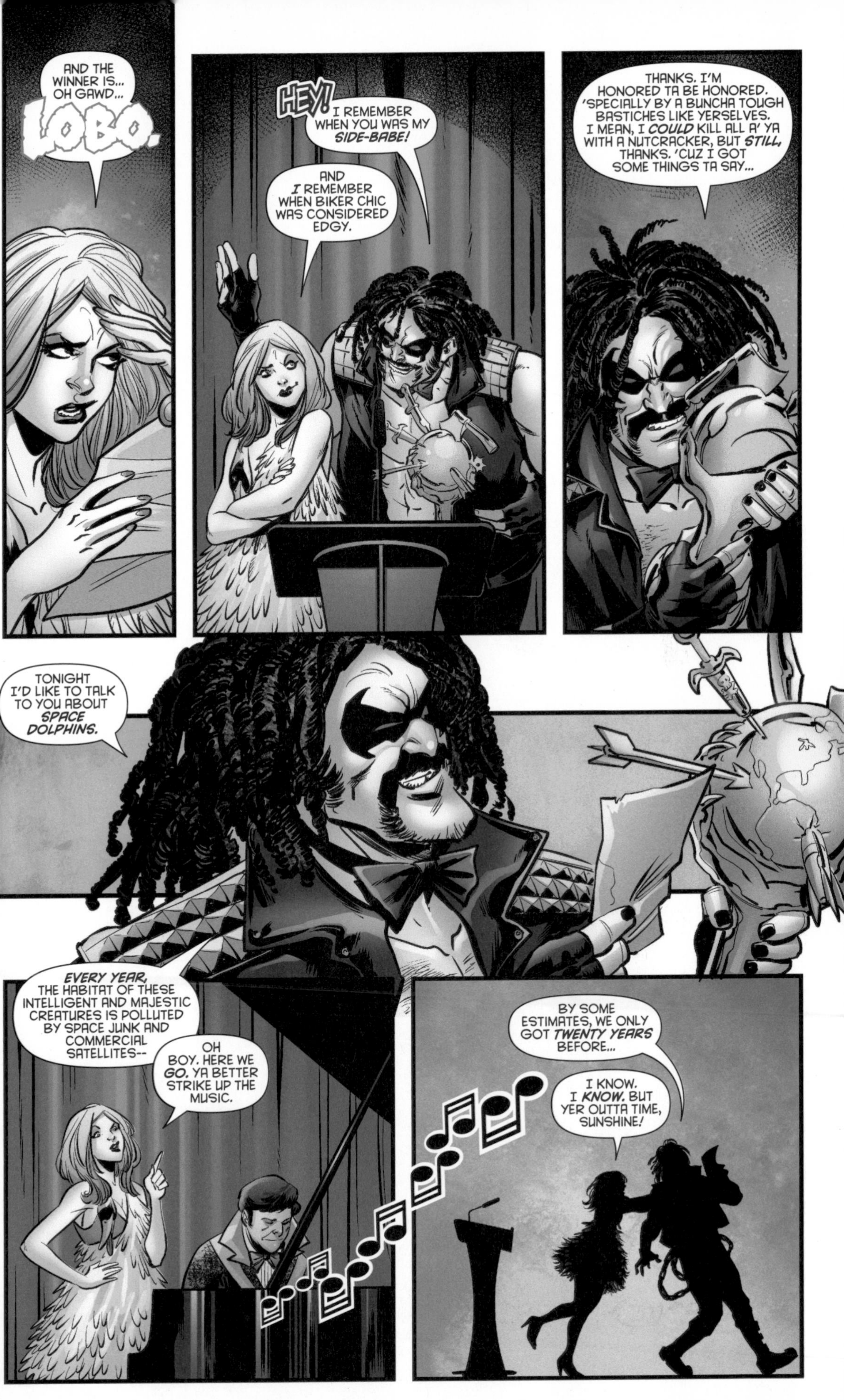
AND THE WINNER IS... OH GAWD...
LOBO.
HEY!
I REMEMBER WHEN YOU WAS MY SIDE-BABE!
AND I REMEMBER WHEN BIKER CHIC WAS CONSIDERED EDGY.
THANKS. I'M HONORED TA BE HONORED. 'SPECIALLY BY A BUNCHA TOUGH BASTICHES LIKE YERSELVES. I MEAN, I COULD KILL ALL A' YA WITH A NUTCRACKER, BUT STILL, THANKS. 'CUZ I GOT SOME THINGS TA SAY...
TONIGHT I'D LIKE TO TALK TO YOU ABOUT SPACE DOLPHINS.
EVERY YEAR, THE HABITAT OF THESE INTELLIGENT AND MAJESTIC CREATURES IS POLLUTED BY SPACE JUNK AND COMMERCIAL SATELLITES--
OH BOY. HERE WE GO. YA BETTER STRIKE UP THE MUSIC.
BY SOME ESTIMATES, WE ONLY GOT TWENTY YEARS BEFORE...
I KNOW. I KNOW. BUT YER OUTTA TIME, SUNSHINE!

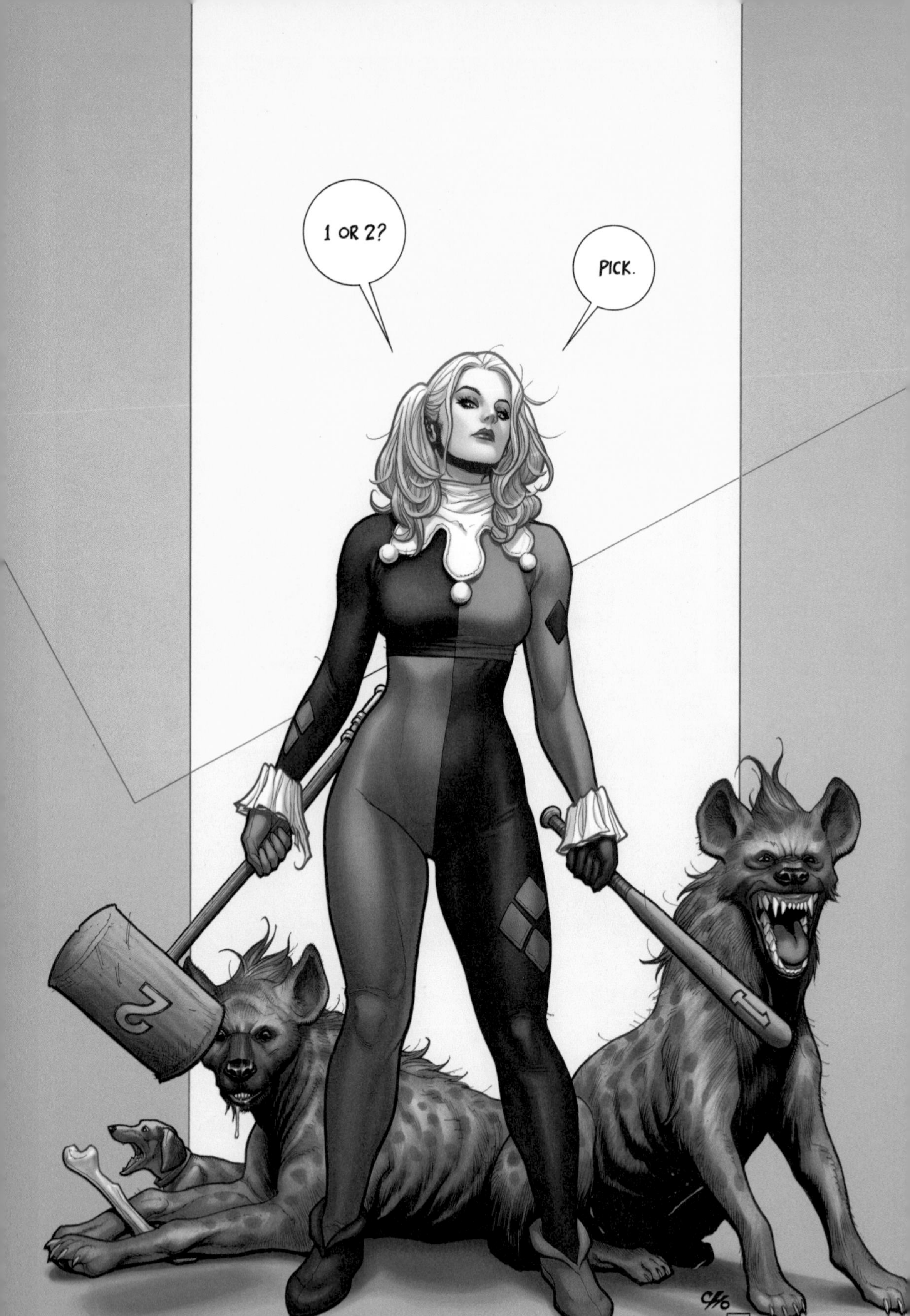
1 OR 2?
PICK.

***Harley Quinn* #64** variant cover
by FRANK CHO and SABINE RICH

Harley Quinn **#65** variant cover
by FRANK CHO and SABINE RICH

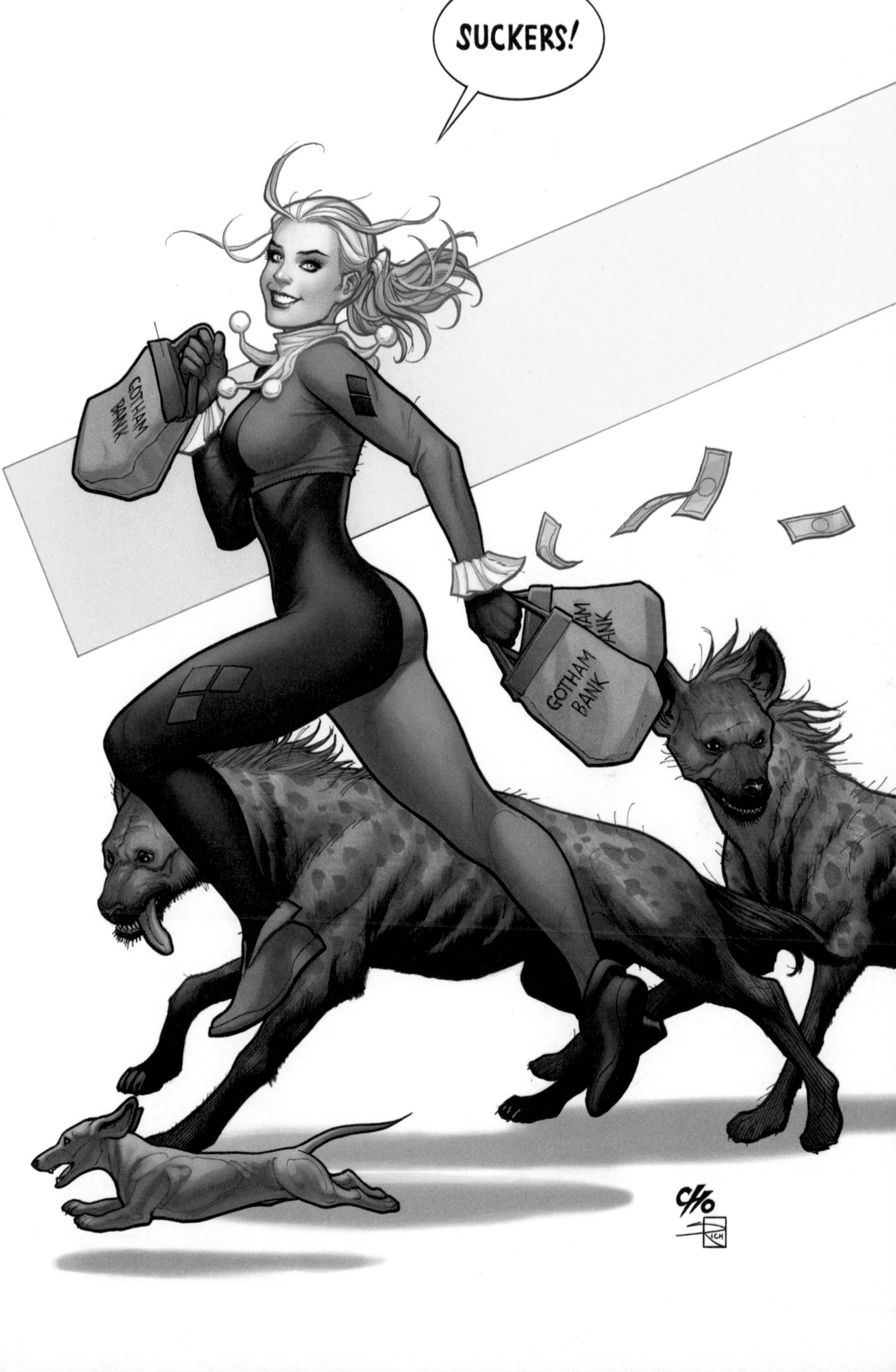

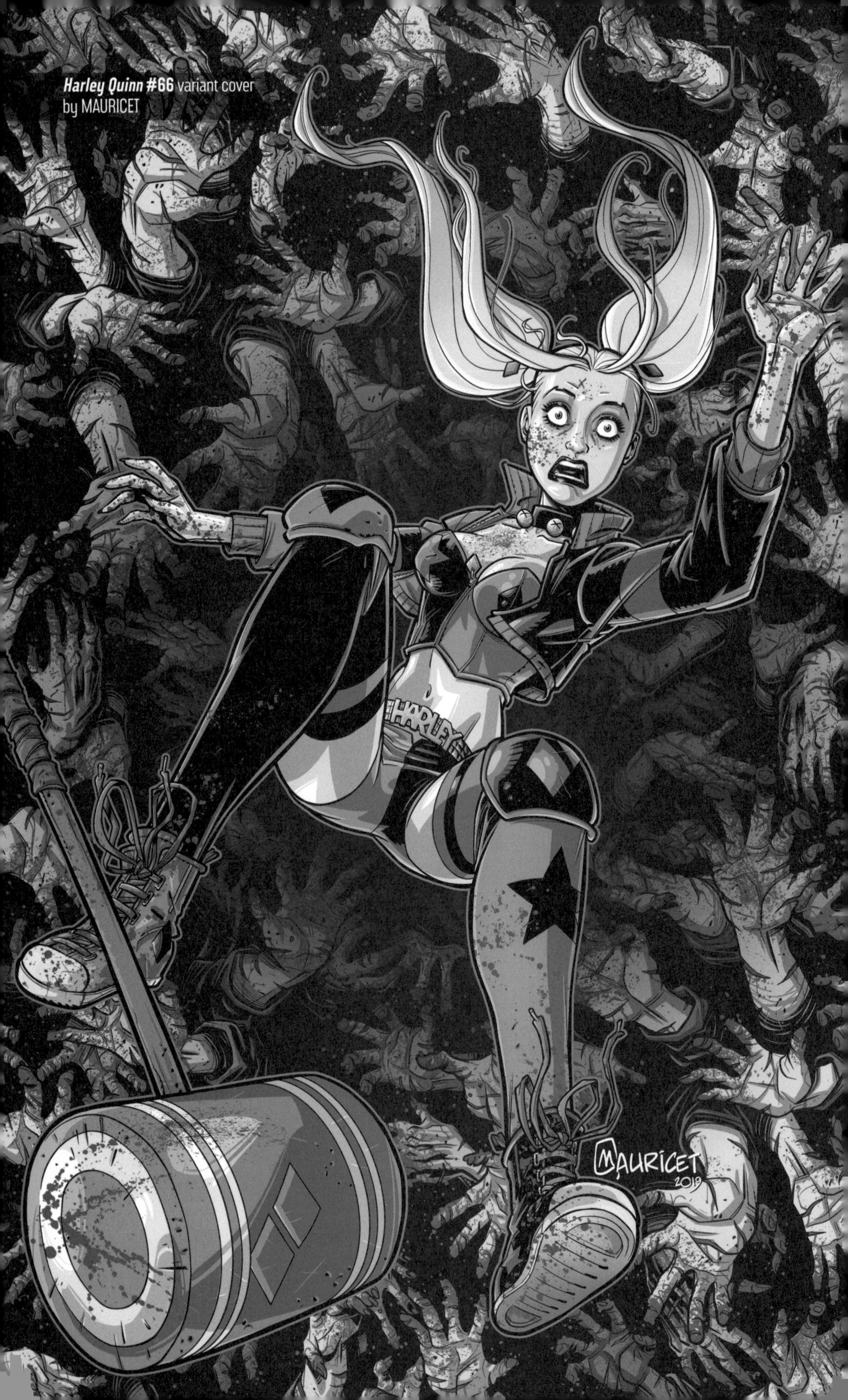
HARLEY
MAURICET
2019

***Harley Quinn* #66** variant cover
by MAURICET

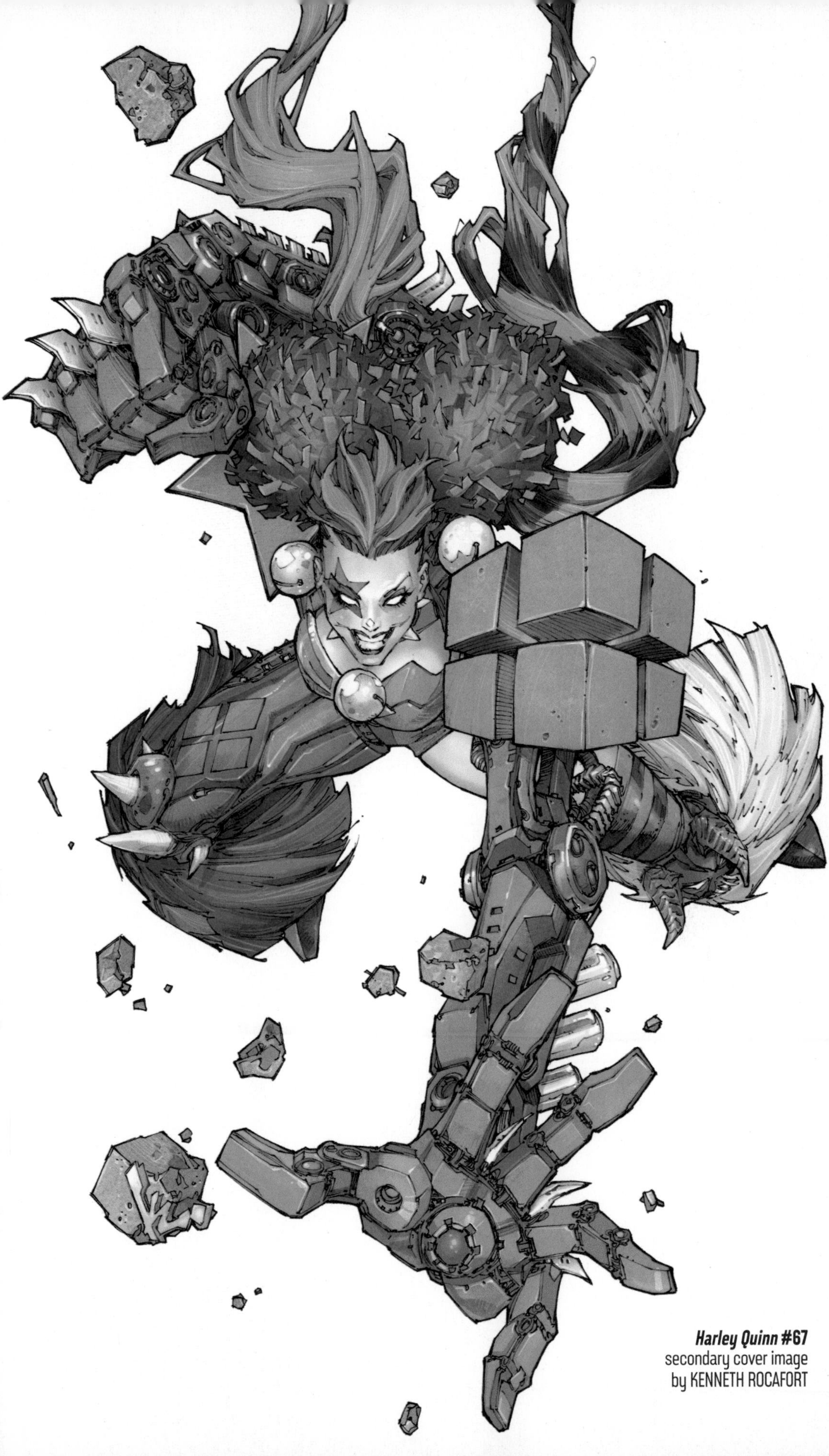

***Harley Quinn* #67**
secondary cover image
by KENNETH ROCAFORT

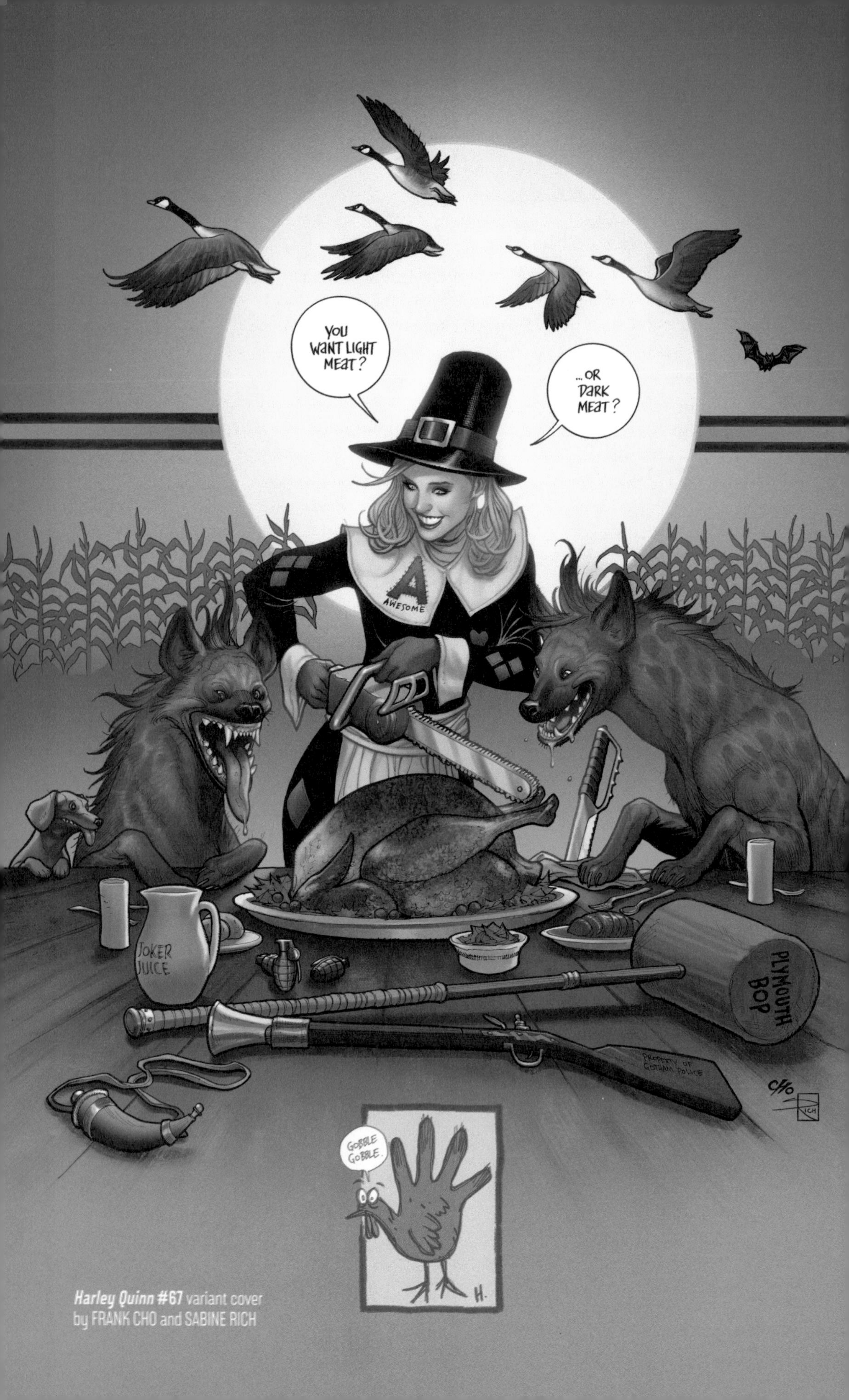

YOU WANT LIGHT MEAT?
...OR DARK MEAT?
A
AWESOME
JOKER JUICE
PLYMOUTH BOP
PROPERTY OF GOTHAM POLICE
GOBBLE GOBBLE.
CHO
RICH
H.

Harley Quinn **#67** variant cover
by FRANK CHO and SABINE RICH

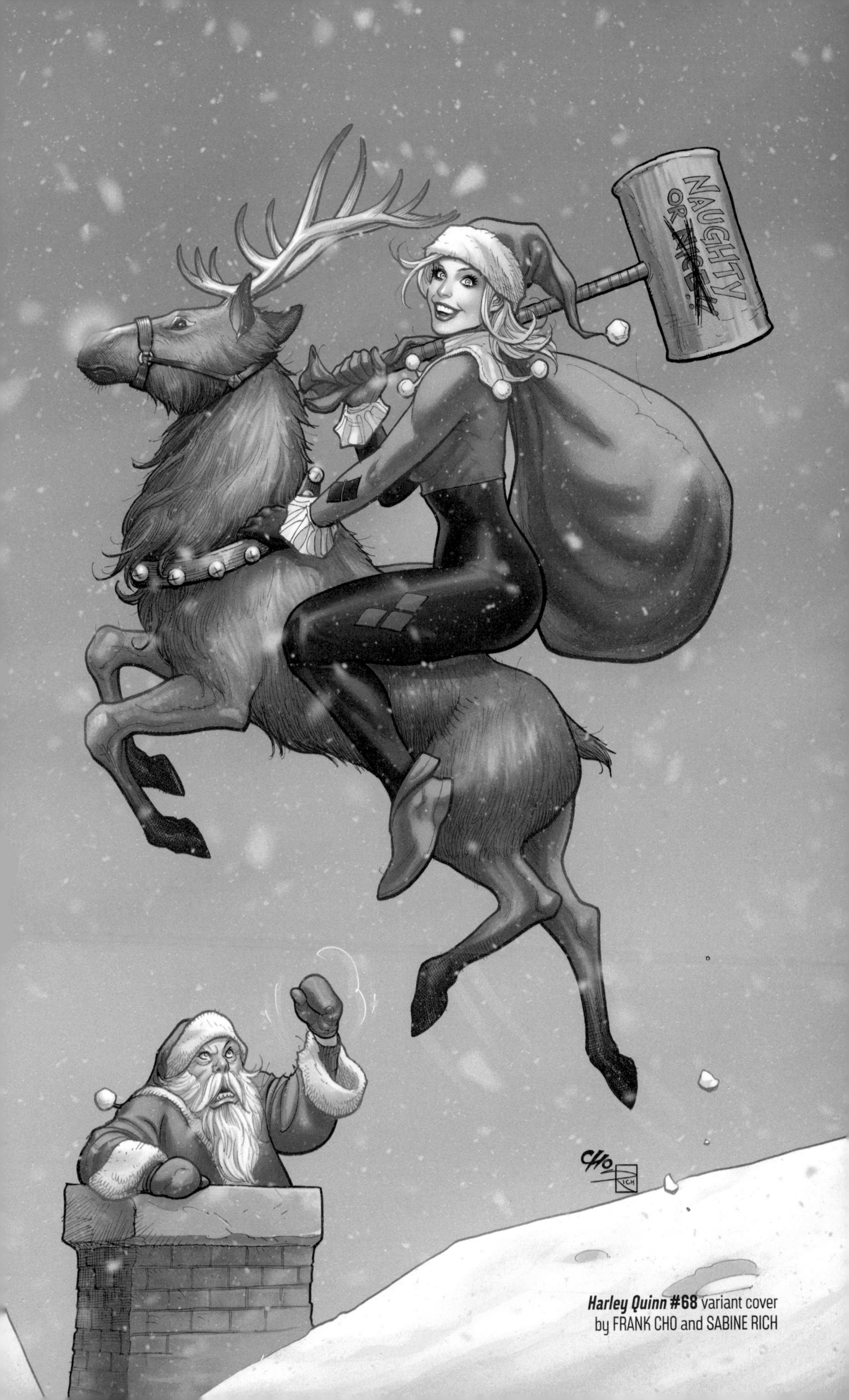
NAUGHTY
OR

***Harley Quinn* #68** variant cover
by FRANK CHO and SABINE RICH

***Harley Quinn* #69** variant cover
by FRANK CHO

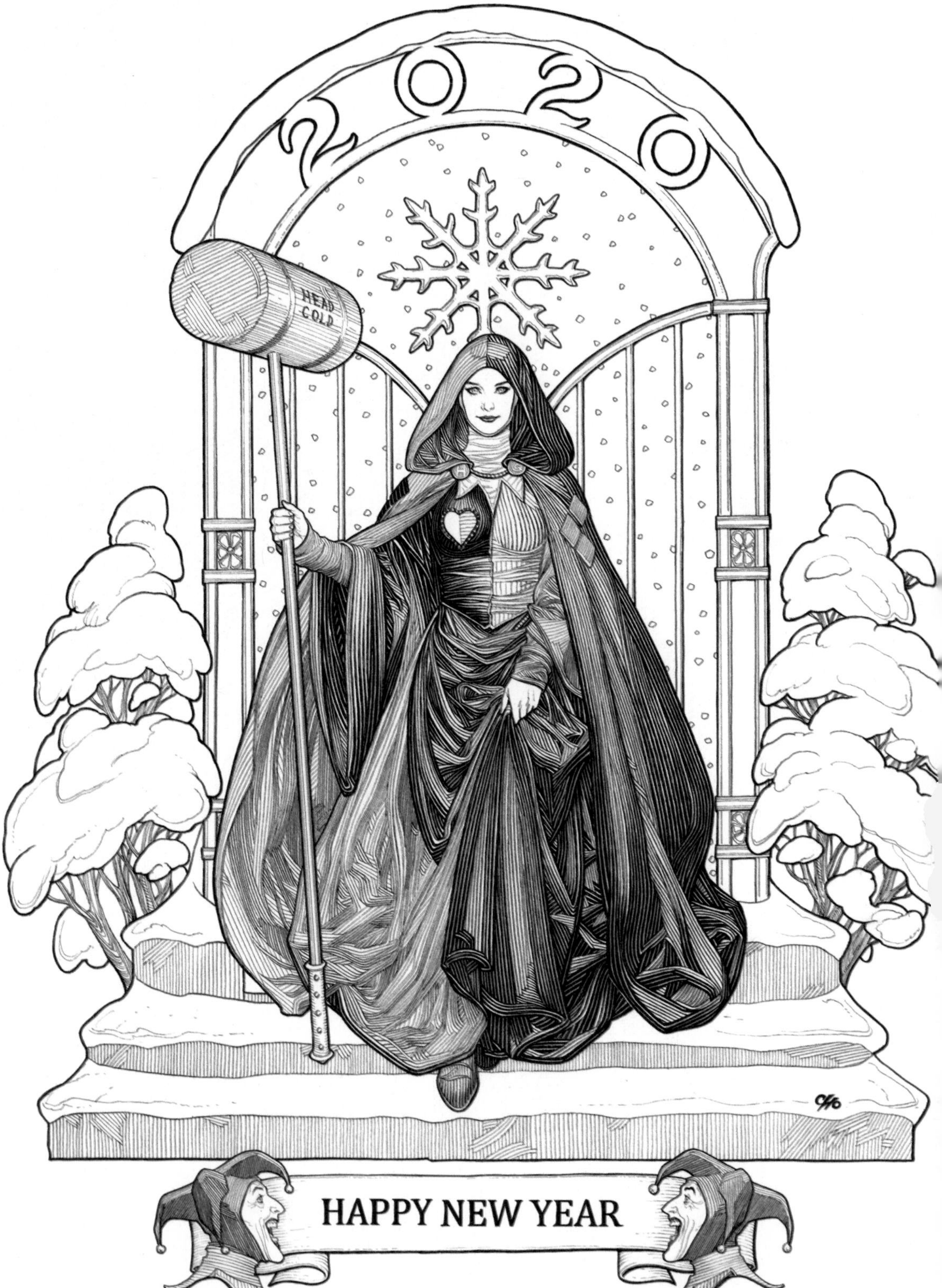
2020
HEAD COLD
HAPPY NEW YEAR